MUSICA ÆTERNA
PROGRAM NOTES
1961-1967

Da Capo Press Music Reprint Series
GENERAL EDITOR
FREDERICK FREEDMAN
VASSAR COLLEGE

MUSICA ÆTERNA PROGRAM NOTES 1961-1967

By Joseph Braunstein

DA CAPO PRESS • NEW YORK • 1973

Library of Congress Cataloging in Publication Data

Braunstein, Josef.
  Musica Æterna, program notes, 1961-1967.

  (Da Capo Press music reprint series)
  "An unabridged and slightly corrected republication
of the first edition ... 1968."
  1. Music—Analysis, appreciation. I. Title.
MT90.B82   1973   780'.15   72-8420
ISBN 0-306-70554-0

154704

This Da Capo Press edition of
Musica Æterna *Program Notes, 1961-1967,*
is an unabridged and slightly corrected
republication of the first edition published
in New York in 1968 by Musica Æterna. It
is reprinted by special arrangement with
Joseph Braunstein.

Published by Da Capo Press, Inc.
A Subsidiary of Plenum Publishing Corporation
227 West 17th Street, New York, New York 10011

Manufactured in the United States of America

MUSICA ÆTERNA
PROGRAM NOTES
1961-1967

PREFACE

These program notes are reprinted in response to the unusually great interest shown during the past six years by the subscribers and other listeners to the series of concerts given by Musica Aeterna, conducted by Frederic Waldman, at The Metropolitan Museum of Art and at Carnegie Hall. The notes also include those expressly written for the recordings made by Musica Aeterna for Decca Records.

The material is arranged by composer names in alphabetical order. An index is provided and the text was generally left intact. The author let a few duplications stand. They constitute quotations from preceding notes on the same composer. The excision of these paragraphs would have affected the flow of the narrative and its continuity. The author most gratefully acknowledges the help given him in the task of proofreading by his former students and friends Mary Anderberg, Sarah Beatty, Lynne Goldstein, and Carol Marunas. In preparing the text, the author joyfully remembered the delightful and inspiring evenings the Musica Aeterna Concerts offered him.

J. B.

ACKNOWLEDGMENT

Musica Aeterna is indebted to the Metropolitan Museum of Art for the kind permission to reproduce *Angel playing the organ* from an engraving of St. Cecelia by Sadeler after Martin de Vas (1532-1603).

ADAM, Adolphe (1803-1856), *Overture to "Si j'étais Roi"*

Adolphe Adam was the son of Louis Adam, an excellent Alsatian musician, gifted pianist, and serious student of Bach and Handel, who achieved an eminent position as a piano teacher during his long tenure as professor at the Conservatoire in Paris (1795-1842). Although opposing Adolphe's wish to embark on a musical career, Louis Adam finally yielded, and the boy entered the Conservatoire in 1817. The teacher who influenced him most was François-Adrien Boieldieu. A very close relationship developed between teacher and student. When Boieldieu put the finishing touches on his masterpiece *La Dame blanche* (1825), he entrusted Adam, then twenty-two, with the task of "compiling" the overture from chosen musical ideas of the opera.

Adam's first great success as a stage composer was *Le Chalet* (1834), which achieved a run of 1400 performances in Paris before 1900. *Le Postillon de Longjumeau* (1836) propelled him to international fame, and the ballet *Giselle*, based on a story by Heinrich Heine, is still successfully maintained in the repertory of leading ballet companies. Viewed artistically, Adam created in a glorious period of the French Opéra-Comique, which was represented by Auber, Boieldieu, and Hérold. Although both Berlioz and Wagner poured irony and sarcasm over Adam, his melodic inventiveness and rhythmic gracefulness secured for him considerable success. The opera *Si j'étais Roi* (*If I Were King*), first produced in the Théâtre-Lyrique on September 4, 1852, held the stage in Germany until the 1920s. The overture became immensely popular. It is a typical potpourri overture, which presents several important melodies of the opera in a very effective manner.

BACH, Carl Philipp Emanuel (1714-1788), *Magnificat*

This work of Carl Philipp Emanuel Bach is the result of an interesting case of hereditary disposition. The common notion that great men never have great sons has been seldom disproved. Yet the eighteenth century offers two outstanding exceptions: Domenico Scarlatti and Philipp Emanuel Bach.

The circumstances under which the *Magnificat* came into being have not been fully clarified. According to Friedrich Rochlitz (1769-1842), a competent writer on musical subjects and an influential critic in Leipzig, Philipp Emanuel composed the *Magnificat* to qualify for the St. Thomas cantorate, a post his father had held. It is a little difficult to accept this story at face value, because Johann Sebastian Bach was alive on August 29, 1749, when the autograph of the *Magnificat* is dated. However, Johann Sebastian was beset by increasing blindness in 1749, and at the same time rumors that his health was severely impaired found wide circulation. The mayor of Leipzig received a letter from the powerful Saxon minister, Count Brühl who, referring to J. S. Bach's impending departure, recommended Johann Gottlob Harrer (1703-1755) of Dresden for the cantorate. The count also suggested that a concert should be arranged forthwith to offer his protégé the opportunity to demonstrate his qualifications by the performance of a cantata. The town council complied with the "suggestion" and the concert took place on June 9, 1749. But Johann Sebastian refused to succumb, and Harrer, tired of waiting, returned to Dresden. No doubt Philipp Emanuel heard of this scandalous event, and was prompted to write his *Magnificat* in order to have a test piece ready. However, when Johann Sebastian died on July 28, 1750, the city fathers of Leipzig appointed the "quiet, accommodating" Harrer, who promised to be a manageable schoolteacher.

The *Magnificat* is a canticle: a monodic setting of a text from the Old or New Testaments. The words, which ancient antiphonaries styled the "Gospel of Mary" or "Canticle of the Blessed Virgin Mary" were uttered by Mary when she visited her cousin Elizabeth, as narrated in the first chapter of Saint Luke. Her greeting to Elizabeth was "Magnificat anima mea Dominum" ("My soul doth magnify the Lord") and the first word gave the canticle its name. Luther retained the Latin *Magnificat* in its traditional place in the Vesper liturgy, which explains its setting by "official" Protestant church composers such as Dietrich Buxtehude, Johann Kuhnau, and Johann Sebastian and Philipp Emanuel Bach.

Philipp Emanuel's *Magnificat* parallels his father's in the choice of key (D major) and by and large in the orchestration. Philipp Emanuel employed a four-part chorus and four soloists; Johann Sebastian a five-part chorus and five soloists (soprano, mezzo-soprano, alto, tenor, and bass). The compositions differ substantially in textual disposition and length. Although Johann Sebastian's *Magnificat* consists of twelve numbers, and Philipp Emanuel's of only nine, the latter is twice as long as the former. Johann Sebastian aimed at compactness and concentration, qualities required for the liturgy of the Christmas service. At Easter and Whitsuntide, however, a more elaborate Vesper service took place, which presumably governed the over-all design of Philipp Emanuel's *Magnificat*.

The first chorus, with the exuberant orchestral introduction suggesting the opening tutti of a concerto or concerto grosso, is vigorous and exhibits a distinct festive splendor. It contrasts sharply with the tranquillity, lyrical style, and minor mode of the ensuing soprano aria with discreet string accompaniment. The spirit of the contemporary Italian opera dominates the florid tenor aria, which reveals a certain heroic quality. The mood changes once more in the choral number that follows; with the exception of the final fugue it is the only section lacking an instrumental introduction. The alternation of pieces in the major and minor modes that we have observed thus far proves a well-calculated pattern that is maintained throughout the work. Thus the aria "Fecit potentiam" reverts to the major key (A major). It discloses a thematic relationship to the corresponding number in Johann Sebastian's *Magnificat*:

J. S. Bach

Fe-cit po- ten- ti- am   fe-cit po-ten-ti-am

C. P. E. Bach

Fe-cit po- ten-ti-am,   fe-cit po-ten-ti-am

The preponderance of dotted rhythm is the outstanding feature of this aria and points unmistakably to Handel. The ensuing duet for tenor and alto consists of two sections: verse 52, in A minor, and verse 53, in F major. Philipp Emanuel followed the paternal model closely in the choice of voices and key. Johann Sebastian treated verse 52 in a tenor aria in F sharp minor, and verse 53 in an alto aria in E major. Philipp Emanuel's setting of verse 52, which contrasts the deposition of the mighty with the exaltation of the humble, displays a gigue-like quality and also, influenced by Johann Sebastian, shows good examples of word painting in the realistic description of both deposition and elevation. The energetic and vigorous mood of the A minor section yields to softness and restraint in the F major part of the duet. Here melodic phrases appear that foreshadow Gluck (*Orfeo,* first chorus) and the preclassical style.

The alto aria "Suscepit Israel" (D minor) concludes the text from the Gospel of Saint Luke. Its tender mood is enhanced by the use of the muted string orchestra and is effectively contrasted with the "Gloria Patri," the invocation of the lesser doxology which is, musically speaking, a modified restatement of the opening chorus and thus creates the spiritual connection between the Gospel text and the lesser doxology. Once more the son followed to a certain degree the road laid down by his father, who closed his work with thematic reminiscences from the opening chorus. Yet the son, not hampered by the need for brevity that kept the imagination of the father in check, proceeded to build up an imposing musical structure on the lesser doxology, in a double fugue of unusual extension. All vocal and instrumental forces are marshaled to hail the glory of God.

The fugue shows a three-sectional design which could be described with the formula A-B-AB: A indicating the fugal elaboration of the first subject, B the exposition of the second, and AB the combination of both. The first, and dominating, theme which appears thirty-four times

Si- cut er- at in prin-ci- pi-   o

is by no means an original idea of Philipp Emanuel Bach, but an old heirloom of the baroque, found in outstanding compositions of this period, as for example in the *Messiah* (1742),

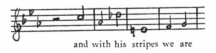

and with his stripes we are

and in Handel's *Joseph* (1743).

Hal- le- lu- jah! Hal-le- lu-jah!

True, the *Messiah* version differs from the *Magnificat* and, for that matter, from the *Joseph* version, in one important detail. It contains the conspicuous diminished seventh, which does, however, appear in the *Magnificat* in nine statements of the theme:

It must be added that Handel, too, used the version with the minor sevenths (*Joseph*, Philipp Emanuel's *Magnificat*) in the same chorus of the *Messiah*.

The frequent use of a characteristically altered version of the theme in the middle of Philipp Emanuel's fugue was prompted by artistic wisdom. It fore- stalled the attrition of a musical idea which had to carry the fugal process of a movement running through 246 measures. The version with the diminished seventh was familiar to Philipp Emanuel from the A minor fugue of the *Well-Tempered Clavier*, Part II, which begins thus:

The second subject in Philipp Emanuel's fugue is a florid coloratura in eighth-notes, which injects an irresistible element of motion:

Except for a few measures, the motion in eighth-notes keeps up until the end and imposes heavy demands on the vocalists. The lesser doxology forms the textual basis of the first exposition (sixty-four measures) while the other sections (twenty-two plus 180 measures) elaborate solely on the word "Amen" thus reviving the ancient synagogue "Hallelujah" jubilations. The fugue ends with a powerful statement of the first theme as the crowning peroration.

In this ambitious piece Philipp Emanuel Bach speaks to us as the great son of a great father. The *Magnificat* was to advance his candidacy for his father's post. He failed, and although this may have caused him bitterness, he un- doubtedly did not regret the turn of events later, and certainly always looked at his *Magnificat* with justifiable pride.

BACH, Johann Sebastian (1685-1750)
Brandenburg Concerto No. 3 in G major
Allegro; Allegro

The new *Complete Edition* of Bach's works now in progress sheds recent light on the history of the Brandenburg concertos in the critical report of the editor Heinrich Besseler. This report is a volume of 170 pages and is the main source of the following paragraphs.

In the fall of 1717 Bach went to Berlin as director of the musical establish- ment of Prince Leopold of Anhalt, at Cöthen, to order a new harpsichord for the court. He visited the Margrave Ludwig Christian of Brandenburg, the most prominent patron of music in the Prussian capital, and played with the princely musicians. It was on this occasion that the Margrave requested that a work by Bach be composed for him personally. This request may have been in the nature of a commission, but Bach was in no hurry to meet his obligation. Once reminded of it, he felt he could fulfill the task by assembling works from stock on hand and, guided by variety, he combined six concertos into a set that he called *Six Concerts avec plusieurs Instruments*. The dedication copy was presented to the Margrave in 1721.

In view of the scoring of the set, for a variety of instruments, it was taken for granted that the Margrave had a sizable number of capable musicians in his employ. But documents recently unearthed reveal a different picture. In 1734 there were only six musicians in the service of the Margrave, and not many more in the preceding years. Thus all items of the set except the last, that requires only seven players, were beyond the capacity of the Margrave's small musical establishment. The autograph, or dedication copy, gives no indication of a practical use. No doubt, the concertos originated from Bach's own practice as *Kapellmeister* in Cöthen. They were first published in Berlin by C. F. Peters, in 1850, under a French title *Six Concerts composés par Jean Sébastian Bach* prompted by Bach's dedication in French. When the *Bachgesellschaft* published the concertos in the first *Complete Edition*, in 1871, it placed the set without title in a volume under the heading "Chamber Music." The name Brandenburg concertos, with which we are so familiar, was coined by Philipp Spitta in his Bach biography (Vol. II, 1880) about 160 years after their completion.

The third Brandenburg concerto is scored for three violins, three violas, three violoncellos, and figured bass (double bass and harpsichord). It is performed with one player to a part. Technically, it is a concerto grosso in which the different instrumental categories (violin, viola, violoncello) alternate as a concertino group or play together as a concerto grosso. Naturally, the individual members of the concertino are also treated soloistically. The piece consists of only two fast movements. The first grows out of the motif heard at the beginning and displays the Vivaldian ritornello principle. That is to say, the idea which opens the movements is frequently stated in different keys. A peculiar cadence characteristic of the baroque establishes the connection with the second movement; this being in the nature of a gigue is propelled as if by perpetual motion.

Concerto for Harpsichord (Piano) in E major
Allegro; Andante; Allegro assai

The individual movements of this composition were utilized by Bach in other works where they appear completely transformed in different surroundings. Bach resorted to the use of pre-existing material—a very old practice of which the Renaissance composers availed themselves and which we also find frequently in the works of Handel, Gluck, and others—when he lacked time or when under pressure of trying circumstances. Nearly all of his seven harpsichord concertos represent arrangements of violin concertos that came into being during his Cöthen period (1717-1723), when he officiated as Kapellmeister and director of the Kammermusik. (Most recent investigations have advanced the opinion that some of the harpsichord concertos are based on concertos for oboe.)

The originals of the harpsichord concertos in D major, G minor, and F major have survived as the violin concertos in E major, A minor, and the fourth Brandenburg concerto (G major), while the originals of the concertos in D minor (2) F minor, and A major are lost.

The case of the E major concerto is different. All three movements of it appear in cantatas, the first as the opening sinfonia of No. 169 (*Gott soll allein mein Herze haben*), the second converted into an aria in the same work, while the last serves as an instrumental prologue to No. 49 (*Ich geh und suche mit Verlangen*). This is not an isolated case. To mention another example, the first and second movements of the harpsichord concerto in D minor, originally written for violin, were adapted for the introduction and first chorus of the cantata No. 146 (*Wir müssen durch viel Trübsal*).

The first movement of our E major concerto discloses the pattern of the *da capo* aria. That is to say, there is an opening main section in E major, a middle division in C sharp minor followed by the repetition of the first section. In applying the pattern of the *da capo* aria, Bach deviates somewhat from the Vivaldian concerto form, but he does not introduce new material in the middle division and confines himself to the manipulation of the ideas presented in the opening section in steady alternation of tutti and solo. The middle movement upholds the Vivaldian scheme of presenting an "aria" that is framed by orchestral ritornellos. It is the domain of the solo instrument. The last movement corresponds formally and stylistically to the first Allegro.

Concerto for Harpsichord, Recorders and Strings in F major
Allegro; Andante; Allegro Assai

All of Johann Sebastian Bach's **seven** harpsichord concertos, with one possible exception (E major, No. 1059 in Schmieder's catalogue), are converted violin (or oboe) concertos.

The original of our piece is the fourth Brandenburg Concerto, in G major, scored for a solo violin, two recorders, string orchestra, and harpsichord which effected the realization of the figured bass. The name "Brandenburg Concertos," with which we are so familiar, was actually coined by Philipp Spitta in his Bach biography, on account of the dedication of the series to Christian Ludwig, Margrave of Brandenburg.

It is interesting to note that Bach usually transposes the violin concertos into harpsichord (piano) pieces one second down, thus the E major concerto into D major, the A minor concerto into G minor and the concerto for two violins in D minor appears in C minor in the version for two harpsichords.

The metamorphosis of the music of the violino principale and the integration of the new harpsichord part into the organism of the work is a fascinating achievement. Bach assigned the harpsichord a dual role: it appears as a solo instrument but has also to provide the realization of the figured bass. Note the echo effects between the tutti and harpsichord in the lyrical Andante, which is closely tied to the fugal finale (Allegro assai). Because of its brilliancy, vigor, animated spirit, driving force, and extraordinary craftsmanship, this movement ranks among Bach's finest of this kind. The wealth of contrapuntal combinations and the variety in the grouping of the instruments keeps the listener in suspense until the final chord.

Concerto for Violin in A minor
Allegro; Andante; Allegro assai

Johann Sebastian Bach the violinist is somewhat overshadowed by Bach the organist. We have come to associate Bach, the creator of *The Well-tempered Clavier*, primarily with the keyboard and particularly with the organ. We know that he was one of the greatest organists of his time—in our imagination we visualize him sitting at the organ of the St. Thomas church in Leipzig surrounded by awe-struck sons and pupils. Yet this unique master of the keyboard was at the same time a fine violinist, who also loved to play the viola. The first salaried position he held was that of violinist in the orchestra of Johann Ernst, brother of the reigning duke of Weimar.

Bach did not represent the glamorous virtuoso, but he was a very proficient player. As a polyphonic thinker, he aimed at polyphony also in his compositions for violin—witness the sonatas and suites for violin alone. In this respect he was a strict antipode to Antonio Vivaldi and other great Italian violinists who excelled in virtuosity.

Bach was not a trail blazer in matters of form in his concertos; he followed the road laid out by Vivaldi, whose concertos exercised great influence on his contemporaries as well as on Bach. Fruits of Bach's study of Vivaldi's works are also his violin concertos, of which only three (one for two violins) are extant. We have no precise information as to when they were composed, but all available evidence points to 1719/20, when Bach was Kapellmeister and director of the *Kammermusik* of Prince Leopold of Anhalt at Cöthen (about thirty miles northwest of Leipzig).

The autograph score of the violin concerto in A minor has not survived, but the original parts have. They lack the tempo indication for the first movement, which displays interesting modifications of the Vivaldian pattern. Compared with the transparent setting of Vivaldi's concertos, Bach's texture is far more complex and polyphonic in nature.

The Andante in C major combines the songful treatment of the solo instrument with the basso ostinato technique. The half-measure ostinato phrase, announced at the very beginning, occurs forty-six times in the bass part.

The quick finale has the quality of a gigue. Note the contrast between the rather polyphonic treatment of the tutti sections and the simplicity of the solo passages.

Concerto for Violin in E major
Allegro; Adagio; Allegro assai

The violin concerto in E major was written about 1719 when Bach officiated as *Kapellmeister* and director of the *Kammermusik* to Prince Leopold of

Anhalt at Cöthen. He held this position from 1717 until 1723. In this capacity, he was obliged to contribute a great deal to the musical establishment of the court, and also to include important contemporary novelties in the repertory of the *kapelle*. The creative genius served his employers with concerti grossi (*Brandenburg Concertos*), solo concertos for violin, and sonatas, while as the director of the *Kammermusik*, Bach tapped the current Italian publications including the works of Antonio Vivaldi (1678-1741) for the benefit of the *kapelle* and for himself. The violin concerto in E major is a case in point. It is cast in the Vivaldian scheme. We know from authoritative sources, among them Johann Sebastian Bach himself, that he was a diligent student of the works of the prolific and ingenious Venetian master. Says Johann Nicolaus Forkel, Bach's first biographer, who received a great deal of information from the sons of the Thomas Cantor:

> He [Bach] realized that musical ideas need to be subordinated to a plan and that the young composer's first need is a model to instruct his efforts. Opportunely Vivaldi's Concertos, then recently published, gave him the guidance he needed. He often heard them praised as admirable works of art, and conceived the happy idea of arranging them for clavier. Hence he was led to study their structure, the musical ideas on which they are built, the variety of their modulations, and other characteristics. [C. S. Terry's translations of Forkel's biography]

The Vivaldian concerto is a three-movement organism, with both the first Allegro and the finale generally comprising four tutti and three solo sections. The former constitute the thematic backbone of the first movement and the reappearance of the opening tutti, partly or in its entirety, at the conclusion, strongly resembles the rondo design. Bach elevated the Vivaldian scheme to a higher level through integration of tutti material into the solo passages. The first movement of the E major concerto displays this technique through the manipulation of the head motif, the broken E major chord. The movement discloses the tripartite design of the *da capo aria* with the insertion of a short Adagio cadenza of the solo violin prior to the repetition of the first section.

The ensuing Adagio in C sharp minor employs the technique of the *basso ostinato*. The melody, sometimes extended, sometimes reduced, or ceasing altogether, moves through different keys. In form and spirit the Adagio clearly reveals its provenance—the operatic aria. It includes a prelude for orchestra that introduces the *ostinato* melody, a songful main part rich in coloratura embellishments, and finally a postlude (repeat of the opening). The finale strictly observes the ritornello principle: the orchestra always plays the same passage in five sections. The soloist does not face the difficult technical problems (and hardly need go beyond the first position) while the listener can easily grasp the musical content of this joyful movement because of the transparent texture and absence of polyphonic complexity.

Concerto for two Violins in D minor
Vivace; Largo ma non troppo; Allegro

Bach spent happy and fruitful years (1717-1723) in Cöthen, the small capital of a tiny principality. As Kapellmeister and director of the *Kammermusik*, he presided over the musical establishment of Prince Leopold of Anhalt-Cöthen. In this capacity, he was obliged to contribute a great deal of his own music, which he performed with his thirteen-piece band for the pleasure of his princely employer, who was a good musician and greatly appreciated the performing and creative achievements of his Kapellmeister. In the Cöthen period Bach composed a variety of concerti grossi and at least seven concertos for violin. He also wrote sonatas for violin and figured bass and sonatas and suites for unaccompanied violin and violoncello.

Only two of the violin concertos (in A minor and E major) have come down to us in their original form. The concerto for two violins in D minor, composed about 1718, is a concerto grosso in which two violins form the soloistically treated concertino. Although Philipp Spitta, eighty years ago, rejected the term "double concerto," it has become customary to speak of this very popular work as the "double concerto." This time-honored colloquialism is definitely at odds with Bach's own unmistakably expressed terminology. The heading on the autograph reads "Concerto a 6, 2 violini concertini, 2 violini e 1 viola di ripieni, violoncello e continuo di J. S. Bach." The wording indicates the very nature of the work. It defines it as a concerto grosso in which the two soloists emerge as prominent members of a larger unit.

In the three-movement structure Bach followed closely the Vivaldian models. Two fast movements frame a very expressive Largo. The outstanding features of the outer movements (in 4/4 and 3/4 respectively) are boundless energy and continuous motion that does not allow even a fleeting lyrical episode. The motion, propelled by motives in sixteenth-notes, comes to a halt only in the concluding measures. This tendency to continuous motion is also apparent in the Largo (12/8), though considerably mitigated. Here the concertino violins dominate in a dialogue, or duet, from the beginning to the end, following each other in a steady flow of imitations and songful phrases, while the ripieno discreetly provides harmonic and rhythmic support.

Suite for Orchestra No. 3 in D major
Ouverture; Air; Gavotte I — Gavotte II; Bourrée; Gigue

The suite evolved from the old popular custom of following a slow dance with a quicker one or pairing a dance with two or four beats to the measure with one in triple time. This custom was practiced on the village green, in modest inns, and in the castles of the aristocracy and the ballrooms of royal palaces. The adaptation of dance forms proved a very suitable means for instrumental music of a higher plane and led to a piece that was an assortment of several stylized dances. This assemblage received different names in different countries: called *ordre* by Couperin, it was designated as *lesson* by Purcell. The German composers used the term *suite* as well as the Italian word *partita* and its German derivative *partie*. Partita ("lot" or "quantity") actually indicates the basic character of the suite, yet the term mostly used in Italy for the suite was *sonata da camera*.

Bach wrote suites for keyboard, string instruments (violin, viola da gamba, violoncello), and four for orchestra. The orchestral suites originated in Leipzig for performance by the Musikverein ("musical association") founded by Georg Philipp Telemann in 1704. Bach directed this amateur orchestra, whose members were mostly students at the university, from 1729 until 1736. Under his leadership it became an important factor in Leipzig's musical life.

Bach's orchestral suites consist of two disparate elements—an overture, patterned after the "slow-fast-slow" design inaugurated by Lully, and the dances proper. The inclusion of the French type of overture constituted yet another phase in the evolution of the suite, for which the term *ouverture* became common. Yet in using this term the German composers, ironically enough, minimized the very essence of the suite and pushed its purpose—the combination of dances—into the background.

Bach's third orchestral suite is scored for two oboes, three trumpets, kettledrums, strings, and harpsichord, and it includes an overture, an air (aria), and three dance pieces. The air is a songful piece that displays the two-section pattern of a stylized dance movement with repetition of each section. The ensuing gavottes conform to the "minuet-plus-trio" pattern, which demands the repetition of the first gavotte after the second. The bourrée is closely related to the gavotte. Both dances are in 4/4 time, but the gavotte begins on the third beat and the bourrée starts in the last quarter of the measure. The concluding item is a gigue that, in contrast to most of Bach's harpsichord suites, is devoid of fugal complexities and is simple in texture.

The suite fell into oblivion after Bach's death and was not heard for a century. Mendelssohn found parts of it in the holdings of the Berlin Singakademie, where he conducted the historic revival of the *St. Matthew Passion* in 1829. When he visited Goethe in Weimar in 1830, he played the overture for him. In a letter to his teacher Karl Friederich Zelter, who counseled Goethe in musical matters, Mendelssohn mentioned that Goethe liked the overture very much, and that it brought to his mind a picture of very aristocratic and pompous gatherings; the poet visualized a file of people in full dress descending a large staircase.

It was left to Mendelssohn to reclaim the suite for modern concert life on February 15, 1839, in Leipzig. He made some changes in the score, however, and added clarinets to facilitate the playing of the difficult trumpet parts. This makeshift practice has been, of course, completely abandoned.

The air achieved a particular popularity through August Wilhelmj's arrangement for violin, which was to be played only on the G string. In the wake of his virtuoso transcription, numerous adaptations for all kinds of instruments flooded the musical market.

Suite for Orchestra No. 4 in D major
Ouverture; Bourrée I — Bourrée II; Gavotte;
Menuet I — Menuet II; Réjouissance

Bach's fourth orchestral suite is scored for three oboes, bassoon, three trumpets, kettledrums, strings, and harpsichord. It includes an overture and six dance pieces. There is no autograph extant and the authenticity of the piece, first published as late as 1881, had been for a long time a matter of dispute. Bach used the slow opening of the overture as an instrumental prologue to his Cantata No. 110 (*"Unser Mund sei voll des Lachens"*) and ingeniously converted the fugal main body of the overture into the first choral number.

As for the dance pieces there are three in common and three in triple meter.

There are two bourrées (1 and 2), which conform to the minuet-trio pattern, and one gavotte. Both dances are in 4/4 and closely related, but the gavotte begins on the third beat and the bourrée starts in the last quarter of the measure. The second bourrée contrasts with the first in the scoring. The absence of the trumpets and kettledrums decreases the sonorities. This device is paralleled in the minuets: the second minuet is played by strings only while the scoring of the first includes oboes and bassoons. The entire orchestra is heard in the finale, a *réjouissance*. Réjouissance, denoting rejoicing and merriment, was a designation for movements in a light vein. In placing the réjouissance, Bach may also have been alluding to a special meaning of the word in French everyday life: *réjouissance* means the bones that go with the meat, and thus indicates an encore for the framework of the suite.

Cantata No. 43 "Gott fähret auf mit Jauchzen"

Bach composed this cantata in Leipzig for the Feast of Christ's Ascension. The text is based on Psalm 47:6, 7; Mark 16:19; and on verses that Albert Schweitzer, while referring to Spitta, ascribed to Marianne von Ziegler, a Leipzig poetess. The cantata is numbered forty-three, which has no chronological meaning, but refers to the order, now a universally accepted catalogue, in which Bach's 199 church cantatas were published by the Bach-Gesellschaft in the second half of the nineteenth century.

Of larger dimensions than most of the other cantatas, the Ascension Cantata is divided into two parts, containing in all an elaborate opening chorus; five recitatives and four arias, sung consecutively by the tenor, soprano, bass, and alto; and the customary concluding Chorale. The first chorus, based on the Psalm verses, suggests by its slow introduction and fugally treated main body a French overture, lacking, however, the concluding *lentement*. The chorus evolves in three stages: the opening Adagio hints melodically at the things to come, the beginning of the fugal movement presents orchestrally the theme and counterpoint, and finally the chorus enters with force amid the clash of trumpets and kettledrums. The treatment of the voices is reminiscent of an ancient, florid Hallelujah. There are coloratura passages on the diphthong *au* in Po*sau*nen and J*au*chzen that stretch over thirteen measures. The tenor aria (No. 3), accompanied by the combined violins playing in unison, one violoncello, and the harpsichord, upholds the motoric tendency of the first chorus. The following soprano aria (No. 5) continues the motion in a somewhat restrained manner.

The second part of the cantata begins with a *recitativo accompagnato*, that is, a recitative with a thematically significant orchestral accompaniment. The rich sonorities provided by the orchestra here, which a *recitativo secco* with harpsichord accompaniment could not supply, ingeniously match the opening chorus. In this recitative Bach pictures the dispersion of the enemy by the use of broken chords in contrary motion, one group of instruments moving upward and the other in the opposite direction. Schweitzer draws attention to an identical treatment of a similar passage, Matthew 26:31, in the *St. Matthew Passion* (cantata No. 20): "Ich will den Hirten schlagen und die Schafe werden sich zerstreuen (I will smite the shepherd and the sheep of the flock will be scattered)." In the following difficult aria, also for bass, the human voice competes with a virtuoso trumpet. While the tenor and bass arias are in the major key, those for female voices are in the minor. The alto aria (No. 9) is characterized by a constantly maintained rhythm,

indicating once more the motoric quality that is a distinct trait of this cantata, a trait stemming from the very first line: "God is gone up ... "

Mendelssohn conducted sections of the Ascension Cantata at the Lower Rhine Music Festival in Cologne in 1838, to which he invited his friend Alfred Joseph Novello, the London publisher. In a letter dated April 7, 1838, he speaks of a "glorious cantata of Sebastian Bach with a double chorus in it, which would repay for the journey by itself." In 1904 this reference aroused the curiosity of an English musician who dealt with the matter anonymously in the *Musical Times*. He was puzzled by the letter because there is no Bach cantata that includes a double chorus, with the exception of *Nun ist das Heil* (cantata No. 50). However, this chorus is all that remains of the cantata, the other pieces being lost, and for this reason it does not fit Mendelssohn's description of a cantata "with a double chorus *in* it." The anonymous Bach specialist finally obtained a program of the festival, containing the texts of the music performed, that partly cleared up the mystery of the "glorious cantata." The opening chorus was that of our Ascension Cantata; it was followed by two arias for tenor and soprano, which could not be identified as Bach compositions, and the recitative for soprano of our cantata set to Mark 16:19. The ensuing double chorus turned out to be the now famous *Nun ist das Heil*. A chorale concluded this strange assortment. At this time little was known of Bach, practically no research having been done about him, and one can therefore understand how Mendelssohn, the Bach apostle, did not recognize this cantata as a concoction.

Cantata No. 169, "Gott soll allein mein Herze haben"

Bach's vast production of sacred cantatas was the outgrowth of his official duties. As cantor of the St. Thomas School he was in charge of the music for two churches in Leipzig, St. Thomas and St. Nicolai. In this capacity he was obliged not only to rehearse the music to be performed, but also to create a great deal of it. The great number of cantatas he wrote in Leipzig was the core of his liturgical output. Cantatas were sung every Sunday except during Advent and Lent and on great holidays. Bach thus needed about sixty cantatas yearly.

The musical forces, soloists, chorus, and orchestra, at the command of Bach were, in the main, alumni of the St. Thomas School. They were classified as *Concertisten* (vocal and instrumental) and *Ripienisten* (chorus and orchestra). The vocal *Concertisten* sang the arias, duets, recitatives, and reinforced the chorus. Listening nowadays to Bach's cantatas and passions performed by famous singers, we should not forget the conditions that prevailed in his time. Bach's interpreters were teenagers who had to grapple with exacting solo parts studded with technical difficulties such as trills or long coloratura passages. The composition of a solo cantata such as the work heard tonight can be explained by a particular condition, namely the availability of a capable singer. The solo cantata limits the participation of the chorus to the delivery of the concluding chorale; the soloist carries the main load in arias and recitatives. In our cantata the usual expanded opening chorus is replaced by an orchestral Sinfonia.

According to the findings of Dr. Alfred Dürr, whose researches brought about the most drastic changes of the Bach chronology as formerly established by Philipp Spitta, the cantata *Gott soll allein mein Herze haben* was written in Leipzig in 1726. The number 169 has no chronological meaning. It stems from the order in which the cantatas were published by the Bach Gesellschaft in the second half of the past century. The autograph of the work indicates that it was written for an *Alto Solo e tre voci ripieni* which means that the soloist had to sing as ripienst in the four-voice chorale. The orchestra, which includes oboes, English horn, and strings, is joined by the organ, which is treated as a solo instrument.

The greater part of the music was utilized by Bach in another composition. The Sinfonia is identical with the first movement of the harpsichord concerto in E major if we disregard the different keys (D major-E major) and the excision of two measures in the cantata. Furthermore, the aria No. 5 (*Stirb in mir*) appears as the middle movement of the harpsichord concerto aforementioned in a shorter version (forty-eight measures in the cantata, thirty-seven in the concerto) and in F sharp minor instead of B minor. Arrangements and recastings of this kind were usual in the eighteenth century. Handel often availed himself of this method, and some of the best airs in Gluck's French operas of the 1770s were taken from his Italian products of the 1740s.

It was chiefly lack of time that compelled Bach to resort to this practice. The question he had to face on such occasions was whether the pre-existing piece selected for transplantation fit the basic mood required in the new surroundings. How did the situation present itself in our particular case? The Sinfonia posed no problem. The opening movement of a concerto cast in the pattern of a *da capo* aria, with the repeat of the first division after a middle section in minor key, could very well serve as an instrumental prologue to a cantata. More difficult technically was the utilization of the second movement of the harpsichord concerto because it had to be converted into an aria. However, the middle movements of the baroque solo concertos were mostly "arias" for an instrument. And the emotional quality of the Siciliano in F sharp minor of the concerto is not out of harmony with the thoughts expressed in the aria of the cantata.

Cantata No. 21, "Ich hatte viel Bekümmernis"

Ich hatte viel Bekümmernis is one of Bach's earliest cantatas. It was composed in Weimar in the spring of 1714, and performed on June 17 in the Schlosskirche to celebrate the reconstruction of the organ in that church. The text is presumably by Salomo Franck (1659-1725), secretary to the Superior Con-

sistory in Weimar, and librarian and curator of the collection of coins of
the duke of Weimar. The translation used in this program is, with a few
deviations, that of Henry S. Drinker.

The slow introductory sinfonia in C minor sets the emotional and spiritual
keynote. It is a moving lament in which the oboe, treated as a solo instrument,
and the violins join in a richly ornamented interplay. Their elegiac, melodic
line is markedly contraposed by the sober "walking bass." This combination,
and the frequent use of poignant dissonances create a mood that is carried
through to the first chorus, expressed by the words: "My heart and soul were
sore distressed." This meaning is driven home relentlessly by an obstinate
motif which is heard more than fifty times in the first section of the chorus:

ich hatte viel Be-   kümmernis, ich hatte viel Be-   kümmernis

Bach returned to this motif several times: in the Sonata for Unaccompanied
Violin in G minor (about 1720); the transcription of this sonata for lute
(after 1720); the Prelude and Fugue for Organ in D minor (Leipzig, 1724/25);
and the Prelude and Fugue for Organ in G major (1724/25).

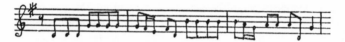

He obviously had come to look with affection upon the contrapuntal potentialities of this motif, which are strikingly evident in the opening chorus of
the cantata. The contrapuntal treatment produces a multitude of dissonances:
major and minor seconds, sevenths, and ninths that keep the listener in
suspense and create an enormous tension. When this process reaches the
boiling point, a decisive turn occurs, corresponding to the words: "O Lord
by Thy comforting my spirit is delighted."

The soprano aria that follows is emotionally and technically reminiscent of
the sinfonia. Also in the key of C minor, the piece is actually a duet for
soprano and oboe.

Bach's great melodic power is shown in the recitative, which leads to an
aria for tenor. Bach never treats the recitative in a schematic way: he always
gives it a strong musical accent. His recitatives are as closely knit to the arias
that follow them as are the preludes to the fugues of his keyboard works. The
tenor aria discloses Bach's predilection for word painting in the melodic
description of the ceaselessly streaming tears. One detail merits a brief consideration. It concerns the composer's treatment of the sentence: "Hier
versink ich in den Grund," which translated literally means "Here I sink into
the ground," and thus it was realistically expressed by Bach:

Hier   versink ich   ın   den   Grund

The second part of the cantata opens with a recitative in the form of a dialogue in which the protagonists are Jesus and the Christian soul. They are also represented in the duet that follows.

The operatic gestures of the duet are swept away by the chorus, in which the concerto grosso technique and contrapuntal choral treatment are employed with consummate workmanship. It should be noted that the autograph of the cantata is actually entitled *Concerto a 13,* which permits a twofold interpretation: it can be an allusion to the older meaning of the term, which implied playing together, or it can refer to the "modern" concerto style. Three solo voices (soprano, alto, bass) enter quasi as a concertino, to which all tenors contrapose a chorale melody by Georg Neumark (1621-1681).

was hel- fen uns die schwe- ren sor- gen

was hilft uns un- ser Weh und Ach?

This pattern is repeated in the middle section, whereas in the concluding portion the entire vocal force participates and the chorale melody is proclaimed by the sopranos. The orchestra, silent in the first two sections, joins forces with the full chorus.

A joyful tenor aria effects the transition to the final chorus, which enters with powerful exclamations along with three trumpets that have been silent throughout the piece. The text is based on Revelation 5:12; Revelation 7:3 is utilized for the concluding fugue.

Lob und Ehre und Preis und Gewalt sei unserm Gott von Ewigkeit zu Ewigkeit

The exposition is projected in concerto grosso manner by the four solo voices. Entering as a concertino, they gradually merge into the choral mass, in conjunction with the orchestra. The trumpets make an important contribution by blaring the fugal theme above the jubilant "Hallelujah" and "Amen" coloraturas of the human voices.

Cantata No. 140, "Wachet auf, ruft uns die Stimme"

The cantata *Wachet auf, ruft uns die Stimme* was composed in Leipzig presumably in 1739. It is based textually and musically on the hymn by Philipp Nicolai (1556-1606), who was pastor at St. Catarin's Church in Hamburg. Bach felt a strong attachment to Nicolai's mystical lines that were included in his book on the *Joys of Eternal Life* (1598). The cantata was written for the twenty-seventh Sunday after Trinity, in November. The Gospel for the day is taken from St. Matthew 25:1-13 and contains the tale of the five wise and the five foolish virgins. Only the first stanza of Nicolai's poem, which consists of three strophes, refers to this parable. The rest alludes to the Canticles and Revelation of St. John 21:2-21.

The cantata also includes lines composed as a recitative and duet that are interspersed among the three stanzas. The poet of this text is not known. Yet these lines are of utmost importance for the spiritual content of the cantata, which deals with the concept of Christ as bridegroom of the believing soul. This mystical union, espoused by medieval theologians, could hardly be understood by the congregations of the eighteenth century, who were inclined to see the matter materially rather than symbolically. To be precise: the mystical union was seen by the congregations as an ideal relationship of love on a real foundation. And Bach, the musician, did not discriminate between earthly and heavenly love.

The musical basis of the cantata is the melody of Nicolai, which appears in the extended opening chorus, in the very middle of the piece, and at the conclusion. Bach's treatment of the melody differs in every stanza and clearly demonstrates the turn from the complex to the simple. In the opening chorus the chorale melody, which is projected by the soprano, is woven into the contrapuntal fabric that is produced by the other choral voices and the instrumental forces. This piece, one of Bach's most remarkable achievements, is organized into twelve sections that correspond to the twelve divisions of Nicolai's chorale. They are preceded by orchestral preludes or interludes of various lengths except for the ninth division. Here the music is set to the word "Alleluia," and the altos, tenors, and basses engage in florid coloratura work before the sopranos enter with the sedate chorale melody.

The second stanza is presented by a solo tenor backed by an embroidery of rich contrapuntal figurations executed by the violins and violas in unison with organ accompaniment. The last strophe is sung by the congregation as a simple four-part chorale in which the instruments reinforce the singers. The duets of the bridegroom and soul (bass and soprano) are both entitled "aria," probably because they are cast in the pattern of the *da capo* aria (A-B-A). They are love duets, and Bach underscores the "earthly emotions" by introducing concertizing solo instruments: a violin and an oboe weave a net of coloraturas and ornaments around the voices precisely as in the contemporary opera.

Magnificat

Johann Sebastian Bach wrote his *Magnificat* for the first Christmas festival after he had taken charge of the music at St. Thomas's church in Leipzig late in the spring of 1723. The *Magnificat* is a canticle (*canticum*), a musical setting of a text from the Old or New Testaments. Canticles were incorporated into the Christian liturgy during the fourth and fifth centuries in the Greek, and later, Roman churches.

Our text, (Luke 1, 46-55) is very similar in thought and language to various psalms. It is recited during the Vesper liturgy with the burning of incense. Most of the great renaissance composers wrote one or more polyphonic versions of *Magnificat*: Dunstable, Dufay, Binchois, Busnois, Gombert, Obrecht, and later, Willaert, Giovanni Gabrieli, Tallis, Byrd, Victoria, Lassus (about fifty settings), and Palestrina (thirty-five settings). Probably the *Magnificat* has been set to music more often than any other hymn or psalm. It is joined to the *Doxologia parva*, the Lesser Doxology, a liturgical formula in praise of God which, stemming from an old synagogal custom, was attached to the recitations of psalms. Luther retained the Latin *Magnificat* in its traditional place in the Vesper liturgy, which explains its setting by "official" Protestant church composers such as Dietrich Buxtehude, Johann Kuhnau, Bach's predecessor in Leipzig, and also Bach's son Carl Philipp Emanuel.

We do not know Bach's success with the congregation that attended the service on December 25, 1723, in St. Thomas's church. Yet we may assume that the *Magnificat* made a strong impression and Bach's later revision of the score testifies to his wish to retain the work in the repertory.

The regular Vesper service was of short duration and only at Easter and Pentecost was a more elaborate *Magnificat* sung. Bach also used this practice for Christmas Day and even expanded the text of the *Magnificat* by inserting four vocal pieces in deference to the local custom of the service. These were Christmas hymns with German and Latin texts, which Bach did not enter in the scores in the places where they were to be sung, but below the *Magnificat* music on the bottom staves. Since the performance of these pieces was suitable only at Christmas, Bach did not regard them as organic elements of the *Magnificat* proper. Thus he did not include them in the second version of the work which came into being between 1728 and 1731. Put in biographical perspective, the second version originated after the composition of both the St. John and St. Matthew Passions. It is in D major, while the earlier version was in E flat major. Evidently Bach encountered some difficulties at the performance and decided to facilitate them by transposing the entire work down a minor second. In addition, he enriched the orchestration by adding two flutes and made several changes in the part writing.

The *Magnificat* is set for a five-part chorus, soprano I and II, alto, tenor, and bass. The orchestra includes flutes, oboes, bassoon, trumpets, kettledrums, strings, and organ. There are also vocal solo numbers (arias, a duet, a terzetto) in which all five voice categories participate. The opening chorus is constructed on the concerto principle and maintains the alternation of tutti and solo. Like a regular concerto movement the chorus is framed by a powerful ritornello of the orchestra. The ensuing aria for mezzo-soprano (No. 2) parallels the instrumental solo concerto, as perfected by Antonio Vivaldi, in the marked reduction of the instrumental body that is here restricted to strings and harpsichord. The following soprano aria (No. 3) represents the type of concerted aria in which the voice alternates with a solo instrument "in concert," in this case, with an oboe d'amore, the mezzo-soprano of the oboe family. Here Bach, the religious thinker, put a particular stress on the words *omnes generationes*, which are not sung by the soprano but by the entire chorus (No. 4). He wanted to underline that all generations should call Mary blessed and realized this thought in a mighty and complex choral number in which only the words *omnes generationes* are proclaimed. This chorus is contrasted with a bass aria constructed on an ostinato motif sounded by the instrumental basses.

A duet of alto and tenor follows (No. 6), a very gentle piece accompanied by muted strings and flutes. An interesting feature is the chromatic descending bass line, which is akin to those characteristic ostinato phrases we encounter in several cantatas and in the *Crucifixus* of the B minor Mass. The use of a persistently recurring motif in the bass is also evident in the chorus *Fecit potentiam* (No. 7). The deposition of the mighty and the exaltation of the humble is realistically described by means of descending and rising scale motives in the ensuing aria (No. 8). Its energetic mood yields to softness and restraint in the alto aria *Esurientes implevit bonis* accompanied by flutes, basses, and harpsichord.

Bach's theological thinking is most evident in the ingenious treatment of the terzetto *Suscepit Israel* (No. 10). Philipp Spitta has pointed out that the Vesper sermon was keyed to the concept that the redemption was the ultimate aim of Christ's incarnation. The only reference to it in the *Magnificat* is the verse reading: "He has holpen his servant Israel in remembrance of his mercy." (Luke I, 54). Bach projects it in a tender terzetto against the old Lutheran chorale melody *Mein Seele erhabt den Herrn* blown by the trumpet in the first version, and oboe in the second. The text of the chorale is actually the first verse of the *Magnificat*, and thus we observe here a "Magnificat" within a *Magnificat*. The text and melody of the chorale go back to Luther's time, and were published in a collection by Georg Rhaw, the one-time Thomas Cantor who went to Wittenberg and founded a printing plant to further Protestantism.

The five-part setting is applied to both the last verse from the Gospel (No. 11, *Sicut locutus est*), which is treated fugally, and to the Lesser Doxology (No. 12), which after powerfully intonated coloratura passages, in the Alleluia tradition, closes with a modification of the melodic material of the opening chorus. Thus the artistic and spiritual unity is perfectly achieved.

BARBER, Samuel (1910—), *Concerto for Violoncello*
Allegro moderato; Andante sostenuto;
Molto allegro e appassionato

As one of the prominent figures in the contemporary American musical scene, Samuel Barber, born 1910 in West Chester, Pennsylvania, requires no special introduction. He is the recipient of several prizes: a Pulitzer Traveling Scholarship, a Guggenheim Fellowship, and the American Prix de Rome. His *Adagio for Strings* enjoys great popularity with concert audiences, and the success of the opera *Vanessa*, with a libretto by Gian Carlo Menotti, has enhanced his prestige considerably here and in Europe. Barber was a student of Rosario Scalero (1870-1954) who was trained in Vienna in the Brahms tradition. Compared to the experimental tendencies of today, which point either to the 20th century Vienna school (Schönberg, Webern) or to the music of Stockhausen or Boulez based on serial technique and utmost freedom of rhythm, Barber's style with its stress on lyricism must be regarded as rather on the conservative side. But while his themes are basically tonal, his harmonic treatment is by no means "conservative," and distinctly shows traits of contemporary idioms. The concerto for violoncello is a case in point.

The concerto was completed on November 22, 1945, at Capricorn, Barber's home in Mount Kisco, N. Y. (Westchester County). It was played for the first time by Raya Garbousova in Boston, who championed the work in subsequent performances in New York (Philharmonic Society), Louisville, and other cities. It is a very demanding piece for the soloist, and takes the high technical standard of the orchestra for granted. Structurally maintaining the traditional three-movement design, the concerto also displays many *cantilena* passages and imaginative technical devices.

The first movement is cast in the classical concerto form with an orchestral ritornello which exposes the two principal themes. An interesting feature is the position of the cadenza which precedes the recapitulation. In this respect, Barber follows the precedent set by Mendelssohn in his violin concerto. The Andante sostenuto in C sharp minor, in which the string body is muffled, has the quality of a placid *siciliana*. Its gentle ending is contrasted sharply with the rapid rugged figure of the violins which opens the finale. A dialogue between the soloist and orchestra develops, terminated by a general rest. Then the second theme enters in a recitative-like manner built upon an *ostinato* bass. Once more the composer adheres to the classical scheme (exposition-development-recapitulation) and provides fine opportunities for the soloist, particularly in the coda where the capabilities of the violoncello are fully utilized.

BARTÓK, Béla (1881-1945)
Divertimento for String Orchestra
Allegro ma non troppo; Molto adagio; Allegro assai

War clouds had begun to darken the political horizon over Europe when in the summer of 1939 Béla Bartók found himself in Switzerland as the guest of Paul Sacher, the conductor of the Basel Chamber Orchestra whom he had met in 1929. A lasting friendship formed between the two, a happy relationship that bore fine artistic fruit. The Basel Chamber Orchestra had become an important factor not only in the musical life of the old Swiss city, but in the furtherance of contemporary music. The orchestra cultivated new creations and commissioned works that, of course, received their first performances by this fine body under Sacher's direction. For this orchestra and the local chapter of the International Society for Contemporary Music Bartók wrote three of his most outstanding pieces: the Music for String Instruments, Percussion, and Celesta (1936), the Sonata for Two Pianos and Percussion (1937), and the Divertimento for String Orchestra (1939).

Sacher lodged Bartók and his wife in a chalet in the village of Saanen. From there the composer wrote to his son Béla on August 18, 1939:

Somehow I feel like an old-time musician summoned as the guest of a Maecenas. As you know, I am the guest of the Sachers here, who look after everything — from a distance . . . . As to excursions, I can of course not start anything in spite of the kindness of the weather: I must work. And specially for Sacher: commission — something for string orchestra; even this makes my situation like that of the musician of yore. Luckily the work went well; in 15 days I have already turned out a work about 25 minutes long; just yesterday I finished it . . . .

The "old-time musicians" Bartók alluded to are probably composers of the eighteenth century like Haydn and Mozart, who often wrote under conditions like those Bartók faced when he composed the Divertimento between August 2 and 17, 1939. Why did he call the composition a "divertimento", or "entertainment"? To make an analogy between the classical composer and the twentieth century musician? The divertimento emerged in the classical period as an important medium for music in a light vein for social occasions. It was a piece of several movements, of simple texture, mostly in the major key, and devoid of contrapuntal complications. It contained two dance numbers (minuets) and concerted sections. It was not conceived orchestrally, but written for single players; that is to say, the part of each instrument in the score was usually executed by one musician.

Bartók's divertimento follows the classical tradition only in the broadest sense. Basically gay, it contains simple melodies and dance tunes, yet it displays passages of a contrapuntal nature and its middle movement is in a serious mood. An interesting technical aspect is the application of the technique of the baroque concerto grosso in the frequent alternation of a small unit of solo players (concertino) and the full complement (concerto grosso). According to the composer the latter should comprise twenty-two players.

The opening Allegro discloses the traditional three-sectional design of exposition, development, and recapitulation. The vivid extended main theme

is introduced by the first violins while the other instruments provide a simple accompaniment in tapping triplets. A rather gay mood is immediately established. The first violins generally lead, despite the occasional reduction of the entire body to a small concertino. The thematic flow is interrupted by a short unison exclamation, whose rhythmical design proves to be of great structural importance:

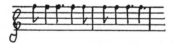

Occurring often, this statement creates the bridge to the second theme, announced by the concertino:

It also furnishes the thematic material for the closing group. Thus, while at the beginning the main accent is on the melody, it is the rhythm that defines the closing of the exposition. Just as entanglements and intricacies are vital elements in light comedies, so Bartók shows us that in a basically serene divertimento there is room for contrapuntal work, and he spices the development section with imitations and canonic passages. Once more the rhythmic energy of example 2 proves its strength and structural importance in the transition to the recapitulation. The latter presents the thematic material in new manipulations and instrumental combinations. While the movement fades away with a sustained *C* of the first violins the other instruments pluck the now familiar obstinate rhythm of example 2.

The somewhat somber Adagio employs the concertino only sporadically. It parallels the first movement to a certain extent in that the opening main idea, given by the second violin

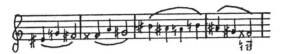

contrasts sharply with an incisive rhythmic passage by the viola:

The main theme is developed from a little motif (E sharp—G—F sharp) that reveals a remarkable generating power later on. Bartók elaborates on it extensively to build up to a great climax. This is a passage of dramatic intensity that seems to break asunder the framework of the gay divertimento. There are two more moments of agitation in the concluding portion, one shortly before the movement dies away in a soft pianissimo.

The somberness of the Adagio is quicky dispelled by a fast-moving finale whose main theme is in the spirit of a rustic peasant dance:

The composer does not hesitate, however, to use this simple melodic material for imitations, and to flavor the thematic process with the insertion of fugal passages. The subject of these passages is derived from a forceful unison statement:

The fugal procedure, once interrupted by an inverted unison statement, is not allowed to go far. It is cut short by a solo episode of the violoncello and violin. The latter consolidates its dominance and even indulges in a cadenza in gypsy fashion, which signals the entry of the recapitulation. Now the listener is in for a surprise: the main theme presents itself in a new shape— its inversion:

The pace seems to become quicker through the triplet motion. After the speed has increased to Vivacissimo the tempo slows to prepare for a polka-like episode; rolling triplets interfere and lead to the rapidly moving conclusion.

Hungarian Sketches
An Evening in the Village; Bear Dance; Melody;
Slightly Tipsy; Swineherd's Dance

Béla Bartók spent the summer of 1931 in Mondsee, a village on the lake of the same name located in the Salzkammergut. This lovely Austrian alpine district is immensely popular as a vacation country and has become famous on this side of the Atlantic as the country of "The White Horse Inn." An Austrian-American conservatory was established in Mondsee, which held sessions during the summer months. Its teaching staff was composed of musicians from Austria, Hungary, Germany, Poland, and the United States (Josef and Rosina Lhévinne). Although Bartók had joined the faculty as a teacher of composition, he expressed criticism of the enterprise, describing it as badly organized. But the job had its compensations—Bartók's teaching obligations required only eight hours a week, he was well paid, and he received his salary with "beautiful punctuality." This comfortable assignment gave him ample time for creative work, and he took full advantage of the opportunity. The result was the suite *Hungarian Sketches*. It is not an original composition and constitutes, in fact, an assemblage of five orchestrated piano items: Nos. 1 and 2 are from *Ten Easy Piano Pieces* (1908), No. 3 from *Nenies* (1908), and Nos. 4 and 5 from the large collection *For Children* (1908-1911). The latter was the fruit of Bartók's intensive folk song research.

Bartók expected numerous performances and broadcasts of the *Hungarian Sketches;* he orchestrated these items "on account of the money." It should be borne in mind that the Bartók of 1931 showed a different artistic physiognomy from the Bartók of 1908. Such works as the first four string quartets, the opera *Duke Bluebeard's Castle,* the ballets *The Wooden Prince* and *The Miraculous Mandarin* displayed his individual style and had established him as one of the leading contemporary composers and as a true representative of the "New Music" that developed as a reaction against neoromanticism and its sensualism and sentimentalism. Opponents of the New Music spoke of its barbarism and, significantly enough, Bartók entitled one of his piano pieces Allegro barbaro. Bartók's terse style and bold harmonic combinations have sometimes antagonized critics and public alike. By using for the *Hungarian Sketches* noncontroversial pieces dating back more than twenty years, Bartók ruled out the danger of opposition and formed a suite that offers a diversity of interesting and easily perceptible musical images.

BEETHOVEN, Ludwig van (1770-1827)
Die Geschöpfe des Prometheus
(Excerpts: Overture and Nos. 1, 2, 3, 5, 9, 15 and 16)

The score of *Die Geschöpfe des Prometheus* was Beethoven's contribution to the Viennese ballet pantomime, which achieved a renaissance at the turn of the eighteenth century, some years after a flourishing period during the reign of the empress Maria Theresa in the 1760s. Both periods owed their bloom to the activities of eminent choreographers in the imperial residence. Gasparo

Angliolini and Jean Georges Noverre dominated the first era; Antonio Muzzarelli and Salvatore Viganó competed for the favor of the Viennese in the second. Yet their numerous creations departed with the day and were soon laid to rest in archives. Only two works survived as the result of the collaboration between the choreographer and a composer of historic consequence: Angliolini's *Don Juan*, set to music by Gluck in 1761, and Vigano's and Beethoven's *Die Geschöpfe des Prometheus*.

The Neapolitan Viganó (1769-1821) and his wife Josepha Maria Medina (née Mayer in Vienna), both dancers, were enthusiastically acclaimed when they appeared at the Viennese court theater in 1793, and their instant success seriously threatened the prestige and position of the incumbent choreographer, Antonio Muzzarelli. This situation brought about a division of the public, but the admirers of Viganó, incidentally a nephew of Luigi Boccherini, constituted the majority. He triumphed not only because of his and his wife's extraordinary dancing and pantomimic gifts, but also for his choreographic ingenuity, which aimed at a dramatic sense, deep expression, and beauty in movement and action.

One of his great admirers was the empress Maria Theresa, second wife of the emperor Francis I, a lady with fine musical training and taste to whom Beethoven had dedicated his famous septet (Opus 20). It is not farfetched to assume that the empress may have influenced the selection of the composer for Viganó's scenario.

Beethoven's position as a composer was well established in Vienna by 1800. The compositions bearing the opus numbers 1-17, 19, and 20 had been published or publicly played, and his first symphony had already been heard. He undoubtedly received the commission for *Prometheus* with great satisfaction and approached his task with deep interest. He had already tried his hand at ballet music in 1790 and 1791 in his native Bonn, when he wrote the music to a *Ritter-Ballet* ("Knight Ballet") that had a scenario drawn up by his friend Count Ferdinand Waldstein. The performance of that work was a rather private affair and the name of the composer was not even mentioned.

Things were now completely different in Vienna. Naturally the name of the renowned composer and piano virtuoso Herr van Beethoven adorned the program. The bill of the first production of *Prometheus* on March 28, 1801, at the Burgtheater defined it as a "heroic-allegorical ballet in two acts, in which two statues come to life and are made perceptive to all passions of human life through the power of harmony." Prometheus guides the statues up to Parnassus to be taught about poetry, drama, dance, and music. On this occasion the ballet was preceded by *Der Dorfbarbier*, a very successful Singspiel by Johann Schenk, who had been in 1793 secretly Beethoven's counterpoint teacher.

Prometheus had a moderate success. There were thirteen repeats in 1801 and nine in 1802, yet Viganó had much confidence in the piece and remodeled it in 1813 for the Scala theater in Milan with the inclusion of pieces from Haydn's popular oratorios *The Creation* and *The Seasons*. This procedure was again applied to *Prometheus* thirty years later in Vienna by August Hus and Matthias Strebinger, who also garnished Beethoven's music with pieces from oratorios by Haydn. This version achieved no less than eighty repeat performances in Milan. Beethoven published a piano edition of the work under the title *Gli Uomini di Prometeo* in 1801.

The piece comprises an overture, an introduction to the first act, and sixteen numbers. The overture, Beethoven's first essay in this field, reveals a conspicuous kinship to the First Symphony: both are in C major, have an Adagio introduction that commences with a seventh chord, and show the repetition of the first quick motif in the higher second in the Allegro section. It should be noted that the overture lacks an elaborating middle section; a short bridge connects the exposition and recapitulation. The ensuing introduction (Allegro non troppo, C minor), which bears in the piano score the heading "La Tempesta," in some ways foreshadows the storm scene of the Pastoral Symphony.

A brief synopsis of the numbers may be helpful. In No. 1 (Poco Adagio) the two statues appear and Prometheus shows his delight (Allegro con brio). An Adagio in F major and an Allegro in D minor comprise No. 2. In No. 3 (Allegro vivace, 3/4, F major) the first rhythmical motif is identical with the motif we hear at the beginning of the second act of the *Meistersinger*, which is purely coincidental. No. 5 constitutes one of the most remarkable pieces Beethoven ever penned, on account of the employment of the harp (the only case in Beethoven's output), and the delightful instrumental combinations. The opening Adagio (4/4) is followed by an Andante section (6/8) with a violoncello solo characterized by a transparent accompaniment to which the other instruments contribute their individual color. No. 9, which commences in E flat (Adagio, 3/4), eloquently reveals Beethoven's dramatic powers in a compassionate recitative-like section and concludes with an Allegro in C minor. The language of the later Beethoven (the *Eroica*) is here anticipated. No. 15 (Andantino, B flat—Allegro) discloses a serene and lyric quality with a delightful instrumental treatment. No. 16, entitled Finale (E flat, 2/4), will no doubt surprise many a listener. The opening theme is the melody familiar to us from the finale of the *Eroica* and also from the Variation and Fugue in E flat for Piano, Opus 35, published in 1803. Beethoven used this theme four times: in a *contredanse* (No. 7 in an assortment of twelve), in both the ballet and the piano variations, and finally in the *Eroica*. In the ballet finale the melody is used as a rondo theme and contrasted to another dance (No. 11). Many features anticipate corresponding passages in the *Eroica* finale, and thus the Prometheus music becomes an important musical, technical, and spiritual link to that symphony.

Concerto for Piano No. 1 in C major, Opus 15
Allegro con brio; Largo; Rondo: Allegro

The numbering of Beethoven's five piano concertos does not agree with their chronology. The concerto in C major is not his first, but his third essay in this field. He composed a piano concerto in E flat major in 1784 in Bonn, and no doubt played it on several occasions. It was in his bag when he went to Vienna in 1792. But Beethoven, aware of the superiority of his more mature works and the towering importance of Mozart's concertos, decided to shelve this early work, which came to light, after his death. Only the piano part was preserved, and the orchestral score for two flutes, oboes, and strings had to be reconstructed on the basis of relevant entries in the piano part to make this early piece available for performance.

Beethoven's second attempt in this medium is the concerto in B flat, which was published as Opus 19 late in the fall of 1801 in Leipzig, after the C major concerto had appeared as Opus 15 in March, 1801, in Vienna. Beethoven had revised the earlier score, which may partially account for the delay in publication. It should be noted that the first editions of both concertos lack any numbering. The familiar numbering stems from later nineteenth-century editions. The C major piece appeared as *Grand concert pour le piano*, while that in B flat was entitled *Concerto* (*sic*) *pour le pianoforte*.

The artistic growth of the concertos is reflected in the orchestration and the use of wind instruments. The concerto in B flat requires one flute and pairs of oboes, bassoons, and horns, while the C major piece is scored for full symphony orchestra with pairs of flutes, oboes, clarinets, bassoons, horns, trumpets, and kettledrums.

Beethoven sketched the C major concerto in 1795/96 and completed the composition in 1798. It is assumed that he played it for the first time in Prague and that he included it in the program of a concert he gave on April 2, 1800, in the Burgtheater in Vienna. The poster simply announced "a grand concerto for the pianoforte, played and composed by Herr Ludwig van Beethoven." (This *Akademie* also featured the first performance of the first symphony.) The review of the *Allgemeine musikalische Zeitung* (Leipzig) stated that "he [Beethoven] played a new concerto of his own which contains many beautiful pages particularly in the first two movements."

The C major concerto was composed before the C minor sonata (*"Pathetique"*), the first symphony, and the string quartets, Opus 18. Formally and technically, Beethoven followed the road Mozart laid out in his Viennese concertos. That it to say, he fully adopted the concept that saw the concerto as a symphonic commonwealth in which the clavier appears not as a ruling member, but as a prominent one with a special task. He adopted the three-movement structure and the formal designs Mozart applied to the individual movements.

The basic mood is one of energy and vigor; it is determined by the march-like main idea, which opens the long orchestral exposition, but, curiously enough, is never assigned to the piano. The solo instrument enters with a new idea of rather gentle quality. The piano tenderly alludes to the main idea only rhythmically in the passages that precede the recapitulation, while in the recapitulation the orchestra states the main idea forcefully. The main idea also prevails in the short but vigorous postlude after the cadenza. Beethoven supplied three cadenzas for the first movement, taking into account the possibilities of the improved piano models with extended range.

In the slow movement (Largo, A flat major), Beethoven followed Mozart's practice in excluding the trumpets and kettledrums, and he also silenced the flute and oboes to achieve tender sonorities and to avoid bright colors. The gentle lyricism of the Largo is contrasted with the gaiety of the rondo finale, in which Beethoven's capricious temperament is evidenced by the strange dynamic accents he imposed on the second theme.

Concerto for Piano No. 3 in C minor, Opus 37
Allegro con brio; Largo; Rondo: Allegro

The original manuscript of this concerto bears the following heading: *Concerto 1800 Da L.v. Beethoven*. Though authoritative to the highest degree, the entry is nevertheless chronologically misleading; and it refers only to one stage of the composition of this concerto, since some of its musical ideas appear in a sketchbook used in 1796. The piece was not quite ready for publication in 1800, and the solo part was not fully committed to paper when Beethoven played the concerto in the famous *Akademie* on April 5, 1803. The concert took place in the Theater an der Wien, where he occupied an apartment at that time. It offered an all-Beethoven program, for which the usual ticket prices were doubled and tripled. The rich bill of fare included the first symphony and the first presentations of the second symphony, the C minor concerto, and the oratorio *Christ on the Mount of Olives*.

The last rehearsal held on the preceding day began at 8:00 A.M. and lasted for six and a half hours. To bolster the energy of the exhausted participants, Prince Lichnowsky, one of Beethoven's most enthusiastic supporters, ordered cold cuts and wine delivered in large baskets. Spirits were revived, and it was agreed to run through the oratorio again. Ferdinand Ries, one of Beethoven's important students, related that on the morning of the last rehearsal nothing of the solo part of the concerto was set down but scrawlings that showed an occasional semblance of notes. This is corroborated by Ignaz von Seyfried, the regular conductor at the Theater an der Wien, who acted then as the page turner for Beethoven. Says Seyfried: "I saw almost nothing but empty leaves; at the most here and there a few Egyptian hieroglyphics, wholly unintelligible to me, scribbled down to serve as clues for him (Beethoven). He played nearly all the solo part from memory. As was often the case, he had not had time to put it all on paper. Whenever he reached the end of an 'invisible' passage, he gave me a secret nod. My evident anxiety not to miss the decisive moment amused him greatly."

The concert was a financial but not an artistic success. The symphony did not fare well with the critics; as for the clavier concerto, one reviewer stated: "Herr von Beethoven, very well known as a superb pianist, did not present the C minor concerto to full satisfaction of the public." Beethoven refused to be daunted and consented to lead the orchestra in the second reading in 1804, with Ferdinand Ries as soloist. It seems that Beethoven was not in a hurry to get the concerto into print, all the less so since he was busy with the "Eroica" symphony (1803) and the opera *Leonore* (*Fidelio, 1804*). The concerto finally appeared in November, 1804, in Vienna.

The C minor concerto, which requires a full symphony orchestra, effected the transition from Beethoven's earlier concertos, in B flat major (Opus 19, 1794/95) and C major (Opus 15, 1795/96), to the great creations in G major (1806) and E flat major (1809). These later concertos displayed important innovations and modified somewhat the concerto pattern devised by Mozart.

Beethoven was thoroughly familiar with Mozart's historic achievement as a composer of clavier concertos. The type of concerto created by Mozart represents a symphonic commonwealth, in which the clavier appears not as a ruler, but as a prominent member with a special task. Mozart emphasized this situation by requiring the soloist to play also in *tutti* orchestral sections like the *maestro al cembalo* in the ensemble music of the baroque and in the opera orchestra. In the Mozartian concerto the clavier also functions as a coloring agent. It will, for example, produce a trill while the clarinets and horns play a melody.

The basic formal design of the Mozartian concerto type and the coloring function of the solo instrument are also evidenced in Beethoven's concertos. Beethoven, however, dispensed completely with the thorough-bass function of the piano. Mozart had to work with a very small orchestra, and he occasionally played concertos with only a string group. Beethoven, on the other hand, demanded a full orchestra, for which no piano support was needed.

The concerto in C minor opens with a theme of march-like quality, a feature also heard in the great E flat concerto. The march rhythm is contrasted with the lyricism of the second theme. However, the gently announced main idea is transformed into an heroic tune in the recapitulation. The cadenza does not lead to the restatement of the main theme but to a highly dramatic episode. In this, after a dialogue between the kettledrum and the clavier, a tension-filled crescendo brings the movement to a conclusion with a powerful unison of piano and orchestra.

Gentle lyricism and instrumental delicacy are the keynotes for the Largo in E major. Oboes, clarinets, trumpets, and kettledrums are silent, and the muffled string body supplies a guitar-like accompaniment to the figurations and arabesques spun out by the clavier. Beethoven demands *gran espressione* even for the delivery of runs in the cadenza. The ending with a fortissimo stroke after the music begins to fade in the concluding measures is an odd innovation. Even a movement in C minor provides opportunities for Beethoven's humor. This is proved conclusively in the capricious final **Rondo**, which ultimately turns into C major.

Beethoven dedicated the concerto in C minor to the Prussian Prince Louis Ferdinand (1772-1806), a musical nephew of Frederick II. The Prince, who knew and admired Beethoven, died on the battlefield in the Napoleonic wars.

Concerto for Piano No. 4 in G major, Op. 58
Allegro moderato; Andante con moto; Rondo: Vivace

The first ideas for the G major concerto were jotted down in a voluminous sketchbook that Beethoven filled with sketches for the opera *Leonore*, later named *Fidelio*. Beethoven worked on the opera during 1804 and 1805. After its completion he concerned himself with the fourth symphony, the string quartets, Opus 59, the piano concerto in G major, heard tonight, and the violin concerto. The concertos were completed in 1806, and the violin concerto reached the public in the same year. Prince Lobkowitz, one of Beethoven's most active patrons (Beethoven honored him with the dedication of the third, fifth, and sixth symphonies, and the string quartets, Opus 18 and

74), arranged two concerts of his music in his Viennese palace. They included the first four symphonies, fragments from the opera *Leonore,* and the G major concerto, with the composer as soloist. The first public reading was given in the memorable *Akademie* of December 22, 1808. The program contained enough music for two concerts. On this occasion the fifth and sixth symphonies were performed for the first time, and sections of the Mass in C major, the aria *Ah perfido,* and the Choral Fantasy were played as well as the G major concerto, with Beethoven as the soloist.

The concerto, published in August, 1808, was dedicated to Archduke Rudolph, the musically gifted prince who became Beethoven's piano and theory student. The prince was a proficient pianist and had studied carefully the works of his teacher. Beethoven honored him with an impressive list of dedications, including, in addition to the G major concerto, the concerto in E flat major; the sonatas in E flat major, Opus 81a, and B flat major, Opus 106; the violin sonata in G major, Opus 96; the trio in B flat major, Opus 97; the vocal score to *Fidelio;* the *Missa solemnis;* and the piano transcription of the Great Fugue, Opus 133.

Technically speaking, Beethoven's concertos followed the road laid out by Mozart. Mozart's great achievement was the fusion of the baroque principle of instrumental dualism (tutti and solo) with the symphonic concept and the thematic dualism of the classical sonata. Thus the clavier appears in the orchestra not as the dominating factor, but as a prominent member with a special task. In his first concertos Beethoven strictly upheld the Mozartian tradition. The G major work, however, discloses some unusual features. At the very beginning the clavier announces the chief idea, and, acting as a member of the orchestra, injects a color that is lacking in the orchestral palette. As unusual as the clavier's opening is the continuation of the orchestra, which occurs with a startling harmonic turn. Another "irregularity" is the absence of the second theme in the orchestral exposition. No less significant is the entry of the solo instrument, which simply takes up the thematic thread and spins it forth. The fascinating details are too numerous to be discussed here. The frequent use of the basic rhythm of the first movement of the fifth symphony will not escape the attentive listener.

Beethoven gave the cadenzas much thought and wrote several for both the first movement and finale. We do not know whether he was satisfied with them in this case, but we do know his ultimate solution of the cadenza problem— in the first movement of the E flat concerto he decreed: "Non si fa una cadenza" (No cadenza should be played).

The middle movement of the concerto, an Andante in E minor, is unique in the concerto literature. Formally, it is a dialogue between the piano and the strings, which play in unison except for a few measures. The classifications of tutti and solo, however, seem meaningless in view of the integration of the piano sound into the orchestral sonority. There is a tradition that sees in the orchestra the pitiless forces of Hades and in the piano the lamenting and imploring voice of Orpheus. Putting aside poetic hermeneutics, we feel, as listeners, utterances of spiritual forces that carry us into sublime spheres. In the finale we are brought down to earth again. The trumpets and kettledrums, silent so far, join the orchestral forces and contribute to the rhythmic flow that carries us irresistibly along.

Concerto for Violin in D major, Opus 61
Allegro ma non troppo; Larghetto; Rondo

The history of Beethoven's violin concerto and the life of its first interpreter form an absorbing tale. Beethoven wrote the piece for violinist Franz Clement (b. 1780), one of the most remarkable Viennese musicians, who was also respected by Haydn, Weber, and Cherubini. As a child prodigy he created a sensation in London, where he played in a concert directed by Haydn. His relations with Beethoven date from the time when Clement, as *primo violino* (concertmaster), witnessed the first performance of Beethoven's opera *Fidelio* (1805). The necessity of revising the opera was realized, and at a session held at the palace of Beethoven's patron, Prince Lichnowsky, Clement played by heart the leading voices of the entire opera on his violin. Spohr narrated that Clement, after hearing Haydn's *The Creation*, made up, with the help of the libretto, a complete piano score of the oratorio that the composer declared fit for publication. He accomplished a similar feat with Cherubini's opera *Faniska,* and the amazed composer professed that he had never come across a similar musical memory. Clement was for a time assistant conductor to Weber in Prague, but his restlessness drove him to become a roving virtuoso. His last years were dark, and he died destitute in Vienna in 1842.

As a conductor of an amateur orchestra he programmed Beethoven's first two symphonies and was bold enough to dare a reading of the "Eroica" with his group. He then included the symphony in the program of one of his own concerts and invited Beethoven to conduct it. Thus the first public performances of the "Eroica" were the achievement of Clement. No wonder Beethoven felt very much obliged to Clement and reciprocated by composing the violin concerto for him. Its humorous title reads: "Concerto par Clemenza pour Clement primo violino e direttore al theatro di Vienna. Dal L. v. Bthvn. 1806."

Clement played it on December 23, 1806, according to contemporary reports without even a rehearsal, as Beethoven had finished the piece hardly two days before the performance. The public applauded it, but the experts showed a somewhat critical attitude that, strangely enough, affected the composer. He decided to convert the piece into a piano concerto and to publish this version also (1808). He dedicated it to Julie von Breuning, wife of Steffen, his friend from the early Bonn days, who was later (1809) honored with the dedication of the original violin version.

The violin concerto fell into disrepute in Vienna as being unrewarding and unperformable. Clement championed it abroad without substantial success. Pierre-Marie Baillot (1771-1842), a Beethoven herald in Paris, played the concerto twice in the Conservatoire in 1828, but also without success. As a result, French violinists shied away from the work for almost half a century, until 1847 when Jean-Delphin Alard (1815-1888), who had succeeded Baillot as violin teacher at the Conservatoire, tried to break ground for the concerto. Meanwhile it had found a youthful champion in Henri Vieux-temps (1820-1881), a Belgian of French extraction who had come to Vienna to study counterpoint with Simon Sechter. Having learned of Beethoven's violin concerto, Vieuxtemps studied it and played the work on March 16, 1834. It seems strange and almost inexplicable that such Viennese violinists as Joseph Böhm, teacher of Joachim, Joseph Mayseder, and Ignaz Schuppanzigh, who played Beethoven's quartets under the composer's direction, had failed to play his violin concerto, and it fell to a foreign boy of fourteen to rediscover the concerto for the Viennese and break the spell on the work that had lasted for so long.

The autograph of the concerto was acquired by Carl Czerny, who willed it to the Court Library, now the Austrian National Library. It is perhaps Beethoven's most interesting manuscript because of the numerous additional entries. These can be divided into two categories: alterations in the solo part, perhaps suggested by Clement, and adjustments connected with the conversion of the work into a piano concerto. The printed version does not show the changes in the violin part entered in the autograph.

The violin concerto, with the exception of the suppressed piano concerto of 1784, is Beethoven's fifth creation in this form. Technically speaking, he followed Mozart's great Viennese clavier concerti. Mozart's historic achievement was the fusion of the baroque principle of the instrumental dualism of orchestra and solo with the thematic dualism of the classical sonata form and the symphonic concept. The solo instrument appears not as a ruler in the symphonic commonwealth, but rather as a prominent member with a special task.

A few of the many individual and novel features in Beethoven's violin concerto may be noted here. In the first movement four kettledrum strokes, which are soon revealed to be thematically important, form a startling beginning. As in the preceding G major concerto for piano, the solo part grows out of the orchestral texture; note, for example, how the trill passages of the solo violin are a coloristic element in combination with a transparent group of wind instruments or strings. The recapitulation makes a triumphant entry with the four mighty strokes that were gently indicated at the beginning. In the Larghetto the flutes, oboes, trumpets, and kettledrums are silent and the violins are muted, giving the movement a delicate orchestral fabric. The transition to the final Rondo is terse; the main theme is effectively announced on the G-string, followed by a markedly contrasting repetition of the theme in the high position on the E-string. The listener is not prepared for the two sudden closing strokes that follow the gradual dying away of the main theme. There is hardly any need to continue the enumeration of the concerto's fascinating details, nor to stress the beauty and intrinsic values of the work. Its symphonic character is never impaired by purely virtuoso passages, for the solo violin speaks movingly as the soul and eloquent voice of the orchestral commonwealth.

Overture to "Coriolanus," Opus 62

Beethoven's overture to *Coriolanus* was not composed to Shakespeare's well-known drama, but to a play by Heinrich von Collin (1771-1811), an influential official in the court administration and a respected author and dramatist in Vienna. Matthäus von Collin, the playwright's brother, asserted that Shakespeare's tragedy was unknown to Heinrich when he wrote his *Coriolanus*. In Shakespeare's play Coriolanus falls a victim of intrigues, but in von Collin's version the hero perishes by his own sword.

Von Collin had achieved popularity as author of the *Wehrmannslieder* (Soldier Songs), inspired by Austria's wars against Napoleon. He was also successful with his drama *Regulus* (1801), which centers on the Roman hero in the First Punic War. *Coriolanus*, which is spiritually related to *Regulus*, was given in 1802 in the Burgtheater. It was published in 1804 and had a successful run in Vienna until 1805; it was performed in other cities. Matthäus wrote in the *Collected Works* of his brother that Abbé Maximilian Stadler (1748-1833), a close friend of Mozart, had arranged interludes from the pages of Mozart's opera *Idomeneo* for the Burgtheater production. This easy way of furnishing incidental music to plays was customary in those days.

Beethoven was attracted to the plot of *Coriolanus* and its chief characters and decided to provide the drama with a musical prologue. This was first played in an all-Beethoven program in one of two subscription concerts that took place in the mansion of Prince Lobkowitz in March, 1807. The overture was probably performed in connection with the play on April 24, 1807, and it was published as Opus 62 in 1808 with a dedication to Heinrich von Collin.

In the years 1805-1810 Beethoven's mind was intensely focused on the overture problem; he laboriously and ingeniously wrestled with it in the overtures to *Leonore* (*Fidelio*), *Coriolanus*, and *Egmont*. The core of this problem was the relationship between the program (the poetic or dramatic idea) and the form. Beethoven abandoned the combination of a huge design and realistic descriptive elements, as seen in the *Leonore* overtures Nos. 2 and 3, in favor of a highly concentrated form, based on the sonata pattern, that aims to express the basic features of the drama and its ending.

Alexander Wheelock Thayer, Beethoven's biographer, professed that he, as a fervent admirer of Shakespeare's *Coriolanus*, experienced feelings of dislike as he heard Beethoven's work for the first time. This sentiment gave way to admiration when he read von Collin's drama. Wagner wrote beautifully about Beethoven's overture on several occasions, once in connection with a performance he conducted in Zürich in 1852. Regarding the ending, a remark of the Russian Beethoven scholar Wilhelm von Lenz (1809-1883) merits quotation: "No other overture dies as this one."

Symphony No. 4 in B flat major, Opus 60

Adagio- Allegro vivace; Adagio; Allegro vivace;
Allegro ma non troppo

The genesis of Beethoven's fourth symphony is only vaguely known. After the completion of the "Eroica" in 1804, Beethoven's creative efforts were concentrated on the opera *Leonore* (1805), known as *Fidelio*, the piano sonatas in C major and F minor (Opus 53 and 57 respectively), the piano concerto in G major, and the symphony in C minor. The work on the C minor symphony was comparatively far advanced when Beethoven decided to interrupt it in favor of another symphony and to move with the piece in a different direction. This was the symphony in B flat major, which bears on the autograph the simple heading *Sinfonia 4ta, 1806. L.v. Bthvn.* Alexander W. Thayer ventured the assumption in his monumental Beethoven biography that the severe criticism heaped on the "Eroica" prompted Beethoven to abandon the project of the C minor symphony for the time being and to write the simpler symphony in B flat major so not to overtax his followers with another creation of such emotional and dramatic intensity. The fourth is the only Beethoven symphony that has no surviving sketchbook to enlighten us on the gradual emergence of the ideas and their elaboration.

In the early fall of 1806 Beethoven was the guest of Prince Lichnowsky in Silesia in Grätz. Both paid a visit to Count Franz Oppersdorf, a great music enthusiast, who kept a little orchestra that regaled Beethoven with his second symphony. Count Oppersdorf became the dedicatee of the fourth symphony, which was premiered in Vienna in March, 1807, at two subscription concerts arranged by Prince Lichnowsky for Beethoven. The concerts took place in the princely palace (today the Czechoslovakian Embassy) and featured only the works of Beethoven: the first four symphonies, the overture to *Coriolanus*, the piano concerto in G major, and several arias from *Fidelio*. The fourth symphony, the overture, and the concerto were novelties. They were presented to a highly exclusive audience that consisted of Beethoven's sincerest admirers. We do not know how the new and old works were grouped, but we can assume that the new symphony was well received.

Robert Schumann described the fourth symphony as a "slender Greek maiden between two giants from the North," meaning the "Eroica" and the C minor symphony. Here Schumann spoke poetically in metaphorical terms and expressed the stylistic difference between these three symphonies. The third and fifth are revolutionary creations, while the fourth appears as an enlarged specimen of the symphonic type developed by Beethoven's predecessors Haydn and Mozart. It is a symphony of a more lyric character and carefree attitude than the "Eroica" and C minor symphonies, with their bold innovations, contrapuntal complexities, dramatic climaxes, and more massive orchestration. The B flat symphony was very dear to Mendelssohn, who included it in the program that signaled the beginning of his activities as conductor of the Gewandhaus Concerts in Leipzig in 1836. The choice is significant of Mendelssohn's artistic temperament.

Richard Wagner, on the other hand, who once conducted the B flat symphony, never referred to it in his theoretical writings although he dealt in some instances extensively with Beethoven's other symphonic creations and the problem they posed to the performer and interpreter. Yet the fourth symphony is by no means a technically easy piece. The cellists, double bass players, and bassoonists of Beethoven's day and later cried out in desperation because of the requirements of their parts in the second and last movements. Beethoven actually wrote a bass passage that was unplayable unless the lowest string was tuned down to achieve an extension of the range so the required notes could be obtained. Beethoven had made the acquaintance of the Venetian double bass virtuoso Domenico Dragonetti (1763-1846), who in a private session had revealed to him the potentialities of the huge instrument, and orchestra musicians from the early nineteenth century to the present day who play Beethoven's symphonies have had to suffer the consequences of this session.

An analysis of the symphony cannot be offered here; only a few details can be pointed out. The first Allegro is prefaced by a somber Adagio; its harmonic vagueness does not presage the very pleasant and serene things to come, particularly the sudden vanishing of the misty atmosphere and the abrupt entry of the Allegro in a brilliant mood. Note the appearance of a new idea in the middle section and the gradual slackening of the motion until it seems to come to a standstill:

A mistyness develops that seems to duplicate that of the introductory Adagio, yet it is solved differently. The fog is not lifted suddenly, but gradually, and an extended crescendo passage finally brings about the re-entry of the main idea. Berlioz appropriately compared this passage to "a peacefully flowing river, which suddenly disappears and [then] leaves the subterranean bed in a foaming cascade which falls down roaringly."

According to Berlioz the Adagio defies any analysis. It is an immensely broad cantilena, containing expressive motifs with small note values. The melody is, to quote Berlioz again, "angelic and of irresistible tenderness." It is pushed aside only once, about midway, by the rhythmically incisive motif of the accompaniment in the measures that precede the recapitulation. The listener will notice that the melodic thread is spun over the entire orchestra, and nearly all the instruments share in the melodic contour. This technique is conspicuous in the frolicsome Scherzo, where the melodic line jumps from instrument to instrument and from section to section.

The speedy finale is akin to some of Haydn's witty last movements and to that of the second symphony. There is no juxtaposition of darkness and light as there is in the first movement; the gaiety is never seriously threatened. Berlioz speaks of a "continuous chatting, which is interrupted by a few stern and fierce chords" that reflect occasional irate outbreaks by the composer, but without any harmful consequences in the long run. At the very end, however, Beethoven smiles at us good-naturedly and dismisses us tersely with a hearty laugh.

Symphony No. 8 in F major, Opus 93
Allegro vivace e con brio; Allegretto scherzando;
Tempo di Minuetto; Allegro vivace

Beethoven worked on the eighth symphony during 1811 and completed the fair copy of the autograph in Linz in October, 1812. He had the parts copied in the winter of 1813. This symphony originated nearly simultaneously with the seventh, in A major, and both received a tryout on April 20, 1813, in the residence of Beethoven's devoted student Archduke Rudolph. The A major symphony had its public premiere, a great success, on December 8, 1813, and its sister work in F major was heard for the first time on February 27, 1814, in an all-Beethoven program presented in the large Redoutensaal of the imperial palace. Anton Schindler, Beethoven's first biographer, asserts that five thousand persons were in attendance.

This figure is probably somewhat exaggerated, yet on this occasion Beethoven had succeeded in assembling an orchestra whose string body consisted of sixty-nine professional and amateur musicians. The main attraction was neither the A major symphony nor the new one in F major, but *Wellingtons Sieg*, or *Die Schlacht bei Vittoria*, usually referred to as the "Battle" Symphony, which employs numerous trumpets, big drums to produce the thunder of the cannons, and rattles to imitate rifle fire. The F major symphony, sandwiched between the powerful one in A major and the sensational *Wellingtons Sieg*, achieved only a *succès d'estime*, whereas the first movement of the "Battle" Symphony generated such enthusiasm that it had to be repeated. Today, *Wellington Sieg* is almost forgotten and is regarded as a curiosity. *Sic transit gloria mundi.*

The eighth symphony occupies a position within Beethoven's symphonic work similar to that of the fourth in B flat major. Schumann described the fourth as a slender Greek maiden flanked by two giants from the North (the "Eroica" and the C minor symphonies). Similarly, the eighth is preceded by the powerful A major symphony and followed by the grandiose ninth. Berlioz pointed out, in a critical survey of Beethoven's symphonic work, that the eighth is hardly longer than the first, but excels it in instrumentation, rhythm, and melody. It could not be otherwise because the first marks the beginning of Beethoven's career as an orchestral composer.

Comparatively short, and of an intimate character in the middle movements, the eighth differs markedly from the preceding symphonies in C minor, F major, and A major, and, of course, also from the ninth. It does not connect the seventh with the ninth, but represents, in the words of Paul Bekker, a serene epilogue to the preceding seven. More than a decade lies between the completion of the eighth and of the ninth, and there is no spiritual or material connection between the lovely, serene landscape painting and the huge, dramatic, and powerful historical canvas.

Freshness and humor are the basic qualities of this symphony. The absence of an extended and pathetic middle movement is consistent with the serene and humoristic vein. Witness the conclusion of the opening Allegro and the unique Allegretto scherzando. In the words of Berlioz: "[This movement] is one of those creations that have no model and no companion piece: they fall perfect as they are from heaven into the lap of the artist. He writes them down at one stroke and when we listen to them we are stunned." The movement displays the finest type of miniature work with amazing details. For its conclusion Beethoven reserved a surprising move: he repeated the commonplace Italian cadence, which he certainly despised, six times, in a crescendo from *pianissimo* to *fortissimo*. Berlioz and others, who evidently failed to understand that this was meant to be sardonic and sarcastic, viewed it with critical eyes.

Beethoven also dispensed with the scherzo and fell back on a somewhat heavy eighteenth-century minuet. In conformity with the Austrian serenade tradition, the gentle trio provides virtuoso solos for the clarinet, horns, and violoncello.

In the finale Beethoven cast aside the pleasant and light vein of the serenade, which dominated the middle movements, and returned to the symphonic spirit with a very extended rondo. There is a melodic and spiritual relationship between the main ideas of the second and fourth movements. This movement, which runs through 502 measures, also served as a playground for his humor and the diversity of his rhythmic imagery. One very characteristic feature of the finale is the multitude of *piano, pianissimo*, and even triple-*piano* passages. These are juxtaposed with *fortissimo* passages, but pages with delicate orchestral combinations are more frequent than those marked by instrumental massiveness. Beethoven's laugh is not always hearty, and his humor shows sometimes a touch of fierceness. The finale of the eighth reflects all shades of humor, wit, and facetiousness.

Mass in C major, Opus 86

Beethoven acquired in his boyhood considerable knowledge of liturgical and church music, as did Haydn and Mozart. Haydn was a choirboy in St. Stephen's Cathedral in Vienna; Mozart practically grew up in the church and was only thirteen years old when he became concert master of the musical establishment of the Salzburg Archbishopric. Beethoven was not even twelve when he was allowed to deputize for his teacher, Christian Gottlob Neefe, at the organ of the court chapel in Bonn. In the following year, 1783, he was added to the court theatre orchestra as harpsichordist, though he did not receive any compensation until he was appointed to the official status of assistant court organist in 1784, a post he held until moving to Vienna in 1792. The income from this position, combined with what he earned after 1788 from his services as violist for the court theater, secured his livelihood.

We are very well informed about the operatic repertory of the court chapel during Beethoven's incumbency, but we are on a less firm ground regarding the liturgical repertory—the masses, vespers, and litanies—Beethoven accompanied. Mozart, in Salzburg, composed freely for the church, as he expressed in a letter to Padre Martini, the foremost musical scholar of the century. In contrast, Beethoven, the organist, apparently regarded his task completely fulfilled with his service at the organ and was not inclined to apply his creative talent to liturgical music.

Even after he had arrived in Vienna, Beethoven's creative mind was focused on piano, chamber, and orchestral music. His lack of active interest in church music is explained by the serious crisis in Austrian liturgical music caused by the church reforms of Emperor Joseph. Issued between 1783 and 1784, the Emperor's edicts sharply curtailed the length of the masses and specifically limited the use of instruments, thus obliterating the musical splendor displayed in the great Austrian churches. The effects of the Josephinian reform were gradually overcome in the 1790s, and the composers who had been most affected were, of course, Mozart and Haydn. Mozart, finding no opportunities to compose new masses, also refrained from completing the great C minor Mass, K. 427, which he had begun in 1782.

Though the Josephinian decrees were partly rescinded by the Emperor's successors, Leopold II and Franz I, the position of *musica sacra* in Vienna was not significantly altered, because of the attitudes of Emperor Franz and Hofkapellmeister Salieri, who wielded the baton in the court chapel for thirty-six years (1788-1824). It was the ambition of every Austrian composer of repute to have a liturgical work performed in the court chapel, yet because of the very conservative repertory under Salieri's tenure, which showed no consideration for those Austrian composers who enjoyed European reputation, Haydn and Beethoven had no chance whatsoever for such a performance. Although Salieri's activities reached far into the nineteenth century, and Beethoven outlived him by only two years, he personified all but the closing decades of the eighteenth century. Nothing is more indicative of Salieri's musical and aesthetic credo than this statement, "The world should have stopped with Gluck." He rejected Mozart's Requiem because it "went beyond the rules," and he dismissed Haydn's great masses as mishmash (*"mescolanza di tutti generi"*) and a grave sin against the church.

When Emperor Franz let it be known that he definitely did not wish to hear Haydn masses in the court chapel, Salieri was delighted to be supported in his repertory policy by the supreme authority. The door to the court chapel was, of course, also closed to Beethoven and so was that to St. Stephen's Cathedral, where Johann Georg Albrechtsberger (1736-1809) held the post of Domkapellmeister, a position, incidentally, that Mozart was to receive. Highly esteemed as a contrapuntist and theorist, Albrechtsberger was by nature a very conservative musician, not prepared to invite protest by performing works of a composer censured by the Emperor. This situation is paradoxical, as Beethoven was a student of both Albrechtsberger and Salieri, the former his counterpoint teacher and the latter, to whom the violin sonatas, Opus 12, are dedicated, his instructor in vocal writing. However, the men did not feel obliged to further Beethoven, either personally or in their common profession of *regens chori*. They viewed critically the rugged personality of their former student, and, to say the least, disapproved of his creations.

Ignoring the tendencies that governed church music in the imperial residence, Prince Nikolaus Esterházy, who ruled over a tiny principality, took a step of far-reaching artistic results. In 1796 he commissioned a mass from his Kapellmeister, Joseph Haydn, then a composer of world fame, to be performed in Eisenstadt at a birthday celebration for his wife. His renewal of the commission in the following years resulted in Haydn's last six great masses, composed between 1796 and 1802. A similar commission was given to Johann Nepomuk Hummel (1778-1837), who succeeded Haydn as Kapellmeister in Eisenstadt, and in 1807 Beethoven was invited to contribute to the by then firmly established custom.

Beethoven accepted the commission and started working on the mass in the spring, occupying himself chiefly with this composition during the summer months, which he spent in Baden, the famous spa about fifteen miles south of Vienna, and in Heiligenstadt, located on the slopes of the Vienna Woods he loved so dearly. At the end of July he received an inquiry from Prince Esterházy, reminding him of the approaching deadline. Promising delivery of the manuscript for August twenty-sixth, Beethoven confessed that submitting the mass would cause him great anxiety because Prince Esterházy was accustomed to "the inimitable masterpieces of the great Haydn." The Prince graciously replied that he set great hopes in the mass and Beethoven's fear of having the work compared with the masses of Haydn rather increased its value.

Beethoven's explicit references to the masses of his teacher are of artistic significance, for they prove conclusively that the attitude of the Emperor and the repertory policy of Salieri could not obscure the historic importance of Haydn's achievements in the field of *musica sacra*. His contemporaries fully realized the greatness of the masses, which were heard, though banished from the court chapel and the venerable St. Stephen's, in other churches of the Viennese diocese, drawing capacity congregations. Handwritten copies of the masses were circulated all over the Empire. Breitkopf and Härtel in Leipzig published five masses between 1802, and 1808, and Beethoven owned the scores of two.

The first performance of Beethoven's Mass in C major, in the Bergkirche of Eisenstadt, took place under an unlucky star. A directive issued by Prince Esterházy on September 12, 1807, one day before the performance, reveals the low morale of the ensemble and the difficulties Beethoven had encountered. The Prince attended the last rehearsal and observed that only one of the five alto singers of the chorus was present. Deeming it necessary to take a hand in the matter, he commanded the Vice-Kapellmeister, Johann Fuchs, to secure the attendance of the entire personnel at the next day's service.

It stands to reason that under these circumstances an adequate reading could not be obtained, and the Prince was indeed disappointed. It was customary after the service for local and foreign musical dignitaries to congregate in the princely suite to exchange their views about the works performed. When Beethoven entered the chamber, the Prince turned to him and asked, "My dear Beethoven, what have you done here?" Irritated by the question and noticing that Hummel, who stood beside the Prince, laughed, he felt deeply hurt by the strange remark of the Prince and the offending behavior of a fellow composer. He left immediately and returned to Vienna. Though an amicable relationship between Beethoven and Hummel was restored after a few years, Beethoven was always seized by anger when he remembered the incident in Eisenstadt.

Beethoven himself thought very highly of the mass, and when he offered it to Breitkopf on June 8, 1808, he contended that he had treated the text in a manner seldom applied to masses before and that the mass had been presented in "several places" and also in Eisenstadt with "much applause." The technical remark is beyond dispute, but the rest is advertising, pure and simple, without any factual foundation. The second reading of the mass was only a partial one and occurred in the Theater an der Wien in the famous *Akademie* on December 22, 1808, which overwhelmed the audience with novelties and an enormous amount of music. The program included the first presentations of the fifth and sixth symphonies, the G major clavier concerto with the composer as soloist, the Choral Fantasy, the concert aria *A! perfido,* as well as the *Gloria* and *Sanctus* from the Mass in C major.

The *Gloria* was not billed as a part of the mass, but as "Hymn with Latin text in church style with chorus and solos." This disguise was to avoid a conflict with the ecclesiastical authorities and the police, who would have interceded if the transplanting of a holy text from a house of worship to a place of entertainment had been announced. The camouflage of the *Sanctus,* however, was less ingenious. This section was proclaimed as "*Heilig* with Latin text in church style with chorus and solos." The word "solos" implies that this performance of the music also included the *Benedictus,* as the *Sanctus* lacks solo passages. As for this memorable performance of portions of the mass, contemporary reports indicate that Beethoven was again out of luck.

However, convinced of the intrinsic values of the mass, he pursued its publication, having added to the Latin a new German text adapted to an organization of the mass into three Hymns, the first comprising the *Kyrie* and *Gloria,* the second the *Credo,* and the third the remaining parts—the *Sanctus, Benedictus,* and *Agnus Dei.* In quest of an acceptable German translation Beethoven declared: "It does not need to be a masterpiece if it only fits the music well." He was actually not interested in a literal translation, but in a new text that would, while transmitting the spiritual content of the holy words, be poetic and singable.

He found a translator in the theologian Dr. Christian Schreiber, whose lines were used for the first edition of the mass, published in Leipzig in 1812 as Opus 86. That Schreiber's "translation" has no verbal connection with the Ordinary can be seen, for instance, from the *Kyrie* which contains thirty-four words in comparison with the six words of the original. The title of the first edition displays a strange pairing of headings in Italian and German: "Messa a quattro voci . . . composta da Luigi van Beethoven; Drei Hymnen für vier Singstimmen . . . von Louis van Beethoven." The purpose of the edition is obvious. The designation "messa" would direct the composition to the Catholic *regens chori,* while the term "hymn" would appeal to the Protestant church musicians and also open doors to concert halls. The copy of the mass Beethoven had sent to Eisenstadt in 1807 contains a dedication to Principe Nicolo Esterházy de Galantha. However, after the incident in Eisenstadt, Beethoven understandably changed his mind and dedicated the mass to Prince Ferdinand Kinsky, one of his very devoted admirers.

The mass was composed during a lustrum when Beethoven created numerous important works, including, significantly, a series of pieces in the key of C major: the Waldstein sonata (1804), the three *Leonora* overtures (1805-1806), the Finale of the opera *Fidelio* (1805), the String Quartet, Opus 59, No. 3 (1806), our mass, the C major Finale of the C minor symphony (1807-1808), and the chief portion of the Choral Fantasy (1808).

Beethoven himself alluded to the technical noteworthiness of the mass when he remarked that he had treated the text in a manner for which only a few examples existed. These examples were provided by Haydn who, definitely abandoning the Italian type of the so-called "cantata mass," created the classical mass pattern that was adopted by Beethoven, Schubert, and Bruckner. In the cantata mass, of which Bach's Mass in B minor, Haydn's *Missa Sanctae Caeciliae,* and Mozart's unfinished Mass in C minor, K.427, are the best-known examples, the individual sections of the Ordinary —the *Gloria* and *Credo* in particular—are split into several self-contained units, such as arias, duets, and choral pieces. The classical mass disposes of these self-contained sections within the six divisions of the Ordinary; the *Gloria* and *Credo* are organized as three-sectional units following the fast-slow-fast pattern, the slow middle portion being cast in a different meter and key. Haydn introduced a solo quartet, which fulfills a function similar to that of the concertino in the concerto grosso, acting as a tonal segment in alternation with a larger body, in this case the chorus. The manipulation of the musical ideas occurs along symphonic lines, particularly in the two most extended sections, the *Gloria* and the *Credo.* Contact with the baroque tradition is maintained, however, by the fugal passages in these two sections, and also in the "Hosanna" of the *Sanctus* and *Benedictus.*

These are some of the important stylistic features to observe in Beethoven's C major Mass. A few additional musical and technical details may be pointed out here. The tempo indication of the *Kyrie* must have caused Beethoven much trouble, for he needed no less than ten words for the prescription: "Andante con moto assai vivace quasi Allegretto ma non troppo." The entire *Kyrie* grows out of the scale-like idea presented in the first measures.

Except for the entry of the *Christe* (in E major), the *Kyrie* is cast in a kind of restrained perpetual motion. The importance of scale motifs and their symphonic manipulation is evident in the *Gloria,* particularly in the "Gratias agimus."

The quick tempo is somewhat lessened in the "Qui tollis" (F minor, 3/4) which is of a rather somber quality. The original tempo, meter, and key reappear with the "Quoniam tu solus sanctus" that is proclaimed in a mighty unison, a word picture created by the accentuation of "altissimus" (the Highest) on the highest note. There is a fugato on "cum Sancto Spiritu" that is not, however, worked out according to the textbook. It is interrupted by the twofold reappearance of the "Quoniam" where the word painting device is once more applied to "altissimus," the second time underscored harmonically by an E flat chord. There is an extended Amen projected alternately by the soloists and chorus.

The first section of the *Credo* evolves from the motif that is heard in the first measure (bass), manipulated in a truly symphonic and, at the same time, dramatic manner.

Note the tone painting in the treatment of "descendit de coelis."

The "Et incarnatus est" (E flat major, 2/4) is the only long Adagio passage in the mass; however, the treatment of the Incarnation is only episodic. Beethoven concentrates rather on the Crucifixion, placing the main accent on the passion by reiterating the word "passus" above dissonant chords. The sepulcher is painted gently in the major mode, but a distant key (D major) announces the Resurrection. The main key is reached with the description of the Ascension.

The *Credo* also concludes with an extended "Amen."

After the short Adagio episode of the *Sanctus*, a distinctly motoric tendency seems to dominate until the end of the mass. The gentle *Benedictus*, devoid of broad lyrical melodies, is characterized by the steady flow of short motifs, as, for example:

and the frequent alternation of the solo quartet and chorus. The steady motion continues into the *Agnus Dei*, from the opening triplets to the greater part of the "Dona nobis pacem." Note the dramatic reappearance in the "Dona" of the "Agnus," with frequent exclamation of the word "miserere." Schubert followed Beethoven in this respect in his E flat major Mass. This episode is also the precursor of a similar passage in Beethoven's *Missa solemnis*. The "Dona" is prolonged through a restatement of the beginning of the *Kyrie* set to the words "Dona nobis pacem." Thus, the *Kyrie* melody, the alpha of the mass, becomes its omega.

BIZET, Georges (1838-1875), *Symphony in C major*
Allegro vivo; Adagio; Allegro vivace; Allegro vivace

About thirty years ago the musical world received the astonishing news that an early symphony was found among the unpublished manuscripts of Georges

Bizet. Considering that this find was made fifty-eight years after the death of Bizet, it seems strange indeed, because posthumous editions of several works such as the "Roma" symphony and the second *L'Arlesienne* suite had already been brought out. The latter was compiled and edited by Bizet's close friend Ernest Guiraud (born 1837 in New Orleans, died 1892 in Paris), who also composed the recitatives for *Carmen*. Bizet's widow Geneviève, the daughter of his teacher Halévy, entrusted Guiraud with the handling of her husband's musical estate.

The question arises: did the symphony escape Guiraud's attention, or did this fine musician not put much stock in this work of his deceased friend? Geneviève, who later married the banker Emile Strauss, presented a substantial number of Bizet's manuscripts to the Paris Conservatoire after the first world war. The rest were kept by her son Jacques Bizet who, in turn, handed the material over to his close friend Reynaldo Hahn (1875-1947). Hahn made his mark in Parisian musical life as a fine critic, notable composer, and successful opera director. He decided, in 1933, to part with the Bizet autographs and presented them to the Conservatoire, whose rich library is now part of the Bibliotheque Nationale. Among the manuscripts that Hahn donated to the Conservatoire was the C major symphony Bizet had composed in 1855 when he was a student at the venerable institution.

The following intriguing facts stand out in this brief narrative. First, the composer showed not the slightest ambition to bring this creation before the public. He actually "suppressed" it. Second, Guiraud, who conscientiously took care of the musical estate of his friend, did not find it worthwhile to champion the symphony. Third, Geneviève Bizet-Strauss withheld the symphony when she made her gift to the Conservatoire. Finally, Reynaldo Hahn kept the symphony for years and did not tell his confrères anything about it or call it to the attention of a conductor. Even after the publication of an article, in 1933, dealing with the unpublished Bizet piece, no one showed an active interest in it. But Felix Weingartner, apprised of the discovery of the symphony by D. C. Parker the first English biographer of Bizet, lost no time in performing it. He conducted the symphony in Basel on February 26, 1935.

The background of the symphony was revealed by Howard Shanet in a paper published in the *Musical Quarterly* (1959). Bizet wrote the piece between October 29 and the end of November 1855, stimulated by the first symphony of his friend Charles Gounod (1818-1893) which was performed in the spring of 1855. Bizet knew it intimately because he made the four-hand arrangement. Shanet offered striking examples of parallelism in the second and third movements of both symphonies.

To place Bizet's C major symphony in its historic perspective, we must remember that in 1855 Schumann's creative activity had ceased and Brahms was only twenty-two years old. Liszt, in 1855, espoused program music in his symphonic poems and monumental "Faust" symphony, and Schubert's B minor symphony was still undiscovered. Anton Bruckner, aged thirty-one, had not yet gone beyond simple dances in his instrumental essays.

Although the work of a student, the symphony heard tonight is, nonetheless, the creation of a genius; engaging because of its melodic inventiveness, and amazing in its well-balanced architecture, formal perfection, and masterly handling of the orchestral resources. Bizet refused to emulate either the monumental symphonies of Beethoven or the stupendous musical canvasses of Berlioz. The question that logically presents itself is: whether or not the musical language of this symphony does presage the composer of *Carmen*. It must be answered negatively. Yet this youthful piece introduces Bizet the craftsman most advantageously. We clearly perceive, in retrospect, that out of this amazing beginning the mature dramatist and creator of *Carmen* would emerge.

"Roma" Symphony
Andante tranquillo-Allegro agitato; Allegretto vivace;
Andante molto; Allegro vivacissimo

With the composition of the "Roma" Symphony in 1866, Bizet realized an idea that he had conceived when he left Rome in the winter of 1861, after a three-year stay. He had come to the Eternal City as the winner of the coveted Prix de Rome. The Prix de Rome is much more than a reward: it is a French institution of national significance and historic importance. Probably the oldest institution of this kind, its tercentenary was celebrated in 1966. The concept originated with the French statesman Jean Baptiste Colbert, minister of Louis XIV, in connection with the organization of the French Academy, now commonly called *l'Institut*. Colbert founded a branch of the Academy in Rome, which was to be the home for twelve young representatives of the visual arts, who were to be sent yearly to Rome at the expense of the government to develop their talents in the artistic atmosphere there. The candidates chosen were to spend five years there.

Evidently neither the founder of the Prix de Rome nor the authorities who administered it thought much of Rome as a place to stimulate the musician, and this gap was filled only in 1805. However, for the musician the Roman sojourn was fixed at three years, with one year to be spent in Germany for the study of symphonic music and one in Paris, which had become an important operatic center. Lack of space forbids describing the procedure of the competition, its mechanics, and the protocol of the announcement of the award. These matters have been set forth vividly by Berlioz in his memoirs.

The seat of the French Academy in Rome is the Villa Medici on the Monte Pincio. It was once owned by Cardinal Alessandro de Medici, who reigned for twenty-five days in 1605 as Pope Leo XI. Napoleon bought the villa in 1803, when he was First Consul, and assigned it to the Institut. The palace, whose inner façade was designed by Michelangelo, has accommodated a host of famous men. The great Velázquez lived there and so did Galilei, at the order of the Holy Office. The number of French artists who lodged there as winners of the Prix de Rome is legion: it suffices to recall the musicians Halévy, Berlioz, Thomas, Gounod, Bizet, Massenet, Debussy, Charpentier, Rabaud, Florent Schmitt, Paul Paray, and Ibert. The Villa Medici is saturated with historic memories, and to dream away one hour in the beautiful little garden is an unforgettable experience.

Bizet became very much attached to the Villa Medici, and his heart was heavy when he had to bid farewell to it and to Rome in 1861. He then resolved to write a symphony whose movements were to symbolize Rome, Venice (Andante), Florence (Scherzo), and Naples.

He visualized a spiritual companion piece to Mendelssohn's "Italian" Symphony. The original plan was altered considerably in 1866, when Bizet decided to abandon the idea of picturing four Italian cities and to compose a Roman symphony instead. One movement was already in existence, namely the Scherzo, which he had written in Rome in fulfillment of an obligation to the Institut. (Each winner was bound to send yearly an *envoi de Rome* to the Institut, in order to prove that he was not squandering his time and that the residence in the Villa Medici had stimulated his creative activity.) One of Bizet's *envois* was a scherzo in E flat major, which Jules-Etienne Pasdeloup, the conductor of the successful Concerts Populaires de Musique Classique, programmed in 1863 sandwiched between works of Mozart and Beethoven. The public expressed its dislike, and the enterprising conductor received many letters of complaint from critical subscribers. But one week later the piece was acclaimed in a concert of the Société Nationale des Beaux Arts and reviewed positively as well. Bizet later resolved to incorporate it into his "Roma" Symphony between the first and third movements. He entitled the former "A Hunt in the Forest of Ostia" and the latter "A Procession." The finale he designated "Carnival in Rome," here clasping hands with Berlioz, whose imagination had likewise been kindled by the Roman carnival, witness his overture *Le Carnaval romain*. By a twist of fate, Berlioz, who had kind words for Bizet in his last piece of journalistic writing, died a few days after the first performance of the "Roma" Symphony. It was given in the Cirque Napoleon on February 28, 1869, under Pasdeloup, who insisted on presenting the work without the ominous scherzo. The program announced the piece as *Souvenirs de Rome*.

Strangely enough, the Parisian publisher Choudens changed the title once more, to *Roma, troisième suite de concert*, when he issued the composition in 1880. Changing the title was an arbitrary act—Bizet had died in 1875— and at the same time a piece of shrewd salesmanship. Calling the symphony the "third suite," Choudens was no doubt referring to the two successful suites made up from the incidental music to Daudet's play *L'Arlésienne*. "Roma" would make the third suite in the sequence, which would give it a good start on the road to success. This edition also suppressed the original titles of the individual movements and designated the finale simply as *Carnaval*.

For reasons difficult to understand the "Roma" Symphony, which the choreographers have appropriated as an effective medium for their specific ends, is not a frequently heard concert item. Does it foreshadow *Carmen*? In the first three movements there are hardly any moments that would clearly point to Carmen, Don José, or Escamillo, but perhaps some lyrical phrases in the opening section and in the Andante reveal a kinship to the mood of Micaela's aria (Act III). Yet there are passages that seem to anticipate elements of the music of *L'Arlésienne*. When Bizet composed the

"Roma" Symphony he was, as an opera composer, not an unknown quantity in Paris. *Les Pêcheurs de perles* had been produced in 1863 and *La Jolie Fille de Perth* was to be mounted.

The original title of the first movement, "A Hunt in the Forest of Ostia," does not apply to the solemn opening and concluding passages in 4/4 time, but rather to the Allegro agitato in 6/8 in between. Here the language of the stage composer is frequently heard. The symphonic idiom is more pronounced in the fugal treatment of the scherzo and its perfect formal balance. We should not be surprised at that. The C major symphony of 1855, by the seventeen-year-old Bizet, which was discovered only in 1936, revealed the youthful composer as an accomplished craftsman. The choice of keys for the Scherzo and Trio of the "Roma" Symphony (A flat and D flat) is remarkable and without precedent in the important works of the classical and romantic symphonic literature.

The first melody of the slow movement, "A Procession," gentle and solemn, foreshadows a similar passage in the music to *L'Arlésienne*. It reappears transformed into a rousing and energetic tune in the carnival episode of the Allegro vivacissimo that in a moment or two presages the composer of *Carmen*. Has the procession theme in the finale a deeper meaning? Should it perhaps be taken as a reminder of the religious aspect of Eternal Rome, ever present even in the bustling and boisterous happenings of the Roman carnival? Maybe, for it is this melody that marks the climactic and jubilant conclusion.

BOCCHERINI, Luigi (1743-1805)
Concerto for Violoncello in B flat major
Allegro moderato; Adagio; Rondo: Allegro

Luigi Boccherini was born in 1743 in Lucca. This picturesque Tuscan town has been the home of several distinguished musicians—Francesco Geminiani, the opera composer Alfredo Catalani who was championed by Toscanini, and Giacomo Puccini, whose family lived in Lucca for generations. Boccherini's instrument was the violoncello. A concert tour with the violinist Filippo Manfredi, a fellow townsman, brought him in 1768 to Paris, where he reaped a sensational success with his chamber music compositions and was besieged by publishers. He then went to Madrid where he settled as court composer. From 1787 to 1797 he wrote exclusively for Frederick William II of Prussia (the nephew of Frederick the Great and a very competent cellist), who was honored by the dedication of quartets by Haydn and Mozart, and sonatas by Beethoven. Boccherini stayed only occasionally at the court in Potsdam and Madrid remained his place of residence. However, after the demise of the Prussian king, Boccherini's salary was suspended and his economic situation went from bad to worse. He died in poverty in Madrid in 1805; in 1927 his remains were brought to Lucca and laid to rest in San Francesco.

Boccherini was a prolific composer who left about four hundred works representing typical Italian instrumental music of the *settecento*. He is also a phenomenon that musicology has not yet been able to explain, in that he seems to have skipped the beginner's stage in composing. He wrote his first quartets in 1761 when he was eighteen years old. The texture of his earliest works is well balanced and their setting displays a genuine quartet style that is far more advanced than that of Haydn's first essays in this field. The originality of Boccherini's early works is amazing: as products of the early 1760s, their style appears strikingly "modern."

Boccherini in Madrid lost contact with the musical production in other countries and the result was complete artistic isolation. "One would be tempted to believe," says the famous Belgian musicologist and lexicographer François Joseph Fétis (1784-1871), "that he knew no other music than his own." Nevertheless, his virtues are many. His works mirror his Tuscan origin, but they also show, as one Italian writer remarks, that Boccherini had close contact with the most ceremonious of all courts—that of Spain. Independent of Haydn, he cultivated successfully the string quartet, and the quintet for two violins, one viola, and two violoncelli was his very own creation. Enormously popular in his lifetime, Boccherini fell almost into oblivion from which he was resurrected by the phonograph record. Yet his fatherland still owes him a complete critical edition of his widely scattered works.

Boccherini's concerto for violoncello in B flat is cast in the three-movement pattern developed by Tommaso Albinoni, Giuseppe Torelli, and Antonio Vivaldi, and offers the soloist good opportunities for displaying technical proficiency. Its musical language is clear, the melodies are graceful and endowed with refined ornamentation.

BRAHMS, Johannes (1833-1897)
Gesänge für Frauenchor, Opus 17

After a roving life filled with adventurous concert tours and long stays in Düsseldorf, Hanover, and Detmold, Brahms decided, in 1860, to settle down in his native Hamburg. He was then 27 years old and had built a fine reputation as a pianist and composer of piano and chamber music as well as vocal compositions (lieder and choral pieces). In Hamburg he organized a women's singing association, a small group recruited from well-to-do patrician families. The advantages of this activity were twofold: he could improve his conducting technique, which was to be valuable to him later on as leader of large choral forces in Vienna; and the work with his "kleinen Singverein" (little singing society) stimulated him to augment the literature to which Schubert, Mendelssohn, and Schumann had made beautiful contributions for women's voices. Such are the Gesänge für Frauenchor with the accompaniment of two horns and harp. Composed in 1860, they were published in 1862 as Opus 17. After a private reading for his friend Joseph Joachim, Brahms brought three songs (Nos. 1-3) before the Hamburg public in a program which included the Waldstein sonata and Schumann pieces played by Brahms. He had originally offered the four songs to the renowned Leipzig music publishing house of Breitkopf & Härtel, but they did not put much stock in the young composer after the disastrous failure of his D minor piano concerto in Leipzig in 1859.

The texts selected by Brahms range from Ossian, the legendary Irish warrior and bard of the third century, and Shakespeare to Joseph von Eichendorff

(1788-1857)—for whom both Schumann and Hugo Wolf showed a strong attachment—and Friedrich Ruperti. One wonders how Brahms came across the verses of Ruperti, an obscure figure about whom no information can be found in important German reference works. Strangely enough, the employment of the harp may have been suggested by the first line of Ruperti's poem—while the harp is associated with Ossian, it is not a symbol of the jester in Shakespeare's *Twelfth Night*.

The series has a three-part setting which is abandoned in the fourth song, the lament for the young hero Trenar, for a four-part setting. Yet Brahms gave the three-section song a consoling ending in C major. In this respect the *Song from Ossian's Fingal* contrasts with the preceding *Gardener*. Max Kalbeck, who wrote an authentic Brahms biography and was very close to the composer, suggests that the gardener was a romantic disguise of Eichendorff, one of Brahms' favorite poets. Brahms once revealed that he had "set the whole [of] Eichendorff to music," but prompted by rigid self-criticism he had destroyed many of the songs. Mendelssohn also set *The Gardener* to music (1844), but by changing the title into *Greetings*, and leaving out the last stanza, he completely nullified the concept of the poet upheld by Brahms.

Nänie, Opus 82

The idea of setting Schiller's poem *Nänie* to music lingered long in Brahms's mind, but he refrained from realizing the plan for personal considerations. Hermann Goetz (1840-1876), a composer whose activities Brahms observed with sympathy, had used Schiller's verses for a choral work, which was published in 1874 and found a warm reception. Brahms abhorred the thought of competing with his younger confrère. Even after the untimely death of Goetz, Brahms entertained feelings of doubt as to whether he could try his hand with Schiller's lines without being accused of irreverence toward the deceased. But this attitude changed when Brahms learned of the passing of the well-known painter Anselm Feuerbach. Brahms and Feuerbach had known each other since 1865, and they shared human and ethical fundamentals and artistic convictions. Although they felt a great mutual respect and esteem, they never entered a cordial comradeship. Feuerbach was appointed professor at the Vienna Art Academy in 1873, but left three years later for Venice, where he died in January 1880, at variance not only with the world but also with himself.

Feuerbach's death affected Brahms greatly. Now he made up his mind to compose Schiller's *Nänie,* which seemed to express precisely the feelings of grief that overwhelmed him when he received the sad news. During his stay in Ischl in the summer of 1880 he occupied himself with the composition. He completed the piece the following summer, in the lovely Pfalzau, about fifteen miles west of Vienna.

Then he addressed himself to Anselm's stepmother, who had loved Anselm deeply. Henriette Feuerbach was an extraordinary woman. She read the Latin and Greek classics in the original, was an accomplished pianist, conducted a small choral group, and wrote several biographical essays. After Anselm's death Brahms could not write her a conventional letter of condolence, and he remained silent. Now he asked for permission to connect her name with the new work, and implicitly with that of her stepson and with his own, in the form of a dedication. She consented to the request. *Nänie* appeared, with the dedication, as Opus 82 in 1881 and was first performed on December 6, 1881, in Zurich under the direction of the composer, who played his new Piano Concerto in B flat major on the same evening.

Schiller's poem consists of seven distichs (fourteen verses), which the composer organized into three groups. The first—preceded by a moving introduction dominated by the wind instruments—is formed by four distichs. The second, of two pairs of verses, is musically contrasted in tempo and key with the first. Only one distich was left for the third section, which resumes the original tempo and key. To counteract the textual and musical imbalance, Brahms used repetitions of words in the third section and concluded the work, as Goetz had done, with the penultimate line and its consoling thought that a song of lament, if intoned by a beloved, will be glorious.

Variations on a theme of Haydn, Opus 56a

In the fall of 1870 Brahms paid a visit to Carl Ferdinand Pohl, a Viennese musicologist, of whom he was very fond. At that time Pohl was occupied with collecting documentary and musical material for a Haydn biography. His work lay on his desk, and he invited Brahms to look at several scores that he had made up from single parts. Among them was a divertimento for wind instruments with a short Andante entitled "Chorale St. Antonii." Brahms read the work and immediately copied the chorale, even entering the date (November 1870) on his copy. We do not know whether Brahms then had conceived the idea to use the chorale as a theme for variations.

Haydn had probably heard the theme from pilgrims, although Dr. Karl Geiringer ventured the possibility that the chorale was a genuine Haydn melody, which later became a folk tune. Be that as it may, in the late nineteenth century only a few musicians and concertgoers had had a chance to hear the chorale within its original framework of the divertimento, and one fact stands out: the tune became famous because of Brahms.

The religious significance of the work is uncertain; the tune could have been devoted to St. Antony of Padua or to the Egyptian Prince of Heraclea, who left his palace, went into the wilderness, and, castigating himself, lived there on roots and plants. Max Kalbeck, an intimate friend and biographer of Brahms, relates that Brahms was familiar with the story of the temptations of St. Antony. Kalbeck even goes so far as to see in Brahms' variation cycle a musical description of certain episodes of St. Antony's life in the desert.

The variation series exists in two versions: one for orchestra and one for two pianos. Brahms authorized the publication of the former with the Opus number 56a and assigned 56b to the piano version, although the latter appeared in November 1873 and the former was not published until January 1874. It is reasonable to assume that Brahms conceived of the variations as an orchestral piece, but that in the first phase of the composition the idea of a piano version grew more and more pressing, until he decided to complete the piano version first. Its manuscript is dated July 1873. Then Brahms continued to work on the orchestral version, which he showed to Otto Dessoff, the conductor of the Vienna Philharmonic Orchestra. Dessoff requested the premiere of the variations for the opening of the 1873-1874 season and invited the composer to conduct his work. Brahms accepted, rehearsed carefully, and made some changes in the orchestration. The enthusiastic reception of the work in Vienna, on November 2, 1874, ushered in a chain of successes, which stimulated Brahms to concern himself seriously with the completion of his C minor symphony.

The variation technique is one of the most important elements of musical composition. It has been applied to countless works on a small scale or large, in a simple and ornamental manner or with harmonic, rhythmic, and contrapuntal complexities. Like the classical composers, Brahms wrote independent variation cycles and variation movements in piano sonatas and chamber music works; he crowned this facet of his creative activity with the imposing finale of the fourth symphony. The variations played tonight are of the type defined as character variations; that is to say, the shape of the theme is fundamentally different in each appearance. The more the series progresses, the more it deviates from the simple pilgrim's tune. The rapid fifth variation, or the sixth with the horn signals, contrast sharply with the delicate Grazioso in the manner of a siciliano, an old dance type. There is frequent change between the major and minor modes (Variations II, IV, and VIII), and between the duple and triple meters. The fourth variation is in 3/8, the fifth in 6/8, the sixth in 2/4, the seventh in 6/8, and the eighth in 3/4 time. Brahms concluded the series with an extended finale, whose artistry foreshadows the last movement of the fourth symphony. He applied to it the baroque ostinato technique, using as the ground a five-measure phrase derived from the theme. Sixteen variations are built on the ground before the triumphant return of the chorale melody.

BRITTEN, Benjamin (1913—)
Serenade for Tenor, Horn, and Strings, Opus 31

The title of Benjamin Britten's song cycle is somewhat puzzling. We usually speak of a serenade as a song sung at night before a lady's window by one or several admirers. The serenade of Don Giovanni, or of Sixtus Beckmesser in Wagner's *Meistersinger*, are well-known examples, as is the serenade that the Cypriots offer Desdemona in Verdi's *Otello*. This old custom generated the instrumental serenade, a form that enjoyed a great vogue during the classical period. The term serenade means "evening song," and the instrumental serenades were open-air music of a pleasant and entertaining nature. Their concerto-like features displayed an enchanting variety. We do not find anything of the sort in Britten's song cycle, although it does show a spiritual connection with the serenade of old. The connection is apparent in the texts that refer to nocturnal elements. Take the first stanza of the Pastoral, which reads: "The Day's grown old; the fainting sun/Has but a little way to run" or the line from the Dirge: "This ae nighte, this ae nighte."

The mood and qualities we associate with night are the spiritual basis and at the same time the generating forces of Britten's Serenade. The texts he selected span almost four centuries of English poetry. There is another interesting link in his score to the classical serenade and the circumstances under which it was usually presented. The musicians arrived at the house where the serenade was to be offered to the strain of a march, and they played the tune again as they went away; in Britten's score this function is entrusted to the horn soloist.

Another trait that Britten's work has in common with the classical instrumental serenade is its metrical, rhythmical, and melodic variety and the delicate treatment of the string orchestra. The music follows the text closely, conveying the basic mood and significant details of the poem. Witness the signal motif of the "horns of Elfland" (No. 3) or the description of the hunt in the Hymn (No. 6), whose original title was Hymn to Diana. The Elegy (No. 4) is the domain of the horn, the participation of the voice being limited to a short recitative. The Nocturne (No. 3) contains interesting cadenza-like passages, and the Dirge (No. 5) displays a highly imaginative construction. The singing voice announces an ostinato melody of six measures, which is repeated eight times. In the orchestra the thematic process occurs in the fugal development commencing with the bass and continuing in the viola, and second and first violins. The entry of the horn marks the dynamic climax, after which a gradual decrease in tension follows, the song ending with the low repetition of the first stanza. Following the classical tradition, the cycle closes with an Epilogue, an exact replica of the Prologue, which is blown from off stage.

Britten composed the Serenade in 1943. It was first performed in London on October 15, 1943, in Wigmore Hall, the late Walter Goehr conducting, with Peter Pears, tenor, and Dennis Brain, horn. Britten composed the Serenade with these two soloists in mind.

BRUCH, Max (1838-1920)
Concerto for Violin No. 1 in G minor, Opus 26
Allegro moderato; Adagio; Finale: Allegro energico

Max Bruch, born in Cologne, launched his career as a composer at the age of fourteen with the performance of a symphony in his hometown, where in 1858 he also produced his first stage work, based on Goethe's singspiel *Scherz, List und Rache* (Joke, Cunning and Revenge). Bruch held several teaching positions in Berlin, Leipzig, Dresden, and Munich. He spent three years in England as conductor of the Liverpool Philharmonic (1880-1883), and he visited the United States in 1883. He was professor of composition at the Musikhochschule in Berlin from 1881 until his retirement in 1910, and he received many academic honors: the University of Cambridge conferred upon him the honorary degree of Doctor of Music in 1893; the French Academy elected him a corresponding member; and in 1918 he received the honorary degree of Doctor of Philosophy from Berlin University.

Bruch was a prolific composer whose chief interest was choral music. In this field he was very successful not only in Germany but also in England and America. Nevertheless, his choral works, which show the hand of a fine craftsman and an outstanding technique in effective vocal writing, have disappeared from the concert hall; some of his instrumental pieces, however, the concerto in G minor among them, have successfully maintained themselves even in the current concert repertory.

Bruch jotted down the first sketches of the concerto in 1857 when he was nineteen years old, but concerned himself seriously with the piece only nine years later in Koblenz, where he held a conductor's post. It was first played almost precisely one hundred years ago, on April 24, 1866, by Otto von Königslow, deputy director of the Cologne conservatory, with Bruch conducting.

Afterwards Bruch thoroughly revised the concerto and sent it to Joseph Joachim, who was then concertmaster at the court theater in Hanover. Joachim made several suggestions for changes and improvements and had a share in the final shaping of the concerto. He organized a tryout for Bruch in the theater in 1867 and subsequently played it in Bremen, Aachen, Brussels, and Cologne. The composer reciprocated with the dedication to Joachim.

Bruch's G minor concerto is a composition of considerably smaller dimensions than those of the violin concertos of Beethoven and Mendelssohn. It is not as brilliant as Mendelssohn's masterpiece, and markedly deviates from the symphonic design of Beethoven, particularly in the comparatively short opening Allegro moderato, about 170 measures long as compared to Beethoven's 535. Bruch's first movement, originally named *Introduzione-Fantasia,* was finally designated as *Vorspiel.* This indicates the deviation from the classical concept that assigns a commanding role to the first movement. Formally speaking, one could describe the *Vorspiel* as an incomplete sonata movement with a short exposition and development, which leads with a very brief cadenza to the extended songful Adagio. The energetic finale provides splendid opportunities for the soloist, technically as well as melodically. The appealing lyricism and melodic charm of the piece explain why the concerto became a favorite with audiences. It is the only concerto between those of Mendelssohn in 1844 and Brahms in 1878 that has successfully withstood the ravages of time for the past hundred years.

CHARPENTIER, Marc-Antoine (1636-1704)
Pestis Mediolanensis

Marc-Antoine Charpentier lived during the reign of Louis XIV. The French proudly speak of this epoch as the *Grand Siècle,* the great century. Among Charpentier's contemporaries were Corneille, Molière, Racine, La Fontaine, Poussin, Lorrain, Lully, and Couperin le Grand. The Académie Royale de Musique, the court opera, was opened in 1671 and renowned architects were busy beautifying Paris in order to make it a symbol of France's greatness. Charpentier, who came from a family of artists, wanted to become a painter and following the established tradition went to Rome to study. There he met the famous composer Giacomo Carissimi (1605-1674) who, recognizing Charpentier's musical gifts, persuaded him to give up painting in favor of music. Thus Charpentier became a student of Carissimi and returned to Paris after a three year stay in the Eternal City. He collaborated with Molière in contributing music to plays performed at the Comédie Française. His successes aroused the jealousy of the powerful Lully, the king's favorite, who did all he could to block Charpentier's activities at the Comédie Française.

Meanwhile Charpentier built up a fine reputation as a composer of masses and motets which had received performances in Parisian churches and monasteries. He was put in charge of the music in the Saint Louis church and obtained a teaching position at the Collège Louis-le-Grand, frequented by the sons of prominent French families. Charpentier reached the height of his career as church musician with his appointment as *maitre de chapelle* of the Sainte Chapelle in 1698.

Charpentier was an industrious composer. In addition to works such as masses, motets, psalms, and other liturgical items he had to furnish pieces for state affairs, military victories, receptions of foreign rulers, and ceremonies for important people. The bulk of his works fills twenty-eight folio volumes which, gracefully written and called *Meslanges*, are housed in the Bibliothèque Nationale in Paris. Most of his music remained unpublished and when Claude Crussard published a biography of Charpentier in 1945 he deemed it appropriate to entitle it *Marc-Antoine Charpentier, A Forgotten Composer.*

Charpentier's sacred music betrays the influence of his teacher Carissimi but it also reveals his own individuality in surprising modulations, dissonant chords, and marked chromaticism. These features are conspicuous in "Pestis Mediolanensis" which is one of twenty-four *Historiae sacrae.* In a textbook on composition, Charpentier devised a code of the aesthetic and emotional nature of the individual keys. He characterized B minor, the key of this piece, as *solitaire et mélancolique* (forlorn and melancholic) which in this case seems to describe the situation aptly.

CORELLI, Arcangelo (1653-1713)
Concerto grosso in F major, Opus 6, No. 6
Adagio-Allegro; Largo; Vivace; Allegro

Arcangelo Corelli was born in Fusignano, a small town about thirty miles southeast of Bologna and ten miles west of Ravenna. He received his violin training in Bologna, and went to Rome in 1671 to study composition. His teacher Matteo Simonelli, a singer in the Papal Chapel, was a highly conservative musician and firm believer in the artistic principles of Palestrina. Much of the Eternal City was then rural in appearance. There were large gardens, and cows grazed on the Forum. The people called the Forum *campo vaccino* (cow pasture). Corelli lived in Rome under the Popes Clement X, Innocent XI, Alexander VIII; Innocent XII, and Clement XI. They were not great patrons of music. There were no good institutions for musical education as those which existed in Naples and Venice. Nor were there fine orchestras as those at St. Mark's in Venice or San Petronio in Bologna. Rome could not compete with Naples or Venice in the operatic field.

Rome's population then amounted to about 150,000 and most of them lived in misery. The cultural life was dependent on the Vatican, its hierarchy, and the very wealthy landed aristocracy. The patronage of the wealthy was vital to the musician. Private concerts given in the palaces of the nobility provided the musican with an appreciative and influential audience, and assured him his livelihood. Corelli's career was made in the *accademie*, sponsored by Christina, former queen of Sweden, Cardinal Benedetto Pamphilji, and Cardinal Pietro Ottoboni. Pietro Ottoboni's official residence was the Palazzo della Cancelleria, built by Bramante. Corelli took up quarters there as a member of the household. He organized the weekly concerts offered by the Cardinal to his guests. Every musician of promise, Italian or foreign, was invited into the Ottoboni circle. Handel was frequently entertained there. Corelli never left Rome and died there in 1713. Hailed as "the major glory of the century," he was enshrined in Santa Maria Rotonda, better known as the Pantheon.

Never pressed by deadlines, contractual obligations, and schedules, Corelli created in leisure and peace. His output is small. Only seventy-two authenticated pieces are included in the complete edition: forty-eight trio sonatas (Opus 1-4), twelve sonatas for violin and figured bass (Opus 5), and the set of twelve concerti grossi, edited by Corelli's pupil Matteo Fornari, and published posthumously in Amsterdam in 1714.

The concerto grosso can be defined as an instrumental piece in which a small unit, called concertino, alternates with a larger body designated as concerto grosso, ripieno, or tutti. Corelli standardized the concertino as a trio sonata ensemble of two violins, one violoncello, and harpsichord. Basically, there are two types of the concerto grosso: the church concerto that includes fugal passages and the chamber concerto presenting an assortment of stylized dance pieces. Sometimes we encounter a mixture of both types, as in the case of the concerto heard tonight—which may enrapture the listener with its freshness, vitality, and rhythmic diversity.

Corelli may have written the concerto for an Easter service when the community was celebrating the Resurrection of the Saviour. The introductory Adagio discloses a hymn-like quality. If an adequate text were to be provided to the music, the congregation could easily sing it. The plain setting of the hymn is contrasted with the vivid manipulation of the motifs in the tender closing Allegro. The serious spirit of the church concerto reasserts itself forcefully in the ensuing fugal Largo, remarkable for its part-writing and harmonic treatment. The seriousness is swept away by the following speedy movement (Vivace, 3/8) that has the quality of the rapidly running Italian *Corrente*. The final Allegro breathes a joyful spirit and displays no contrapuntal complexities. Here we find ourselves in the sphere of the chamber concerto. For this movement, too, reflects the character of the dance. One thinks of a modified gavotte with which the composer wished to provide a happy send-off for the congregation.

DALLAPICCOLA, Luigi (1904—), *Tre Laudi*

Luigi Dallapiccola was born in the Istrian town of Pisino, then Austria and now Yugoslavia. He went to school in Trieste and Graz before entering the Cherubini Conservatory in Florence as a piano student. He later took up composition, graduating in 1931, and was appointed in 1934 to the faculty of his Alma Mater. Dallapiccola has taught at the Berkshire Music Center in Tanglewood (1951 and 1952) and at Queens College.

One of the first Italian composers to discard the classical harmonic concept and turn towards atonality, Dallapiccola has adopted the twelve-tone method of Arnold Schönberg, combining it with technical devices of his own. He is one of the leading Italian composers of our time, a musician who tries to inject Latin melodiousness into the atonal fabric and "to explore all the possibilities of the system [dodecaphony] and to work patiently towards its clarification, by means of sensibility and not of theory."

His output includes orchestral works, chamber music, vocal compositions, and the opera *Il prigioniero*, which has received international acclaim. He is deeply interested in the Italian music and poetry of the past, as shown in his transcription of Monteverdi's *Il Ritorno di Ulisse in patria*, the *Tartiniana*, a violin piece based on themes by Tartini, and the *Cori di Michelangelo*. Another example is the song cycle offered tonight, which is comprised of three *laudi*.

The *laudi* were songs set to devotional texts and poems in the vernacular and were sung at processions and at gatherings in churches or in oratories. The executants, called *laudisti* or *laudesi*, were plain people—artisans and shopkeepers who organized themselves into confraternities or *campagnie*. In the thirteenth century nine laudesi confraternities formed in Florence, often congregating at vesper services of such churches as Santa Maria Novella, Santa Croce, Santa Reparata (the old Duomo), and Santa Maria del Carmine. From Tuscany and Umbria this movement spread to the north of Italy, propelled in particular by the flagellants or *flagellanti*, also called *battuti* or *disciplinati*. Driven by extreme religious fervor, they sang the laudi during the rite of flagellation or *disciplina*. The poems contain incitations to penance and appeals to divine mercy. Also incorporated into them are narratives of the life of Christ and of the joys and dolors of the Virgin; this emphasis of the laudesi and flagellanti on the cult of the Madonna accounts for the lyrical quality of many laudi. A great many laudi date from the period that also gave birth to the two most venerated religious Latin poems— the *Dies Irae* and the *Stabat Mater*. Prose or verse in form, radiating spontaneity and, in spite of occasional robustness, an appealing grace, the anonymous laudi were circulated from town to town and were a source of consolation to many people.

The source of the text used by Dallapiccola is a *laudario* (collection of laudi) preserved in Modena and dated 1266. It is, in all probability, a precursor of another Modena laudario, dated 1377, that was made accessible through transcription and publication in 1908. This laudario, containing an enlarged version of the texts Dallapiccola set to music, may have already existed in 1266, in which case the composer has presumably selected those passages that suited his intentions. Composed between 1936 and 1937, *Tre Laudi* was first heard at the 1937 music festival in Venice.

Dallapiccola employs, in addition to a soprano voice, a thirteen-piece ensemble: flute, oboe, clarinet, bassoon, horn, trumpet, alto saxophone, harp, piano, violin, viola, violoncello, and bass. The songs are musically connected and organized as a slow-fast-slow combination. The music of the first verses reappears as a coda in the first and second songs, while the first four measures of the third lauda form the conclusion in a retrograde motion, that is, the music of these measures is read backward, producing a new melody. This procedure is, however, not a novelty, but in fact a very old device used by the Flemish Renaissance composers, as well as by Bach and Mozart.

DEBUSSY, Claude (1862-1918), *Children's Corner*

Doctor Gradus ad Parnassum; Jimbo's Lullaby; Serenade for the Doll; Snow is Dancing; The Little Shepherd; Golliwog's Cakewalk

Debussy composed his *Children's Corner* piano suite between 1906 and 1908, the year of the publication. The English titles for the suite and its six individual pieces are, of course, very conspicuous in the work of a French composer. Actually, the original heading of the third item read *"Sérenade à Poupée,"* and the idea of providing English titles seems to have occurred to Debussy during the process of composition. He dedicated the suite to his five-year-old daughter Claude-Emma, lovingly called "Chouchou," with "her father's affectionate apologies for what follows."

Debussy's biographer Léon Vallas suggests that the suite evokes scenes of a playing child under the watchful eyes of a *"miss* or *nurse."* Chouchou, undoubtedly, was evidencing interest in the piano at the time, and Debussy, remembering his own pianistic apprenticeship with Carl Czerny's études or Clementi's *Gradus ad Parnassum,* opened the suite in an ironic vein with "a sort of hygienic and progressive gymnastics," entitled "Doctor Gradus ad Parnassum." Jimbo of "Jimbo's Lullaby" (No. 2) was a toy elephant. "The Little Shepherd," of the tender and delicate fifth movement, was probably a picture or drawing that figured in Chouchou's little world.

With the final movement "Golliwog's Cakewalk," Debussy definitely leaves the children's world. A golliwog was a black doll loved by the little ones. But Debussy, in a sardonic mood, combined the syncopated cakewalk, imported from America, with a quotation from *Tristan and Isolde*—sheer blasphemy. This may justify the characterization of the work by a French critic as "a masterpiece of *esprit et malice."* Debussy was somewhat afraid of the reaction on the part of the public, which he thought would hardly credit the controversial creator of *Pelléas et Mélisande* with a sense of humor. When Harold Bauer played the *Children's Corner* publicly for the first time in Paris on December 18, 1908, the composer preferred to be outside the auditorium. He was very satisfied when Bauer told him that the audience received the piece smilingly.

The orchestration was done by the French composer and conductor André Caplet (1878-1925), a close friend of Debussy and, like him, a winner of the Grand Prix de Rome. (Debussy consented in several instances to the orchestration of his piano works by other musicians.) Caplet, who was with the Boston Opera Company from 1910 to 1914, introduced the orchestral version of the *Children's Corner* in New York in 1910, before Debussy presented it in Paris on March 25, 1911.

Chouchou survived her father by only sixteen months. She died at the age of fourteen in July 1919.

Petite Suite

En bateau; Cortege; Menuet; Ballet

Although comparatively few people knew of Debussy when he wrote the *Petite Suite* in 1888, at the age of twenty-six, those who did considered him a musician of promise. In 1884 he had won the coveted Prix de Rome, which signified official recognition of his creative talent and technical maturity, and established his status as a musician high above the average. He had already traveled a great deal as the house pianist of Madame Nadezhda von Meck, the patroness of Tchaikovsky, and as a winner of the Prix de Rome, he had resided for two years in the Villa Medici on the Monte Pincio where Halévy, Berlioz, Thomas, Gounod, Bizet, and Massenet had previously stayed, and Charpentier, Rabaud, and Ibert were later to live. He had then visited London and in 1888 made a pilgrimage to Bayreuth.

Debussy had become known in ruling musical circles as a difficult young man. He had antagonized the conservative musicians in the Conservatoire by his obsession for inventing chordal combinations that defied the time-honored rules. He also fell out of favor with the French Academy, which awards the Prix de Rome, and consequently lost the opportunity of having one of his works performed publicly under the auspices of this venerable institution.

Prior to the first performance of his String Quartet in 1893 and *Prélude à l'après-midi d'un faune,* which became a landmark in musical history, Debussy, who was an excellent pianist, was known mainly for his piano compositions. He conceived the *Petite Suite* as a piano composition for four hands. During this period, about 1888 to 1889, Debussy's activities were limited to private gatherings, and it was at such occasions that he played the *Petite Suite.* His partner was Jacques Durand, the son of publisher Marie-Auguste Durand, who had been an organist in important Parisian churches before he took up music publishing. When Jacques Durand entered his father's firm, he naturally became Debussy's publisher: he also promoted the works of César Franck, Saint-Saëns, Massenet, Chausson, d'Indy, and Ravel.

The success of the *Petite Suite,* published in 1889, explains the manifold arrangements made of it. That most widely circulated abroad is the orchestral arrangement by Henri-Paul Busser (b. 1872), a student of Widor, Gounod, and Franck who made a brilliant career as organist, composer, teacher at the Conservatoire, and conductor at the Opéra. Debussy, who had the highest professional regard for Busser, authorized him to orchestrate the *Petite Suite,* as well as the symphonic suite *Printemps* (written in Rome between 1886 and 1887). Busser's orchestral arrangement of the *Petite Suite* is copyrighted 1907, and thus we may conclude that Busser, then conductor at the Opéra, undertook the job around 1906 or 1907. The date is important because it explains the style of the orchestration, which approaches that of the mature Debussy. Busser's orchestral setting of the *Petite Suite*—with its display of delicate pastels, arresting mixture of colors, and restrained use of percussion instruments for rhythmical accentuation—is a superb achievement. If it were not for Busser's name on the title page, no one would assume that Debussy had not penned the score.

In Debussy's composition the influence of the traditions of the French clavecinists—François Couperin, in particular—is evident in the programmatic titles given to the individual movements. In the choice of key he took the liberty of deviating from the usual pattern; the first item is in G major, the second in E, the third in G, and the finale in D, the major mode dominant throughout. All four movements are patterned after the three-sectional dance forms in which an opening section is followed by a rhythmically and harmonically contrasting portion, the piece concluded by a precise or modified repetition of the first part. For example, the gentle opening division of "En bateau" has the quality of a barcarolle and is followed by a passage characterized by resolute dactyls. In the brilliant "Cortège" syncopation provides the contrasting element in the middle section. The "Menuet" is not of a rustic type associated with Alpine peasants, but has a delicately refined quality that is typically French. "Ballet," the title of the last piece, simply means "dance." Actually two types of dances are represented here, one in duple time and one a waltz. Yet the chief melody of the former is combined in 3/4 time with the waltz in the coda, where all instrumental means are effectively utilized for the sonorous conclusion.

Prélude à l'après-midi d'un faune

At the beginning of the 1890s Debussy (born 1862) was little known in Paris, and his name was never heard in foreign musical circles. Gounod, Delibes, Thomas, and Massenet dominated the French lyrical stage and were famous abroad. The prestige of Saint-Saëns was high. Gounod, and later Thomas, reigned at the Conservatoire. Gustave Charpentier and Dukas made headway slowly. Fauré (born 1845) was still second organist at the Madeleine, but had attained esteemed stature after the performance of his *Requiem*. César Franck (1822-1890) had finally achieved recognition. His most important student Vincent d'Indy (born 1851) succeeded him in the presidency of the Société Nationale de Musique, which was devoted to the promotion of the *Ars Gallica*, and had become a most consequential factor on the French musical scene. It was in this "forum" that Claude Debussy was launched to fame.

Living in poverty during the early 1890s, Debussy published about twenty songs, mostly set to the verses of Paul Verlaine, and a few piano pieces; among them the *Petite Suite* for four hands, which in time became very popular in the orchestral transcription of Henry Busser. Debussy had his first break on December 29, 1893, when the Société Nationale programmed his only string quartet. This, interestingly enough, was not played by a French group, but by Belgian musicians led by the outstanding violinist Eugène Isaye. The audience was made up of the musical elite of Paris, whom Debussy sarcastically called "les Mandarines de notre class." The quartet aroused great interest, but also irritation because of its new and highly original features. It was soon published and the Parisians began to talk about Debussy. One year later the Société Nationale broke with a long-standing tradition and converted one of its intimate *séances* into a full-fledged concert for the public, when it presented Debussy's *Prélude à l'après-midi d'un faune*.

Like many Parisians of his generation, Debussy had become infatuated with the poetry of Stéphane Mallarmé, who, pushing aside the conventional rules of syntax, aimed at the reduction of words to musical sounds and at the formation of verbal sonorities. This concept was related to ideas championed by the painter Claude Monet (1840-1926), who exhibited in Paris (1863) a picture with the caption "Sunrise—an Impression." In this particular case the word "impression" conveyed the intention of the painter to record with the brush what he saw at a quick glance. From this caption the term "impressionism" originated. Generally speaking, the impressionist painter is less interested in the object than in the play of light upon the object. He seems to create an atmosphere rather than a precise statement. In this respect the idea of impressionism bears affinity with the poetry of Verlaine and Mallarmé.

Mallarmé wrote the poem *L'après-midi d'un faune* in 1876. The actor Benoit Constant Coquelin aîné was to recite it as a monologue on the stage. Debussy's original plan was to express the atmosphere and poetic idea of the poem in a symphonic triptych consisting of a prelude, interlude, and a *paraphrase final*. Only the prelude materialized. The autograph bears "1892" on the title page and "September 1894" at the end—a time when Debussy's mind was already focused on the opera *Pelléas et Mélisande*. He saw fit to include in the first edition of the *Prélude* the following paragraph, which was also printed as a program note:

> The music of this prelude is a very free illustration to Stéphane Mallarmé's beautiful poem. It does not follow the poet's conception exactly, but describes the successive scenes among which the wishes and dreams of the Faune wander in the heat of the afternoon. Then, tired of pursuing the fearful flight of the nymphs and naiads, he abandons himself to a delightful sleep, full of visions finally realized, of full possession amid universal nature.

The piece was an immediate success, and the Swiss conductor Gustave Doret (1866-1943), who led the orchestra, had to yield to the demand for an encore. The unusual conception and striking features in matters of melody, harmony, and orchestration aroused opposition among the critics, the academicians, and conservative elements who held important teaching positions. The propriety of the subject matter was questioned in some quarters on moral grounds. Edouard Colonne, the famous conductor, actually ordered the omission of the program note quoted above "because too many young ladies attend these concerts."

Viewed historically, the presentation of Debussy's *Prélude*, which ushered in musical impressionism, is recognized as the most important event in the history of French music after the first performance in 1830 of the *Symphonie fantastique* by Hector Berlioz. These works wrote a new chapter in the history of music.

The piece by Debussy reached these shores on April 1, 1902. It was introduced by the Boston Orchestral Club under the baton of the French oboist Georges Longy, who had played it in the earliest performances in Paris.

That the leading American symphony orchestras (New York, Boston, Chicago) failed to evince interest in Debussy's unique creation should not surprise us, since the venerable Société des Concerts du Conservatoire waited eleven long years before it admitted to its program Debussy's exquisite, delicate, and colorful description of the desires and dreams of a faun on a hot afternoon.

Danse sacrée et Danse profane for Harp and Strings

The composition of Claude Debussy's *Dance sacrée et Danse profane* was the result of particular circumstances: in 1904 the renowned Brussels Conservatoire instituted a class for chromatic harp, and the manufacturing firm of Pleyel et Compagnie in Paris, founded in 1807 by Haydn's pupil Ignaz Josef Pleyel, commissioned Debussy to compose a piece. The harp in use until then was the so-called double-action pedal harp, invented about 1810 by the famous Parisian piano maker Sébastien Erard, which permitted raising the pitch of every string by either a tone or semitone by means of seven pedals. Attempts to simplify this procedure led to the invention of the *harpe chromatique* by Gustave Lyon, the director of Pleyel.

His invention failed to gain general acceptance, but succeeded in setting Debussy's pen in motion: the dances for harp and string orchestra were the result. They were first played in Paris on November 6, 1904, by the Colonne orchestra. Lucille Wurmser-Delcourt was the soloist; she also introduced them to America on December 28, 1919, in New York. The dances were dedicated to Gustave Lyon.

The title is somewhat intriguing since there is not much difference between the sacred dance and its profane counterpart. Both display small melodic phrases, a transparent texture, shifting harmonies, and richness of dissonances, and at the same time arresting effects obtained by the harp in combination with the sonorities of the string orchestra. There is no break between the sacred dance

which emanates modal flavor and the profane companion piece:

Although moving a bit faster, the latter is devoid of the passionate emotion or ecstatic moments the title may perhaps lead us to expect but the delicacy of sound and the effects obtained by the harp keep our unceasing interest.

Première Rapsodie for clarinet and orchestra
Moderato; Molto adagio-Allegro

Claude Debussy, the dreaded musical revolutionist, received an official position in February 1909. Gabriel Fauré, the director of the Conservatoire, appointed the creator of *Pelléas et Mélisande* a member of the *conseil supérieur*. The opera was still a very controversial topic, and the appointment reached Debussy shortly before he departed for London to supervise the production of *Pelléas,* which, incidentally, was successful. It is to the credit of Fauré that he took a positive attitude in the violently discussed *Cas Debussy.*

The membership of the *conseil supérieur* obliged Debussy to attend certain contests. In 1909 he was a juror at the contest for wind instruments. He did not consider this duty a chore. On the contrary, he enjoyed it and observed keenly the sonorities of flutes, oboes, clarinets, and bassoons. Stimulated by these experiences, he wrote two clarinet pieces for the audition of the contestants in 1910: the *Première Rapsodie* and the *Petite Pièce.* The contestants did not perform well in sight reading the rhapsody, which we, half a century later, understand completely. Only one, a certain Vandercruysse, passed with flying colors and came out with the first prize and a compliment from the composer, Debussy having said that he interpreted the piece as a *"grand musicien."*

Debussy composed the rhapsody at the end of 1909 (December 1909-January 1910) for clarinet and piano and orchestrated it later. He entitled the orchestral version *Première Rapsodie pour orchestre avec clarinette principale,* which means he considered the soloist an agent in the rich instrumental palette of the orchestral framework. The original meaning of the term *rhapsody* implied the recitation of a passage from a larger work. Musically speaking, it was applied to a composition of no specific form. Debussy's rhapsody, however, shows a certain formal design and introduces the clarinet as a singing instrument, displaying its virtuoso qualities. The clarinet appears as a lyrical voice in the dreamy opening, supported by harps and clasped by the delicate laces of the strings. The agility of the clarinet is demonstrated in a quick section, designated as "scherzando," which leads to a return of the opening before the scherzando is resumed.

Debussy enriched the clarinet literature with this enchanting piece; it rewards the soloist and is at the same time a remarkable orchestral composition, endowed with melodic charm, transparency, and a colorful instrumental fabric. Debussy dedicated it to P. Mimart, who was the first to play the original version with piano, on January 16, 1911, in Paris at the Société Musicale Indépendante.

DVOŘÁK, Antonin (1841-1904)
Concerto for Piano in G minor, Opus 33
Allegro agitato; Andante sostenuto; Allegro con fuoco

Dvořák wrote his only piano concerto in the summer of 1876. He was then forty-five years old, and at long last his fortunes had taken a favorable turn after a hard economic struggle. In 1875 he was awarded the Austrian State Prize, instituted in 1863 to aid "young, poor, and talented painters, sculptors, and musicians in the Austrian half of the Empire." (The other half belonged to the crown of Hungary.) Dvořák's reputation from the award was all the more enhanced by the prestige of the judges—Eduard Hanslick, the influential

Viennese music critic, Johann von Herbeck, the powerful director of the court opera, and Johannes Brahms, who became Dvořák's most successful champion.

In 1876 Dvořák's opera *Vanda* was produced in Prague, and in the same year he wrote the *Strains from Moravia,* which made his name known abroad. He was prompted by the pianist Karel von Slavovsky (1845-1919) to try his hand on a piano concerto. Slavovsky, whose career has escaped the attention of lexicographers, took an active interest on behalf of the rising generation of Czech composers; he was the soloist at the first hearing of Dvořák's piano concerto on March 28, 1878, in Prague. Alas, however satisfactory the event may have been for the composer, it actually marked a dead end for the concerto, since no local publisher showed interest in the work. In 1883, when the name of Dvořák had become internationally known, it was finally accepted by a German firm, Hainauer, in Breslau. Oscar Beringer (1844-1922), a student of Moscheles and Tausig, who had introduced Brahms's piano concerto in B flat in England, gave several readings of Dvořák's concerto there, and was host to the composer on his first stay in London in 1884.

What were Dvořák's models? A great deal of the concerto literature fashionable in the 1870s has been forgotten today, for instance the concertos by Anton Rubenstein and Adolf Henselt. The elegant creations of Saint-Saëns did not attract Dvořák. He may have known Tchaikovsky's concerto in B flat minor, which, composed in 1874/75, was heard in Boston as early as October of 1875. Dvořák did not follow the lead of the early romantic concertos by Mendelssohn and Schumann, nor did he choose the Lisztian design. He adopted instead the classical symphonic concept of Beethoven (concerto in E flat major) and Brahms (concerto in D minor).

The composition of the concerto was prior to Dvořák's "Slavic" period, which comprises such well-known pieces as the first set of the *Slavonic Dances,* three *Slavonic Rhapsodies,* the *Czech Suite,* and the string quartet in E flat major, Opus 51, in which the artistic stylization of national folk dances is very prominent. Yet the concerto, especially its finale, does not lack Czech traits. On the other hand, it also contains passages that seem to point to Schumann and Brahms. The first movement assumes a heroic aspect in certain passages, which Dvořák wanted to be interpreted "grandioso," particularly in the recapitulation about half-way through the opening theme and in the cadenza. The heroic character of the first movement is contrasted with the tender lyricism of the Andante, in which the trumpets and kettledrums are silenced. Yet at the end, the gentleness is interrupted violently by another "grandioso" episode. The finale, seasoned by an unmistakably Slavic flavor, speeds along with melodic and rhythmic diversity.

The autograph of the concerto reveals that Dvořák had a hard time composing it. He made many corrections and changes. Whole pages are pasted over with new versions, and many passages of the solo part were reworked several times. Dvořák's expectation to enrich the literature with a musically attractive and pianistically effective score was denied the fulfillment by the pianists. They pronounced the solo part as disadvantageous to the virtuoso. Such opinions, once expressed, become in time a formidable deterrent and mark the study of the piece as an unrewarding task. Vilem Kurz (1872-1949), professor at the Prague conservatory, conscious of the musical value of Dvořák's piano concerto and also well aware of the virtuoso psychology, suggested a partial revision of the original piano part to dispel the cautious attitude of the concertizing pianist and his preconceived ideas.

Kurz's revision, which does not touch the musical substance but only the setting of certain passages, was accepted by the editors of the complete edition of Dvořák's works as useful for the interpreter. Both Dvořák's version and that of Kurz are given in juxtaposition, and the pianist is left to take his choice. Rudolf Firkusny, an enthusiastic champion of the work, plays the composer's text and follows in certain places the version of Vilem Kurz, who happened to be his own teacher.

Czech Suite

Praeludium: Pastoral; Polka; Minuetto;
Romanza; Finale: Furiant

After Dvořák left the orchestra of the National Theatre in Prague and became organist of St. Adalbert's Church there in 1873, some important events led to a favorable turn in his fortunes. In 1875 he was awarded the Austrian State Prize and his Serenade for Strings (E major) was performed in Prague in December of 1876. That Christmas he received as a gift from friends money to finance a private printing of duets for soprano and alto, based on Moravian national songs. He sent the duets to Vienna when he applied for a renewal of the State Prize.

After Brahms had read them, he alerted his publisher, Simrock, in Berlin and urged Dvořák to dispatch a copy immediately to Simrock. During that time Dvořák wrote his second serenade (D minor, Opus 44), scored for wind instruments. The duets, accepted by Simrock and published in 1878 as *Airs from Moravia*, were instantly successful. Simrock suggested that Dvořák write some Slavonic dances as a pendant to Brahms's very popular *Hungarian Dances*. Accepting the proposition, Dvořák soon composed a set of eight *Slavonic Dances* (published in a piano duet version as Opus 46) and proceeded to orchestrate them. While he received three hundred marks for them, the *Slavonic Dances* earned Simrock a fortune.

In the winter of 1879, as he was working on the String Quartet in E flat major (Opus 51), Dvořák decided to amend his pair of serenades to form a triptych. He sketched a *tempo di marcia* and a *minuet*, following the pattern of the D minor serenade, as well as of an old Austrian tradition according to which the execution of a serenade is preceded by and concludes with a march. However, he later abandoned the serenade idea altogether and wrote a five-movement piece that he entitled "Suite" and later, in the program of the first performance on May 16, 1879, in Prague, designated *Czech Suite*. The bill of fare at that concert also included the first reading of the orchestral version of the *Slavonic Dances*, Opus 46.

Published as Opus 39 in Berlin, 1881, the *Czech Suite* belongs to Dvořák's "Slav Period," which comprises the first set of *Slavonic Dances*, three *Slavonic Rhapsodies* (1878, Opus 45), the String Sextet in A major (1878, Opus 48), an E flat major quartet (1879), and a *Mazurek* for violin (1879, Opus 49); in all these works the artistic stylization of national folk dances is a conspicuous trait. Though entitled "suite," this pleasant work displays the light mood of the classical serenade, couched in a thoroughly Czech musical language. With the opening "Praeludium" Dvořák alludes, if only nominally, to the baroque suite, while the "Romanza" refers to the classical serenade. Note, for example, the inclusion of romances in Mozart's *Eine kleine Nachtmusik* or his great Serenade for thirteen wind instruments (K. 361). The Czech element is most pronounced in the three national dances: the "Polka" (2/4), the "Sousedská" (3/4, a rather slow round dance), and the concluding "Furiant" (3/4), for which the composer reserved the greatest volume of sound, while the preceding movements are given a more gentle and light orchestral garb.

Notturno for Strings, Opus 40

The designation notturno implied different meanings in the classical and romantic periods. In the time of Haydn and Mozart notturno was almost synonymous with serenade and indicated a piece of open air music. Linguistically speaking, serenade could be defined as evening music, while notturno could signify night music. The common denominators were the practice of original performance in the open air and the light musical fare. Haydn, for example, wrote eight notturnos for a small ensemble, including a hurdy-gurdy, and Mozart composed serenades, notturnos, and *Eine kleine Nachtmusik*. He also applied the title notturno to five terzets for two sopranos and bass with clarinet and basset horn accompaniment to verses by Pietro Metastasio.

Songs of tender, dreamy, and sentimental quality for one or two voices were frequently entitled notturno. Giuseppe Blangini (1781-1841), a composer, once very successful, but now forgotten, achieved enormous popularity with his 170 notturnos for two voices. But his notturnos were insipid *salon* music, and it was left to his Irish contemporary John Field (1782-1837) to raise the notturno, or nocturne, to a high artistic level as a composition for piano. Field's nocturne is a slow piece with a graceful and frequently ornamented melody and a simple accompaniment of broken chords, sustained by the pedal. Chopin, who wrote twenty nocturnes, is greatly indebted to Field.

Dvořák's *Notturno for Strings* follows the line taken by Field and Chopin. It shows the tender, ornamented melody, the triplet accompaniment, and the sustained pedal tone that runs halfway through twenty-four measures (on F sharp). Composed in 1870 as an Andante religioso for a string quartet in E minor, it was included in 1875 as the slow movement in the string quintet, with double bass, in G major (Opus 77). But the composer had second thoughts and replaced the Andante religioso with another slow movement. The discarded piece remained untouched until the end of 1882. Dvořák then revised it and had it performed as a notturno on January 6, 1883, in Prague.

Serenade for Strings in E major, Opus 22

Moderato; Tempo di Valse; Scherzo; Larghetto;
Allegro vivace

Antonin Dvořák composed the serenade for strings within a fortnight (May 3-May 14, 1875) in Prague. A favorable turn of his fortune accounts for its quick completion. As organist at St. Adalbert's church, he had more time for his creative work than during the preceding decade, when he earned his living as violist of the National Theater in Prague. Moreover, he found official recognition as a composer when he received the then newly created Austrian state prize for the symphony in E flat major.

The first performance of the serenade took place on December 10, 1876, in Prague. A piano arrangement appeared in 1877, and two years later the score and parts were published in Berlin, where Dvořák had found a great following after the publication of the *Slavonic Dances*. With the composition of the serenade, Dvořák continued an old Austrian musical tradition. The term *serenade* is derived from the Provençal word *serena*, which means evening song; the connotation of the medieval Latin word is "late." The most frequent interpretation of the term *serenade* is that of a lover's song beneath his lady's window. It was also applied to instrumental pieces performed as open-air music. There is a large literature of serenades, to which a host of Austrian composers, including the classical masters, contributed a variety of works. The multi-movement structure with two dance pieces links the serenade to the baroque suite, while the outer movements usually show some symphonic traits. The execution of a rococo serenade was preceded by and concluded with a march. Dvořák upheld this tradition in a modified way by quoting the opening theme of the first movement at the conclusion of the finale.

Dvořák's serenade for strings is deeply rooted in the folk music and dance tunes of his native Bohemia. It displays his extraordinary inventiveness, rhythmic vitality, appealing lyricism, consummate craftsmanship, and gift for bewitching sound, which string players know so well from his chamber music.

Serenade in D minor, Opus 44

Moderato, quasi marcia; Minuetto; Andante con moto;
Finale: Allegro molto

Dvořák composed the D minor serenade in Prague between January 4 and 18, 1878, when he was organist at the St. Adalbert church. It was his second work of this kind, being preceded by a serenade for strings written in 1875 and published as Opus 22. Our serenade received its first performance in Prague on November 17, 1878, and was published as Opus 44 by the renowned Berlin firm of Simrock in April, 1879. Dvořák dedicated the work to the German composer and writer Louis Ehlert (1825-1884), who had written an enthusiastic review in 1878 of Dvořák's *Strains from Moravia* and the first set of the *Slavonic Dances* in the Berlin daily *Nationalzeitung*. The sales of Dvořák's compositions increased substantially in the wake of Ehlert's review.

The scoring of the piece for pairs of oboes, clarinets, bassoon and a contra-bassoon (optional), three horns, violoncellos and double-bass contrasts with that of Mozart's great Serenade in B flat, K. 361, which calls for pairs of oboes, clarinets, basset-horns, bassoons and a contra-bassoon, and four horns. In contrast to Mozart's and Beethoven's multi-movement serenades, Dvořák limited the number of movements to four; however, he followed an eighteenth-century usage in the shape of the first movement. The rococo serenade was usually open-air music: the musicians entered playing a march and after performing the serenade proper, left to the strains of another march. Mozart composed special marches for this purpose. Dvořák upheld this tradition by giving the opening movement the character of a march. It is a three-section piece with a trio in F major. The repeat of the first section closes deftly in D major.

The second movement combines in an imaginative way the moderate pace of the minuet with the quick motion of the scherzo. As the late Otakar Sourek, in the foreword to the score of the *Complete Works,* has pointed out, the minuet has the quality of the *sousedska* ("neighbors' dance"), while the fast trio is in the nature of the furiant.

The warm lyricism of the Andante and its richness of sound that is characteristic of Dvořák's slow movements in his chamber works (chiefly the string quartets) needs no particular commentary. In the fast-moving finale Dvořák again uses a device he had employed effectively in his earlier string serenade: the quotation of, and elaboration on, the opening melody of the first movement. We are not surprised that the following coda abandons the minor mode and closes jubilantly in a bright D major.

Requiem
The Background

Antonin Dvořák's operas and large scale vocal works, secular and sacred, are little known and rarely performed outside the Slavic countries. The regular concert goer who loves Dvořák's orchestral and chamber music hardly knows of his achievements as a dramatic composer or as a master of the oratorio, cantata, and *musica sacra.* Curiously enough it was a choral piece, the Hymnus, *The Heirs of the White Mountain,* that brought Dvořák his first great success (Prague, 1873). It was also a vocal work which carried Dvořák's name beyond the Czech musical circles: the *Moravian Duets.* Published by Simrock in Berlin in 1876 at the recommendation of Johannes Brahms, the *Moravian Duets* "laid the foundation for Dvořák's world renown," as his biographer Otakar Sourek asserts.

The huge American musical community takes pride in the fact that Dvořák spent about three years in the New World as director of the National Conservatory in New York (from 1892 to 1895) but it is forgotten today that the first new work the Czech master presented to the American public was a sacred choral composition, a *Te Deum.* Dvořák had been requested to compose a piece for the approaching quadricentennial of the discovery of

America. When the promised text—*The American Flag* by Joseph Rodman Drake—failed to arrive and the time had run out, Dvořák made his own choice and found the ancient prose hymn *Te Deum laudamus* of the fourth century appropriate to meet the great occasion. It was characteristic of the man and his deep religious sentiments that he felt the momentous historic event and the memory of Columbus should be honored artistically with a hymn of praise, *ad majorem Dei gloriam.* When Dvořák landed in New York on September 26, 1892, he brought with him the *Te Deum* for soprano and bass soli, chorus, and orchestra, and conducted it four weeks after his arrival in New York. (*The American Flag* received a reading only in 1895.)

Like Haydn, Mozart, Beethoven, Schubert, and Bruckner, Dvořák had considerable experience in matters of liturgical music and practice. It may be pointed out parenthetically that the lives and art of both Bruckner and Dvořák show very noticeable parallels. Both were country boys; both played in the village bands before they obtained exalted positions on the organ loft; both drew from the inexhaustible source of folk music and used its tunes with highest artistry; both were deeply religious men whose sacred creations form an essential part of their life work; both received doctorates *honoris causa*, and while Bruckner dedicated his First Symphony (actually his third) to his alma mater, Vienna University, Dvořák presented at Cambridge as a dissertation his G major Symphony and the *Stabat Mater*, thus indicating the importance of the *musica sacra* within his creative achievements.

In 1861 Dvořák had become a member of the orchestra of the Czech National Theatre in Prague. To supplement his meager salary he played the organ in several churches. In 1872 he left the theater and assumed the position of organist at the St. Adalbert church. This was not a large house of worship and its musical and financial resources were insufficient for the presentation of large-scale works. Nevertheless, Dvořák had ample opportunity to familiarize himself thoroughly with the liturgy. He wrote two masses that have not been published yet.

In 1886 he was commissioned by the architect Josef Hlávka to write a mass for the consecration of the chapel on his estate in Luzany. Dvořák conducted the mass at the consecration ceremonies on September 1, 1886. The local conditions had ruled out the participation of an orchestra and necessitated an organ accompaniment. Yet the mass was dear to Dvořák who felt that it "could have been called Faith, Hope, and Love toward God the most High, and Thankfulness for the great gift which was granted to me to finish so felicitously this work in the praise of the Most High and in honor of our art." He was determined to bring the mass before a larger public and he decided to give it an orchestral garb, hoping that it would duplicate the resounding success of the *Stabat Mater* in England. Yet his hope failed to materialize because the orchestral version, which Dvořák completed shortly prior to his embarcation for New York in 1892, became known only after the performance of the Requiem (1891). Since the mass is a creation of small dimensions and intimate character, the British audiences missed in it the grand sweep and ecstatic expressions that are characteristic of Dvořák's great choral works.

We do not know the circumstances that may have prompted Dvořák to write a Requiem Mass. Jarmil Burghauser, in the preface to the score, published in the monumental complete edition of Dvořák's works, seems to rule out the possibility of a commission by stating that the Requiem "was not perhaps actually commissioned by one of the English festival committees." What lies behind this vague statement? In Dvořák's time there were three regularly held music festivals that played an important role in the musical life of the British nation: the Three-Choir Festival of the choirs of Gloucester, Hereford, and Worcester (initiated in 1734), the Birmingham Festival (organized in 1768), and the Leeds Festival, first held in 1858. Dvořák had been associated with all of them as conductor of his own works. In 1884 he conducted his *Stabat Mater* in Worcester at the celebration of the 800th anniversary of the cathedral. In 1885 he presented in Birmingham his dramatic cantata *The Specter's Bride*, which was a commissioned work. In 1886 Dvořák was the star of the triennial music festival in Leeds and presided over the world premiere of his oratorio *Saint Ludmilla*.

These appearances generated an enthusiasm Dvořák had never experienced before and confirmed that he had made a decisive impression on the music world as a great choral composer. It is evident that the festival committees tried to grace their programs with new works from his pen. There are indications that the Birmingham committee had negotiated with Dvořák for the performance of the Requiem at the end of 1889. He must have acquainted the directors with his intention to compose a mass for the dead since negotiations with Birmingham are mentioned in Dvořák's correspondence of January 1890. From this point on there are no further doubts about the history of the composition since the sketches and the autograph score provide precise dates.

Dvořák began the Requiem on January 1, 1890, but interrupted the work about midway because he journeyed to Moscow and St. Petersburg in March, and to London in April. That the Requiem was nevertheless always in his mind is reflected by a short note entered in the sketch to the *Lacrimosa* which reads: "Written in Cologne on the Rhine."

After his return from London Dvořák resumed work on the Requiem in Vysoká, a quiet village, about forty miles southwest of Prague, near the silver mining town of Příbram. Vysokà was Dvořák's beloved vacation spot where he had built a home. Deeply attached to nature, he was in the habit of going out at daybreak and roaming the woods like Beethoven, listening to the concerts of the birds. Here he collected his thoughts and developed his musical ideas. It was in this pastoral setting that he finished the sketch of the Requiem on July 18, 1890.

After two weeks of rest, Dvořák began the orchestration on August 2, brought it up to the *Sanctus* and completed it in Prague. With a feeling of relief he entered in the manuscript which served as the master copy for the engraver: "Thanks God, the scoring is finished, Prague X,31,1890." Then the orchestral and piano scores were dispatched to his London publisher Novello. The first reading of the Requiem was given in Birmingham on October 9, 1891. Dvořák, Doctor of music *honoris causa* of Cambridge University, presided over the Festival Chorus and Orchestra and the response was overwhelming. Thereafter, whenever the Requiem was performed, it continued to make a deep impression. That the success was anticipated in American musical circles months prior to the first presentation in Birmingham can be gathered from the first draft of the contract which defined Dvořák's obligations as director of the National Conservatory in New York and conductor of his own works (to be presented in ten concerts). The offering of the Requiem was stipulated therein (July 1891).

Yet the Requiem was heard in the new world before Antonin Dvořák had set foot on American soil. The organization which undertook the performance of so demanding a work was the Church Choral Society of New York. Founded in 1886 by Richard Henry Warren (1859-1933), it presented the American premières of large-scale choral works by Liszt, Gounod, Saint-Saëns, and others. The performance of Dvořák's Requiem with an orchestra of sixty-five under Warren's direction took place on February 25, 1892, in the Episcopalian St. George Church on Stuyvesant Square.

The impression was profound. The critics paid tribute to the technical virtues of the work, the masterful orchestration and choral writing, and stressed the Slavonic color. Theodore Thomas included the Requiem in the program of the Cincinnati Biennial Music Festival (May 28, 1892) and Dvořák conducted it in Boston on November 29 and 30, 1892. He was not able to attend the Chicago performances on April, 10 and 11, 1893, which were led by Theodore Thomas. The reading given by the Oratorio Society under Frank Damrosch's direction in Carnegie Hall on April 4, 1901, was probably the first New York full-scale rendition of the Requiem after the presentation by the Church Choral Society in 1892. Strangely enough, the successful American presentations in the 1890s were overlooked by biographers and reference works and are also bypassed in the list of the initial performances given in the foreword to the score of the complete works (1961).

The presentation in Vienna (March 1901) in the concerts of the Society of Friends of Music under the baton of Ferdinand Löwe, the great Bruckner apostle, brought Dvořák a triumph. And when this venerable organization (founded in 1812) gave a reading in memory of the deceased composer in November 1904, Franz Schalk, the other renowned Bruckner herald, led the musical forces.

While we address ourselves to the discussion of the liturgical and technical aspects of Dvořák's Requiem, it will not be amiss to preface this examination with a few historical and liturgical observations and also to explore the relationship of Dvořák's work to other masses for the dead, written by various illustrious composers, which have attained pre-eminence in the history of the *musica sacra*.

Dvořák and the Liturgy

The Roman Catholic service of the Mass, which exercised an immense influence on the development of music, was gradually evolved through almost a thousand years. The sections sung by the chorus are (a) *Introitus*, (b) *Kyrie*, (c) *Gloria*, (d) *Graduale*, (e) *Credo*, (f) *Offertorium*, (g) *Sanctus*, (h) *Benedictus*, (i) *Agnus Dei*, and (j)*Communio*. Of these *Kyrie, Gloria, Credo, Sanctus, Benedictus* and *Agnus Dei* form the invariable Ordinary (*Ordinarium Missae*). In the Mass for the Dead, however, (*Missa pro defunctis*, generally called

"Requiem" after the first word of the Introit: *"Requiem aeternam dona . . ."*) the joyful *Gloria* and the dramatic *Credo* are omitted. They are replaced by the Sequence: *Dies irae*. Sequences in the liturgical sense are hymnlike sacred poems which were interpolated into the original liturgy of the Roman Catholic Church.

A large literature of Sequences had accumulated, but only five, including the *Dies irae,* are sanctioned today. This Sequence is a poem which consists of nineteen three-line stanzas in trochaic meter, each of the three lines rhyming in triplets. The rhyme scheme is abandoned in the last two stanzas, which are made up of verses from the Response *Libera me Domine de morte aeterna,* (Save me, O Lord, from eternal death), sung at the end of the service. The Response is spiritually akin to the Sequence (*Dies irae*) which it antedates. Thus the lines of the Response were probably not part of the poem but were added to it at some later date.

The authorship of the *Dies irae* has been the subject of many treatises and conjectures. It has been ascribed to Saints, Popes, and Cardinals, to Gregory the Great, St. Bernard of Clairvaux (died 1153), St. Bonaventure (died 1274), and Pope Innocent II (died 1216). Most authorities now attribute the authorship to Thomas of Celano (circa 1200-1255), a Franciscan Friar Minor, poet, and hagiographical writer who had joined the order in his teens and, after a stay in Germany, had become a close associate and first biographer of St. Francis of Assisi. The historical and ideological background of Thomas—incidentally a contemporary of Thomas of Aquino and Jacopone da Todi, the reputed author of the sequence *Stabat Mater*—is of cardinal importance for the understanding of the *Dies irae,* which was to become a source of inspiration to such great composers as Mozart, Cherubini, Berlioz, and Verdi. Weaving three stanzas into the church scene of *Faust,* Goethe drew a sheer frightening impact from the simple lines of the poetizing Franciscan Friar.

Thomas of Celano was a son of the turbulent thirteenth century which mercilessly heaped political disasters and national misfortunes upon the Apennine peninsula. It was the century when, under the influence of Franciscan and Dominican preachers who incessantly admonished their flocks to be prepared for the day of reckoning, the Last Judgment became an important subject of painting. The famous frescoes in the Camposanto in Pisa, Giotto's *Last Judgment* in Santa Maria dell' Arena in Padua, those of Luca Signorelli in the Duomo of Orvieto and of Michelangelo in the Sistine Chapel, all reflect the sentiments expressed by Thomas of Celano in his *Dies irae.*

The ascription of his poem to so many venerated churchmen eloquently testifies to the high esteem the verses enjoyed among the faithful. Praised as "the chief glory of the sacred poetry and most precious treasure of the Latin Church," the *Dies irae* has been translated countless times into many languages. More than 200 English renderings are known and some very illustrious names figure among the translators, as for example John Dryden, Sir Walter Scott and Lord Macaulay. The translation which is supplied here is by Rev. William Josiah Tirons. He wrote it after he had attended the rites for the Archbishop of Paris who had died at the barricades in the revolution of

1848 on a peace mission. The recitation of the *Dies irae* in Notre Dame deeply impressed Tirons, who resolved to translate the poem at once. His rendering was published in the same year and went with slight modifications into many hymn books.

The interpolation of the *Dies irae* after the Graduale in the *Missa pro defunctis* evoked innumerable musical settings. Yet the liturgical practice was not uniform before the turn of the sixteenth century. In France for instance the *Dies irae* was not an officially established part of the Requiem Mass before 1500 and, generally speaking, the Renaissance composers— Palestrina and Victoria for example—did not feel obliged to provide a polyphonic setting of the Sequence in their masses for the dead. The *Dies irae* had to be executed in plain song whose melody, incidentally, proved to be of strong attraction to Romantic composers who used it in instrumental works (Berlioz, Liszt, et al). Yet the *Dies irae* is the core of the Requiem and, seen from the artistic and musical point of view, it is the section which appeals most to the fantasy and imagination of the composer. It is the section whose musical treatment fully reveals the spiritual approach of the composer and lends the work its characteristic musical and artistic profile. For these reasons a brief consideration of the four famous Requiem Masses that Dvořák undoubtedly viewed as possible models will bring his spiritual approach and musical technique sharper into focus. They are the Requiems of Mozart (1791), Cherubini (1816), Berlioz (1836), and Verdi (1874).

They have common features and also reveal basic differences. The latter stem primarily from the treatment of the *Dies irae*. Mozart, Berlioz, and Verdi adopted for the Sequence the pattern of the so-called "cantata mass" of which Bach's Mass in B minor, Haydn's *Missa Sanctae Caeciliae*, and Mozart's unfinished Mass in C minor, K.427, are the best known examples. In the cantata mass the individual sections of the Ordinary, particularly the *Gloria* and *Credo*, are split into musically self-contained units which are thematically independent from each other. Mozart organized the *Dies irae* in six divisions, Berlioz in five, and Verdi in nine.

Berlioz tore the poem apart, muddled the stanzas and transplanted altered lines from the *Offertorium* into the *Dies irae*. He was chiefly interested in the creation of overpowering tone pictures and stunning contrasts. (In addition to his huge main orchestra with sixteen kettledrums and ten cymbals he needed four extra brass bands.) Except for a tenor solo in the *Sanctus*, Berlioz adopted the vocal disposition of Cherubini by writing for the chorus only, excluding solo passages and ensembles (duets, trios, quartets). Verdi, on the other hand, returned to the technique of Mozart and provided the four soloists with arias, duets, etc. He used the technical devices of the operatic finale. He connected the individual sections of the *Dies irae* through transitory passages; and, by the recurring use of certain phrases and motifs as well as by the two-fold quotation of the text and music of the first stanza, he succeeded in unifying the heterogeneous textual elements and the many musical episodes. In contrast to Mozart, Berlioz, and Verdi, Cherubini's *Dies irae* is 'through-composed' with the strict observance of the basic tempo, meter, and tonality.

What was Dvořák's approach? Several ways were open to him. He could follow the Austrian classical tradition of Mozart, whose Requiem shows strong influences of the Baroque melodically and in the sharply accentuated dotted scales in the *Rex tremendae majestatis*. Dvořák undoubtedly studied Cherubini's C minor Requiem which, the *coup de tamtam* in the *Dies irae* notwithstanding, is written in the classical style. Could Dvořák have followed the road of Berlioz, whose *Grande Messe des Morts* does not express the sorrow of the individual but instead was conceived as a manifestation of the masses with the intention "to produce a cataclysm of sinister harmonies and noise from another world." Such a notion never entered Dvořák's mind. Otakar Sourek said of him: "In his great and boundless wonder at all manifestations of nature and of life, [he] believed that the will and power of the supernatural ruled over all." This attitude definitely ruled out Berlioz' pictorial concept. In his *In Memoriam of Antonin Dvořák* Leos Janácek recounts an interesting incident which occurred before it had become known that Dvořák had composed a Mass for the Dead. Once Janácek had found Dvořák in an irritable mood while turning the leaves of Berlioz' Requiem. This occurrence clearly reveals Dvořák's attitude towards an important creation of a predecessor whom he admired. However, Berlioz' approach was at odds with Dvořák's conception, which put the spiritual aspect of the Requiem before the romantic-descriptive possibilities the text may offer to the composer.

Expressing himself strongly against the forceful accentuation of the terror of the Last Judgment in the musical treatment of the *Dies irae,* Beethoven once stated that he would take Cherubini's Requiem as a model in case he should ever write a Mass for the Dead. It was his conviction that the faithful should not be terrified by the music. Witness the *Crucifixus* episode in his *Missa solemnis.* There are no fortissimo outcries, no "sinister harmonies" projected by the brass section, and no agitated runs and wild tremolos executed by the strings. We must understand, however, that composers who had close connection with the operatic stage and developed a refined technique of illustrating dramatic situations could hardly find fundamentally different musical means if they were confronted with the task of setting the *Dies irae* to music. This holds true not only of Verdi but also of Dvořák, who had written eight operas prior to the composition of the Requiem.

Yet to Dvořák, the church musician, the strict observance of the liturgy was a foregone conclusion; and in this respect, Cherubini's C minor Requiem appears to have served as a guide to Dvořák. He followed Cherubini not only by including the *Graduale* and *Pie Jesu* (preceding the *Agnus Dei*), which were not composed by Mozart, Berlioz, and Verdi, but also in the delicate orchestration of these pieces in which Cherubini silenced the violins. Furthermore, Dvořák adopted Cherubini's (and Verdi's) basic architectural proportions. While in the case of Berlioz, the Introit, *Kyrie,* and Sequence form two-thirds of the work, the Requiems of Cherubini, Verdi, and Dvořák display a perfect architectural symmetry: *Introitus, Graduale, Kyrie* and *Dies irae* form one half, while the other sections taken together equal it in size.

Some Analytical Observations

While the general liturgical organization of Dvořák's Requiem closely resembles Cherubini's C minor Requiem, the treatment of the Sequence (*Dies irae*) follows the tradition of the cantata mass. In one respect Dvořák deviates completely from the works of his predecessors and his contemporary Verdi: he uses a short basic motif which, recurring again and again from the first measure to the concluding passage, establishes the musical coherence of the work and also secures its spiritual unity. This technique of motivic unification was familiar to the masters of the fifteenth and sixteenth centuries. Dvořák was in all probability not a great student of Renaissance polyphony and the method he employed in the Requiem is in essence the application of the leitmotif. His motif is very short, consisting of one note and its upper and lower neighboring notes.

It occurs in the exact intervallic configuration about 120 times in all twelve minor keys in 4/4, 3/2, 9/4, 3/4, and 6/8 time. Appearing also in several derivations, it could be called "Requiem motif." It reflects sorrow and resignation, and its chromatic quality is in marked contrast to the diatonic lines of the Gregorian melodies. This programmatic aspect of a basic motif or theme was to become an important factor in Dvořák's future orchestral and dramatic works. In the application of the leitmotif, Dvořák proceeds along Wagnerian lines. It is true that Mozart's Requiem shows certain thematic and motivic relationship among its individual sections. Scalelike phrases and motifs, ascending and descending, appear abundantly in Verdi's *Messa da Requiem*. But in the use of a leitmotif, Dvořák's Requiem Mass is probably unique in the liturgical literature.

This motif even went beyond its original conception, as Jarmil Burghauser has pointed out. It appears in Dvořák's *Othello* Overture and is also quoted in Josef Suk's *Asrael* Symphony and in the Third Symphony of Bohuslav Martinu. It became a national symbol and its use in Suk's symphony is of particular significance. He wrote *Asrael* in memoriam of Antonin Dvořák, his teacher and father-in-law. While working on the symphony his wife, Dvořák's daughter, died, and thus the composition became a lament for his wife and her father.

This brings us to another outstanding trait of Dvořák's Requiem. Although abhorring political and national radicalism, Dvořák was proud to be a Czech musician. Conscious of his artistic mission as a son of the Czech people, he spoke their musical language in his Requiem perhaps no less pointedly than in the lyrical passages of his chamber music and symphonies. Those warm melodies and appealing lyrical phrases that have conquered the world prove anew their charm and power in the spiritual sphere of the *musica sacra*. Dvořák composed the Requiem in observance of the liturgical laws but he succeeded, due to his melodic genius, in mitigating the anxiety of the faithful and in imparting hope and confidence to their souls.

Dr. Josef Zubaty, an eminent philologist, president of the Czech Academy of Art and Sciences, a professionally trained musician and close friend of Dvořák, described his approach to religion as a "religiousness which came from the heart, from conviction of one devoted to God and not to any definite religious organization." Yet Dvořák, the church musician, took pains to observe the liturgical laws in his sacred works. As we have pointed out already, we do not know the circumstances which finally led to the composition of the Requiem. This writer ventures the assumption that Dvořák felt the inner necessity to approach the text as a creative musician after he had written masses and a *Stabat Mater.* He arrived at a decision after he was convinced that he was artistically ready for it.

Another motive might have influenced his determination to compose a Requiem. Great representatives of great musical nations had written masses for the dead. It was perhaps Dvořák's idea to demonstrate the artistic maturity of the Czech musicians by composing a Requiem Mass that he hoped would be considered a great work and worthy to be included among the admired creations of his famous predecessors.

In the following paragraphs a short analysis of the Requiem will be given, with some particularly interesting details pointed out. Dvořák employs a solo quartet, four-voice chorus, and a large orchestra: two flutes and piccolo, two oboes and English horn, two clarinets and bass clarinet, two bassoons and contra bassoon, four horns, four trumpets, three trombones and tuba, kettle-drums, tam-tam, organ, and strings. An entry in the autograph piano score indicates that Dvořák contemplated the use of large and small bells in a passage of the *Tuba mirum* but the autograph orchestral score lacks a note to this effect. The basic key, B flat minor, rules out the use of the open strings for the violins and basses and permits only the open C string for the viola and violoncello. It is a tonality which darkens the sonorities of the string sections and generates a sombre color which is appropriate for a Requiem Mass.

1. Introitus—Kyrie

It commences with the Requiem motif, which, announced pianissimo by the muted violins and violoncellos, appears in varied shapes.

The passage *"Te decet hymnus"* is treated in a chordal, hymn-like fashion in contrast to Mozart, who used the corresponding plain song melody entwined with figurations, while Verdi applied imitative polyphony to these lines.

The *Kyrie* is tightly knit to the Introit and developed from the Requiem motif. Witness for instance the use of shorter note values:

2. Graduale

The solo soprano begins the intonation with the Requiem motif which, in

Dvořák's words, should be delivered *con afflizione,* with sadness.

N. B. Read B flat.

The soloist is joined by a three-part women's choir. The strings do not play for the greater part of the *Graduale,* a practice which recalls Cherubini's device of silencing the violins during the *Introit, Kyrie,* and *Graduale.*
The middle section is dominated by the solo soprano, and the four-part men's choir brings about the gentle and surprising conclusion in G major, which is sharply contrasted with the Allegro impetuoso of the *Dies irae.*

3. Sequence a) *Dies irae*

The setting of the first two stanzas has a marchlike quality which ultimately loses its force and the music fades away almost inaudibly.

di- es i- rae, di-es il- la

b) *Tuba mirum*

The musical treatment of this stanza is based on the Requiem motif from which another persistently repeated motif is developed.

It is not used as the thematic main factor but as a coloristic counter voice to the melody of the alto. However, it generates a strong driving power which leads to the sheer volcanic eruption upon the words *"mors stupebit et natura."*
The fifth stanza (*Liber scriptus*) resumes the theme of the *Dies irae* in A minor

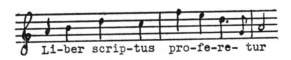

Li-ber scrip-tus pro-fe-re- tur

and then, following the precedent established by Verdi, Dvořák repeats the music of the *Dies irae* set to the text of the first three stanzas of the Sequence, including the *Tuba mirum.*

c) *Quid sum miser*

The Requiem motif is joined to the theme of the *Quid sum miser*

and the new variant is ingeniously used for the bridge passage to the *Rex tremendae.*

There is a frequent alternation of solo voices and chorus. The use of the dotted rhythm in *Rex tremendae majestatis* reveals a kinship to Mozart and also to Verdi in the proclamation of the theme by the basses. Dvořák connects this passage with *Tuba mirum*, musically as well as spiritually, by quoting the obstinate motif aforementioned.

Note the harmonic richness. The passage starts in A flat major and turns to C sharp minor for the forceful *Rex tremendae* which, however, gradually losing its impetus, dies away (*morendo*) on the sustained C sharp in the lower strings with the C sharp major chord.

d) *Recordare*

Framed by the lines of the mighty *Rex tremendae* and the agitated *Confutatis*, the stanzas of the *Recordare* emanate a certain mildness that tends to evoke a rather lyrical musical treatment. Employing a solo quartet without the participation of the chorus, Dvořák follows here the road of Mozart. Here is the domain of Dvořák the lyricist who expresses himself in a musical language which, simple but appealing, stems from the soil of his homeland.

e) *Confutatis*

The opening lines are proclaimed by the bass, which is also the case in the Requiems of Verdi and Mozart. The leitmotif appears in a new shape.

This section begins in G minor and closes in B major.

f) *Lacrimosa*

The fluctuation of the harmony continues until the main key is reached. New variations of the Requiem motif are introduced

and references to the preceding sections made. The signal motif after *"homo reus"* stems from the *Recordare*.

Of particular significance is the reappearance of the rhythmic motif which is heard throughout the first two stanzas of the Sequence. It now returns in a diminution:

Injected first into the *Amen* passage by the strings, it is taken up by the kettledrums in the concluding measures. It is the Alpha and Omega of the *Dies irae* as set forth by Dvořák.

4. Offertorium a) *Domine Jesu*

A marchlike prelude of the wind instruments precedes the statement of the first words, intoned by the choir bass. The phrase

which discloses a Slavic flavor is repeated later by the alto section of the chorus. There are also references to the leitmotif.

Observing an old tradition (Mozart, Cherubini) Dvořák treated the sentence *"Quam olim Abrahae promisisti"* in an imposing fugue of 200 measures in length. As Jarmil Burghauser has pointed out, the beginning and general contour of the "jubilant" fugal subject conforms to the Czech fourteenth-century hymn "Let us sing joyfully, let us praise God the Father," which was still sung in the churches in Dvořák's time. It is preserved in a manuscript of 1410 and in all probability Dvořák chose this historic tune because of its rhythmical and metrical relationship to the melody of *"et lux perpetua luceat eis"* in the Introit.

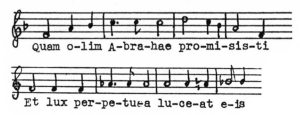

The second part of the Offertory repeats, though modified, the intonation, words, and music referred to above, and concludes with the repetition of the fugue.

b) *Hostias*

5. Sanctus

Going beyond the traditional three invocations Dvořák wrote seven which, intoned piano, prepare the mighty entrance of the eighth with its constantly fluctuating harmonies.

6. Benedictus

Closely joined to the Sanctus (B flat major) the gentle *Benedictus,* which also restates the Requiem motif, is in the key of B major. It turns to B flat major for the *Hosanna* section which, however, is not identical with that of the *Sanctus.* This constitutes a deviation from the classical practice.

7. Pie Jesu

The words refer to the last stanza of the Sequence and also anticipate the *Agnus Dei.* Following the jubilant *Hosanna* the transparent and tenderly orchestrated *Pie Jesu* appears as a study in contrast. Except for a few measures, it is sung a cappella either by the four-part men's chorus, joined by the altos, or by a trio, formed by the soprano, alto, and tenor soloists. The Requiem motif appears several times.

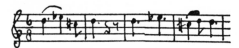

8. Agnus Dei 9. Communio

This section is in the main key. The frequent use of the Requiem motif in different shapes once more reflects its importance as a supreme spiritual element as well as an effective means of achieving a thematic coherence which encompasses the work as a whole. The dynamic climax is built upon the first statement of the words *"Lux aeterna luceat eis"* ("Light eternal shine upon them...") where a new shape of the Requiem motif is woven into the orchestral fabric.

There are also references to the *Lacrimosa* and Introit.

Et lux per-pe-tu-a lu-ce-at e- is

After a quotation of the Requiem motif the conclusion in **B** flat minor is deftly effected.

ELGAR, Edward (1857-1934)
Concerto for Violoncello in E minor, Opus 85
Adagio moderato; Allegro molto; Adagio; Allegro ma non troppo

Edward Elgar, who was born at Broadheath near Worcester, England, and died at Worcester, was the son of an organist and successful music dealer. A proficient violinist, he also played the piano, organ, violoncello, double bass, bassoon, and trombone. He acquired experience in conducting as a bandmaster on the staff of the County Lunatic Asylum, a post that he held for five years. Elgar slowly gained acceptance as a composer, and only the success of the *"Enigma" Variations* in 1899 placed him in a position of prominence among English composers at the close of the Victorian era. He wrote for nearly all fields of music except the opera, and his most famous piece is a march, *Pomp and Circumstance, No. 1,* conceived to reflect the glory of imperial England. This march has the same symbolic and emotional importance for England that the *Stars and Stripes Forever* has for the United States. During his lifetime, Elgar was the recipient of many honors. He was knighted, received the Order of Merit, became Master of the King's Musick, and was made a baronet.

The concerto for violoncello was composed in the country during the summer and early autumn of 1919. It was performed shortly after its completion on October 27, 1919, in Queen's Hall, London, by Felix Salmond (1888-1952), who later taught at the Juilliard School of Music from its founding in 1924. Elgar's concerto does not attempt to set off the virtuoso; its basic quality is tranquility. In spite of the use of a rather romantic orchestra that includes four horns, three trombones, and three kettledrums, it resembles chamber music more than symphonic music. But Elgar abandoned the three-movement design of the classical concerto in favor of a four-movement structure.

The deviation from the classical tradition becomes immediately apparent in the opening measures that present a short recitative of the solo instrument. This recitative functions as a motto, that, modified, reappears in later movements and serves as a melodic source for other themes. The main body of the first movement (Moderato, 9/8) reflects the pastoral quality. The second movement, prefaced by a short recitative, constitutes the scherzo. Remarkable are the light orchestration, the lovely cantabile melody that represents the trio and the declamatory cadence at the end. The Adagio (B flat major, 3/8), gently orchestrated, displays a lyrical quality that is contrasted with the emotional middle section. The tranquil mood returns in the closing portion that is linked to the dance-like Finale (2/4). Once more we encounter the recitative motto. A rapid crescendo leads to the vivid and incisive ending.

FAURÉ, Gabriel (1845-1924)
Pelléas et Mélisande
Prélude; Andantino quasi Allegretto; Sicilienne; Molto adagio

Maurice Maeterlinck's play *Pelléas et Mélisande*, published in 1892 and first produced in 1893, attracted several important composers: Claude Debussy, Gabriel Fauré, Arnold Schönberg, and Jean Sibelius. Debussy conceived the idea of a "lyrical drama" shortly after the appearance of the play—his score could be considered complete in 1898, when Fauré wrote his incidental music for a production of the play in London. Schönberg composed his symphonic poem *Pelléas und Mélisande* in 1902-1903 and Sibelius followed with his incidental music in 1905.

An enormous amount of incidental music has been written in the past hundred and fifty years. This music served the purpose of the day, sometimes, but often without, arousing great interest, and was ultimately buried in theater archives. But the contributions of outstanding composers found their way into the concert hall in the form of suites. We may think of Mendelssohn (*A Midsummer Night's Dream*), Bizet (*L'Arlésienne*), Grieg (*Peer Gynt*), Richard Strauss (*Der Bürger als Edelmann*), and Korngold (*Much Ado about Nothing*). Fauré is another case in point: from his music to *Pelléas et Mélisande* he assembled a suite first heard at the celebrated Concerts Lamoureux in Paris in 1902, the same year that Debussy's lyric drama was first staged at the Opéra Comique. Fauré's suite, published as Opus 80, consists of four movements. It opens with the original Prélude

in which the composer tries to depict the essential elements of the drama: the gentleness of Mélisande, the somberness of the story and its tragic ending. The Andantino quasi Allegretto that follows refers to the first scene of the third act. The pertinent stage direction reads "A room in the castle, Pelléas and Mélisande are discovered. Mélisande is spinning with a distaff at the back of the room." The spinning is indicated musically by constantly moving sextolets in the string section while the melodic development is entrusted to the wind instruments, chiefly the oboe:

The third movement, entitled Sicilienne,

was originally a piece for violoncello and piano (Opus 78) and its orchestrated version was later incorporated in the incidental music. The last movement (Molto Adagio), characterized by an intensity of emotion, mirrors the ending and the death of Mélisande.

Ballade and Fantaisie for Piano and Orchestra

Fauré was a versatile composer who wrote for the stage, for the church, and much instrumental and secular vocal music. He began his brilliant musical career, like many renowned French musicians, in an organ loft. A student of Camille Saint-Saens, Fauré received his first employment at twenty-one, in 1866, at Rennes, about two hundred miles west of Paris. He later occupied organist's posts in churches in the French capital, building up a fine reputation. When Saint-Saens gave up his position as first organist at the Madeleine in 1877, Fauré was appointed second organist there. He became chief organist at this famous church in 1896 and professor of composition at the Conservatoire. His prestige as a teacher was enormous. His most prominent students were Maurice Ravel, Georges Enesco, and Nadia Boulanger. In 1905 Fauré was appointed director of the Conservatoire. He kept this illustrious position until 1920, when ill health and growing deafness necessitated his resignation.

In 1877 Fauré accompanied his teacher Saint-Saens to Weimar to attend the first production of the opera *Samson and Delilah,* which Saint-Saens was unable to place in his own country. Saint-Saens owed the acceptance in Weimar to Liszt, whose influence in the small capital of the tiny duchy was still very great. Saint-Saens introduced Fauré to Liszt, and Fauré showed him the original version of the *Ballade,* a piece for piano solo. Liszt, then sixty-six, tried it and pronounced it "too difficult." This is hard to understand because the *Ballade* is by no means studded with pianistic fireworks like those with which Liszt in his youth held his fashionable audiences spellbound. As Fauré's son Philippe expressed it, his father "had a horror of virtuosity, of rubato and of those effects in performance which send shivers down the spines of the audience."

The instrumental *ballade* has no direct connection with the old English *ballad,* in narrative verses and set to dance tunes, nor with the *ballades* by Franz Schubert and Carl Loewe, which rank as outstanding achievements in the German art song. The instrumental ballade is freely constructed, and can be described as an extended song without words. Introduced by Chopin and adopted by Liszt, Brahms, Grieg, and others, charged with emotion and often showing heroic traits, the instrumental ballade is a creation of the romantic movement.

In the *Ballade* Fauré followed to a certain extent the tradition of Chopin. *Ballade* employs a small orchestra without trumpets and kettledrums; the main accent is placed on lyricism.

The *Fantaisie,* published as Opus 111 in 1919 and separated from the *Ballade* by more than forty years, displays different features. These two score years sparked great developments in French music and saw the creation of the most important works of César Franck, the entire creative activity of Claude Debussy, and the emergence of Maurice Ravel. Although some critics credited Fauré with the introduction of a "prédebussyste" element, and the *Fantaisie* actually displays passages with the whole-tone scale, Fauré developed his own musical language with clarity and delicate lines as the characteristic features. The fineness and poetic qualities of his music earned him the nickname "French Schumann."

In contrast to the *Ballade*, to which the orchestral garb was later added, the *Fantaisie* was orchestrally conceived. It is scored for a full symphony orchestra with four horns, trumpets, and kettledrums, and also employs the harp in an original manner by pairing it with the piano. The *Fantaisie* consists of three sections: the first and third (Allegro moderato, 4/4), are thematically linked, and frame the rapid and rhythmically incisive middle section in 3/4 time. The composer dedicated the piece to Alfred Cortot, who as pianist as well as writer energetically promoted Fauré's piano works.

Requiem

Introit and Kyrie; Offertory; Sanctus; Pie Jesu; Agnus Dei; Libera me; In Paradisum

Gabriel Fauré's *Requiem* is the product of a great Parisian tradition. There is perhaps no other capital or metropolis where so many important musicians have occupied organist's or church conductor's posts. A galaxy of names, spanning three centuries and representing the glory of French music, eloquently testifies to the vital role that the churches of Paris played in the muscial history of France. Marc-Antoine Charpentier, Couperin, Rameau, Lesueur, Gounod, Franck, Saint-Saens, Widor, Fauré, Delibes, D'Indy, and others were organists or conductors in the churches of the French capital.

Fauré began his career as an organist in 1866 at Rennes and went to Clignancourt, a northern suburb of Paris, in 1870. In 1871 he was at the church of Saint-Honoré Eylau and was assistant to Widor at Saint-Sulpice. In the following years Fauré often substituted for Saint-Saens at the Madeleine. In 1877 when Saint-Saens, who traveled and concertized frequently, quit his post at the Madeleine, he was succeeded by Théodore Dubois, and Fauré was appointed as his deputy. Fauré became chief organist at the Madeleine in 1896, when Dubois received the directorship of the Conservatoire. About ten years later history repeated itself: Dubois resigned and was succeeded by Fauré. Fauré's appointment as director of the Conservatoire in 1905 marked the end of his activities as a church musician.

Fauré's professional association with the church of almost two score years was artistically productive. His contributions to the *musica sacra* are on a modest scale and include only thirteen works; of these, the *Messe de Requiem*, published as Opus 48, is the outstanding one. It is one of Fauré's most important creations. He was moved to compose it by the passing of his father in 1885. The composition occupied him throughout 1886, and in 1888 he had the satisfaction of having the mass performed at the Madeleine.

The Roman Catholic service of the mass, which exercised an immense influence on the development of music, was gradually evolved through almost a thousand years. The mass as a musical category, which is performed by the chorus, and in some cases by soloists and orchestra, consists of the *Kyrie, Gloria, Credo, Sanctus, Benedictus* and *Agnus Dei*. These sections form the invariable Ordinary (*Ordinarium Missae*). However, in the mass for the dead (*Missa pro defunctis*, generally called "Requiem" after the first word of the Introit: "*Requiem aeternam dona . . .*"), the joyful *Gloria* and the dramatic *Credo* are omitted. They are replaced by the sequence *Dies irae* (Day of

Wrath). Sequences, in the liturgical sense, are hymnlike sacred poems that were interpolated into the original liturgy of the Roman Catholic Church. A large literature of sequences had accumulated, but only five, including the *Dies irae,* are sanctioned today.

The verses of the *Dies irae,* permeated with imagery, drama, and remorse, kindled the fantasy and inspiration of Fauré's great contemporaries Berlioz and Verdi. Fauré was certainly familiar with the *Requiems* of Berlioz and Verdi, but maintaining that art and above all music should elevate us as much as possible from the world as it is, he rejected the pictorial approach that led to the huge canvasses painted by the two composers in the Dies irae.

He was not the only prominent composer who held this view. Cherubini showed a similar attitude in his famous *Requiem* in C minor of 1816. Beethoven expressed himself strongly against the forceful accentuation of the terror of the Last Judgment in the musical treatment of the *Dies irae.* It was his conviction that the faithful should not be terrified by the music: fortissimo outcries, "a cataclysm of sinister harmonies" (as desired by Berlioz), agitated runs, and wild tremolos of strings, which certainly have a terrifying effect and are the vital stock in trade of the dramatic composer.

Fauré waived these devices. As his most devoted student Charles Koechlin declared, he rejected "the cruel anthropomorphism of the divine justice modeled after sanctimonious prudery of human courts" and stressed instead "tenderness, pardon, and hope."

These convictions account for Fauré's omission of the *Dies irae.* Yet an advantage accrued from the execution of the sequence in chant: namely, a reasonable performance time within the rites; and this, as Fauré knew too well, was a point of eminent practical value. Composing the *Requiem,* he had in mind liturgical readings rather than concert presentations. However, he disregarded the liturgical exigencies by the omission of the *Benedictus,* which, incidentally, is also lacking in the *Messe des Morts* by Berlioz. Following the example set by Cherubini in his famous *Requiem,* Fauré inserted a *Pie Jesu* before the *Agnus Dei* and also provided, as did Verdi, a *Libera me,* which is usually sung in those Requiem Masses that precede the burial. Finally, Fauré added the old *In paradisum deducant angeli* ("May the angels lead you into Paradise"), which underlines the comforting aspect.

Fauré's work differs most conspicuously from the famous masses for the dead by Mozart, Cherubini, Berlioz, Verdi, and Dvořák in the orchestration. Fauré abandons the customary division of the string body into violins I and II, viola, violoncello, and bass and scores for viola I and II, violoncello I and II, and bass, sometimes divided, with an occasional use of the violins. The violins mainly reinforce the violas and are given an independent melodic line only in the *Sanctus.* Even here they are muffled in order to tone down their brightness, because Fauré's orchestral palette consistently avoids brilliantly shining colors and aims rather at dark-toned, gentle, velvety sonorities. Fauré dispensed with the oboes, and the participation of the flute and clarinets is limited to a dozen measures in the *Pie Jesu.* Kettledrums go into action briefly in the *Libera me.* The organ, however, plays throughout, and harps enter in the *Sanctus* and the final measures.

The elimination of the violins was not exactly a novelty. Cherubini had set a precedent in the *Pie Jesu* of his C minor *Requiem,* and Etienne-Nicolas Méhul excluded the violins entirely from his opera *Uthal* (1806) in order to achieve the dark and melancholic mood of Ossian, which was the basis of the libretto. Fauré faced a somewhat similar situation, and his scoring reflects his spiritual and musical approach.

Fauré's *Requiem* is a choral work despite the baritone solo passages in the Offertory and *Libera me* and the soprano solo in *Pie Jesu.* These are not aria-like passages but are in the nature of a prayer said by the officiating priest. This is a *Requiem* without fugues, and there are only short contrapuntal passages in the Offertory. The simple and chordal texture as well as the syllabic manner of the part writing seems to go back to a technique of the thirteenth century, *conductus.*

The omission of the *Dies irae* was criticized, and voices were heard that suggested that the work was pagan rather than Christian in tone. Charles Koechlin firmly opposed this view, contending that it was "pointless (to say) that his (Fauré's) art did not concern itself with a detailed image of Hell..." It is the avoidance of the element of terror and even of the idea of Purgatory that evokes the feeling of comfort. Norman Sucking, a British author, has drawn attention to the prominence Fauré gives the word "requiem" (rest) and the idea of rest through the insertion of the *Pie Jesu, Libera me,* and *In paradisum,* all of which include a prayer for rest. "Requiem" is the first and also the last word of Fauré's mass for the dead. This remarkable fact sets his *Requiem* apart from those of his great predecessors as well as those of his famous contemporaries.

FITELBERG, Jerzy (1903-1951),
Concerto for Trombone, Piano, and String Orchestra
Allegro; Variations; Allegro energico

Jerzy Fitelberg was born in Warsaw in 1903. His father, Gregor, was a distinguished conductor who had championed the works of the Polish contemporary musicians, and was himself a composer. Fitelberg received his musical education from his father, and also took courses in the Hochschule für Musik in Berlin. From 1933 until 1940 he lived in Paris, where his creative work was influenced by contemporary French musicians, as well as by Stravinsky. Fitelberg was a successful composer whose orchestral and chamber music was frequently performed and published in Europe. He came to the United States in 1940, before France collapsed under the German onslaught. He was not unknown in America, for in 1936 he had received an Elizabeth Sprague Coolidge award for a string quartet, which was performed at the Coolidge Festival of Chamber Music in Washington in 1937.

Fitelberg's style, which only rarely displays a Polish melodic flavor, has been termed "cosmopolitan" by Nicolas Slonimsky. Formerly a percussionist in the orchestra led by his father, he emphasized the rhythmical element in his creations. The concerto for trombone, piano, and string orchestra, written in New York in 1947, is a case in point.

The coupling of the trombone and piano is unusual. In this work the technical demands of the former are exacting because of the perplexing entangled rhythmical situations. In the 201 measures of the first movement, there are more than a hundred changes of meter (2/4, 3/4, 4/4, and 5/4). By and large, Fitelberg stays within the traditional framework of the three-movement concerto. The first Allegro is freely constructed, while the middle movement offers a variation series with frequent changes of tempo and rhythm. The finale, which has a less intricate rhythmical character and texture, displays a dance-like quality. Jerzy Fitelberg died in New York in 1951. He was outlived by his father (1879-1953).

GABRIELI, Giovanni (1557-1612)
Sonata a tre chori
"Dulcis Jesu," sonata con voci

Giovanni Gabrieli was born in Venice about 1557. He was a nephew and pupil of the famous Venetian organist and composer Andrea Gabrieli (c. 1520-1586), who in turn was probably a student of the Fleming Adrian Willaert (c. 1490-1562). During Willaert's thirty-seven years as *maestro di cappella* at St. Mark's, he exercised great influence on the Italian musical scene, having many students to whom he imparted the art of Franco-Netherlandish vocal polyphony. It was this tradition in which Giovanni Gabrieli was reared. He spent several years in Munich, one of the great centers of Renaissance music, engaged as a member of the court chapel by Orlando di Lasso. From 1584 until his death in Venice in 1612, Gabrieli was an organist and composer with the musical establishment of St. Mark's.

Gabrieli lived at a crossroads in musical history, when a decisive stylistic change occurred. Having matured in the late Renaissance, he then witnessed the inception of the baroque, which introduced the monodic style, brought about the creation of the opera, and last but not least, generated the rise of instrumental music. Because of his "manifold innovations, all of which were adopted by other composers sooner or later," the role that Gabrieli played, particularly as instrumental composer, was epoch-making. Concerning this we will be enlightened by Egon Kenton's forthcoming biography of Gabrieli, the first full-fledged book on this great Italian composer since 1834; Gabrieli's widely scattered artistic legacy will be made accessible through a complete edition of his compositions, now in progress.

The composers associated with St. Mark's were required to write not only for the usual services of the ecclesiastical year, but also for the official festivals and affairs of state. In the time of Gabrieli the Serenissima Repubblica was at the height of its political power, and the splendor of the solemn masses and vespers in the cathedral was mirrored in the music executed by the famous chapel. It was probably for an occasion in the chapel that *Dulcis Jesu,* designated as *sonata con voci,* was written. Needless to say, the term "sonata" meant quite a different thing in 1600 than it means today. It indicated an instrumental piece, and Gabrieli also applied the term to a composition employing human voices as well. Though not necessarily intended for liturgical purposes, such a piece was meant to be performed in church, where its devotional quality permitted its execution within or after the service.

While in earlier times organ pieces had alternated with choral music within the liturgical service, Gabrieli availed himself of the rich musical means of St. Mark's and composed longer instrumental pieces for the great holidays and festivals that were attended by the Doge, the dignitaries of the government, and the powerful Venetian aristocracy. These pieces, the *sonate*, were heard in alternation with the choral groups posted in the two organ lofts that faced each other in the choir of the cathedral.

Gabrieli preferred for his orchestral sonatas the three-choir organization, with five parts for each choir. In our *Sonata a tre chori* these parts are specified as violino—meaning viola—or wooden cornetto, and four trombones. However, the sonatas were never performed in just this manner, as the names of the musicians and their respective instruments, preserved in treasury notes, indicate. Gabrieli was given to experimentation, as was Antonio Vivaldi a hundred years later, and would conduct the same piece on various occasions, using different performers and instrumental arrangements each time. According to a wide-spread belief, Gabrieli used brass instruments preponderantly in his performances. Egon Kenton does not subscribe to this notion, yet it does account for the over-stuffing with brass instruments of modern arrangements of Gabrieli's works. It is true that Gabrieli's manuscript scores seldom define the orchestration exactly and thus leave much leeway to today's orchestrator.

The *Sonata a tre chori* belongs to *Canzoni et Sonate,* published posthumously in 1615, where it appears under the heading "Sonata XIX a 15." Kenton's orchestration places the strings and harpsichord in the first choir; the woodwinds—flute, oboe, clarinet, bass clarinet, and two bassons—supported by a harmonium, in the second; and in the third choir the brass instruments—trumpet, two horns, and two trombones—assisted by the organ.

Dulcis Jesu, presumably composed prior to 1610, is a particularly instructive example of Gabrieli's late style and also of significant trends in the early baroque. Its subtitle, *sonata con voci,* places it among those compositions that combined instruments with human voices and were designed for liturgical use or devotional purposes. The only surviving copy is preserved in the Landesbibliothek of Kassel. The piece calls for six voice and fourteen instrumental parts, organized in three choirs. Only some of the required instruments are indicated; those that are undefined are notated in the tenor and bass clefs. The casting was left to the conductor, whose choice hinged on the available means.

For the first choir there are precise indications only for a soprano solo, cornetto, and viola, while the four remaining parts are written in the tenor and bass clefs. Thus four instruments have to be used to realize these parts; Kenton employs three celli and a double bass. The second choir is led by the tenor, accompanied by a cornetto, viola, two baryton tubas, and a bass trombone. The third choir is comprised of a vocal quartet—soprano, alto, tenor, and bass—and a trio of two trumpets and a bass trombone.

A previous arrangement by Egon Kenton of the *Sonata a tre chori* was performed at the Gabrieli Festival in Venice in 1957, after a convocation delivered by Cardinal Giuseppe Roncali, later Pope John XXIII. *Dulcis Jesu* has probably not been heard since the days of Gabrieli.

GOUNOD, Charles (1818-1893), *Petite Sinfonie*
Adagio et Allegretto; Andante cantabile; Scherzo: Allegro moderato; Finale: Allegretto

The production of *Le Tribute de Zamora* (Paris, 1881) marked the end of Gounod's career as an opera composer, the staging of the revised version of his first opera *Sapho* (1851-1884) notwithstanding. Although *Faust* was moving rapidly to its five-hundredth performance, and *Roméo et Juliette* was sustaining Gounod's international prestige, he refused to rest on his laurels, henceforth devoting his creative energies mainly to large-scale sacred and liturgical works. The *Petite Sinfonie* constitutes a remarkable exception. Gounod had written two symphonies (1855 and 1856) during the first stage of his operatic career. (A piano arrangement for four hands of the first symphony was made by Georges Bizet.) Gounod's return to the symphonic genre was stimulated by the concerts of the Société de Musique de Chambre pour Instruments à Vent, founded in 1879 and directed by the flutist Paul Taffanel, who became a successful conductor at the Conservatoire and the Opéra. Gounod wanted to contribute a piece to the repertory of this ensemble, and Taffanel's group was honored to have a piece by the composer of *Faust*.

The *Petite Sinfonie,* was first performed on April 30, 1885, in the Salle Pleyel. To place it in historical perspective, César Franck's Symphonic Variations for Piano were first played on the following day, Massenet's *Manon* had been premiered one year before, Debussy was living in the Villa Medici in Rome as winner of the coveted Prix de Rome for 1884, and d'Indy, who had won the Prize of the City of Paris in 1885, was recognized as one of the important modern French composers.

Because he could not exclude Taffanel from the performance, Gounod added a flute to the classical ensemble of pairs of oboes, clarinets, bassoons, and horns; he succeeded splendidly in making a virtue out of necessity. The *Petite Sinfonie* is in form similar to the classical pattern, and in this respect Gounod paid homage to Mozart, whom he deeply revered.

HANDEL, George Frideric (1685-1759)
Concerto Grosso in E minor, Opus 6, No. 3
Larghetto; Andante; Allegro; Polonaise; Allegro ma non troppo

The principle of the concerto grosso evolved in the earliest stages of orchestral music in Italy, when the technique of the *cori spezzati* (split choruses) was transferred to the field of instrumental music. The use of the double chorus, whose divisions sing in alternation, reflects an ancient antiphonal practice. The concerto grosso, which emerged fully developed in Italy about 1680, can be defined as an instrumental piece in which a small unit, called concertino, alternates with a larger body (concerto grosso, ripieno, tutti). It must be emphasized that the term "concerto grosso" does not denote a certain formal pattern but indicates a distinct manner of orchestration.

Arcangelo Corelli (1653-1713) standardized the concerto grosso by organizing the concertino as a trio sonata ensemble of two violins, one violoncello (or bass viol), and harpsichord. When Handel went to Italy at the end of 1706, the concerto grosso was a firmly established type of orchestral music, organized by analogy to the two sonata types as church concerto (*concerto da chiesa*) or as chamber concerto (*concerto da camera*). The former generally displays a "slow-fast-slow-fast" order in the sequence of its movements, with the inclusion of fugal passages, whereas the chamber concerto represents basically an assortment of stylized dance pieces—the Italian counterpart of the French, English, and German suites. Numerous concerti grossi are hybrids that display elements of the *sonata da chiesa* and also include dance forms that point to the *sonata da camera*, such as Handel's Concerto grosso in G minor heard tonight.

Handel had studied models of the concerto grosso in Italy. He imbued the Italian scheme with the spirit of his personality and applied as much of his eminent craftsmanship to the small dance forms as he did to his powerful choral works. We do not know the circumstances that prompted the composition of the set that appeared as Opus 6 in 1739—the same year in which Handel finished *Israel in Egypt* and wrote both the *Ode for St. Cecilia's Day* and the opera *Jupiter in Argos*. He turned out the entire set of twelve "Grand Concertos" between September 29 and October 20; it was an amazing feat of concentration and creative power, although he did use older material, "borrowing" from piano works by Gottlieb Muffat (1690-1770). It should be mentioned here that the opus number 6, assigned to the set by Handel's publisher John Walsh is utterly misleading from a biographical and chronological point of view, since the compositions Handel had created before 1739 comprise about eighty folio volumes of the complete edition of his works.

On October 29, 1739, the London *Daily Post* ran the following advertisement: "This day are published proposals for printing by subscription with his Majesty's royal license and protection twelve Grand Concertos in seven parts for four violins, tenor [viola] and a violoncello, with a thoroughbass for harpsichord. Composed by Mr. Handel. Price to subscribers, two guineas. Ready to be delivered by April next. Subscriptions are to be taken by the author at his house in Brook Street, Hanover Square and by Mr. Walsh." (Handel had designated John Walsh as his official publisher in 1730 in order to protect himself against Walsh's notorious pirating practices.) Evidently, there was a market for the concerto grosso in the British capital around 1739/40. The situation changed in 1759, when Handel passed from the scene; the heyday of the concerto grosso was over, and the dominance of the symphony had begun.

The use of dance types places our piece in the category of the chamber concerto. The solemn Larghetto introduction, indicating the sarabande rhythm, is based on a six-measure group that reappears three times in variations with a recurring, though slightly modified, bass line. Thus the movement conforms, to a certain extent, to the passacaglia. The melodic line of the opening measures is identical with that of the first chorus of Bach's cantata *Jesu der du meine Seele*, which by an amazing coincidence, also displays variation and *basso ostinato* technique. Baroque contrapuntal art is manifest in the second movement (Andante) while the following Allegro is characterized by forceful unison passages and a continuous motivic interplay. The ensuing dignified polonaise is a far cry from the brilliant polonaises of the romantic composers. The extended drone bass suggests the music of the pifferari, which Handel as well as Corelli had heard in Rome. The Polonaise is rhythmically contrasted with the short bisectional concluding dance movement that displays the echo effects Corelli used so often.

Concerto grosso in G minor, Opus 6, No. 6

Largo e affetuoso; A tempo giusto; Musette: Larghetto; Allegro; Allegro

The G minor concerto strikes a balance between the *concerto da chiesa* and the suite. The opening Larghetto e affetuoso, solemn and sorrowful, emanates the spirit of the church sonata. Romain Rolland interprets this movement as the expression of deep melancholy in the spirit of Dürer and Beethoven. Here it was Handel, the organist, who applied a steadily alternating registration to the string body: piano against forte, high against low, soli against tutti, long halts (chords) against pauses. The mystical conclusion of the Larghetto sharply contrasts with the ensuing fugal Allegro, in which there is no alternation of the concertino and ripieno. The following Musette has always been one of Handel's most famous instrumental pieces. As the title suggests it imitates the bagpipe, with its long sustained drone. Handel was very fond of this musette and is said to have introduced it frequently between the parts of his oratorios, even before it was published. It is a three-section piece, whose middle portion is enlivened by robust figurations. The following energetic Allegro places the first concertino violin in the limelight. To please the listener, the composer concluded the concerto with a short dancelike piece for only three voices (violin, viola, bass), which presents music easier to absorb than the polyphonic texture and somber mood of the first half of the work.

Concerto Grosso in B flat major, Opus 6, No. 7

Largo-Allegro; Largo e piano; Andante; Hornpipe

When Handel's Grand Concertos appeared in 1739 in London new artistic tendencies were developing in Italy, that would push the concerto grosso into the background. Prior to 1740, Giovanni Battista Sammartini (1701-1775) produced his first symphony, and a new age dawned.

In London there was evidently still an interest in, and a market for, the concerto grosso, a circumstance that did much to add to the flourishing trade of Handel's publisher, John Walsh, and his son John.

Our concerto in B flat major, whose opening movement reveals the slow-fast (fugal)-slow design of the French overture, is of particular interest for structural and instrumental reasons. It conforms to the four-movement scheme of the *concerto da chiesa* but closes with an extended dance piece. Note the unusual shape of the fugal subject whose first note is repeated thirteen times (two half, four fourth, and eight eighth-notes):

The spirit of baroque polyphony also dominates the ensuing serious Largo. We come to a more serene passage with the steadily flowing Andante that is Italian in character. Handel turns to the north for inspiration with the concluding Hornpipe. Originally the name of an instrument, probably made from an animal horn, the term has meant since the sixteenth century a type of English folk dance. Typical of the hornpipe of Handel's time is the irregular accent on the second beat:

The listener will certainly notice that there is not one passage in the entire piece that shows the alternation of a soloistically treated small group (concertino) with the larger body (ripieno). Thus this work is actually no concerto grosso at all. It approaches the orchestral concerto as created by Antonio Vivaldi, a type that represents the early phase of the pre-classical symphony.

Concerto grosso in D minor, Opus 6, No. 10
Overture: Lento-Allegro; Air: Lento; Allegro; Allegro; Allegro moderato

The concerto in D minor, whose opening movement reveals the "slow-fast (fugal)-slow" design of the French overture, discloses features of the church concerto in some movements and elements of the chamber concerto (suite) in others. Take for instance the pathetic Air in 3/2 time. The term "Air" if applied to a suite movement meant either a real dance or a piece with the structure of a dance movement but without the rhythmical traits of a certain dance type. Although the opening measure of the Air indicates the sarabande rhythm, the whole piece is rather grave and mystical in the spirit of the church concerto. The following Allegro displays the binary organization of dance pieces. The alternation between concertino and concerto grosso, which thus far has been applied to the Air only, is evident in the ensuing movement, designed after the Vivaldian ritornello principle based on the frequent recurrence of the main idea in different keys. The alternation technique is abandoned once more in the short final Allegro. The Allegro, simple in texture and only ten measures long, is in the nature of a gavotte (4/4) and is repeated in a varied form. The concerto, which began with the seriousness and pomp of the church concerto in the minor mode, closes with the lightness and grace of a dance piece in the major key.

Concerto grosso in B minor, Opus 6, No. 12
Largo; Allegro; Larghetto; Largo—Allegro

The B minor piece, the last item of Handel's set, conforms generally to the pattern of the church concerto. It opens with a Largo marked by rhythmical impetus. A lively Allegro follows. The third movement is a songful Larghetto, which could be termed Theme and Variations. Each of the two sections of the theme is varied twice. A short Largo effects the transition to the concluding fugal Allegro whose main idea is later contrasted with triplets that are characteristic of the gigue. Yet the triplet motion does not gather sufficient strength to push the basic rhythm into the background. The latter prevails in the end.

Concerto for Harp and Orchestra in B flat major
Andante—Allegro; Larghetto; Allegro moderato

The harp is one of the oldest instruments. Its history, which spans over five thousand years, dates from the time of the Sumerian civilization. In more modern times the harp was part of the instrumental body that contributed music to plays in the late Renaissance. It was also employed in the earliest operas, for example in Monteverdi's *Orfeo* (1607), but it disappeared from the opera houses in the seventeenth and eighteenth centuries, although it was still used sporadically in orchestras prior to the nineteenth century. Bach never employed it, but Handel introduced the harp in his masque *Haman and Mordecai* (1720), which he transformed in 1732 into the oratorio *Esther*. But is is interesting to note that Handel disposed of the harp solo in *Esther* and demoted the instrument to the doubling of the bass line. In all probability it was particular circumstances that had permitted Handel to assign a prominent role to the harp in *Haman and Mordecai*. Presumably there was a fine harpist available and the use of the instrument was logical in view of the lines "Zion now her head shall raise, tune your harp to song and praise."

The original manuscript of our piece, an item of the King's Music Library and part of the Handel Collection of the British Museum, bears the heading *Concerto per la Harpa*. When Handel set out to write a harp concerto, he had not forgotten the solo passage in *Haman and Mordecai*. The concerto calls for muted strings and plucked basses in the first movement. We observe a similar picture in the aria of the masque where the harp is accompanied by muted violins. Handel wanted to prevent the thin tone of the instrument of 1720 from being covered by the violins.

Although the harp concerto was first published in 1738 as a concerto for either organ or harpsichord (Opus 4, No. 6), London music lovers heard it in the original version as a harp concerto in 1736 when Handel inserted it as an interlude in a performance of the oratorio *Alexander's Feast*. At that time he could secure the participation of the excellent harpist John Powell. Recorded in Sir John Hawkins' monumental *General History of the Science and Practice of Music* is an advertisement from the London *Daily Post* of February 27, 1741 that gives notice of "A concerto of Mr. Handel's on the harp played in Hickford's Great Room by Mr. Parry." It was undoubtedly the work considered here. The inclusion of this composition in Handel's complete works in the organ rendition almost obliterated the original version for harp. Marcel Grandjany has revised the work for modern harp and included a cadenza in the middle movement with motivic references to the first Allegro.

Concerto for Oboe and Orchestra in G minor
Grave; Allegro; Sarabande; Allegro

The history of this piece is shrouded in darkness, and the autograph, which could provide a clue to the time and place of its origin, has not survived. Even Friedrich Chrysander, who spent a lifetime in Handel research and single-handedly, for the most part, collected and edited the material for the hundred folio volumes of the monumental Handel edition (1856-1894), has very little to contribute. His scanty information is based on an edition of the work brought out by the Leipzig publishing firm of J. Schuberth, around the middle of the nineteenth century. According to this publication, which was used for Chysander's edition in 1865, the concerto was written in 1703, at which time the eighteen-year-old Handel was a member of the Hamburg opera orchestra. On what external evidence Schuberth based this date we do not know.

The piece differs in two important respects from the three-movement concerto type established by the Italian pioneers Albinoni, Torelli, and Vivaldi, and also adopted by Bach. In the first place, it upholds the slow-fast-slow-fast pattern of the church sonata. Secondly, the piece is, strictly speaking, not a concerto for oboe with orchestral accompaniment and clearly defined extended solo and tutti passages, since the oboe is not given a dominating role and is rather engaged in a dialogue with the violins. It is submerged fully in the ensemble in the third movement (Sarabande). The inclusion of a sarabande links the concerto to the suite.

The most striking feature of the work is the thematic connection between the opening movement and the concluding Allegro, the main idea of which is a rhythmically transformed version of the chief theme of the pathetic Grave:

Organ concerto No. 13 in F major, "The Cuckoo and the Nightingale"
Larghetto—Allegro; Adagio; Larghetto; Allegro

Handel's concertos for organ and orchestra represent a musical category *sui generis,* which, unknown in Germany, Italy, and France, arose out of the composer's managerial practice. At the first performance in 1733 at Oxford of his oratorio *Athalia,* Handel appeared as an organ virtuoso and enraptured the audience of 3700 with his unexcelled art of improvization. He then believed that his appearance as an organist would attract more people to his oratorios, particularly to the performances of new works. Since he had an orchestra at his disposal on those occasions, he conceived the idea of combining the organ and orchestra, and thus the organ concerto came into being.

Handel wrote twenty works of this kind. Twelve were published in his lifetime in two sets with six items each: one bearing the opus number "4" in 1738; the other without opus number in 1740. A third assortment of six concertos prepared by Handel appeared posthumously in 1760. Two more organ concertos reached the public in the deluxe edition that the British composer Samuel Arnold (1740-1802) issued from 1786 on. Handel scored a remarkable success with his organ concertos, which in his day were very popular with both organists and harpsichordists, professional and amateur.

The concerto in F major, which was played by Handel at the premiere of *Israel in Egypt*, is the first item of the 1740 set. In the monumental complete edition of Handel's works it appears in the third set after those of 1738, Opus 4, and 1760, Opus 7. This accounts for the number "13." Yet the set, which includes the items 13 through 18, does not comprise pieces originally conceived as organ concertos, but transcriptions from previous compositions: Handel's famous Concerti grossi, Opus 6, of 1740 and his Trio Sonatas for two violins, or flutes, and figured bass, Opus 5, of 1739.

The opening Larghetto and the final Allegro of the Organ Concerto in F major were derived from the sixth sonata of Opus 5, and the Concerto grosso No. 9 in F major was tapped for the middle movements of the organ piece. It is interesting to observe that the outer movements of the organ concerto are more extended than their sources in the trio sonata, while the middle movements are less elaborate and shorter then the related sections of the concerto grosso.

The Organ Concerto in F major conforms structurally to the "slow-fast-slow-fast" design on the Italian church concerto without displaying its contrapuntal texture. The fast movements reflect the application of the Vivaldian ritornello principle: the frequent recurrence of the main idea in different keys. The motifs in the second movement that allude to the call of the cuckoo and the song of the nightingale led to the nickname "The Cuckoo and the Nightingale."

Overture to Berenice

The opera *Berenice* was Handel's fortieth creation for the stage and the last in a series of three that originated between August 1736, and January 1737. Handel wrote *Berenice* in the incredibly short time of forty-one days. This feverish activity was necessary in order to provide fresh material for the Covent Garden theater and thus to compete successfully with the Haymarket theater where his rival Nicola Porpora and the famous *castrato* Farinelli attracted an enthusiastic public. There was no victor in this hard-fought battle: in 1737 both opera houses had to close and Handel, overworked and nearly ruined financially, suffered a paralytic stroke.

The story of *Berenice*, often used as an opera plot before, takes place in Egypto-Roman surroundings. Its ingredients are love and jealousy, misunderstanding and political intrigue. The cast contains two female and five male characters; three of the latter were portrayed by a woman and two *castrati*.

Berenice was produced at Covent Garden on May 17, 1737, with the royal family in attendance. There were only three repeat performances at Covent Garden; however a staging in Brunswick in 1743, with changes and "arrangements," is recorded.

The overture is a kind of a four-movement suite. The dotted rhythm of the slow introduction, Grave, and the contrapuntal style of the ensuing Allegro relates the first two movements to Lully's "French Overture." The Andante–Larghetto in 3/4 time, and the closing gigue in 12/8 point to the suite, or sonata da camera.

In spite of the catastrophic events of 1737, Handel was victorious in the end. The lives of Giovanni Bononcini and Nicola Porpora, his great rivals on the operatic scene, ended in misfortune. The former spent his last years in Vienna living on a small charity pension and the latter died in direst poverty. The expense of Porpora's burial had to be met by means of a subscription among his friends, while Handel was enshrined in Westminster Abbey.

L'Allegro ed il Penseroso

Handel's First Oratorios

Handel's first journey to Italy (1707-1709) was of momentous importance to his artistic development. In Italy he became familiar with the great achievements of the baroque—the opera, the oratorio, the lyrical chamber cantata for one or two voices, and the various instrumental forms for ensembles, the concerto grosso in particular. Driven by ambition and creative urge, he wrote Catholic church music, operas, cantatas, and, in 1708, two oratorios. The first, *La Resurrezione*, performed in Rome with Corelli as concertmaster, was a brilliant success. The other, *Il trionfo del tempo e del disinganno (The Triumph of Time and Disappointment)*, was a flop. Handel revived it in 1737 in London, and in 1757 revised it with an English text and the title *The Triumph of Time and Truth*. These two Italian oratorios were emulations of current models by a genius who wanted to test his gifts in a new field. Like his early operas, they consisted of recitatives, arias, and a few duets and trios but did not include choral numbers.

Twelve years were to elapse before Handel turned once more to the oratorio. The circumstances were immensely different. He had gone to London in 1712. In 1714 he decided to live in England and became a British subject in 1726. His first oratorio written in England was *Esther*, also known as *Haman and Mordecai*. Handel was then (1720) in the employ of the Duke of Chandos, and *Esther* was probably staged in the ducal palace in Cannons near London. Since the autograph did not survive, we do not know the exact title, but the term "oratorio" was unknown in England around 1721. According to Dr. Charles Burney in his *General History of Music* (1776-1789): "Oratorios, though common in Italy during the last century, were never attempted in England, either in public or private, till the year 1720, when Handel set the sacred drama of Esther...."

This performance remained an isolated event. But when the singer and composer Bernard Gates (1685-1772) arranged a revival of *Esther* in honor of Handel's forty-seventh birthday on February 23, 1732, with two repeats on March 1 and 3, there were important repercussions. The performance took place at the Crown and Anchor Tavern in the Strand and was a private affair sponsored by music clubs that met there regularly. Though the libretto designated *Esther* as *"Oratorio"* or *"Sacred Drama,"* nobody's religious feelings were hurt by the presentation in a tavern. Handel was delighted but troubles arose. Six weeks later another reading of *Esther* was announced as *"Never perform'd in Publick before."* Somebody had pirated a copy of the score used by Gates and tried to profit from it. Handel was aroused and he acted with determination. He arranged for a staged, full-dress performance of *Esther* at the King's Theater in the Haymarket on May 2 with the opera company and the Chapel Royal chorus. Then he received an unexpected blow. Dr. Edmund Gibson, the Bishop of London, prohibited the chapel boys and chorus from participating in any theatrical production. Handel met the situation shrewdly. In the issue of the *Daily Journal* of April 19, which advertised the pirated performance of *Esther*, he announced that at the King's Theater in the Haymarket *Esther* would be "performed by a great Number of the best Voices and Instruments. N.B. There will be no Action on the Stage, but the House will be fitted up in a decent Manner for the Audience."

The second of May, 1732, which inaugurated a series of 22 performances of *Esther,* was the birthday of the English oratorio. The use of English was to affect Handel's future oratorios greatly. It made the Handelian oratorio a particularly English musical medium and separated it from the contemporary Italian opera. With the presentation of *Esther* in 1732, Handel established a pattern that he would strictly adhere to in the future: his oratorios were usually presented in the theater but without action and costume. Handel, however, employed in his oratorios opera singers who probably could not desist from making gestures and occasionally from acting; Handel himself organized the oratorios in *acts* and entered stage directions into his autographs.

The Double Track: Opera and Oratorio

In spite of the artistic and financial success of *Esther*, Handel did not give up his career as a stage composer. In the decade between May 2, 1732, and the premiere of *Messiah* in Dublin on April 13, 1742, Handel produced 17 operas and only seven oratorios. In 1741 he terminated his creative work for the stage, and from 1743 until 1751 he composed 15 oratorios. If blindness had not overtaken him completely in 1753, he would have undoubtedly continued to produce oratorios.

Yet Handel's heart was in the opera, and it was his ambition to win the English over to the Italian opera, a medium of which he was the most powerful representative. But the fortunes of his artistic career were affected by social and political conditions. The wealthy Tory aristocracy favored the opera but was chiefly interested in the vocal virtuosity of the prima donna and the castrato. The bourgeoisie and the lower middle class, which supported the Whigs, organized their own musical life and convened in taverns. Handel had made enemies among the aristocrats by taking away their subscription privileges. They imposed upon Handel the competition with the famous Italian opera composer Giovanni Bononcini (1670-1747), who was called to London. They even prevailed on Nicola Porpora (1686-1768), a competitor in the operatic field, to compose an oratorio. This did not draw sufficiently to beat Handel, and Handel's supremacy remained unchallenged for a century until Mendelssohn presented *Elijah*, which captured the hearts of the British and acquired a firm place beside the works of Handel.

The machinations of the powerful cliques took effect. Ruined financially and losing strength, Handel, in 1737, suffered a stroke that paralyzed his right hand. He went to Aix-la-Chapelle, regained his health, and returned to London determined to face his enemies. A pamphlet poked fun at his misfortunes and joyfully anticipated the fall of a "great bear." Friends deserted him, but he found "consolation in being undisturbed in his thoughts by the accosting of his acquaintances when he walked down Piccadilly". The opera *Jupiter in Argos* billed for May 1, 1739, was withdrawn. Handel had practically run out of funds, and he realized that the opposition to him had grown so strong after the failure of *Israel in Egypt* that he could not risk another disaster that spring.

Meanwhile, storm clouds gathered on the horizon, and England went to war with Spain. This was not a favorable climate for opera, and Handel charted his course accordingly. He set John Dryden's *Ode for St. Cecilia's Day* to music, and to cut his expenses he moved the performance from the Haymarket to a smaller theater in Lincoln's Inn Fields. The attendance was very good, and Handel successfully revived *Alexander's Feast* and *Acis and Galatea*. But in mid-December a cold wave swept over London. The Thames became a frozen field. The poor died in their flimsy buildings or perished in the streets while the wealthier revellers went to the solidly covered Thames, lit fires, and enjoyed barbecues. The weeks passed but not the cold. In January 1740 the situation worsened. Places of entertainment closed down because of lack of heating material. Handel fought desperately against the elements. He warmed his theater and covered the doors with thick curtains and advertised his precautionary measures in the newspapers. But the audiences diminished, and winter seemed to win out. The weather was aided by a group in social circles that wanted to drive Handel again into bankruptcy. They sent a gang of ruffians to the theater to riot there. Chairs were overturned and stones thrown. Music lovers who braved the weather were intimidated by the disorder outside the theater.

In those turbulent days Handel composed *L'Allegro ed il Penseroso*. He produced it on February 27, 1740, in Lincoln's Inn Field Theater and gave it four more times but could not recover his expenses. The attacks on the theater and the molestations of the audience continued. Finally, Handel was forced to close the place down but did it with a noble gesture. He donated the proceeds of a performance of *Acis and Galatea* and the *Ode for St. Cecilia's Day* to the Decayed Musicians Fund. Then he was a poor man himself.

"L'Allegro ed il Penseroso"—An Interlude

When Handel took up the composition of *Israel in Egypt*, he turned away from the dramatic oratorio represented by *Esther*, *Deborah*, *Athalia*, and *Saul*. He later continued the series with *Samson*. Dean Winton considers the works created between *Saul* (1738) and *Samson* (1743)—*Israel in Egypt, Ode for St. Cecilia's Day, L'Allegro ed il Penseroso,* and *Messiah*—an "interlude." *Israel in Egypt* is a huge canvas of biblical history and the great epic of the struggle and victory of suppressed nations symbolized by the Jewish people. Yet the work can also be interpreted as an artistic expression of an autobiographical nature. Handel was involved in a bitter struggle for artistic and economic survival and he was determined not to compromise. After the failure of *Israel,* Handel saw himself completely defeated: he had failed on the lyric stage and was turned down as an oratorio composer. Harassed by his enemies and the elemental forces he could not control, he turned to two odes by John Milton and delved into their vernal feelings while London was suffering from a deadly cold.

Milton probably wrote *L'Allegro* and *Il Penseroso* in 1632, when he stayed at his father's house in Norton, near Windsor, amid the greenery of the English countryside. The two poems comprise 338 lines, and about 100 were omitted by Handel. We do not know whether the choice of Milton's lines was Handel's or if somebody else had directed his attention to the poems. Handel's literary collaborator was Charles Jennens (born 1700). Jennens moved among writers, musicians, and painters, and since he was popular in the segment of society that had cultural interests, he may have met Handel in some salon. He was big and heavy, a bachelor like Handel, and very rich. The collaboration with Handel on *Saul, L'Allegro, Messiah,* and *Belshazzar* secured immortality for the immensely conceited Jennens. He drove to his publishers in a magnificent carriage with a lackey sitting behind him who had to sweep the pavement before Jennens stepped down, while Handel always walked until rheumatism prevented him from doing so.

The task of preparing a text from poems and of coordinating the selected lines and integrating them into one unit demanded considerable skill and understanding for the requirements of the composer. The omissions were mostly mythological references, and the changes and modifications were dictated by musical reasons. The juxtaposition of two polar temperaments, of gaiety and pensiveness, anticipated to a certain extent Schumann's imaginary characters Florestan and Eusebius, who represented the active and reflective sides of his personality. Jennens's disposition of the text favors the composer immensely through the steady alternation of contrasting moods.

The music reveals a particular trait of Handel's personality, the understanding of nature and love of the English landscape, which Milton evoked in his poems. Whereas the poet described the variety by employing alternating voices, Handel offers a united view of the meadows, rivers, hills, towns, sun, moon, and stars. This reveals, in the words of Winton Dean, "sympathy with English life and the English scene which is perhaps the most profound tribute Handel ever paid to the land of his adoption."

A Few Analytical Observations

The score of *L'Allegro ed il Penseroso* includes 44 numbers: 13 recitatives, 23 arias, and eight choral items. Jennens added a third section to Milton's verses under the heading *Il Moderato,* which commended the merits of moderation. Handel set Jennens's verses to music in nine numbers: three recitatives and arias, one duet, and two choral pieces. He was not satisfied with the amendment, however, and even replaced it in later performances by the *Ode for St. Cecilia's Day*. *L'Allegro* was not a long piece and was not regarded by the audiences as an adequate value for their money. Even presentations of long oratorios were padded with concerti grossi and organ concertos.

Speaking of *L'Allegro ed il Penseroso*, the French Handel scholar Victor Schoelcher said: "It required all the boldness of genius to attempt a subject so eminently undramatic. Never had music to depend upon herself so entirely." The libretto challenged Handel to resort to all melodic, harmonic, and rhythmic means his immense craftsmanship could provide. The variety of musical components that form the score of this outwardly undramatic oratorio is enormous. There are pieces of simple texture and some of true baroque polyphony. Some arias display a simple melodic vocal line while others are studded with difficult coloraturas. There are concerted arias with solo parts for flute, violoncello, horn and trumpet. There are marches and dance tunes (minuet and siciliano). The use of 3/4, 4/4, 3/8, 6/8, and 12/8 meters ensures rhythmical variety, and the nine major and six minor tonalities achieve harmonic diversity. This kaleidoscope is enriched by the mood contrast, and taking into account the imagery of landscape painting and the illustration of natural phenomena, Handel's work appears as a microcosm of music.

This annotator cannot detail the individual numbers here but is limited to the brief consideration of a few salient points. Handel did not identify the two polar temperaments with a definite voice category: some of the *L'Allegro* arias are sung by the soprano, tenor, and bass (baritone), and the soprano also sings *Il Penseroso*. Handel revised the voice parts several times, and some of the soprano arias were transposed three times to fit the range of the contralto, tenor, and bass. If the circumstances required a singer whose range failed to conform to the original tessitura of the part, Handel did not hesitate to make the necessary adjustments.

Nos. 1–4   (The work lacks an overture.) Two recitatives and two arias constitute the opening statements of the two temperaments.

No. 5   *L'Allegro* sings the once famous laughter aria, which is taken up by the chorus (No. 6) in four-voice polyphony.

No. 7   *L'Allegro* tenders an invitation to dance, which the chorus accepts (No. 8).

Nos. 9–12   A complex dominated by *Il Penseroso* consists of a recitative (No. 9), aria (No. 10), recitative and aria (No. 11), and chorus (No. 12). It is unified musically by a motif, which is treated as basso ostinato but appears modified in later statements.

Nos. 13–15   Recitatives and arias of *L'Allegro* with imitations of the warbling lark.

Nos. 16–17   Recitative and aria of *Il Penseroso*. This is a specimen of a nightingale aria that was a favorite type of the Italian opera and cantata in the settecento. Whereas Handel achieved the imitation of the lark by using violins, he illustrates the warbling of the nightingale by trills and runs of the flute. Note that in the middle section in D minor the rising of the moon is depicted by the slow rising of the vocal line from *e'* (above middle *c*) to *a"* above the staff.

Nos. 18–19   *L'Allegro* appears now as a hunter (baritone) and takes us on a chase in which the horn plays an important part. The vocal line and the accompaniment are integrated in the signals of the hunting horn.

No. 21   *Il Penseroso's* aria illustrates the chirping of the cricket and horn call of the night watchman.

Nos. 22–23   *L'Allegro* guides us into farm and dairy land accompanied by the pastoral siciliano rhythm.

No. 24   *L'Allegro's* ensuing soprano aria in the manner of a slowly danced minuet shows a peculiar application of the da capo design: the middle section appears as a strange baritone recitative (No. 25) in which a mountain landscape is portrayed; then we are led back to the place where nibbling flocks graze.

No. 26   The following aria (*L'Allegro*) indulges in an enthusiastic description of country dancing. The bells ring and the fiddles (rebeck) sound.

No. 27   The chorus joins in the merrymaking and enters rather surprisingly with a sudden change from forte to piano. The feast is over, the dancers go to bed, and the "whispering wind" sings a lullaby. The wind abates and all sleep soundly.

Nos. 28–29   Recitative and aria of *Il Penseroso* in praise of the power of music.

Nos. 30–31   This is contrasted with *L'Allegro's* description of the life in the "populous cities" (recitative and chorus). The chorus conforms to the da capo pattern with a D minor middle section in 3/8.

No. 32   The aria "There let hymen appear" (*L'Allegro*) expresses "pomp, and feast, and revelry" at a wedding, and Handel injects his humor with gusto, especially in a protracted coloratura passage set to the words "in saffron robe."

No. 35   *L'Allegro* reveals in a "pomposo" aria his literary taste (Ben Jonson and Shakespeare). The incisive march music is markedly contrasted with No. 36.

No. 36   *L'Allegro's* G minor aria (Andante, 3/8; the lyricism of this aria is opposed by the quick motion of the ensuing coloratura aria (No. 37).

No. 38   The trumpet players are placed in the limelight and compete in this aria with the tenor who is joined by chorus (No. 39). *L'Allegro* was favored with four arias in a row but *Il Penseroso* has the last say.

Nos. 40–43   *Il Penseroso* speaks out in a place of worship (recitative, chorus, and organ) and leads us through cloisters into a church. Meditating (aria No. 42), he finds pleasure in the peaceful atmosphere of a hermitage and quiet of a cell. He prays to melancholy to bestow these pleasures upon him and this prayer is said by the chorus (No. 43) in a solemn double fugue, a genuine apotheosis of melancholy, which *L'Allegro* had condemned at the very beginning of the oratorio. The conclusion reflects Handel's frame of mind in the weeks when he composed the work. He longed for peace and with the passage of time he probably came to consider Jennens's *Il Moderato* ending as spiritually inappropriate.

Two Arias

"Furibondo spira il vento" *(Partenope)*
"Stille amare, già vi sento" *(Tolemeo)*

The second decade of the eighteenth century saw in England a steadily rising enterprising spirit and an economic growth, which greatly affected Handel's fortunes. It was a period of mercantile foundations and speculation, which also drew opera into its whirlpool of activity. Rich music lovers and greedy investors united to form an organization for the production of operas. A founding capital of fifty thousand pounds sterling was subscribed. The King headed the subscribers' list and allowed the new enterprise to grace its name with the word "royal." Thus in 1719 the Royal Academy of Music as a privately managed opera theater came into being, and Handel was appointed one of its musical directors. The home of the Academy was the King's Theater on the Haymarket. It opened its doors in 1720, and in the first nine seasons Handel contributed twelve operas with 245 performances out of a total of 487.

The last production of the ninth season was *Tolemeo,* which was completed on April 19 and staged on April 30, 1728. Obviously, the singers received and learned their music piecemeal, and the orchestra and stage rehearsals had to be compressed into a week. The plot revolves around the Ptolemys, who ruled Egypt from the death of Alexander the Great to Cleopatra. The improbable story introduces four pairs of lovers and their intrigues. The aria "Stille amare, già vi sento" presented tonight is a monologue by Tolemeo, who, condemned to death by drinking poison, is about to empty the cup. It is an elegy in B flat minor, a tonality little-used in Handel's day, and it depicts the feelings of a man who awaits his death. A revival of *Tolemeo* was attempted at the Handel Festival in Göttingen in 1933.

The Royal Academy of Music suffered severe financial losses following the enormously successful presentation of *The Beggar's Opera* in January 1728. The audiences had lost interest in the deeds and sentiments of mythological figures with their stilted language; they were delighted to watch the doings of contemporary low characters and of the thieves and highwaymen that John Gay brought onto the stage, for whom Dr. John Christopher Pepusch provided catchy tunes. *The Beggar's Opera* drew capacity audiences, and the Royal Academy was empty.

The situation necessitated the reorganization of the Academy, and Handel was given increased power in the management. The Academy began a new season in December 1728, and on February 24, 1730, Handel presented *Partenope,* which had a libretto that had been set to music in Italy thirty

years before by Luigi Manzo. Handel's work was also given in Brunswick in
1731 and in Hamburg in 1733; it was revived in Göttingen in 1935.

The story centers on the love life of Parthenope and events that were connected with the foundation of Parthenopolis, today called Naples. The plot
deals with the tangled affairs of various mythological characters. One of the
protagonists is the Corinthian prince Arsace, whose part was originally sung
by a contralto. The very agitated aria "Furibondo spira il vento" 'expresses
the rage of Arsace against Rosmira, a princess betrothed to him, whom he
deserts. It is a typical *da capo* aria in which the passages in sixteenth-notes
storm up and down in perpetual motion to underline Arsace's fury.

Israel in Egypt
The Evolution of the Oratorio

The oratorio, like the opera, is an achievement of the baroque. It is usually
defined as a semidramatic musical composition on a sacred theme performed
by soloists, chorus, and orchestra without action, scenery, or costume. Aside
from secular oratorios, of which Haydn's *The Seasons* offers a classical
example, this definition aims at a clear-cut separation between opera and
oratorio. Yet this view was not universally accepted. One school of thought
regarded the oratorio as an opera without stage and, conversely, advocated
theatrical performances of oratorios. Even Mendelssohn occasionally inclined
to this point of view, and in Düsseldorf he conducted several choral numbers
of *Israel in Egypt* with *tableaux vivants* designed by painters of the Düsseldorf school, a group to which he felt a strong attachment. He found the
union of Handel's music and the Düsseldorf paintings "indescribably
beautiful."

The Düsseldorf experiment, although it later was extended even to
Messiah, constituted a rather isolated case. It had forerunners in one particular instance in the practice of Handel, as we will see presently, and also
in the *sepolcro,* a form cultivated in Vienna in the early 1700s. The *sepolcro*
was a dramatic presentation of the passion of Jesus staged in churches during
Passion Week in front of a specially built Holy Sepulcher. The Viennese
sepolcri were performed on Good Friday within the liturgical ceremony in
the court chapel and were attended by the court. This ephemeral mixture
of oratorio, opera, and liturgy was actually a private affair for the imperial
family and was without lasting artistic consequences.

Outstanding German literary figures and scholars opposed the concept of
the oratorio as a kind of sacred opera. Johann Gottfried Herder, the great
thinker, poet, aesthete, and an ardent admirer of Handel, saw in the oratorio
"a pure art species which is separated from the opera." Expressing himself
poetically, he said: "It descends from heaven without that distracting
theatrical decoration which attracts the eye."

Philipp Spitta, the eminent Bach biographer, underlined the fact that
Handel's oratorios deal with the destiny of peoples and problems that concern
mankind. Georg Gottfried Gervinus, the noted literary historian who wrote
a valuable book on Handel and Shakespeare and collaborated with Friedrich
Chrysander in the preparation of the monumental Handel edition, spoke of

the "oratorian drama" (*oratorisches Drama*). This expression reflects the intention to exclude operatic notions from the aesthetic consideration of the Handelian oratorio. Thus the question "Is there any connection, formal, technical, or spiritual, between opera and oratorio?" presents itself with justification.

True, the oratorio employs features that evolved in the operatic sphere, namely the recitative and the aria. But in spite of this, the oratorio is a product *sui generis* whose evolution differs fundamentally from that of the musical drama. The latter came into being as the result of theoretical discussions and practical experiments with an avowed purpose. To the Florentine intellectuals, scholars, poets, and musicians, who at the end of the 16th century gathered at the palaces of the counts Bardi and Corsi and debated the recreation of the Greek drama in terms of music, the destination was clear and they charted the course accordingly. With the creation of the monodic recitative style the basis for the musical drama was laid. Like Pallas Athena, who in her armor was born from the head of Zeus, the opera came into being in a developed stage. Events then moved rather quickly: the evolution from Peri's *Dafne*, the very first opera (1597), to Monteverdi's *Orfeo* (1607) occurred within a decade, and the Florentine innovators must have observed matters with deep satisfaction. Yet while the opera was "invented" by following up definite ideas, the oratorio by way of contrast evolved as an unexpected by-product of religious activities initiated by Filippo Neri (1515-1595), a Florentine nobleman in the 1540s in Rome.

Neri assembled his followers, mostly young men, in the Oratorio, a small prayer chapel in the church San Girolamo della Carità. The gatherings took place in the evening and included prayers, a sermon, and religious music drawn chiefly from the popular *laudi spirituali* that were sung before the statue of the Virgin. A large literature of *laudi* had accumulated, since singing of *laudi* had been practiced by well-organized fraternities for centuries. As Neri's following grew, the need for a larger assembly hall became a matter of concern. Finally Neri, who had taken holy orders in 1551 at the urgent request of the church authorities, secured the support of the pontiff and obtained sufficient means to raze the old church, Santa Maria in Vallicella, and to build a spacious and lavishly adorned new house of worship. Commonly called Chiesa Nuova, it became the center of the farflung activities of Neri's adherents who formed the "Congregation of Oratorians," which received the papal confirmation in 1575. Branches of the congregation were organized all over Italy, and at the end of the 17th century the Oratorians (*Fratres Philipini*) convened in 36 *Case filippine* for their devotional exercises in which music had assumed a larger role with the passage of time. The frequent attendance of high church dignitaries and musically trained visitors at the Oratorian exercises had a certain effect on the musical practice of the confraternity.

Included in the repertoire of the Filippini were the so-called *dialoghi*, which in time displayed the essential elements of the future oratorio, namely the narrator, treated soloistically or chorally; the utterances and rejoinders of Biblical or allegorical persons; and the chorus, as an active or contemplative element, which at the end pronounces the moral of the piece. In short the *dialoghi* developed the narrative, dramatic, and lyrical and reflective components of the oratorio.

The introduction of the narrator, called *testo* in Italian or *historicus* in Latin, proved to be a technical device of the first order. It was to become one of the basic pillars of the oratorio. Neri did not live long enough to observe the emergence of the oratorio as an artistic medium. He died at the age of 80 in 1595, one year after the deaths of Palestrina and Lasso. His earthly pilgrimage had come to its end at the momentous stylistic change in musical history that brought about the creation of the opera.

The new monodic recitative style also penetrated the sphere of the *laudi* and *dialoghi* and when around 1640 the title of "Oratorio" was given to the *laudi* and *dialoghi* the term implied then the artistic-musical as well as the sacred proceedings or the synthesis of the spoken word (sermon, gospel reading), and music.

If we compare the early history of both the opera and oratorio we clearly perceive the different approaches to the presentation of the two media. The opera was an aristocratic art, the oratorio democratic. The first operatic productions were private affairs of the courts and nobility and in general could be attended by invitation only. The situation changed when the first public theaters were opened in Venice in 1637. Now opera became accessible to anyone who was willing to pay the admission. Yet the oratorio could be heard by everyone who attended the exercises in the house of worship. It is interesting to observe that even in the early stage of the oratorio consideration for the common people played an important part. This tendency conformed to the principles of the Filippini. Two types of oratorio developed: the *oratorio volgare* in the vernacular (Italian) and the *oratorio Latino*. The former was cultivated in Santa Maria in Vallicella by the Filippini, while the home of the latter was San Marcello and its champion the Archconfraternity of the Holy Cross.

The Latin oratorio appealed to the upper stratum of the society and the educated class familiar with Latin. The Archconfraternity of the Holy Cross counted the noblest gentlemen of Rome as its members. It stands to reason that the Latin oratorio was less popular than the *oratorio volgare*. Yet it was in San Marcello that the oratorios of Giacomo Carissimi (1605-1674) were performed. They are not works of large dimensions and do not bear comparison with the creations of Handel, Haydn, or Mendelssohn, but they anticipate distinct Handelian traits: the functional importance of the chorus, the epic significance of the narrator (*testo*), and the dramatic quality. Naturally the cultivation of the oratorio was not limited to Rome; the Oratorian confraternities were instrumental in spreading the new artistic medium over Italian soil. The numerous oratorio scores of the late 17th century differ markedly from the modest pieces sung in the early exercises of the *Case filippine*. The oratorios created in Bologna particularly reflect the boldness and the splendor of baroque architecture and the inclination toward decorative effects. It was an "art of the dazzling façade." These effects are obtained by the instruments in orchestral pieces, by the increase of solo numbers, and by a highly polyphonic choral setting. In short the Bolognese oratorio displays traits that are characteristic of Handel's style.

At the end of the 17th century the age of the singer arrived and profoundly affected the development of both opera and oratorio. Now the latter availed itself of essential operatic elements: the *recitativo secco* with harpsichord accompaniment, the *recitativo accompagnato* with orchestra, and the *da capo* aria and the coloratura. Castrati sang in oratorios as well as in operas. These were, roughly sketched, the conditions when Handel arrived in Italy at the beginning of 1707.

Handel's First Oratorios

The importance to Handel's artistic development of his first sojourn in Italy cannot be overestimated. There he became thoroughly familiar with all the great achievements of the baroque—the opera, the oratorio, the lyrical chamber cantata, and the various instrumental forms, in particular the concerto grosso. Driven by an elemental creative urge, he wrote two oratorios in 1708. The first, *La Resurrezione,* performed with the participation of Corelli, achieved a brilliant success. The other, *Il trionfo del tempo e del disinganno (The Triumph of Time and Disappointment)* was a flop. Handel revised it almost half a century later under the title *The Triumph of Time and Truth.*

These two Italian oratorios were emulations of current models by a genius who wanted to test his gifts in a new field. Twelve years were to elapse before Handel turned once more to the oratorio. The circumstances were immensely different. He had gone to London in 1712. In 1714 he decided to live in England and became a British subject in 1726. His interest centered on the opera, to which he devoted his creative forces and also his personal life by assuming managerial responsibilities. Despite the tremendous work load he had to carry he keenly observed the musical scene and became familiar with the works of Henry Purcell and also with the anthem, that particularly British musical genre, which, disclosing the features of the motet and the cantata (in recitatives and solo passages), became a part of the liturgy of the Anglican Church. The twelve anthems Handel wrote for the Duke of Chandos between 1716 and 1719 and those he wrote for the coronation of George II (1727) appear as important precursors of his oratorios and mirror Handel's personality to a considerably higher degree than the Roman products of 1708. Handel's anthems are not dogmatically directed sermons but the profound expression of the people. They are the spiritual foundation of the great oratorios and their ethic ideas and represent the last stage in the process of attaining consummate musical craftsmanship.

Handel's first essay in the field of the oratorio written in England was *Haman and Mordecai,* produced in 1720. Handel called it a "masque" because the term "oratorio" was unknown in England. Says Dr. Charles Burney in his *General History of Music*: "Oratorios, though common in Italy during the last century, were never attempted in England, either in public or private, till the year 1720, when Handel set the sacred drama of Esther for the chapel of the Duke of Chandos at Cannons." This performance remained an isolated event, but when the singer Bernard Gates arranged a revival twelve years later on Handel's birthday (February 23) the matter assumed a different aspect with important repercussions. The work received a staged production in Gates' home with the participation of choir boys and choristers, members of the Royal musical establishment assigned to the royal chapel and Westminster Abbey.

After two more private performances a public presentation on the stage of the "King's Theatre in the Haymarket" was announced, and for the first time the work was called "an oratorio or sacred drama." Then Dr. Edmund Gibson, the Bishop of London, issued a prohibition to the chapel boys and chorus to participate in any theatrical production. Thereupon Handel cancelled the dramatic presentation and announced: "There will be no acting on the stage, but the house will be fitted up in a decent manner for the audience. The music will be disposed of after the manner of the coronation service."

These events were recorded by Burney. Though the story lacks documentation its factuality can be accepted without reservation. For the famous British music historian, born in 1726, observed the last stage of Handel's artistic career from close quarters and had ample opportunity to gather firsthand reports from people who were in the audience at that historic performance of *Esther* (as it was now titled), which was graced by the attendance of the royal family. Handel then established a performance pattern to which he strictly adhered in the future: his oratorios were usually presented in the theater, but without action and costume. Another important factor stemmed from the *Esther* presentations and was to affect Handel's future oratorios, namely the use of English for the text. It made the Handelian oratorio a particularly English musical medium of strong appeal and at the same time separated it from the Italian opera.

The fortune of Handel's artistic career was to a large extent affected by social and political conditions. The wealthy Tory artisocracy favored the opera, which was in Handel's time the Italian opera. They were chiefly interested in the vocal virtuosity of the prima donna and the castrato. The bourgeoisie and the lower middle class, which supported the Whigs, organized their own musical life and convened in taverns. Samuel Jeacock, a baker, founded a madrigal society and Thomas Britton (1644-1714), who sold "small coal" converted a loft in his coal house into a music room with a small organ and a fine virginal. There he arranged musical productions attended by the most cultured Londoners, who had the pleasure of hearing Handel at the organ and, at the virginal, Dr. Pepusch, who was to achieve fame through *The Beggar's Opera*.

Handel's heart was tied to the opera and it was his great ambition to win the English to Italian opera, of which he was the noblest representative. In this endeavor he failed due to the machinations of powerful cliques. Ruined financially and losing strength, in 1737 he suffered a stroke of paralysis that maimed his right hand. He went to Aix-la-Chapelle, regained his health, and returned to London determined to face his aristocratic enemies and their malevolent coteries. Within 17 months he created three operas and two oratorios—namely *Saul* and *Israel in Egypt*.

Israel in Egypt and its Artistic Significance

Israel has a strange history. Handel commenced the work with Moses' Song, which now forms the second part of the oratorio, completing it within eleven days (October 1-11, 1738). Then he composed the Exodus, now the first part, in the incredibly short time of two weeks (October 15-28). Exodus tells of Israel's slavery in Egypt, of the plagues and tribulations, and of the liberation. Exodus completed, Handel was not satisfied because he thought that it lacked the historic background which he now deemed necessary to provide. Once more he compiled a text that treats "The Lamentations of the Israelites" for the death of Joseph. The words were then adapted to the funeral anthem for Queen Caroline (1737), which in this version served as the first part of *Israel in Egypt*. The procedure Handel adopted for the composition was paralleled about 120 years later by Richard Wagner in the writing of the poem of the Nibelungen tetralogy. He began with *"Siegfrieds Tod"* (*Götterdämmerung*), then wrote *Siegfried, Die Walküre*, and finally *Das Rheingold*. Since the Funeral Anthem had appeared in print first, Handel preferred not to include the make-shift version for *Israel in Egypt* in the score of the oratorio and substituted the first part of *Solomon* (1749) in later performances of *Israel*. The present performance follows the Handelian tradition to a certain degree with the offering of the overture to *Solomon*.

The choice of subject matter was not without political and ideological significance. Handel took up a topic that was paramount in *Esther* (1732) and *Deborah* (1733)—the fight for liberty. *Israel in Egypt* is a "song of liberty," and it was so interpreted by Handel's thoughtful and sensible contemporaries. It is the great epic of the struggle and victory of suppressed nations of which the Jewish people are the symbol. We find a similar political manifestation couched in musical terms in the Risorgimento operas of Verdi, particularly in *Nabucco,* which deals with the Babylonian captivity of the Jews. The Italian generation of the 1840s especially recognized their own national plight in the happenings enacted on the stage.

The Biblical verses Handel selected for *Israel in Egypt* are from Exodus and Psalms 78, 105, and 106. Their use was branded as a profanation of the Scriptures, particularly in view of Handel's practice of presenting oratorios in the theater. Needless to say, his enemies were strongly critical of the choice of Biblical topics.

The first performance of *Israel in Egypt* took place on April 4, 1739, "with several Concertos on the Organ and particularly a new one," as announced in the London *Daily Post*. There were repeats on April 11 and 17 "at the desire of several persons of distinction" and on May 1 the Funeral Anthem and Moses' Song were presented. The success Handel had hoped for did not materialize. Political reasons and lack of understanding account for the failure. The aristocracy and the Tories had a personal ax to grind, because Handel had abolished the subscription system that favored the rich people. He received encouragement only from the liberal papers and journals, which carried kind reviews and poems in praise of Handel. Nearly all of his personal friends were in the Whig camp. Yet, as absurd as it may seem to us, it was its intrinsic values and the extraordinary artistry that doomed *Israel* to failure. The power and intensity of Handel's musical language sometimes generated a nearly paralyzing effect on his contemporaries and even on well-disposed listeners. The music of *Israel* impressed the audience enormously, but at the same time it terrified the tender-hearted people because of its elemental force. Torn between his high artistic ideals and the hard realities, Handel decided to make the repeat performances of *Israel* a success by cutting a number of choral items and by inserting several favorite arias from earlier works. Yet this attempt, which can not be defended on artistic grounds, could not turn the tide in his favor. The London public of 1739 was not ripe for *Israel in Egypt*, neither musically nor spiritually.

It suffices to glance briefly at the table of contents to realize that Handel wanted to create something exceptional. The result of his efforts was without precedent. The score of *Israel* includes four short recitatives, four arias, three duets, and 28 choral numbers of varied length, of which 18 are set for eight voices. The most unusual feature, however, is the absence of the fashionable *da capo* aria, which dominated contemporary opera. Thus Handel ruled out the possibility of vocal display on a grand scale. Instead he shifted the emphasis to the chorus, which in those days barely existed in opera. Thus *Israel*, which deals not with the fate of personages but with the destiny of a people, became the choral oratorio par excellence. Only a few grasped the ethical aspect: in a lengthy letter to the liberal London *Daily Post*, a correspondent, whose identity has not been established, arrived at the conclusion that a country in which such a work as *Israel in Egypt* was produced was strong and that "Protestant, free, virtuous, united Christian England need little fear if the whole force of bigotry should rise against her."

Thus, Handel's bold artistic experiment to create a people's oratorio did not succeed. Sensitive observers were afraid of the consequences. A reader of the *Daily Post* expressed his deep concern about the unhappy situation and deplored "that so excellent a work of so great a genius was neglected, for though it was a polite and attentive audience, it was not large enough, I doubt, to encourage him in any future attempt." This proved to be true; Handel took the setback very seriously. He wavered in his decision about the road to follow in the future. Should he separate himself from the opera and shift the emphasis to the oratorio? Then, after writing three more operas, he created a pattern that permitted the assimilation of certain operatic features into the oratorio.

Abandoning the lofty concept of the choral oratorio, Handel gave the *da capo* aria considerable space in his later oratorios. To cite only two examples, there are 19 choral numbers and fifteen *da capo* arias in *Messiah* and the corresponding ratio in *Judas Maccabaeus* is 17 to 22. Viewed historically, the failure of *Israel* is less a personal misfortune for Handel than an artistic disaster that deprived us of similar works. Bach once had to cope with a similar situation—or crisis?—that compelled him to abandon the cantata type based on scriptural words, the *Actus tragicus*, for example, and to compose texts that in most cases would be dignified if we called them poetry.

This annotator does not propose to detail the individual numbers (39) of "the greatest choral epic which exists" (Romain Rolland) but limits his task to the brief consideration of a few salient points. To begin with there is the much discussed matter of Handel's "borrowings," or the use of pre-existing musical material from the pens of other composers. In *Israel in Egypt* occur the most barefaced of these cases, as Rolland put it. Interestingly enough, most of the foreign musical ideas used in *Israel* were transplanted from works by two totally forgotten composers, from a *Magnificat* by Dionigi Erba and a *Te Deum* by Francesco Antonio Urio. Information about Erba and Urio is very scanty. They lived around 1700 and were clerics. Erba was a prelate attached to the cathedral in Milan, and Urio, a Franciscan, officiated at one time at Santa Maria Gloriosa dei Frari in Venice. We do not know the circumstances under which Handel became acquainted with the music of these cleric-composers. He also tapped Urio's *Te Deum* for *Saul* (1739), for *L'Allegro, il Penseroso ed il Moderato* (1740) and for the *Dettingen Te Deum*. The scores of Erba's *Magnificat* and Urio's *Te Deum* are printed as important melodic sources in the monumental Handel Edition prepared by Friedrich Chrysander, who also included a *Serenata* by Alessandro Stradella (1642-1682) from which Handel drew several passages for *Israel in Egypt*. He took some ideas of the famous German organist Johann Caspar Kerrl (1627-1693) and by his teacher Friedrich Wilhelm Zachow (1663-1712).

Last but not least he re-used his own music. The most interesting case appears in the chorus "They loathed to drink" (No. 4). The theme with the conspicuous leap of the diminished seventh has several ancestors in Pachelbel, Buxtehude, and Bach (*Actus tragicus, Well-tempered Clavier*), and was the parent of other fugal subjects that appear in the works of Handel (*Messiah, Joseph*), Philipp Emanuel Bach (*Magnificat*), Haydn (String Quartet in F minor, Op. 20, No. 5), Mozart (*Requiem*), and others.

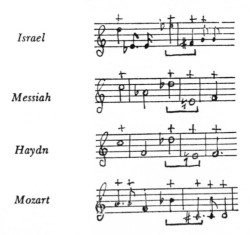

Advised by his teacher Zachow, Handel had copied much music and entered it in his "study books"—from which he later drew when the necessity arose and if the musical material held out the promise of an attractive and interesting elaboration. It seems that Handel felt that only manipulation made a melody or motif important and artistically valuable. He sometimes did not change the borrowed musical material, but he transformed its quality and emotional character completely. A theme which in its original setting was to be projected in a very fast tempo becomes in the hands of Handel a moderately moving melody of pastoral character and emanates calm, peace, and serenity. To speak of plagiarism reflects a rather superficial attitude. Rolland's poetic interpretation of Handel's practice, which was common in the renaissance and late baroque, merits quotation here: "Handel has evoked from the depth of these musical phrases their secret soul, of which the first creators had not even a presentiment." Expressed in more technical terms, Handel found that the borrowed themes or phrases contained far more potentialities than their original treatments displayed. A musical inventor is not necessarily a great builder, but Handel was both. Bach and Gluck frequently availed themselves of the parody technique, i.e. the use of pre-existing material taken from their own works or from those of other composers. The 18th century was in this matter not as narrow-minded as were the 19th-century critics of Handel who accused him of plagiarism and condemned him morally. The parody method was very convenient to Handel, who created under enormous pressure. Yet looking at Handel's practice projected against his vast output published in 100 folio volumes, and recognizing his extraordinary receptiveness, we nevertheless note primarily his unique gift of making great new creations out of musical material which was not his own and which lacked greatness.

The following paragraphs offer a brief technical survey of *Israel in Egypt*. Generally speaking, the first-part—which opens with a recitative and contains only one aria—upholds the anthem tradition of Henry Purcell.

No. 2 is a choral threnody cast as a contrapuntal fantasy.

No. 4 is based on a harpsichord (organ) fugue in A minor which, published in 1735-36, is derived from an organ fugue by Johann Pachelbel (1653-1706).

No. 5, an alto aria, is devoid of lyrical sentiments but is of descriptive character.

Nos. 6 and 7 are derived from the *Serenata* of Alessandro Stradella. Yet thanks to Handel's genius the conventional material assumes great significance. The result of the transformation procedure is a lively and interesting tone painting.

No. 8 is a harmonically remarkable choral recitative which depicts the Egyptian darkness.

No. 9. Here Handel reverted to a fugue in G minor published in his fourth collection of harpsichord pieces (1735).

No. 10. The melodic source of this idyllic and pastoral episode is a passage in Stradella's *Serenata*. This chorus discloses a ternary pattern with a serene fugue ("He brought them out with silver") as the middle section.

No. 11, a fugue, is a transcription of an organ canzona by Johann Caspar Kerrl (1686) and was probably taken from Handel's "study books."

No. 12. This effective eight-voice choral recitative refers to Erba's *Magnificat*.

No. 13, an eight-part double fugue, stems from Handel's *Dixit Dominus* (Psalm 110 in the King James Version) which originated in Rome in 1707.

No. 14, a chorus, portrays the destruction of the Egyptian army in the Red Sea. Handel reverts to the tenth Chandos Anthem *The Lord is my*

Light, particularly for the continuously moving instrumental bass part which depicts the rolling of the waves.

Nos. 15 and 16. A powerful eight-voice choral recitative leads to a four-part fugue which, drawn from Stradella's *Serenata,* concludes the first part of the oratorio.

Part II

Nos. 17 and 18. A short but weighty introduction prefaces an elaborate chorus which is based on the Italian duet for soprano and bass *"Tacete, ohimè* (1711?). There are three chief ideas: a) the rather dignified scale motif at the beginning, b) the flowing coloratura passage which passes through all eight voices, and c) the sharply accentuated motif which dominates at the end.

No. 19, a duet for two sopranos, constitutes an improved version of a duet from the *Magnificat* of Dionigi Erba. Combining the violins in unison and eliminating the viola, Handel gives the attractive piece a transparent texture.

Nos. 20 and 21. This rather massive choral passage (eight voices) taken from Erba, serves as an introduction to the ensuing double fugue in the style of the 17th century.

No. 22, a duet for two bassos, is a remarkable counterpart to the duet for two sopranos (No. 19). Its musical material is derived from three different sources: a) from a choral passage by Urio, b) a duet for two bassos by Erba (*Magnificat*), and c) from a trio for three bassos of the cantata *Triumph Victoria* by Handel's teacher Zachow. Blending the three different melodic ingredients together, Handel miraculously succeeded in achieving the musical, technical, and spiritual unity of the duet.

No. 23. This eight-voice choral arioso is an adaption of material taken from the *Te Deum* by Urio.

No. 24. The Introduction (14 measures) is drawn from Urio, the ensuing contrapuntal fantasy for eight voices presents Handel's powerful ideas in an antiphonal manner.

Nos. 25 and 26. A choral recitative in block harmonies leads to an extended eight-voice fugue transplanted from Erba's *Magnificat.* These four consecutive choral numbers reveal a remarkable architectural symmetry in the pairing of a slow recitative passage and a faster moving contrapuntal section.

No. 27. Handel gathered musical material for this four-voice choral piece from a conventional alto aria in Erba's *Magnificat,* yet the borrowed motifs are remodeled drastically and can hardly be recognized in their new contrapuntal and harmonic surroundings.

No. 28, a deftly orchestrated tenor aria markedly contrasts with the preceding choral arioso.

No. 29, a soprano aria ("Thou didst blow"), stands out because of its orchestral treatment and its construction. The violins are silenced and the accompaniment is provided by oboes, bassoons, violas, cellos, and basses. Handel applied to the aria the basso ostinato technique. The ostinato theme is four measures long, but extended by one measure of rest. There are eight statements of the ostinato theme, which appears in a shortened form in the seventh statement.

Nos. 30 and 31. A monumental choral arioso (eight voice) turning from C minor to A minor is followed by a fugue derived from the *Magnificat* by Erba.

No. 32. Erba's composition was also the source for the duet of the alto and tenor, but Handel provided a new accompaniment for the string orchestra.

No. 33. The eight-part chorus "The people shall hear" is one ot the most stupendous items of the choral literature. Alternating between homophonic phrases and consummate polyphony, it discloses rhythmic strength and sharp dramatic accents. For a passage which forecasts the "melting away of the inhabitants of Canaan" Handel utilizes a phrase by Alessandro Stradella to achieve the effect of a hocket.

No. 34. The chorus with its powerful conclusion is contrasted to the heart-felt alto aria.

Nos. 35 through 39 form a spiritual and musical unit. Handel concludes this colossal creation with an architectural master stroke: the jubilant chorus "He hath triumphed gloriously," which rang at the beginning of Moses' Song, is once more heard at the end as a song of victory and exalting peroration.

Psalm No. 112 for Soprano, Chorus, and Orchestra

"Laudate pueri Dominum"

Handel's contributions to Roman Catholic liturgical music forms but a small part of his vast production. He was a Protestant, and his professional life as an opera composer and impresario precluded serious creative activity in the field of Catholic sacred music. We do not know whether he deemed it unimportant to publish the few pertinent works, or whether his London publisher, John Walsh, failed to show interest in them. At any rate, three psalms, a *Gloria Patri,* and eight other pieces remained unpublished until 1872.

Handel was reared in the severe and learned style of the north German organists. He made such rapid progress under the tutelage of the famous organist Friedrich Wilhelm Zachau (1663-1712) that he was appointed assistant organist at a church in Halle, his home town, when he was only twelve years old. It is assumed, though sometimes contested, that the 112th psalm (113th in the King James version of the Bible) was written in Halle before Handel went to Hamburg and entered the orchestra of the German opera as violinist. It was in Hamburg that his career as opera composer began.

Having reaped success as an opera composer, and with savings of two hundred ducats in his pocket, Handel went to Italy in the fall of 1706 and reached Rome at the turn of the year. He evidently had powerful protectors, or else knew how to become the talk of the town, for a diary unearthed in the Archivio Capitolino contains the following entry for January 14, 1707: "A German has arrived in this city who is an excellent harpsichord player and composer. Today he exhibited his prowess by playing the organ in the church of St. John [in Lateran] to the admiration of everybody."

The significance of this item lies in the fact that a *Sassone* of Lutheran faith was permitted to play the organ in the great, revered basilica, the church of the bishop of Rome. Permission could have been granted or an invitation issued only through the intercession of a member of the Sacred College. It was probably Cardinal Pietro Ottoboni, who resided in the Palazzo Cancelleria and was a patron of the arts and humanities. He kept his own musical establishment, and Arcangelo Corelli (1653-1713) was in charge of the musical productions offered by the cardinal to his guests. Every foreign artist of standing was supposed to call on the cardinal and to appear at these famous gatherings. There Handel met not only Corelli but also Alessandro Scarlatti (1660-1725) and his son Domenico (1685-1757).

Handel studied contemporary Italian productions, wrote oratorios on Italian texts, and considerably revamped his setting of the 112th psalm, which was probably performed during his stay in Italy. The second version, the autograph of which is preserved in the King's Library in the British Museum, is dated July 8, 1707. It is interesting to compare the first version, which is regarded as his oldest preserved composition, with the remodeled form. Handel must have liked his youthful essay. He put it in his bag before he set out for Italy, undoubtedly intending to present his setting of the 112th psalm, which forms a part of the Vespers liturgy, as an artistic credential. Yet once in Italy he realized he would have to revise it considerably to meet Italian standards. And this he did.

The older version is a solo cantata for soprano with a modest orchestral accompaniment, whose setup stems from the trio sonata (two violins and figured bass). It is in F major and consists of arias and recitatives. The later version in D major employs a full string orchestra with two oboes and a figured bass with obbligato passages of the organ. The second soprano makes the fifth voice of the five-part mixed chorus. The part of the solo soprano, with its profusion of coloratura passages, mirrors the influence of the contemporary *opera seria*. The "Italian" version of the psalm is a creation of astonishing variety. It contains concerted arias with oboe or organ soli, recitative-like choral passages, and polyphonic and homophonic settings of the choral numbers. Viewed in hindsight it appears to be a remarkable prediction of the great things to come. Handel remembered it well: the musical material of the concluding number went into the *Jubilate* of 1713 and ultimately into the first chorus of the oratorio *Joshua* (1747).

HAYDN, Joseph (1732-1809)
Concerto for Violoncello in D major
Allegro moderato; Adagio; Rondo: Allegro

Haydn wrote a considerable number of concertos, for all kinds of instruments: violin, violoncello, double bass, flute, horn, trumpet, harpsichord, violin and harpsichord, organ, and the now obsolete *baryton* and *lira organizzata*. Nearly his entire output in the concerto category was composed for home consumption, that is for the musical establishment of his employer, Prince Esterházy. Oddly enough, Haydn's finest achievement, the well-known trumpet concerto of 1796, did not come into being in the line of duty but was a work of the retired kapellmeister. This was written for Anton Weidinger, a Viennese court trumpeter, who constructed a keyed trumpet that permitted the production of all diatonic and chromatic notes. This invention accounts for the composition of this very popular concerto.

The concerto in D major, composed in 1783, found great favor with the cellists, yet its authenticity has been doubted for more than one hundred years. The composition was published twice in Haydn's lifetime; in Offenbach and in Paris between 1803 and 1806. The earlier of these two editions has not been accurately determined. The Offenbach version states on the title page *Edition après le manuscrit original de l'auteur,* but the German lexicographer Gustav Schilling claimed the authorship in his *Universal-Lexikon der Tonkunst* for Anton Kraft (1752-1820). Kraft, a fine cellist, was a member of the Esterházy orchestra. He owed his engagement to Haydn, who favored him with the composition of this concerto.

It was Kraft's son Nicolaus (1778-1858), also an excellent cellist, who inspired the tale of his father's authorship of the Haydn concerto. One wonders how his and Schilling's assertion could be taken seriously in the face of the precise information imparted by the edition previously mentioned. Even the testimony of such a highly respected scholar as Ludwig von Köchel, that he had seen Haydn's autograph in Dresden in the 1860s, could not silence the doubts sowed by Schilling. They lingered on in respectable publications and were squashed once and for all only when Haydn's autograph turned up in Vienna in 1954. Haydn may indeed have followed one or another suggestions of a technical nature offered by Kraft senior, but if this assumption is correct it concerns a small matter, which although of no artistic importance was grossly misrepresented by Kraft junior.

The work follows the three-movement design of the classical concerto with the alternation of tutti and solo. There is an opening Allegro in the sonata pattern, followed by the "coloratura aria" of the Adagio. A fluent rondo with an extended episode in D minor forms the concluding movement.

Sinfonie concertante for Violin, Violoncello, Oboe, Bassoon, and Orchestra in B flat major, Opus 84
Allegro; Andante; Allegro con spirito

The autograph, reposing in the Westdeutsche Bibliothek in Marburg, bears the heading *Concertante di me giuseppe Haydn, mp In nomine Domini London 792.* Haydn entered the work in his own thematic list as *Concertant Sinfonie.* First played in London on March 9, 1792 with Johann Peter Salomon, Haydn's impresario, as violin soloist, it was published in parts in Offenbach in 1796 with the opus number 84. The number is meaningless — at about the same time a Parisian firm issued the work as Opus 81. The score remained unpublished until 1920. It is difficult to understand why.

The sinfonie concertante combines the formal design of a classical type with a baroque manner of orchestration. The early composers in the classical style tried to infuse the concerto principle, one of the most significant features of baroque instrumental music, into the outstanding structural achievement of the classical style — the symphony. The result of this experiment was the sinfonie concertante.

Haydn's Sinfonie concertante discloses a variety of elements characteristic of the baroque and classical styles: the three-movement structure points
to the baroque solo concerto and also the Italian and early classical symphony; the scoring, which provides for a concertino of four instruments,
stems from the concerto grosso; the insertion of a cadenza by the entire
concertino at the end of the first movement is a feature of the classical concerto; the design of the outer movements conforms to that of both the classical
concerto and symphony. All these elements are combined in the spirit and
projected with the craftsmanship the Haydn symphony shows in its most
mature stage.

It is interesting to note that the concertino is employed in the tutti exposition of the first movement. Yet its soloistic activity commences only after
the forceful close of the tutti statement. In the Andante Haydn uses a
baroque device in the reduction of the accompanying tutti, from which the
trumpets and kettledrums are excluded. In the finale Haydn once more avails
himself of a baroque device. After a brisk unison statement of the orchestra
the solo violin executes a recitative; the orchestra interrupts but the violin
is undaunted and insists on being heard. It does so successfully and after a
virtuoso cadenza lauches into the announcement of the main theme, which
is derived from the opening statement. The latter is very interesting in so
far as it is identical with a motif of the first Allegro in Mozart's violin concerto in D major (K. 218, 1775):

Influence or coincidence? Be that as it may, the motif develops under
Haydn's hands into one of his unique rondos that are the playground for
his humor, jokes, and surprises: witness the unexpected turn caused by the
reappearance of the recitative passage of the solo violin. But behind this
playfulness is artistic wisdom: the first recitative preceded the announcement of the chief idea and now the recitative skillfully disguises the beginning of the coda.

Symphony No. 7 in C major, ("Le Midi")
Adagio-Allegro; Recitativo; Adagio; Minuetto; Finale: Allegro

Shortly after Haydn had entered the service of His Serene Highness Paul
Anton, prince of the Holy Roman Empire, at Esterház as *Vice-Capel-Meister*
in the spring of 1761, he wrote three symphonies that, numbered 6, 7, and
8 in the *Complete Works,* bear the individual headings *Le Matin, Le Midi,*
and *Le Soir.*

It is assumed that the prince had suggested a symphonic cycle depicting
the different periods of the day. If this is true, the prince must have been
stimulated by at least two compositions that followed a similar programmatic line. One was Vivaldi's cycle of four violin concertos (included in a

series of twelve) published in 1725, which quickly achieved great popularity as "The Four Seasons." The other piece was by Gregor Joseph Werner (1695-1766), who as *Ober-Capel-Meister* in the service of Prince Esterházy was actually Haydn's superior. Werner wrote a *New and very curious Instrumental Calendar,* an assortment of twelve trio sonatas referring to the twelve months of the year which, published in 1748, were undoubtedly played at the Esterházy palace. Haydn had presumably known Vivaldi's concertos, since Count Wenceslas Morzin, the dedicatee of Vivaldi's Opus 8 which includes the famous Four Seasons cycle, was a close relative of Count Carl Joseph Morzin, Haydn's first employer.

In addition to this circumstantial evidence, there is also strong internal evidence in Haydn's *Tageszeiten* symphonies which definitely indicates the influence of the baroque tradition. This influence is manifest in our symphony in the employment of two solo violins and a solo violoncello and also in the use of the instrumental recitative. The former device stems logically from the concerto grosso, the latter from the baroque opera.

The suggestive power of the baroque is felt at the very start of our symphony in the introductory Adagio, which displays a quality typical of the French overture, a certain solemnity and firmness, underlined by the dotted rhythm we find so often in Handel. This spiritual attitude is sustained by the unison main theme of the Allegro. The most interesting features of the symphony are found in the second and third movements (Recitative and Adagio). Formally speaking, the relationship of the Recitative and the following Adagio corresponds to that of the recitative and operatic aria or duet. Numerous slow movements in the concertos of Vivaldi and Bach and in the early quartets of Haydn are arias for violin.

The instrumental recitative is a baroque feature. Johann Sebastian Bach's Chromatic Fantasy for keyboard contains a movement entitled *Recitativo*. It served as a model for Carl Philipp Emanuel Bach, who included recitative passages in his harpsichord sonatas of 1742. Haydn himself eloquently testifies to the influence of Philipp Emanuel's sonatas by declaring that "whoever knows me thoroughly will find that I owe very much to Emanuel Bach."

In our symphony the recitative passages are projected by the solo violin, accompanied by the oboe and strings. It is a typical *recitativo accompagnato* with important contributions by the orchestra. The soloists in the following duet (Adagio, G major) are the violin (soprano) and the violoncello (tenor), which offer a virtuoso cadenza at the end. The violoncello gets another chance in the trio of the minuet, where the horns participate prominently. The vivid and quickly moving finale, in which the flute plays an important part, foreshadows the gaiety and character of Haydn's later finales.

The symphony, whose autograph is preserved in the Esterházy archive in Budapest, was published in 1881.

Symphony No. 57 in D major
Adagio—Allegro; Adagio; Menuet; Prestissimo

Haydn composed the D major symphony in 1774. Although he was concerned chiefly with music for the stage during this decade, he also wrote thirty symphonies. In addition to producing four operas himself, he was contractually obliged to conduct operas by other composers—a task he took seriously. In some instances Haydn revised and improved the scores of his fellow composers if he found that coaching and rehearsing was not sufficient to mount the opera. The first years of the period 1770-1780 reveal stylistically a new Haydn. Gone are the lightness and serenity of the rococo. Now a musical language emerges that seems to reflect an attitude commonly termed "Storm and Stress" (Sturm und Drang).

Haydn surprised his princely audience with a series of five symphonies in the minor key displaying a passionate and dramatic quality. In these years the string quartet series, later published as Opus 20, came into being, remarkable on account of the fugal movements that eloquently testify to Haydn's ties with the Austrian baroque tradition. Yet the monumental character of the "Storm and Stress" symphonies and the contrapuntal developments in the string quartets failed to find favor with Haydn's employer, Prince Esterházy, and his court. Haydn drew the logical conclusion. He ceased to write string quartets for almost ten years, while in the symphonic field he tried to accommodate the taste of the prince by composing less problematical music.

The symphony under review is a case in point. Its autograph is preserved in the national museum in Budapest which holds the precious manuscript collection of the Esterházy family. The slow introduction (3/4) to the first Allegro (4/4) functions as a curtain raiser which, as H. C. Robins Landon, the renowned Haydn scholar, put it, sets the stage for an evening's entertainment. In this introductory Adagio the "audience may become comfortable and prepare itself for twenty-five minutes of intellectual amusement." Indeed, there is only one moment when a unison run of the strings seems to threaten the calm. The Allegro proceeds according to the sonata pattern, the slow movement is a variation series, and the finale speeds along in moto perpetuo fashion.

Symphony No. 88 in G major
Adagio—Allegro; Largo; Minuetto; Allegro con spirito

Haydn's G major symphony, which bears the number 88 in the painfully incomplete Complete Edition, was composed in 1787, the year that saw the first performance of Don Giovanni. Technically and musically of the highest caliber, the symphony is on a par with those that form the famous set of twelve Haydn wrote for his appearances in London in the 1790s. That Haydn had many admirers in the British metropolis even in the 1780s can be gauged from the fact that a London publisher lost no time in bringing out an edition of our G major symphony after its first publication in Vienna and a performance in London in 1789. The title page of this London edition reads: "A Grand Symphony performed at the Professional Concerts, Hanover Square 1789, Composed by Joseph Haydn of Vienna." Haydn was not then a resident of Vienna, but lived in Esterház and Eisenstadt as Kapellmeister of Prince Esterházy; evidently the publisher deemed it opportune to place the composer in the capital of the Austrian empire since Eisenstadt, a community of five thousand people, had no meaning for the English musicians and prospective buyers.

The first movement, like that of many other symphonies of Haydn's most mature period, opens with a short Adagio of preludial character. Variation technique is applied to the Largo. In spite of the mellow character of the theme, which seems akin to the hymn "Praise the Lord from whom all blessings flow," there are several sharp and serious utterances, the last shortly before the tender close of the movement. Trumpets and kettledrums that have been mostly silent again join the instrumental forces in the typical rustic minuet. The melody of the trio emanates an unmistakable Slavic flavor which is underscored by bagpipe basses.

The finale is one of Haydn's master rondos. The humoristic main theme, entering modestly, charms the listener, who is not prepared for the sudden forte outburst of the full orchestra later on. The transition to the recapitulaion is so inconspicuous and at the same time ingenious that the listener is hardly aware of it; the composer deceives him anew by jumping into the conclusion at a point when we would expect the restatement of the second theme. But Haydn evidently thought he had offered the audience enough, and after a short halt the symphony quickly finishes with the brisk coda.

Symphony No. 89 in F major
Vivace; Andante con moto; Minuetto; Finale: Vivace assai

The F major symphony was composed in 1787, as the autograph, which is preserved in the Fitzwilliam Museum in Cambridge, England, tells us. Prompted by the success of the six symphonies that he wrote for Paris in 1785/1786, generally referred to as the "Paris" symphonies, Haydn wanted to place two others in G major, No. 88, and F major, No. 89, with a publisher in the French capital.

His agent was a certain Johann Tost, whose identity is not definitely established. We encounter a violinist in the Esterházy orchestra from 1783-1789, and also find the name of a Monsieur Jean Tost as the dedicatee of the string quartets Opus 54 and 55 (1789) and of the six quartets Opus 64, composed in 1790. Monsieur Jean Tost was not only a proficient violinist but also a very successful businessman and cloth manufacturer who played a role in Vienna's musical life around the turn of the eighteenth century.

Whether or not Monsieur Jean Tost and Johann Tost of the Esterházy chapel are the same person has not yet been determined. But it was Johann Tost who journeyed to Paris and to whom Haydn gave the exclusive rights for the publication of the two symphonies. Since the composer would certainly not have handed over the symphonies to his former subordinate as a gift, a deal must have been concluded between Haydn and Tost. Be that as it may, the theory that Haydn composed the two symphonies for Johann Tost, a former member of the Esterházy orchestra, is not well founded.

Tost went to Paris and sold the symphonies to Johann Georg Sieber, a German-born horn player and former member of the orchestra of the Opéra, who had built up a thriving music-publishing firm. Meanwhile, the Viennese publishing house of Artaria and Co., with which Haydn had dealt since 1780, acquired a copy of the two symphonies and published them without the authorization of Haydn. Tost angrily accused Haydn of violation of their contract. The matter was never sufficiently explained, but apparently things were smoothed over. Haydn's connection with Artaria was maintained, and so were his friendly relations with the "mysterious violinist Tost." *Habent fata sua symphoniae.*

The F major symphony is one of the two among Haydn's last twenty symphonies that lacks a slow introduction, the other being the C minor, No. 95, of the London series. The opening Vivace exhibits Haydn's extraordinary craftsmanship and fascinating diversity in the manipulation of the melodic material in the middle section. It seems that certain adverse circumstances had plagued the master during the composition of this symphony, and in order to facilitate his task he decided to help himself to movements from earlier works, a method that numerous composers, e.g. Vivaldi, Bach, Handel, and Gluck, had practiced before. Thus for the second movement, Andante con moto, he selected the second movement of the fifth concerto in F major for two *lire organizzate,* horns, and strings, written for Ferdinand IV, king of Naples, who played the *lira organizzata,* a kind of hurdy-gurdy. In present-day performances this instrument is replaced by oboes and flutes.

The orchestration of the symphony (flute, two oboes, bassoons, and horns) required, of course, some changes in the instrumental texture of the "borrowed" movement. Formally speaking, the Andante is a three-section piece with a middle division in a minor key. The rustic minuet is contrasted with the gentle *ländler* melody with the characteristic *one*-two-three accompaniment that foreshadows the Viennese waltz. In the fast rondo finale Haydn once more resorted to the *lira* concerto in F major. But since a symphonic finale moves on a higher plane than the *lira* piece, which was more in the nature of entertaining music, Haydn had to contribute something to elevate the original to the symphonic level. He achieved this by insertion of an impassioned section in F minor, which beclouds for a while the basically gay atmosphere of the movement. This episode is highlighted by the offbeat *forzato* accentuation and characteristic syncopation.

Symphony No. 90 in C major
Adagio—Allegro assai; Andante; Minuetto; Allegro assai

In 1788 Haydn was commissioned to write three symphonies for the Count of Ogny, a music-loving nobleman who supervised the postal service between Paris and Marseilles. Since the French aristocrat owned the series of six symphonies now referred to as the Paris Symphonies (1785-1786), a connection between the count and Haydn must have been established a few years before. The new symphonies achieved resounding success and Haydn's stature as a composer was firmly established in France. *Mercure de France,* the leading magazine devoted to the belles lettres and arts, spoke of Haydn's *vaste génie.*

The three symphonies for the Count of Ogny bear in the accepted listing the numbers 90, 91, and 92 and precede Haydn's last symphonic creations, the

London Symphonies (Nos. 93 to 104). Strangely enough, he also sold these three symphonies under exclusive contract to another nobleman, Prince Öttingen-Wallerstein who kept a little orchestra. The prince found out to his chagrin that these masterpieces, which he had imagined could be heard only at his residence, were played all over. Haydn, acknowledging the complaint, excused his transaction as self-defense against the piracy practiced by publishers everywhere—in those days a composer did not enjoy legal protection. The prince forgot about the incident and Haydn was his guest when he journeyed to England in the fall of 1791. The autograph of our symphony is now in the Library of Congress.

The work shows Haydn the symphonist at the peak of his development. The introductory Adagio is not of merely preludial character but represents the type of organic introduction whose thematic material is used in the main body (Allegro assai) of the movement. There are numerous interesting details that eloquently testify to the ingenuity and craftsmanship of the composer. One passage which occurs towards the end may be singled out. It is the virtuoso string run that commences with the violins, continues in the viola and violoncello, and finally descends to the double basses. Beethoven also employed this effective device in the famous stretta in the second and third Leonora overtures. Variation technique is applied to the Andante. There are two themes, one in F major and the other in F minor, and each is varied twice. The variations maintain the major-minor order. A third variation of the F major theme follows, which is greatly expanded to a coda. The refined minuet is less rustic and designed to please a sophisticated audience. The finale, which races forward at high speed, is spiced with surprising harmonic turns and humorous traits.

Symphony No. 91 in E flat major
Largo - Allegro assai; Andante; Minuetto; Finale: Vivace

Haydn's symphonic production up to the 1780s, which comprised more than eighty works, was in the first place intended for home consumption, i.e. for the musical establishment of Prince Nicolaus Esterházy, called "Nicolaus the splendor-loving." Haydn, as Kapellmeister to the Prince, was duty bound to furnish all sorts of music: compositions for the church and theater and for large and small ensembles, symphonies, concertos for the members of the princely chapel, and chamber music. His symphonies were heard first in the palace in Eisenstadt and the castle in Esterház. He was free to publish them, however, as he saw fit, and so knowledge of his output spread not only to Vienna but also to the music publishing centers of western Europe as Haydn established business connections with Paris, Amsterdam, and London. His works appeared in the programs of Le Concert Spirituel in Paris, and his symphonies were featured in London, where two organizations were engaged in a lively competition for the musical audience: the Professional Concerts, led by Wilhelm Cramer from Mannheim, and the Salomon Concerts, managed by Johann Peter Salomon from Bonn.

The managements of these groups hoped to get Haydn's presence on stage at the performance of his works, and in 1783 they attempted to engage him to come to London. These attempts were doomed to failure, however, for Prince Esterházy would never have released Haydn from his contract. In contrast, the directors of the Concerts de la Loge Olympique in Paris thought it advantageous enough to grace their programs with Haydn's works without having the privilege of the famous master's attendance. When they approached him in 1784 with a commission for six symphonies, he gladly accepted, and he wrote the six that bear the numbers 83 through 87 and are known as the "Paris" symphonies.

During his first stay in London Haydn found that he needed more symphonies than those he was contractually obliged to compose. He urgently requested from a Viennese friend the score of the E flat symphony, which he regarded artistically on a par with the works presented in England.

Showing Haydn's artistic maturity and consummate craftsmanship, the symphony follows the firmly established pattern. The opening Largo is more than a formal introduction to the main body of the first movement. It is connected with the Allegro assai through the ascending and descending scale motifs that furnish the material for the main theme. The Allegro displays Haydn's contrapuntal dexterity.

The following Andante, consisting of five variations, is certainly one of Haydn's finest achievements of this kind. It combines humor, wit, and sophistication. The theme that starts as a march tune is suddenly disturbed by sharp accents, clashing harmonies, and surprising dynamic contrasts. The variations follow the major-minor-major order—the second one is minor—and display a diversity of instrumental combinations. All the instruments have something of importance to contribute, and the theme, which entered gently and modestly, appears in the final variation as an incisive military tune.

The energetic minuet is contrasted with a lilting *ländler* that happily unites folk and art music. The spirited finale moves along without impairing the receptive mood of the listener by contrapuntal complexities or emotional excitement. Everything is serene and sunny.

Symphony No. 93 in D major

Adagio—Allegro assai; Largo cantabile; Minuetto; Presto ma non troppo

Haydn was a musician famous throughout Europe in the 1780's. But his official obligations in his position of *Kapellmeister* in the service of Prince Nicolaus Esterházy precluded extensive travel and appearances in the great musical centers of Western Europe—Paris, Amsterdam, and London.

London was bustling with musical activities in the closing decades of the 18th century. Two German violinists Johann Peter Salomon from Bonn and Wilhelm Cramer from Mannheim played an important part in the musical life of the wealthy British metropolis. They successfully upheld the tradition set by their fellow countrymen Johann Christian Bach and Carl Friedrich Abel who had championed Mozart, when as a child prodigy, he appeared in London in 1764. Wilhelm Cramer was engaged as a leader of the group known as the Professional Concerts, and Salomon organized orchestral concerts generally known as the Salomon Concerts. Salomon had once tried to engage Haydn for London, and failed because of Haydn's pressing duties at Esterház.

In the fall of 1790, en route from Italy where he had gone to enlist singers for London, Salomon in Cologne, learned of the death of Prince Nicolaus Esterházy. The astute Salomon concluded that a change in the leadership of the "tiny principality" of Esterház might involve Haydn's position. Salomon reversed his course immediately and went to Vienna. He was not mistaken. Prince Anton, the successor to the splendor-loving Nicolaus, had dissolved the little orchestra, leaving Haydn a general without an army. Although Haydn was obliged to retain the title of *Kapellmeister,* he was practically a free man and was able to move to Vienna.

One day after he had settled in Vienna, Haydn received an unknown visitor who entered his apartment and said: "I am Salomon from London and I [have come] to take you there. We will conclude an 'accord' tomorrow." The financial propositions made by Salomon were excellent, and a substantial sum was deposited at a Viennese bank as a guaranty. Once everything was settled, Salomon lost no time in publicizing the triumphant success of his negotiations in Vienna. He dispatched to London the announcement of Haydn's impending appearance in the Salomon Concerts.

Haydn and his impresario left Vienna on December 15, 1790. On New Year's Eve they reached Calais having travelled by way of Munich, Bonn, and Brussels. On the following day, after Haydn had attended Mass, they boarded the channel vessel. They landed at Dover at five that afternoon and arrived in London on January 2, 1791. Bound by his contract to compose six symphonies for the Salomon Concerts, Haydn found himself caught in the competition between the Salomon organization and Cramer's Professional Concerts. When Salomon was forced to postpone the first concert of his subscription series, Cramer cleverly took advantage of the situation. He included a Haydn symphony and quartet in the program of the first Professional Concert. Haydn's debut took place on March 11, 1791. It marked the beginning of an uninterrupted series of successes.

The symphony in D major discussed here was probably written in the summer or autumn of 1791. It was first presented on February 17, 1792. Following the English custom, Haydn sat at the piano while Salomon as concertmaster actually led the orchestra. The symphony received such an enthusiastic welcome that the slow movement had to be encored. The press joined the enthusiastic chorus. *The Times* of February 20, 1792, reported: "A new Overture [symphony] from the pen of the incomparable Haydn formed one considerable branche of this stupendous musical tree." *The Diary* of February 18th praised the "fire of Haydn's bold imagination" and termed the symphony "a composition at once grand, scientific, charming, and original." It was repeated in the concerts on February 24th and 27th.

Our D major symphony reflects Haydn's inventiveness, extraordinary craftsmanship, vitality, humor, and Austrian *Gemütlichkeit* (a quality for which no equivalent English expression exists). The first movement opens with the customary slow introduction displaying strong dynamic contrasts which create an air of expectancy that is resolved with the entry of the gay Allegro assai. The slow movement appeals to the listener because of its gentleness and inwardness. The incisive military signal sounded by the winds and kettledrums dominates the trio of the Minuet. It is quite different from the gallant court dance associated with the *ancien régime*. As is frequently encountered in Haydn's symphonies and quartets, the Finale is a vehicle for wit and humor, and for his harmonic and dynamic surprises.

Symphony No. 96 in D major
Adagio—Allegro; Andante; Minuetto, Finale: Vivace

Two German violinists Johann Peter Salomon, from Bonn, and Wilhelm Cramer, from Mannheim, played an important part in London's musical life in the closing decades of the eighteenth century. Wilhelm Cramer was engaged as a leader of the group known as the Professional Concerts, and Salomon organized orchestral concerts generally known as the Salomon Concerts.* A whispering campaign against Haydn began in the circles of the Professionals. The *Morning Chronicle* of January 13, 1791, reported the following: "Upon arrival of HAYDN, it was discovered that he no longer possessed his former powers. Pity is that the discovery did not possess the merit of novelty ..."

After Salomon had announced his series and emphasized that "Mr. Haydn will preside at the Harpsichord, and will compose for every Night a new Piece of Music," the *London Gazetteer* fired a sardonic broadside at the master on February 5, 1791: "The *nine days wonder* about Haydn begins to abate. He has been *exhibited* at the Anacreontic Society and other musical gatherings greatly to the amazement of *John Bull* [(1562-1628) famous virginal and organ player] who expected to hear another *Cramer* [John Baptist, son of Wilhelm] or a *Clementi*. But the truth is, this wonderful *composer* is but a very poor *performer ...*" Parenthetically, it may be noted that the club song performed on every evening when Haydn visited the Anacreontic Society, and which he must have heard, was the tune later used for *The Star Spangled Banner*.

Despite all these intrigues, Haydn worked quietly on two symphonies, the D major, No. 96, and C minor, No. 95. The former was presented at his public debut, which took place on March 11, 1791. It silenced the opposition once and for all. The *Morning Chronicle,* enthusiastically joining the Haydn camp, said that "... never, perhaps, was there a richer musical treat. It is no wonder that to souls capable of being touched by music, HAYDN should be an object of homage, and even of idolatry; for like our own SHAKESPEARE, he moves and governs the passions at his will." The *London Diary* reported "... that by unanimous desire, the second movement was encored and the third was vehemently demanded a second time also, but the modesty of the Composer prevailed too strongly to permit a repetition."

The D major piece opens the series of Haydn's twelve London symphonies, which represent together with Mozart's last four symphonic creations (1786-1788) the peak of the eighteenth-century symphony. Yet for 150 years this symphony was not played in its authentic version. Numerous changes crept into the score, harmonies were altered, the parts of several instruments (flute, bassoon) were considerably changed, and false notes injected. Because of the tireless research carried out by H. C. Robbins Landon, in England, Germany,

---

* See note on Symphony No 93

and Hungary, the authentic text has been restored and made available in a new score. Based on the composer's autograph (in The British Museum) and on several sets of authentic manuscript parts, corrected by Haydn himself, it is used for tonight's performance.

Scored for pairs of flutes, bassoons, horns, trumpets, kettledrums, and strings, the symphony opens with the customary slow introduction, creating an air of expectancy resolved with the entry of the gay Allegro. By using two solo violins in a passage in the Andante, Haydn resorted to the practice of the baroque concerto grosso. The soft conclusion of the Andante is contrasted with the rustic minuet. The trio, however, presents a delightful waltz melody. We can understand why the audiences of 1791 demanded the repetition of this charming tune. The finale moves speedily along in true *moto perpetuo* fashion and amuses the listener from beginning to end.

Symphony No. 99 in E flat major
Adagio—Vivace assai; Adagio; Minuetto; Finale: Vivace

When Haydn left Vienna for his second journey to London on January 19, 1794, he carried along only one symphony of the six he was contractually obliged to compose for the concerts managed by his impresario Johann Peter Salomon. He first appearance was scheduled for February 3, 1794, but he arrived in London only on the following day. The concert took place on February 10, 1794, and featured a "New Grand Overture" by Haydn, namely our E flat symphony, which bears the number 99 in the accepted listing of the Viennese musicologist Eusebius Mandyczewski. (The term "overture" was generally used in England for a symphony.) It was composed late in the fall of 1793.

According to the *Morning Chronicle,* Haydn's new symphony was received with rapturous applause. The animation and accuracy of the orchestra were considered "highly honorable to the leader Mr. Salomon." The review continues: "The incomparable Haydn produced an overture which is impossible to speak [of] in common terms. It is one of the grandest efforts of art we ever witnessed. It abounds with ideas, as new in music as they are grand and impressive; it rouses and affects the emotion of the soul." One week later the symphony was programmed again. The first movement was accorded such a tumultuous applause that it was repeated. The parts of the symphony appeared in 1801 and the score as late as 1808. However, the publication of an arrangement of Haydn's last six symphonies for piano, with optional accompaniment by violin and violoncello, was announced in 1797. Haydn's last symphonies (Nos. 88 to 104), composed between 1788 and 1795, represent, along with Mozart's so-called Prague symphony (1786) and his great triptych of 1788 (E flat, G minor, C major), the peak of the eighteenth century symphony. The scoring—two flutes, oboes, clarinets, bassoons, horns, trumpets, kettledrums, and strings—is that of the Beethoven orchestra. The texture shows Haydn's artistry in the manipulation of small motifs that nevertheless bring about dramatic climaxes. We are moved by the gentleness and inwardness of the slow movement. Note also the contrast between the energetic minuet and the delicate trio. As is often the case in Haydn's symphonies and quartets, the finale is the playground for witticism and humor, but contrapuntal passages convince the listener that counterpoint and humor can, properly guided, walk hand in hand.

Symphony No. 100 in G major ("Military")
Adagio—Allegro; Allegretto; Minuetto; Finale: Presto

When Haydn left Vienna for London on January 19, 1794, he had in his bag only one of the six symphonies he had agreed to compose for the twelve subscription concerts commonly known as the "Salomon Concerts." They had been instituted by the enterprising violinist from Bonn, Johann Peter Salomon (1745-1815), who acted not only as the impresario, but also as contractor, concertmaster, soloist, and business manager, looking after organizational details and press releases. (Take, for example, the following announcement: "The Ladies's Tickets are blue and transferable to Ladies; and the Gentlemen's are red and transferable to Gentlemen only.") The concerts took place in the venerable Hanover Square Rooms, which were the scene of great musical events for a century (1775-1874). Conforming to the English custom, Haydn, as conductor, sat at the harpsichord, while Salomon, the "leader" (whom we call "concertmaster"), actually directed the orchestra.

Arriving in London on February 4, 1794, Haydn soon went into rehearsal of the novelty, the E flat major symphony (No. 99), to be featured at the first Salomon concert on February tenth. He then completed the D major symphony known as "The Clock" (No. 101), presented on March third, and soon finished the G major symphony (No. 100), announced in the program of the eighth concert on March 31, 1794 as *New Grand Overture* with the "Military Movement." The piece was the hit of the season. The *Morning Chronicle* reported on the repeat performance of April seventh: "Another new symphony by Haydn was performed for the second time; and the middle movement was again received with absolute shouts of applause. Encore! encore! encore! resounded from every seat: the ladies themselves could not forebear. It is the advancing battle, the sounding of the charge, the thundering of the onset, the clash of arms, the groan of the wounded, and what may well be called the hellish roar of war increased to a climax of horrid sublimity which, if others can conceive, he alone can execute; at least he alone hitherto has effected these wonders."

It is obvious that the reviewer refers to the trumpet signal in the Allegretto and also to the so-called Turkish music in the Allegretto and the finale, which, played on triangle, cymbals, and bass drum, earned the symphony the nickname, "Military." Haydn's pupil, Ignaz Pleyel, the founder of the Parisian publishing and piano manufacturing firm, issued this work as "Symphonie Turque" (1799). It became a favorite of the London public, which clamored for repetition, and thus it was played at several concerts during Haydn's visit, including his benefit concert on May 3, 1794.

The piece shows its author at the apex of his craftsmanship and abounds in interesting details, of which only a few can be mentioned here. Note the anticipation of the famous "Radetzky March" of Johann Strauss, Sr., in the second theme of the first Allegro. The second movement was transplanted from a concerto for the lira organizzata (No. 3, 1786), an obsolete hurdy-gurdy-like instrument for which Haydn, commissioned by King Ferdinand IV of Naples, wrote several ensemble pieces. Haydn recast the original version of the Allegretto, inserting the military episode. His fondness for cracking jokes and springing surprises is evident in the spirited finale that speeds along with unexpected halts, startling dynamic flashes, and the rousing Turkish music.

Symphony No. 101 in D major, "The Clock"
Adagio—Presto; Andante; Minuetto; Finale: Vivace

On July 24, 1792, Haydn returned to Vienna from a journey to England—a journey that had been very successful in many ways. He had received an enthusiastic welcome and had made many friends. The works he produced in London were acknowledged as masterpieces, and the venerable Oxford University conferred upon him a doctorate of music. It was also a most rewarding financial undertaking. In all probability Haydn's shrewd impresario, Johann Peter Salomon, the fine violinist from Bonn, had discussed the possibility of another trip to London before Haydn left England. Final negotiations were carried out in the fall of 1793, and on January 19, 1794, Haydn was once more under way to the British Isles. His first appearance was scheduled for February 3, 1794, but he arrived in London on the following day. The delay caused postponement of the first concert of a subscription series to be given in the famous Hanover Square Rooms, which had opened in 1775.

Salomon had "respectfully acquainted the nobility and gentry" of this series and announced that "Dr. Haydn will supply the concerts with new compositions, and direct the execution of them at the pianoforte." The roster of the principal performers "who will play concertos and concertantes on their respective instruments" included Signor Viotti, the famous violinist, and Mr. Salomon.

The Symphony in D major was presented at the fourth concert on March 3, 1794, and enthusiastically acclaimed. The reviewer of the *Morning Chronicle* had this to say: "But as usual the most delicious part of the entertainment was a new grand Overture by HAYDN; the inexhaustible, the wonderful, the sublime HAYDN! The first two movements were encored; and the character that pervaded the whole composition was heartfelt joy. [With] every new Overture he writes, we fear, till it is heard, he can only repeat himself; and we are every time mistaken. Nothing can be more original than the subject of the first movement; and having found a happy subject, no man knows like HAYDN how to produce incessant variety, without once departing from it. The management of the accompaniment of the andante, though perfectly simple, was masterly; we never heard a more charming effect than was produced by the trio to the minuet.—It was HAYDN; what can we, what need we say more?" The symphony was repeated on March 10, 1794, and the connoisseurs found it Haydn's best work.

Technically speaking, this symphony demonstrates Haydn's firmly established symphonic pattern. Preceded by a slow introduction in D minor, the main portion of the first movement, Presto, is in 6/8 meter, which although occurring in two other opening movements of Haydn's London symphonies (Nos. 94 and 103), was used chiefly in final rondos. The 6/8 meter in the eighteenth century was associated with the hunt, and the Presto, lacking lyrical passages, moves speedily along. It is contrasted with the slower motion of the following Andante, whose precisely moving accompaniment in "tick-tock" fashion has suggested the popular nickname "The Clock." The clockwork is drowned out by the forceful middle section in G minor, but it resumes its function with the return of the gentle main idea, which is treated as a theme and variations.

The finale reveals a surprising feature. Usually the playground for Haydn's wit, it shows instead a very serious attitude in the middle section in D minor. Still, Haydn has a surprise in store for the audience, but not one of the kind that they might expect. In the recapitulation he offers "learned music" and introduces the theme in a *fugato* with two subjects. But he is kind enough not to burden the listener with contrapuntal complexities too long and returns to a simpler setting in the concluding portion, after a restatement of the gentle main theme.

Symphony No. 102 in B flat major

Largo—Vivace; Adagio; Minuetto; Presto

At the beginning of 1795 there was sensational news for the musical circles of London: Salomon announced that his own concert series would be discontinued and would be replaced by a series called The Opera Concerts. These were to be given in the King's Theater, a larger auditorium than the one in Hanover Square. Haydn was under contract to compose three symphonies for the new enterprise, which was managed by the famous Italian violin virtuoso Giambattista Viotti (1755-1824), who had settled in London in 1792. The orchestra, numbering about sixty players, was led by the German violinist Wilhelm Cramer as concertmaster, who as the one-time leader of the Professional Concerts was a competitor of Salomon. The symphonies that Haydn composed for The Opera Concerts are known as Nos. 102, 103, and 104. They mark the conclusion of his career as a symphonist, which spanned a period of thirty-five years.

Billed as "A New Grand Overture composed on the Occasion, by—Haydn," the symphony in B flat received its first performance on February 2, 1795. The reviewer of the *Morning Chronicle* was not satisfied with the execution, however, and made the following observation: "It cannot be expected that so numerous an Orchestra could play with the same spirit and accuracy on the first night, and indeed the first time of their performance in this Hall, for we understand they did not rehearse here as they will hereafter." Praising the symphony, its harmony, melody, passion, and effect, the reviewer recorded: "The last movement was encored and notwithstanding an interruption by the accidental fall of one of the chandeliers, it was performed with no less effect."

This incident became legendary through the tale that the landscapist Albert Dies (1755-1822) included in his *Biographische Nachrichten von Joseph Haydn* (1810). He had gathered the *Nachrichten* during thirty lengthy visits paid to the master between 1805 and 1808. Putting the incident in 1792, the second year of Haydn's first stay in England, Dies related: "When Haydn appeared in the orchestra and sat down at the pianoforte to conduct the symphony himself, the curious audience in the parterre left their seats and crowded toward the orchestra the better to see the famous Haydn quite close. The seats in the middle of the floor were thus empty, and hardly were they empty when the great chandelier crashed down and broke into bits, throwing the numerous gathering into great consternation. As soon as the first moment of fright was over, and those who had pressed forward could think of the danger they had luckily escaped and find words to express it, several persons uttered the state of feelings with loud cries of 'Miracle! Miracle!...I have heard this incident related in various ways and almost always with the addition that in London they conferred on the symphony the flattering name 'Miracle.' It may be that such is the case, but when I made inquiry of Haydn about the matter, he said, 'I know nothing about it.'"

Obviously there is a mixture of truth, confusion, and slips of memory on the part of Dies and probably of Haydn. The chandelier fell during the performance of the B flat major symphony in 1795, but somebody, nobody knows where or when, connected the "miracle" of 1795 with the D major symphony No. 96 of 1792. Thus it carries its sobriquet unjustly.

The second presentation of the B flat symphony came off without incident and aroused unbounded enthusiasm. The *Morning Chronicle* praised it: "The rapture it gave cannot be communicated by words: to be known, it must be heard." The symphony, admired as one of Haydn's greatest achievements in the field, is one of the peaks of the eighteenth-century symphony. His extraordinary craftsmanship and his technique of manipulating the musical material also in contrapuntal combinations provided the point of departure for Beethoven, whose first symphony was composed in 1800. Some outstanding features are dynamic contrasts and dramatic rests and the use of rugged canonic passages and clashing dissonances, which render ridiculous the commonplace expression of "Papa Haydn." Another notable trait is the muting of the trumpets and muffling of the kettledrums in the Adagio. (This movement, richly endowed with figurations and ornaments, also appears in the piano trio in A major, No. 26, in the key of F sharp major.) Like other Haydn symphonies, the work presented tonight shows the influence of folk music. The light main idea of the animated finale is derived from a march tune frequently played at peasant weddings.

Symphony No. 103 in E flat major ("Drum Roll")

Adagio—Allegro con spirito; Andante; Minuetto; Allegro con spirito

The symphony in E flat major was composed in 1795 in London and is Haydn's penultimate symphonic creation. First performed on March 2, 1795, it was programmed as an "Overture," since this term was generally used in England to define a symphony. The *Morning Chronicle,* reporting on the première, noted: "Another new Overture, by the fertile and enchanting Haydn was performed; which, as usual, had continued strokes of genius, both in air [melody] and harmony. The Introduction excited the deepest attention, the Allegro charmed, the Andante was enchored, the Minuets, especially the Trio was playful and sweet and the last movement was equal, if not superior to the preceding."

The critic of 1795 fully grasped the outstanding features of the symphony. The introduction is not of merely preludial character, but an element of organic importance. It reappears, though abbreviated, before the coda and its thematic germ is woven into characteristic passages of the middle section. The Andante is a variation movement with a melody in C minor and one in C major. In the first variation of the C major tune Haydn approached the sinfonie concertante through an extended violin solo. It may have been a compliment to his impresario Johann Peter Salomon, who was also the concertmaster. The finale, one of Haydn's greatest instrumental achievements, is built on a simple motif of only four notes, similar to that of the first movement of Beethoven's C minor symphony. It was certainly a stroke of genius to retard the entry of the main idea by a horn signal, which then is used as a melodic counterpoint to the spirited main theme. Immediately the play with the four-note motif begins: it is heard in manifold combinations and varieties more than 150 times, and is paired at the powerful conclusion with the opening signal now proclaimed emphatically by the brass choir, oboes, and clarinets. Haydn presented the autograph score to Luigi Cherubini in 1806 and signed wittily under his name "Padre del celebre Cherubini." The manuscript is now in the British Museum.

Symphony No. 104 in D major
Adagio—Allegro; Andante; Minuetto; Allegro spirito

The symphonies which Haydn composed for the Opera Concerts* are known as Nos. 102, 103, and 104. They mark the conclusion of his career as a symphonist that spanned a period of thirty-five years. The exact date of the first performance of the D major symphony is not known. It was the last composed in England, and the very last of Haydn's symphonic output. The symphonies (Nos. 88-104) composed between 1788 and 1795 represent with Mozart's so-called Prague symphony (1786) and the great triptych of 1788 (E flat, G minor, and C major) the peak of the 18th century symphony. They reveal a trend to monumentality and provide the point of departure for Beethoven whose first symphony originated in 1800.

The incisive beginning of the Adagio of the symphony heard tonight, that precedes the main body (Allegro) of the first movement, imparts a serious message to the listener. Set in the minor mode, the slow introduction creates a tension released by the entry of the Allegro that shows Haydn's artistry in the manipulation of small motives. The Andante in G major, to which the variation technique is applied, discloses strong dynamic contrasts, and the same tendency is reflected by the juxtaposition of the robust minuet (D major) and the gentle trio (B flat). The finale clearly reveals Haydn's intention to match the first movement with a broad symphonic Allegro of monumental design. The main theme is derived from a well-known Croatian

---

* See note on Symphony No. 102

folk song that H. C. Robbins Landon identified as *Oj Jelena*.

Subjected to striking symphonic treatment and contrasted with a slower moving melody of a rather mystical quality it appears powerfully orchestrated above the mighty beats on the kettledrum in the triumphant conclusion.

The Creation
Haydn and the Oratorio

Haydn's journeys to England in 1791-92 and 1794-95 greatly affected him personally and were of momentous artistic importance. Praised as the most famous living composer, he returned to Vienna a well-to-do man whose financial resources secured for him a comfortable life. He had purchased a home in the suburb of Gumpendorf, which was then rural in appearance. The surroundings, orchards, fields and meadows appealed to the man who had been born and raised in the country. As Kapellmeister of Prince Esterházy, he had spent the greater part of his life in the countryside and had enjoyed walking through the large park around the princely palace and strolling through the vineyards of tiny Eisenstadt or roaming the wide plains in which Esterházy Castle was located. Yet the pressures of business, rehearsing, conducting and composing, his far-flung activities which encompassed the church, the theater and the concert hall, left him very little time for the enjoyment of nature. Even after he had settled down at his home in Gumpendorf, he was not inclined to spend his time as a gentleman of leisure.

At sixty-three, he considered his career as a symphonist closed with the composition of the second set of six "London" symphonies. He had still much to say, and expressed himself most profoundly in his last eight string quartets (Op. 76 and 77) and choral works: the six great masses, the *Te Deum*, and the oratorios *The Creation* and *The Seasons*. In London he had attended the Handel Festival at Westminster Abbey where he heard *Messiah, Israel in Egypt*, and sections from *Saul, Judas Maccabaeus*, and other oratorios. More than a thousand people performed, and it is said that Haydn wept when the "Hallelujah Chorus" swept through the venerable building and exclaimed: "He [Handel] is the greatest of us all." Impressed with Handel's powerful oratorios, Haydn presumably conceived the idea of composing an oratorio of the highest artistic calibre.

The primary objective of Haydn's engagement in London was his appearance at the presentation of new symphonies expressly created for the concerts organized by Haydn's impresario, Johann Peter Salomon. Nevertheless, Haydn soon found the opportunity to introduce himself as a choral composer, with a piece entitled *The Storm*, based on words by John Wolcot (1738-1811). It was offered in the second concert of the Salomon series and enthusiastically acclaimed. "This piece," said the reviewer of the *Diary* of February 25, 1792, "is an exquisite specimen of imitative harmony, adapted to English words; the horror of a tempest, contrasted with the gradual serenity of a calm, were finally represented and highly admired." The warm reception prompted Salomon to program *The Storm* again in the same season. We should assume that the shrewd Salomon had suggested this composition, and the selection proved to be a fine piece of public relations. In the first place, it presented Haydn, the great symphonist, as a consummate choral composer to an audience steeped in the traditions of Purcell and Handel. Secondly, the use of the English verses testified to Haydn's determination to apply his art to poetry in the language of the people whose hospitality he enjoyed. Thirdly, the choice of lines by a contemporary author was apt to create good will towards the composer. A letter of Haydn addressed to his friend Marianne von Genzinger dated April 29, 1792, eloquently testifies to his great diplomatic success. "I must confess, I have gained considerable credit with the English in vocal music by this little chorus, my first attempt with English words. It is only to be regretted that, during my stay here, I have not been able to write more pieces of a similar nature but we could not find any boys to sing [the choral parts] at our concerts, their having been already engaged for the past year to sing at other concerts, of which there are a vast number."

During his second sojourn in England, Haydn met Lord Abington, a patron of music, who had tried as early as 1783 to engage the master for appearances in the so-called Professional Concerts with which the Salomon enterprise competed. Haydn, at that time in the employ of Prince Esterházy, was unable to accept the offer. In a meeting with Haydn in 1794, Lord Abington suggested the composition of an oratorio and transmitted to him a libretto which was based on *Mare clausum* by John Selden (1584-1654). Haydn evinced interest and composed an aria and a chorus, but then his creative urge waned and he laid the matter aside. It is surmised that the master did not regard his knowledge of the English language as being sufficient for the composition of a large-scale work.

Haydn was no novice in the field of the oratorio. In 1775 he had composed an Italian oratorio, *Il Ritorno di Tobia,* for the concerts of the Viennese *Tonkünstler Sozietät,* a welfare organization for the benefit of widows and orphans of Austrian musicians. Haydn presented the piece to the *Sozietät* free of charge, came to Vienna to conduct it twice, and even brought the soloists with him. This is a work in the typical Italian fashion of the time: an assortment of numerous recitatives and coloratura arias. The original version contained only two choral numbers, which are the strongest elements of the work and foreshadow the Haydn of the last masses and oratorios. Haydn purposely avoided breaking new ground and catered to the fashionable taste in order to secure the financial success of the undertaking. In 1784 he added two more choral numbers to the score, and after the completion of *The Creation* and *The Seasons* he even permitted his student Sigismund von Neukomm (1778-1856) to modernize *Il Ritorno di Tobia* through deletions, abbreviations and instrumental changes. But these and later attempts were of little avail, in the face of the melodic freshness, depth, power and mastery of the two great oratorios that bear the indelible stamp of the late Haydn.

Twentieth-century audiences hardly accept time-bound and outmoded works, even if they bear famous names. Passing over the oratorio-like adaptation of *The Seven Last Words,* originally an instrumental work, written in 1786 for a religious ceremony in Cadiz, Spain, we come to recount briefly the circumstances which led to the composition of *The Creation.*

The Genesis of the Creation

To Sir George Grove, the famous British lexicographer, was related the following episode which occurred during Haydn's stay in England. One day the master visited the French violinist and composer François-Hippolyte Barthélémon (1741-1808), with whom he had become very friendly. In the conversation Haydn expressed his wish "to write something which will make my name last in the world." What would Barthélémon advise him to do? The Frenchman reached for a Bible which was lying on the table and said: "There is the book; begin at the beginning." The story rings true and may have had a bearing on later events.

Before Haydn left London in 1795, Johann Peter Salomon, his impresario, anxious to persuade him to compose an oratorio in English, gave him a libretto by an unknown author. According to August Griesinger, Saxonian diplomat, friend of Haydn, and his first biographer, his name was Mr. Lidley, or Lindley. The poem was drawn largely from Milton's *Paradise Lost* and was intended for Handel.

Griesinger's source for this information was Joseph Haydn himself and a story which appeared in the *Allgemeine Musikalische Zeitung* in 1799, to which we will return presently. Memory probably had failed Haydn when he related the matter to Griesinger, his biographer, who became friendly with the master around 1799. Mentioning a Mr. Lidley, or Lindley, as the author of the English libretto based on *Paradise Lost,* Haydn may have erroneously drawn in the composer Thomas Linley (1738-1796), whom he met in London. It is doubtful, however, whether Handel, after he was stricken with blindness in 1752, had any interest in writing a new work. His last oratorio, *The Triumph of Time and Truth* (1757), was a revision of an Italian work of 1708. If, actually a mythical Mr. Lindley had written a libretto with the intention of submitting it to Handel, he must have done it prior to 1750. Consequently, whether Handel had become acquainted with the poem or not, it must have been in somebody's desk for about forty years before it reached Salomon. The whole story was presumably a stratagem of the shrewd impresario to make the poem attractive to Haydn, the admirer of Handel. Be that as it may, the alleged connection between the poem and Handel could not fail to impress Haydn, who took the libretto without commitment.

Yet the subject matter must have interested him for several reasons. First, it was the Biblical topic which, following the traditions of Handel's Scriptural oratorios, appealed to Haydn's religious feelings. In addition, and no less important, Haydn, the nature-loving man, saw many fine musical opportunities in the descriptive pages of the poem. He also may have found the libretto spiritually related, to a certain extent, to two previous choral pieces on English words: *The Storm* and the oratorio fragment whose subject matter was the sea. Haydn now faced the task of dealing with the universe, and he undoubtedly remembered the suggestion made by Barthélémon: "Begin at the beginning."

About a year after his return to Vienna, Haydn was prompted to take up the libretto again by a remark made by Gottfried Freiherr van Swieten, who said: "Haydn, we would like at long last to hear an oratorio from you." Van Swieten's remark could not be ignored. Born 1734 in Leyden, he served for a time in the diplomatic corps and, in 1778, he became *"Präfect"* of the Court Library. A passionate musician, tall and solemn, he moved like a high priest in musical circles. His opinion carried the weight of infallibility. At concerts he was closely observed, and people formed their judgments on the basis of his facial expressions. Van Swieten became part of musical history because of his relations with Haydn, Mozart, and Beethoven.

Mozart frequently participated in the private musical gatherings, arranged by Van Swieten in his home or in the magnificent baroque palace of the Court Library. Compositions of Bach and Handel comprised the greater part of the musical fare, and Mozart was commissioned to adapt *Messiah* and other Handel works for Van Swieten's private concerts. The study of the baroque composers, in turn, was of decisive influence on Mozart's style, which is reflected in numerous instrumental and vocal (particularly liturgical) works.

Beethoven, too, contributed to the gatherings of Van Swieten's circle and had to satisfy the extraordinary appetite of the host for fugues by Bach and Handel. He generously reciprocated the hospitality by dedicating his first symphony (1800) to Van Swieten. The influential Baron, who was a subscriber to Beethoven's Opus 1 (Three Piano Trios), certainly would not have been an admirer of the later Beethoven. Yet his remark to Haydn about the composition of an oratorio engendered the situation to which Haydn, undoubtedly was looking forward. He showed Van Swieten the English libretto he had received from Salomon. Van Swieten immediately went to work in a three-fold capacity: as translator-editor, self-styled musical consultant, and organizer of the first performance. Whether he did all this for the sake of art or to prove his indispensability to Vienna's musical life does not matter. His achievements benefited Haydn substantially.

Van Swieten's editorial activities are described in an article, mentioned above, which he published in the *Allgemeine Musikalische Zeitung* (Leipzig, 1799), from which the following lines merit being quoted: "I saw immediately that this work would provide Haydn with an ideal opportunity to display the full powers of his inexhaustible genius; and as I had long hoped for this very possibility, I was encouraged to take the libretto and to give the English poem a German setting. In this way the present translation came into being; while on the whole I followed the general outlines of the original, I changed details whenever it seemed prudent to do so out of consideration of the musical line or expression."

A century later it came to light that Van Swieten not only saw fit to adapt and translate the English text, but also to counsel Haydn musically, even in matters of orchestration. A manuscript copy of the libretto, preserved in Eisenstadt, shows numerous marginal entries by Van Swieten. Some suggestions were actually accepted by Haydn.

To give a few examples: Van Swieten dealt with the transition from darkness to light and suggested that "the words *'Let there be light'* should be said only once." Haydn proceeded accordingly. For the bass recitative No. 16, Van Swieten imagined an accompaniment with a "straight" rhythm for the solemn motion of the basses, and Haydn provided a steadily moving bass line. The accompaniment of the terzet "Most beautiful appear" (No. 18) should depict the flowing of the brook, the flight of the birds and the quick motion of the fish. Van Swieten recommended a fugue for the conclusion of of the second part with "sweet sound and pure harmony." He advised the participation of the chorus in the first duet of Adam and Eve (No. 30) in a simple harmonic setting and thought that the music to the very last verses should again be in fugal style.

In fairness to Van Swieten it must be said that his marginal notes were not mandatory, but ideas and suggestions of an expert and fellow musician. Haydn did not think very highly of the symphonies of the gentleman-composer. He termed then "as stiff as the Baron himself," but he was not given to obstinate controversy and accepted Van Swieten's ideas if they seemed useful.

Haydn started work on the oratorio in the fall of 1796, after completion of the *Heilig Messe* and the *Missa in tempore belli*. On December 15, 1796, Johann Georg Albrechtsberger (1736-1809), conductor at St. Stephen's Cathedral, wrote to his student Ludwig van Beethoven: "Haydn came to see me yesterday: he is occupied with the idea of a big oratorio which he intends to call *The Creation* and he hopes to finish the work soon. He improvised some of it for me (at the piano) and I think it will be very good."

The Austrian National Bibliothek preserves a sketchbook used by Haydn for the composition of *The Creation*. This fascinating manuscript reveals two things: first, the intensively carried out detail work in the early stage of the creative process; and secondly, that all had not gone smoothly for Haydn. The repeated drafting of certain passages convincingly proves that the work did not come into being as a spontaneous utterance. but as the result of attempts subjected to constant critical scrutiny. Both Haydn the musical inventor and the musical thinker were at work here. Once when he was asked to explain why it took him almost two years to complete the oratorio, he remarked: "Because I intended it to last for a long time."

When Haydn decided to undertake the composition of *The Creation*, Van Swieten induced "twelve persons of the highest aristocracy" to offer the master the amount of 500 ducats. The gentlemen who contributed to this sum were well-known patrons of arts as, for example, the Princes Esterházy, Lobkowitz, Auersperg, Kinsky and Lichnowsky, whom we encounter in the story of Beethoven's life. Although concentrating on *The Creation*, Haydn was, nevertheless, busy with other matters in those days, e.g., conducting masses and *The Seven Last Words* and working on the string quartets Op. 76. Then he wrote the Austrian national anthem ("Gott erhalte") which was sung publicly for the first time on February 12, 1797. The oratorio kept Haydn occupied throughout the year 1797 and the winter of 1798. Prince Schwarzenberg, who put his palace on the Mehlmarkt (Neuer Markt today) at Haydn's disposal for the first performance, received the notice of the completion on April 5, 1798. The preparations for the first performance, scheduled for April 29 and 30, were initiated immediately.

The première of *The Creation* was strictly a private affair for the Austrian aristocracy, undertaken by amateurs guided by the industrious Van Swieten. To avoid traffic congestion, flour and vegetable vendors removed their stalls and the market was cleared. Twelve policemen and eighteen men on horseback directed the movement of the state coaches of the exclusive audience. Haydn conducted, and Antonio Salieri, the influential court conductor, sat at the piano to play the *secco* recitatives. A poem honoring Haydn, written by the famous Austrian Orientalist Joseph von Hammer-Purgstall, was distributed among the audience. The ten promoters who underwrote the expenses of the performance increased Haydn's compensation from 500 to 600 ducats, and donated to him the receipts of 4088 florins (gulden)—a handsome amount in 1798. Two more readings were given in the Schwarzenberg Palace on May 7 and 10.

The first public performance of *The Creation* took place on March 19, 1799, (Haydn's name day), at the Burgtheater which had seen memorable premières in Haydn's lifetime, e.g., that of Gluck's *Orfeo* and *Alceste,* as well as Mozart's *The Abduction from the Seraglio, The Marriage of Figaro* and *Così fan tutte.* The poster included an interesting remark addressed to the public. Pointing out that while Haydn fully appreciated the flattering applause of the public, he nevertheless requested the audience to abstain from attempts to achieve or force the repetition of certain numbers, because repeats would destroy the coherence of the individual sections and the effect of the work as a whole "and impair the pleasure which the public expects because of a perhaps too-favorable renown of the work." It is evident that Haydn's request was prompted by the experiences he had had at the first private performances; for despite the comparatively small audience at these occasions, the new work had, nonetheless, become a topic of conversation within the Viennese musical community at large.

The performance of *The Creation* on March 19, 1799, took place under dramatic circumstances. A Russian army commanded by Suworov, as allies of Austria against Napoleon, marched through the city. For two hours, the gravity of the situation was ignored, and the audience was carried into a peaceful world by the music. Griesinger, Haydn's first biographer, who also was in attendance, relates the following:

"I had the good fortune to be a witness to the profound emotion and wild enthusiasm with which this oratorio was greeted by the whole audience when it was played under Haydn's direction. Haydn admitted to me, that he could not express the feelings which filled his soul when the performance expressed his every wish, and when the audience awaited every note in profound silence. 'Sometimes my whole body was ice cold,' he said; 'and sometimes I was overcome with burning fever; more than once I was afraid that I should suddenly suffer a stroke.'"

When the *Tonkünstler Sozietät* repeated *The Creation* on December 22 and 23, 1799, it doubled the prices and netted 4474 florins. This reflects

Haydn's drawing power which, tested in London, was not to lessen in years to come.

The Publication and Later Performances

The Creation quickly became known all over Europe with the publication of the score. It appeared with German and English text as well as title in the two languages, of which we quote the English version: "The Creation/An Oratorio composed by Joseph Haydn/Doctor of Musik, Member of the royal Society of Musik in Sweden, in actuel Service of His Highness the Prince of Esterházy. Vienne 1800."

It was published on a subscription basis; 409 subscribers purchased 507 copies of the folio volume of more than 300 pages. The list of subscribers, headed by the imperial and royal families of Austria and England, included well-known names of the Austrian, English and Russian nobility and figures who also played an important role in the life of Beethoven, e.g., Count Rasumofsky and Prince Galitzin, the dedicatees of string quartets Op. 59 and 127, 130 and 132, respectively. We find, of course, Prince Esterházy (6 copies) and Van Swieten (4), Johann Peter Salomon, who subscribed for 12 copies, Muzio Clementi, Dr. Charles Burney, the famous English music historian, and Johann Nepomuk Maelzel, the inventor of the metronome.

Numerous performances were given in the wake of the publication of the score. In this connection a brief account of the presentation of The Creation in Paris would seem in order. The correspondent of the Allgemeine Musikalische Zeitung (Leipzig) reported from Paris in August, 1800: "The patriarch of the new music, the famous Haydn, is expected in our capital. Mr. Pleyel, as it is said and hoped, will bring him into our midst after the return from Germany..." Ignaz Pleyel, a student of Haydn's and very much devoted to him, had settled down in Paris as music dealer and publisher. His attempts to persuade his revered master to conduct The Creation in Paris failed. Daniel Steibelt, the popular piano virtuoso who had secured a copy of the score, was entrusted with the direction of the oratorio, for which a French translation was quickly furnished.

Steibelt aimed at presenting the work in a grand manner with an orchestra of more than 100 players. An enormous display of publicity brought an elegant audience to the opera house on Christmas Eve of 1800. Even Napoleon, then First Consul, was in attendance. Yet the impact of Haydn's work was not overwhelming, the reviews not encouraging, and the second performance on January 2, 1801, attracted only 700 people. Several little Parisian theaters quickly seized the occasion to bring out humorous parodies of the oratorio a few days after the first performance. The following titles are indicative of the spirit of these parodies, for which even Haydn's music was pirated: The Recreation of the World, The First Man and the Creation of Sleepness, The Consequences of the Creation. There were some consequences. The "production" left a substantial deficit, and the director of the opera lost his position because he was declared a violator of police regulations when he threw a party for the prominent artists and theater administration which lasted until the morning hours.

Despite all these tragicomic events, the French Government viewed the performance of Haydn's work in Paris as an artistic and cultural event of the first order and had a medallion struck in remembrance of this occasion and in honor of the composer, who was very proud of it. The medallion was transmitted to Haydn with an address signed by 140 musicians who had participated in the performance. In his letter of thanks, Haydn confidently referred to Horace's lines in *Odes* III, 60, 6: *Non omnis morriar* ("I shall not die entirely"). The action of the French Government was duplicated by the Philharmonic Society in St. Petersburg, which began its activities in 1802 with a performance of *The Creation* and honored Haydn with a medal in 1808 and assured him that the society owed its artistic and material success to *The Creation.*

The composition of an oratorio with a German text seemed unusual in Vienna, where the Italian oratorio was in vogue. There were even people who regarded Haydn as out of step with the times. Giuseppe Carpani, an Italian writer living in Vienna and author of the Haydn biography pirated by Stendhal, translated the libretto into Italian. Although rather Germanic in its musical language, *La Creazione* was successful in Italy. It was conducted in Milan (1834) by a twenty-one-year-old musician, Giuseppe Verdi, who attended a rehearsal of the oratorio in the *Teatro dei Filodrammatici*. When none of the leaders of this amateur group appeared, the director asked Verdi to fill in. He did so well that he was given full charge of the concert.

The most memorable presentation of *The Creation* was on March 27, 1808, given in honor of Haydn, in the *aula* of the old Vienna University (still standing), by the Society of Amateur Concerts, also known as the Cavalier Concerts. The occasion was glorified in poems by Heinrich von Collin and Giuseppe Carpani (in Italian). Prince Esterházy sent a coach to Haydn, so that he be driven from distant Gumpendorf to the city. A big crowd awaited the master at the door of the University. Prominent musicians, including Beethoven, were present. The feeble Haydn, seventy-six, was carried in a chair into the hall and received with trumpet flourishes and cries: "Long live Haydn!" Two ladies presented the poems to the composer, who was deeply moved. Though he was advised to keep his hat on, he complained about the draft and Princess Esterházy put her shawl around him. Several ladies followed her example and soon covered Haydn with shawls.

Strangely enough, the oratorio was sung in Carpani's Italian translation. Antonio Salieri, the "Talleyrand of music," who as conductor of the Court Chapel kept Haydn's masses from the repertory for almost thirty years, presided over the musical forces. After the passage, "And there was light," the audience burst into applause. Haydn raised his hands as if to indicate the source of his inspiration. Overwhelmed by the honors and by the power of his own music, he left after the first part, hardly able to express his thanks to the audience and the musicians. It is said that when he was carried away he made a gesture, as if to bless the assembly. Beethoven bent down and kissed the master's hand and forehead.

It was Haydn's last public appearance and also the last of the Cavalier Concerts. The popularity of *The Creation* and *The Seasons* was enormous. Both became steady features, for half a century, in the repertory of the *Tonkünstler Sozietät* during Advent and Lent. In 1848, Eduard Hanslick, beginning his career as a music critic, felt it necessary to remind Viennese concert circles that there were still other important oratorios and choral works worthy of attention, those of contemporary composers as well as of Bach and Handel. Prompted by feelings of deep satisfaction, Hanslick underlined in his *History of the Viennese Concert Life* (1869) the fact that the very frequent performances of *The Creation* and *The Seasons* not only brought enjoyment to thousands of music lovers but, due to the good returns, helped to alleviate the serious economic plight of many widows and orphans of Austrian musicians for some three-score years.

Technically, Haydn combined in *The Creation* the structural elements of the Italian oratorio of the late 18th century with important components of Handel's style. He retained the *recitativo secco* (11) accompanied by the harpsichord and low strings, the orchestrally accompanied *recitativo accompagnato* (7), the aria (7), the duet (2), and the terzet (2). The story is not told by one narrator, as the Evangelist in the Passions of Bach or in Handel's *Israel in Egypt*, but by the three archangels: Gabriel (Soprano), Uriel (Tenor), and Raphael (Bass). They relate the events not only in recitatives in the language of the Bible but also in arias that paraphrase and ornament the sacred text. In using a soprano, tenor and bass for the narration, Haydn adopted the practice of Handel in *Messiah*, where the narrative in recitatives is distributed among all four voices (soprano, alto, tenor, and bass).

Also following Handel's example, he assigned an essential role to the chorus. It appears in a dual capacity: either in straight choral numbers (7) or in arias (Nos. 2 and 4) and in a duet (No. 30). There are also passages for soloists (3 or 4) in choral pieces (Nos. 13, 19, and 34) which correspond to the device Haydn introduced in his last great Masses, in which the juxtaposition of the chorus and a solo quartet (soprano, alto, tenor, and bass) is one of the outstanding structural features.

All choral numbers except two are hymns of praise of the Lord and the glory of His creation, a panegyric of His greatness and might (Nos. 4, 10, 13, 19, 26, 28, 30 and 34). The exceptions are the passage of the creation of the light and the depiction of the despair and confusion of the evil spirits after the first day dawned. The antithesis of the fall of the evil spirits and the rise of a new world is musically symbolized by the falling and rising of the melodic line (No. 2).

H. C. Robbins Landon, eminent Haydn scholar, suggested that Haydn retained the Italian *secco* recitative for coloristic reasons. "In these brief sections," Landon argues, "the listener has a chance to rest from the vast sound of the choruses and the largest orchestra Haydn ever employed." This is a mistake, because only four out of the eleven *seccos* follow choral numbers. The others are preceded by arias, a soft *recitativo accompagnato* and a duet. In using the "dry recitative," Haydn had a proven device for communicating the story. In this respect he followed tradition; he did not fashion the arias in the endless *da capo* pattern. Occasional coloratura lines give the soloists a chance to display their technique. These passages stem not from the highly ornamented *bravura aria* of the defunct *opera seria* but rather simpler *singspiel*. Haydn the classicist never forgot that he matured in Vienna, where the contrapuntal tradition of Johann Josef Fux and its codification in Fux's

Gradus ad Parnassum (1725) was truly upheld. Many a work by Haydn reflects this attitude, particularly in the *fugato* portions of the choral numbers. His fugal movements seem to flow easily from his pen. Haydn's relaxed treatment of "learned music" with its complexities probably accounts for the success of *The Creation.*

The work is divided into three parts. The topic of the first is the Creation during the first four days; the second recounts happenings of the fifth and sixth days. The third part is more reflective in nature. The story told by the three archangels Gabriel (soprano), Uriel (tenor), and Raphael (basso), in recitatives, is prefaced by an orchestral introduction of 59 measures, depicting the chaos. This is unquestionably the most advanced and prophetic piece of music created in the 18th century. At seventy-four, Haydn declared that the potentialities of the music of the future were far greater than the achievements of the past. He added that he had ideas to advance his art further but his physical condition did not permit it. The instrumental prologue to *The Creation,* with its bold harmonies and extraordinary orchestral treatment, can be taken as a musical illustration of Haydn's revealing statement.

We do not know precisely to what extent Haydn kept in touch, from peaceful Gumpendorf, with the current musical events. Had he become aware that the potentialities he envisioned had become realities in several works of his former student Ludwig van Beethoven? He probably had not come to know the "Eroica" or the "Waldstein" sonata, the string quartets Op. 59, and the "Leonora" overtures Nos. 2 and 3. A spiritual tie connects the last-named works in C major with the overwhelming C major passage set to the words "And there was light." From this stems a long line of spiritual descendants: The finale of Beethoven's fifth symphony, the C major music to *"Heil sei dem Tag"* in *Fidelio,* and the invocation to the light at the end of Mendelssohn's cantata *The First Walpurgisnight.* C major became the tonal symbol for light, the day and the sun. Witness the powerful phrase in Hans Sachs' monologue, "But then came St. John's Day" in *Die Meistersinger* (Act III) and the awakening of Brünnhilde in *Siegfried* (Act III) and Zarathustra's hymn to the sun in *Also Sprach Zarathustra* by Richard Strauss.

The Creation contains a great deal of descriptive music which fills the "accompanied recitatives." This was no new feature in Haydn's work. His interest in program music is reflected in several works. In 1761 he had written a symphonic trilogy that depicted the different periods of the day. He expressed a distinct programmatic idea in the finale of the "Farewell" Symphony. He described an earthquake in *The Last Seven Words* and conjured up in the *Missa in tempore belli* the fearful atmosphere in which the mass was created in the kettledrum solo in the *Agnus Dei.*

In *The Creation* he illustrated the roar of the "tawny lion," the leap of the tiger, the nimble stag, the running steed, and crawling worm. One of the most significant examples of Haydn's approach to descriptive music appears in the recitative No. 16 ("And God created great whales") that opens as a *secco* but continues as a *recitativo accompagnato* employing only divided violas, violoncellos, and the double bass in its lower ranges—set to the words "Be fruitful all, and multiply." Haydn originally set the whole passage as a *recitativo secco* but then decided to provide an *accompagnato* for the lines spoken by God. In order to give this music a mysterious quality, he felt that only dark orchestral colors would be appropriate, and he chose the low instruments of the string body.

Note how Haydn, in Raphael's first aria (No. 6), subtly discriminates between the raging sea, the broad river, and the softly gliding brook: rolling passages in sixteenth-notes describe the roaring sea, short motifs in sixteenth-notes symbolize the river, and the motion in triplets illustrates the soft rippling of the brook.

Also note the contrast between the sunrise and the gliding of the moon (No. 12): a scale moving from d_2 to f_3 in a crescendo from pianissimo to fortissimo paints the sunrise, while a gentle pianissimo passage projected by the strings depicts the moon. A unique passage is the introduction (E major) to the recitative of Uriel that opens the third part of the oratorio. Haydn used three flutes to portray this moment when "in rosy mantle appears... the morning young and fair." Francois-Auguste Gevaert, Belgian scholar, musician, and educator, said that Haydn gave in these pages a description of the earthly paradise. There are numerous pages that remind us of Mozart, not of the "Italian" Mozart but of the Mozart of the German *singspiele* and late instrumental music. When Haydn began *The Creation* he was sixty-three and a wise and very religious man. "I was never so religious as during the composition of *The Creation*," he declared, "daily I fell on my knees and asked God for strength." He was deeply attached to nature, and for this reason both the devotional elements of the libretto and the descriptive passages appealed to him. In treating the former, he moved spiritually along the road he had taken with the two preceding Masses and was to follow in the Masses after *The Creation*. The sequel to the "material" side of *The Creation* was the oratorio *The Seasons* (1800-01).

In conclusion, note the duet of Adam and Eve (No. 32). It expresses the joy of the splendor of nature and the happiness of love. The horn passage at the beginning of the Allegro section (2/4) Haydn incorporated in the *Gloria (Qui tollis)* of the B flat major Mass of 1801. This Mass is generally referred to as *Schöpfungsmesse (Creation Mass)* because of this quotation from the oratorio. The religious aspect of *The Creation* is emphatically underlined in the final chorus in B flat major with the powerful concluding fugue. The choice of the key for this praise of the Lord is probably not accidental: four Masses of the last six are in the key of B flat major.

Missa in tempore belli

The church was a musical alma mater to the great Austrian masters. Beethoven, the son of a church singer, became a deputy court organist before he was twelve. Mozart was born into the musical establishment of the archbishop of Salzburg and became familiar with the *musica sacra* in early infancy. Franz Schubert was a choirboy in the imperial court chapel. Haydn started his musical career as a chorister in the small town of Hainburg, about thirty miles to the east of Vienna. At the age of eight he went to Vienna to sing in the choir of the venerable cathedral of St. Stephen.

When Haydn was a choirboy at St. Stephen's, the music was directed by Georg Reutter, Jr. (1708-1772), who also held the conductorship of the court chapel. These two positions were rewarding to him because he held both on a contractor's basis, and by failing to fill vacancies and by not giving the boys enough to eat, he was able to effect economies that increased his own resources, but at the same time decreased the artistic standard of the institution. Haydn suffered many hardships during the time spent in the chapel house of St. Stephen, yet the fruitfulness of these years cannot be overestimated. He became very familiar with the literature and, as a performer, learned the technique of voice leading and composition.

Haydn spent nine years at St. Stephen's and was dismissed in November 1749. This was not an injustice on the part of Reutter, since Haydn's voice was almost gone. He then supported himself as accompanist, teacher, composer, valet, and by playing in dance bands and houses of worship. He was violinist in the church of the Brethren of Charity and organist in the chapel of Count Haugwitz, and he continued to sing occasionally in St. Stephen's. About this time he wrote the first of his fourteen masses. His activity in the field of the *musica sacra* expanded after his promotion to Kapellmeister of Prince Esterházy in 1766.

Haydn retired from active service as Kapellmeister in 1790. He then made two trips to England, in 1791-1792 and in 1794-1795. These greatly affected him personally and were of momentous artistic importance. Praised as the most famous living composer, he returned to Vienna a well-to-do man, whose financial resources secured for him a comfortable life. At sixty-three he considered his career as a symphonist closed with the composition of the second set of six London symphonies. But he was not inclined to spend his time as a gentleman of leisure at home in Gumpendorf, a suburb of Vienna.

He had agreed to write one great mass every year for the celebration of the name-day of Princess Maria, the wife of the reigning prince, Nicolaus II, and one of Haydn's most devoted admirers. The festivity took place around September 8, in the small Bergkirche in Eisenstadt, the main town of the principality. Haydn usually spent the summer there and worked on the mass whose performance was scheduled for September.

The summer of 1796 was not pleasant because Austria found herself at war against France, whose army, commanded by the young general Napoleon Bonaparte, had been victorious in its eastward march across Europe and was threatening Austria in the west and the south. Thus Haydn called the mass *Missa in tempore belli,* and he entered this title on the first page of the autograph, which is preserved in the Esterházy Archives of the National Library in Budapest.

When he commenced the series of his last six masses in 1796, he approached his task not only as a master craftsman of instrumental writing, but also with the knowledge of Handel's oratorios, which had deeply impressed him in England. The suggestive power of the opera had penetrated the regions of sacred music in Italy after the turn of the seventeenth century. The same development took place in Austria, where numerous Italian composers had settled down and exercised strong influence on the native artists in the opera as well as in the oratorio and church music. It was the historic mission of

Haydn and Mozart to clear both the oratorio and sacred music of the luxuriant operatic features, and retaining important achievements of baroque art, to channel classical elements into church music.

In his late masses Haydn (and also Mozart in the *Requiem*) disposed of the operatic aria and introduced the solo quartet, which fulfills a function similar to that of the concertino in the concerto grosso. That is to say, it is a group of soloists in alternation with a larger body, in this case the chorus. Contact with the baroque is maintained in the polyphonic texture of the choral parts and in the fugal passages that conclude the *Gloria* and the *Credo*. The manipulation of the musical ideas in these masses occurs along symphonic lines, particularly in the textually most extended sections, the *Gloria* and the *Credo*. The spiritual diversity of the *Gloria* and the *Credo* logically led to a three-section design in the musical treatment, and the adoption of the three-part concept of the sonata form. Thus the middle portions of both the *Gloria* and the *Credo* contrast with the framing sections in tempo, meter, key, and mood. The middle part of the *Credo* in particular assumes a dramatic aspect, because it includes the narrative of the Incarnation, Crucifixion, and Burial of Christ. It is obvious that the lines that deal with the Resurrection and the Ascension require a different musical treatment. The *Benedictus* is mostly of a lyrical-contemplative nature, the *Agnus Dei* is solemn, while the concluding passage, on the words *Dona nobis pacem* (Give us peace), is serene in quality. All of these features can be observed in the *Missa in tempore belli*.

The first performance took place on September 13, 1796, and a Viennese reading is reported for December 26, of that year, in the Piaristenkirche in the suburb of Josephstadt. Since the twenty-sixth of December is a big holiday in Austria, St. Stephen's day, the church was filled to capacity. The *Agnus Dei*, with its gruesome kettledrum part and the military signal prior to the *Dona nobis pacem*, impressed the congregation deeply. Here speaks Haydn, the ardent patriot, who, craving peace, turns to God. Beethoven, who was probably present then, remembered this passage well. It was his model for the martial episode in the *Agnus Dei* of the *Missa Solemnis*, with its prayer for inner and external peace.

The Mass in Time of War is now performed in the Viennese orchestration which, employing clarinets and horns throughout, is richer than the original Eisenstadt version. Haydn's original clarinet parts for the Viennese performance were recently discovered in a chimney in the Esterházy palace in Eisenstadt, where they were hidden in 1945 when the Russians occupied the building. The music was found undamaged and could be used by H. C. Robbins Landon for a new, authentic edition of Haydn's score. The information of the unusual vicissitudes of the clarinet parts is imparted by Landon's foreword, to which this writer is indebted.

Mass in B flat major ("Theresien Messe")

Austrian sacred music has a very old and rich tradition. It was nurtured by the Hapsburg emperors who were not only ardent music lovers but in some instances professionally trained musicians and respected composers. Medieval rulers had their musical establishments, and similar institutions, as well as court chapels, were inaugurated in Austria. There were court chapels in Vienna, Prague (Bohemia), Graz (Styria), and Innsbruck (Tyrol), as well as that of the archbishop of Salzburg who, as the primate of Germany, was the ranking church prince in the German orbit. The Counter Reformation was victorious and with no religious problems, the Austrian baroque produced a richness of creation in all fields of art. Music was heard in lavishly adorned palaces of the wealthy aristocracy, in the large baroque churches, and in the spacious monasteries whose libraries accumulated large collections of musical manuscripts, including compositions of Haydn. The art of organ-building flourished.

Vienna itself had two outstanding musical establishments, the court chapel (Hofkapelle) and the choir at St. Stephen's Cathedral (Stephansdom). The former operated as a branch of the court administration and performed in the very small Gothic chapel (it admits about three to four hundred people) in the imperial palace. It was the house of worship of the imperial family and not a church for the common folk: its exclusiveness could be compared with that of the Sistine Chapel. The Gothic Stephansdom is the church of the archbishop of Vienna and, as such, a religious center of first rank.

Numerous Italian musicians and composers came to Vienna and there exercised strong influence on the native artists. The suggestive power of the opera had penetrated the regions of the *musica sacra* in Italy. The same development took place in Austria, where the learned manner of the baroque had to yield to the style of the opera. Vienna was the town of Johann Josef Fux, whose *Gradus ad Parnassum* became the counterpoint bible for five or six generations of musicians. The style of Palestrina was his ideal, but Fux's important treatise could not stem the tide. The vocal polyphonic masses disappeared completely, first supplanted by the concerted style of the baroque, and finally by the classical-symphonic technique. It was the mission of Haydn and Mozart to effect this stylistic metamorphosis in those compositions that they created *ad majorem Dei gloriam*.

Two masses stand out among those composed in Esterház. Both were conceived on so large a scale that the musical forces required were not available there. One is the *Missa Sanctae Caeciliae* (about 1773) for the Brotherhood of St. Cecilia, a work of baroque pomp nearly exceeding Beethoven's *Missa solemnis* in length. The other is the *Missa Cellensis* (1782), written for Maria-Zell, the famous shrine in Styria. The year 1782 was a fateful one for church music because of the ecclesiastical reforms decreed by Emperor Joseph II encompassing the abolition of monasteries and convents, the secularization of church properties, the decrease of festival days, and the institution of changes in the liturgy. The Josephinian reforms had far-reaching effects on church music. They aimed at simple choral singing and the sharp curtailment, and in some instances, the abolition of instrumental music. These conditions hampered the productivity of both Haydn and Mozart; the former resumed his creative activities for the church only in 1796, after some of Joseph's regulations were rescinded.

Meanwhile Haydn's personal circumstances had changed greatly. He had retired from active duty as kapellmeister of Prince Esterházy and settled in

Vienna. He had been twice to England and had become the most famous living composer. Artistically he had reached maturity and the peak of his technical mastery. When he commenced his series of six great masses in 1796 the Viennese classical style was in full bloom, and hundreds of master-pieces in all branches of music had been created. He now approached the composition of the mass not only as a master craftsman of instrumental writing, but also with the knowledge of Handel's oratorios, which had deeply impressed him in England.

Composed in 1799, the *Theresien Messe* was preceded by one of Haydn's most popular works, *The Creation* (1798). The manuscript of the Mass is preserved in the Austrian National Library. Strangely enough Haydn did not publish the Mass, which became known through handwritten copies only; the orchestral score reached the printing press only in 1924, one hundred and twenty-five years after it had sounded for the first time. We do not know the occasion for which the Mass was written. It is assumed that Haydn composed it for the nameday of Princess Maria Esterházy, the wife of the reigning Prince Nicolaus II, and one of Haydn's most devoted admirers. Her nameday was solemnly celebrated in Eisenstadt, the main town of the principality. The festivity took place in the Bergkirche, where Haydn's remains were laid to rest. It is a small church, and taking this circumstance into consideration in the orchestration, Haydn employs, in addition to the strings, only two clarinets, two trumpets, and kettledrums.

The *Kyrie* is in three sections: Adagio, Allegro (contrapuntal), and a shortened repeat of the opening Adagio. The *Gloria* discloses four contrasting divisions: a vivid opening, then a more lyrical section *(Gratias)* with solo passages for tenor and bass, markedly contrasted with the excited *Qui tollis* and the expressive *Miserere,* followed by the optimistic *Quoniam* with the fugato on the *Amen.* The *Credo* is three-sectional. The first portion is characterized by runs of the strings maintained throughout to the entry of the slow second section in B flat minor *(Et incarnatus est).* The quick motion returns with *Et resurrexit* and the closing words *Et vitam venturi saeculi amen* are treated fugally. The *Sanctus* is short in accordance with the rite, and the *Benedictus* truly reflects the spirit of a man led by trust in God. The *Agnus Dei* opens with a powerful unison statement of typical baroque character by the chorus and strings. The expression of grief and solemnity is mitigated in the third exclamation, thus effecting the transition to the *Dona,* which reflects confidence in the prayer for peace and also indicates the festive mood at the close of the holy celebration. Viewed as a whole, we see here the type of composition that laid the foundation upon which Beethoven, Schubert, and Bruckner built their great masses.

Te Deum

St. Paul advocates in Col. 3:16: "Teaching and admonishing one another in psalms and hymns and spiritual songs, singing with grace in your hearts to the Lord." The distinction which separates the hymn from the spiritual songs as well as from psalms is impossible to ascertain. In the fourth century the term hymn was understood to indicate a strophic poem, all the stanzas of which were to be sung to the same melody. St. Ambrose, Bishop of Milan, is the father of the hymnody of the Western Church. There were biblical and non-biblical hymns, and occasionally they were written in prose. The most famous non-biblical hymn in prose is the *Te Deum,* whose authorship has been the topic of numerous scholarly investigations. A legend relates that, in 387, when St. Ambrose (333-397) baptized St. Augustine (354-430), they spontaneously improvised the *Te Deum* in alternate verses.

It is assumed that the *Te Deum* was written in the first half of the fifth century. Southern France has been suggested as the probable region of origin. The text discloses a three-section design: the first part is a paraphrase of Psalm 148; the second is a hymn to Christ and the Holy Ghost, with references to the Incarnation, atoning death, and opening of the kingdom of heaven; the third part is derived from antiphons that are based on Psalms 28, 114, 33, 31, and 71. Many old manuscripts reproduce the text (192 words) without a title, and only sporadically with the heading *Hymnus Ambrosianus* or *Hymnus optimus.* While the former refers to a legendary tradition, the latter clearly reflects the high esteem and veneration these lines enjoyed among the faithful.

The *Te Deum* became an essential feature of the coronation service, particularly in England. Shakespeare took cognizance of this time-honored custom in *Henry V*: Act IV, scene 8, in the lines: "Do we all holy rites, Let there be sung *Non nobis* and *Te Deum.*" *(Non nobis Domine* being a famous canon in the days of Elizabeth I). Originally intended for daily morning use, the *Te Deum* became a spiritual and musical item in religious services connected with affairs of state and official acts. Handel wrote one for the celebration of the victory at Dettingen, Sullivan for Queen Victoria's Diamond Jubilee, and Walter Damrosch composed the so-called "Manila" *Te Deum* for Admiral Dewey's victory of 1898.

Haydn twice set the *Hymnus optimus* to music. Both compositions, separated by 35 years, were connected with the imperial family. The first, commonly referred to as the "little" *Te Deum,* was written to celebrate the return of Prince Nicolaus Esterházy from the coronation of Joseph II as German Emperor. The other, more elaborate *Te Deum* was written for the Empress Maria Theresa second wife of Emperor Franz. She was a musically trained princess "with," according to Haydn, "a pleasant but weak voice." Nevertheless, she once managed to sing the soprano part in *The Creation.* Beethoven dedicated to her his famous Septet. The Empress had been instrumental in removing the difficulties he encountered with the libretto of *Fidelio* which did not pass censorship. Haydn's intention to compose a *Te Deum* for the Empress aroused the indignation of Prince Nicolaus II Esterházy, who wanted to monopolize Haydn's liturgical works for the services held in Eisenstadt, the "capital" of his tiny principality. The solution for this difficulty was, apparently, a compromise. Haydn wrote the *Te Deum* for the Empress, and, presumably, first presented it in Eisenstadt on the occasion of a visit of Lord Nelson and Lady Hamilton.

The work is an achievement of Haydn's sublime maturity. He wrote it in 1800 after the completion of four of his last six great Masses and *The Creation.* He employed a large number of brass instruments (two horns, three trumpets, and three trombones) to accentuate the spiritual significance of the revered lines. The formal design is very much akin to that of the *Gloria* and *Credo* of his Masses. The opening Allegro section is followed by an Adagio part in C minor and an extended portion (Allegro moderato), in which a rich modulatory treatment reveals the influence of the symphony. The fugal style of baroque tradition is applied to the last section, but the texture becomes simple as if to underscore the meaning of the words *Non confundar in aeternum* with power and unshakable belief.

HINDEMITH, Paul (1895-1963), *Cello Concerto*
Allegro moderato; Andante con moto; Allegro marciale

The concerto for violoncello under review is Hindemith's third essay in this field. The first was a very early work, which bears the opus number 3, and, like other pieces of Hindemith's youth, was never published. At that time (in the 1910s) Hindemith, the violist, did not think of his own instrument, but chose instead to compose a concerto for violoncello. About twenty years later, in 1925, he wrote the *Kammermusik No. 3* for violoncello and ten solo instruments. Hindemith was then in his thirtieth year and a musician of international repute. The art of Johann Sebastian Bach and Max Reger, polyphony and linear counterpoint had exercised a decisive influence on his artistic development and the crystallization of his personal style. In the *Kammermusik No. 3* the violoncello is not accompanied by an orchestra, but rather *joined* by ten other solo instruments.

The work under consideration is technically of a different quality. It is a true concerto for violoncello and orchestra and is cast in the classical three-movement framework. Yet the scoring goes far beyond that of classical and romantic models, for Hindemith employs a strong brass section, a number of percussion instruments (kettledrums, a bass drum, a snare drum, cymbal, triangle, tambourine, glockenspiel) and the celesta. He composed the concerto in Lenox in the summer of 1940, when he taught at the Berkshire Music Center at Tanglewood. The piece was first presented by Gregor Piatigorsky in Boston from the manuscript on February 7, 1941. Sergey Koussevitzky presided over the orchestra.

The score displays imaginative modifications of the classical sonata structure. In the opening Allegro there is a short, energetic orchestral exposition. The solo instrument enters with a new idea and later presents a more lyrical theme. About midway there is a virtuoso cadenza, into which the bass drum introduces itself. Yet the cadenza does not lead to the main idea proclaimed by the orchestra at the beginning, but to the lyrical episode of the solo instrument. The main theme, however, reappears later in a powerful restatement, which actually leads into the coda.

The Andante opens with a songful passage of the solo instrument, followed by a very fast section in the nature of a tarantella. In the third section the rapid tarantella motion, maintained by the soloist, appears in contraposition to the slow cantilena of the Andante, projected by the flute and clarinet. The violoncello adopts the slow tempo again in the tender conclusion. The finale is an Allegro marciale, which exposes two themes. The melody of the trio was derived from "an old march" as the composer indicates on the score. There is an expanded but modified recapitulation of the first section, and the movement closes with reminiscences from the trio.

Kammermusik No. 3 (Cello-Konzert), Opus 36, No. 2
Maestoso; Allegro; Andante; Allegro moderato

The *Kammermusik* No. 3 for a violoncello obbligato and ten solo instruments was completed in 1925 and first performed on April 30, of that year in Bochum, Germany, with Hindemith's younger brother Rudolf as soloist. The composer was then in his thirtieth year and a musician of international repute. The performance of Hindemith's works was forbidden in Germany after the rise to power of National Socialism in 1933, when the composer was charged with the intentional destruction of the great tradition of German music. Nothing is farther from the truth: it was, on the contrary, the art of Johann Sebastian Bach and the all-important principle of polyphony and linear counterpoint that exercised a decisive influence on Hindemith's artistic development and formed his personal style.

This is convincingly reflected in the *Kammermusik* discussed here. This work is one of a series of four which, showing a common basic quality, were published as Opus 36. Each one of these "chamber music pieces" features a different solo instrument (piano, violoncello, violin, piano). The designation "cello concerto" in parenthesis in the title indicates the author's technical approach: the violoncello is not accompanied by an orchestra but rather joined by ten other solo instruments. The composer regards the violoncello obbligato as a *primus inter pares,* the first among equals. All the instruments (flute, oboe, clarinet, bassoon, horn, trumpet, trombone, the solo violoncello, violin, another violoncello, and double bass) combine to play a piece in four movements. In spite of the prominence of the solo violoncello the other instruments always have something of thematic importance to communicate and are never treated schematically; as the composer indicates, they are all soloists.

Hindemith here revived the baroque concerto; his models no doubt were Bach's Brandenburg concertos, which Bach defined as *concerts avec plusieurs instruments.* Bach's concertos in turn had Italian ancestors: Bach was very receptive to the achievements and technical devices of the contemporary Italian composers—Antonio Vivaldi in particular. The latter wrote numerous concertos for small ensembles, calling for four, five, six, or seven musicians only (string and wind instruments).

Hindemith's four-movement design points to the old suite. The solo violoncello which opens the work

is not given a dominant role in the first Allegro. It is silent throughout half of the movement and is heard again only at the end. It gets its chance, however, in the gay Allegro, 9/4, that follows:

Here its part is studded with difficult passages and the player has to traverse a polyphonic thicket where he has little opportunity to "sing." In the three-sectional slow movement in 3/2 meter the composer avails himself of the basso ostinato technique of the baroque. The ostinato theme,

abandoned in the middle section, reappears in the closing portion in a complex contrapuntal combination. It is heard simultaneously in three different versions: in the original form (trombone) and in diminutions plucked by the violin and the double bass.

In the spirited finale,

dominated thematically by the opening idea, the solo violoncello reigns from beginning to end.

HONEGGER, Arthur (1892-1955)
Concerto da camera for Flute, English Horn, and Strings
Allegretto amabile; Andante; Vivace

The Concerto da camera was first played in Zürich on May 6, 1949, by the Collegium Musicum under the baton of Paul Sacher. Honegger wrote the piece at the request of Elizabeth Sprague Coolidge (1864-1953), the noted American patroness of music. An accomplished composer, she established the Berkshire Festival of Chamber Music which, first held annually in Pittsfield, Massachusetts, was later transferred to Washington, D. C. There it continued under the sponsorship of the Elizabeth Sprague Coolidge Foundation. Many notable composers including Bartók, Prokofiev, Schönberg, and Stravinsky were commissioned to write for these concerts.

Honegger was born in Le Havre of Swiss parents. A product of the Paris Conservatory and a musician who had spent his whole life in France, with the exception of a few years, Honegger is considered a French composer. Once he was asked: "Are you French or Swiss?" He answered diplomatically: "Both." The lightness and graceful lyrical quality of the Concerto da camera seem to reflect Honegger's attachment to the French music of his time. The work corresponds to the original meaning of the word *concerto* that is derived from *conserere* meaning "to congregate"—of course, for the purpose of making music. The familiar aspect of the word *concerto* stems from *concertare,* "to compete," and is of a later date. Although flute and English horn are treated soloistically in Honegger's *Concerto da camera,* they do not play against each other, but join the strings in a spirited conversation of question and answer. They do not fight for domination.

The composer supplied the following brief characterization of the three traditional movements: 1. Allegretto amabile: "It is based on very simple themes of popular character which stand out against the background of string harmonies from which they arise." 2. The Andante introduces a "melodic theme which progresses from solemnity to a sharp brilliance in an atmosphere of somewhat melancholy calm." 3. The finale "which has the feeling of a scherzo" sharply contrasts with the gentle Andante. Propelled by high spirits, it concludes rather abruptly.

Symphony No. 2 for String Orchestra
Molto moderato-Allegro; Adagio mesto; Vivace non troppo

In 1936 Paul Sacher, conductor of the Basel Chamber Orchestra, requested from his compatriot Arthur Honegger a composition for the impending tenth anniversary of this group, which had achieved a remarkable success in promoting contemporary music. Although Honegger, a resident of Paris, started to work on the project, which was to be a symphony for string orchestra, five years elapsed before he could send word to Sacher of its completion. The score, a war child, is dated Paris, October 1941. Sacher lost no time in programming it. He conducted the symphony not in Basel, but in Zürich on May 18, 1942, in a concert given by the orchestra of the Collegium Musicum of that city. A microfilm of the score, flown to London, provided the opportunity of a war time performance in the British capital. The work reached America (Boston) on December 27, 1946, through the good offices of Charles Münch.

The symphony came into being under most trying circumstances, spiritually and materially, during the time of the German occupation when things needed for every day life were wanting. Honegger relates, "It was very cold when I wrote this symphony and since I could not heat my studio I felt cold." It has been suggested that the symphony embodies much of the mood of occupied Paris. The work assumes this plausible connotation, however, only by the force of circumstances: Honegger began the composition years before the outbreak of the war and took up the slow middle movement, the Adagio mesto or "sorrowful Adagio," first. This procedure was by no means dictated by foresight into the future—Honegger preferred to work that way. But the feeling of grief was well fitting to 1940/41, when, in the words of the composer, "the time in Paris was not too cheerful."

The somber mood is strongly reflected in the slow introduction to the first Allegro. It is a passage of organic importance, and reappears in the middle of the Allegro and once more toward the end. Its thematic germ is a simple motif announced by a solo viola which, persistently repeated, emanates a lamenting quality. The Allegro exposes two contrasting main ideas, the very impetuous theme given out by the basses, and a lyrical phrase, by the violins, which functions as the second theme in the sonata sense. The composer strove to impart to the movement what he called "inner impetuosity," which after violent and convulsive moments abates at the conclusion.

The Adagio mesto (3/2) intensifies the mood that permeated the introduction to the first Allegro. After a dynamic climax accentuated by harsh dissonances, the agitation slowly diminishes, the tension recedes, and the movement fades away deftly.

The fast-moving finale introduces the element of brilliancy and shows manifold rhythmical and harmonic contrasts. There are clashes between duple and triple rhythm and harmonic collisions when passages in distant keys sound simultaneously (polytonality). The tempo finally increases to a rapid presto and the listener asks "Where do we go from here?" The answer is given by a choralelike melody proclaimed by the first violins. Afraid that the violins, contraposed by the forceful storming of the other groups, would not succeed in carrying the chorale through, Honegger strengthened the part with a trumpet. Assuring the tonal domination of the chorale, the entry of the trumpet assumes spiritual significance, for projected against the background of 1941 the conclusions of the symphony carries a message of resolute determination and victorious optimism.

KODÁLY, Zoltán (1882-1967), *Dances of Galánta*

As the Nestor of the Hungarian musicians, Dr. Zoltán Kodály (pronounced koh-dah-é) enjoyed great prestige as composer, educator, musicologist, and author in his country as well as abroad. He was brought up in a musical family, studied composition at the Budapest Academy of Music and acquired a doctorate of philosophy through his thesis *Strophic Structure in the Hungarian Folksong*. He occupied himself with the study of folk music all through his life. He became associated with Béla Bartók in this field. They collected, organized, and edited songs. Hungary, which formed a part of the Austro-Hungarian empire, was inhabited by Hungarians, Slovakians, Croatians, Roumanians, Germans, and Ukrainians. An enormous wealth of folk music waited to be investigated and analyzed scientifically. Kodály and Bartók undertook numerous field trips that brought important scientific results and also proved to be of consequence for their own creative work, which drew upon folk music. On these trips they went first to the ethnographic border sections of Hungary. Later political developments proved this a very wise step because these territories were transferred to the new national states after World War I, and the change of the political complexion of these regions made folk-music research impossible.

Kodály's growing recognition as a composer was considerably enhanced abroad through his *Psalmus Hungaricus,* composed for the commemoration of the fiftieth anniversary of the union of Buda and Pest. For the 250th anniversary of the delivery of Budapest from the Turks, he wrote a *Te Deum.* When the Budapest Philharmonic Orchestra celebrated its 80th anniversary in 1934, Kodály presented it with the *Dances of Galánta.*

Kodály had spent a few years in his boyhood in Galánta, where his father, a traffic officer with the Hungarian State Railroads, was stationed for a time. Some happy memories of those years may have guided Kodály in the composition of the *Galántai táncok,* which are *verbunkos* music. (The word *verbunkos* is a corruption of the German *Werbung,* meaning enlisting or recruiting.) A characteristic Hungarian dance executed on such occasions led to a national style. The dance consisted of slow figures alternating with fast ones. The performers were hussars led by their sergeants while local or regimental gypsy bands played. These proceedings fell into oblivion when conscription was instituted after 1849. But the *verbunkos* dance survived.

The dance shows two easily perceptible sections: a slow beginning (*lassu*) and a quick part (*friss*). This order resembles the old sequence of the slow pavan and the quick galliard. *Verbunkos* music became immensely popular in Vienna at the turn of the 18th century, and many dances and collections were published there. The term *verbunkos* was not generally used then, but the melodies were associated with Hungarian music, and the idiom became popular with the great masters Haydn, Beethoven, Schubert, and Brahms.

Kodály recast and modified the *verbunkos* melodies he used for the *Dances of Galánta.* The *verbunkos* quality is obvious in the structural pattern or, broadly speaking, in the slow (*lassu*) and quick (*friss*) order, which is here considerably enlarged and enhanced musically. There are five principal themes, which appear in the following order:

Lassu	*Friss*
Themes I-II-III-II	IV-II-V-II-Coda

The music reveals, of course, the so-called gypsy quality in the uncommon melodic steps and the characteristic syncopation, rhythmic variety, and vitality. The piece is given a splendid orchestral garb, fashioned to the high standard of virtuosity of the 20th-century orchestra.

LASSO, Orlando di (1532-1594), *Two Motets*
"Timor et tremor," "Tristis est anima mea"

Roland de Lassus, cited mostly under the Italianized form of his name, Orlando di Lasso, represented with his contemporaries Giovanni Perluigi da Palestrina, Tomás Luis de Victoria, and William Byrd the peak of Renaissance vocal polyphony. Although he hailed from a district that is located in Belgium, Lasso belonged to the shining galaxy of Netherlandish composers who during the fifteenth and sixteenth centuries were members of the important musical establishments in France, Germany, and Italy, and whose musical language became universal during the Renaissance. In contrast to Palestrina, who traveled little, Lasso saw a great deal of Europe.

In 1556, when Lasso was only twenty-four years old and already a composer of renown, he was called to Munich to enter the service of the Duke of Bavaria. Lasso settled down in the Bavarian capital. Highly admired and revered as a *princeps musicorum* (prince of musicians), he retained his post until his death in 1594. Lasso spoke French, Italian, and German as well as his native dialect. Witty and likable, he loved wine, fishing, and games. Yet he was fully aware of the futililty of riches and splendor; his spirit was not always serene, and his soul was troubled. The two motets eloquently testify to that.

Lasso's output was astounding and will fill about sixty folio volumes of the complete edition, which is now in progress. He composed sacred and secular texts in four languages: Latin, French, German, and Italian. While the greatest part of Palestrina's production was devoted to the mass, Lasso's interest was focused chiefly on the motet and the madrigal.

The motets under consideration originated before 1565. The text of *Timor et tremor* is taken from the Psalms and expresses fear of and faith in the power of God. *Tristis est anima mea* is taken from the Gospel according to St. Matthew and describes the suffering of Christ in the Garden of Gethsemane. Both motets were regarded as ideals of sacred music during the seventeenth century and were included in text books as models.

MAHLER, Gustav (1860-1911), *Songs of a Wayfarer*

The Songs of a Wayfarer were composed between December 1883 and January 1885. Mahler was then conductor at the court theater in Cassel. Viewed biographically, the songs are the artistic aftermath of an unhappy love affair with the actress Johanna Richter. Mahler described the situation in a letter to his intimate Viennese friend Friedrich Löhr: "I have written a cycle of songs, six for the present, all of which are dedicated to her. She does not know them. What more could they tell her than what she knows already..."

Mahler, who omitted two of the songs in the published version, was the author of three poems of the cycle. The words of the first song were taken from *Des Knaben Wunderhorn*, an anthology of German poems, folksongs, and carols of nearly three centuries, published in 1806-08. Mahler concealed his contribution of poetry because he was afraid that he might be ridiculed for the simplicity of the texts. Even modern editions of the cycle do not give the name of the poet. Mahler's wayfarer resembles the young man in Schubert's *Winterreise*, who disappointed in love and disillusioned with life, sees only death as the destination of his wintry journey. In fact, Mahler follows closely the situation disclosed by the poet Wilhelm Müller in *Winterreise*. He introduces the unhappy lover who is driven to despair because his sweetheart left him to marry another man. Mahler's wayfarer also entertains thoughts of a premature death which, as expressed in the third song, have, according to Hans F. Redlich, "a suicidal ring."

The Songs of a Wayfarer begin the series of Mahler's masterworks. His previous compositions include chamber music, operas, a Nordic symphony, the cantata *Das klagende Lied,* and five songs which form Book I of *Lieder and Gesänge aus der Jugendzeit* (1885). It had been assumed that the young composer conceived the wayfarer songs as an orchestral song cycle that was later given a piano version. The assumption is now disputed—there is no orchestral score autograph extant bearing the date of the composition. The version with piano accompaniment is held to be the original one. No public readings of this version are recorded in the 1880's. Yet Donald Mitchell contends in his book (1958) on Mahler's early years that it is scarcely possible the songs were not performed with piano sometime before the première of the orchestral version. This took place in Berlin as late as March 16, 1896, under the composer's direction with the excellent oratorio and lieder singer Anton Sistermans as soloist.

It seems that Mahler orchestrated the songs after the completion, in 1888, and first performance of the first symphony (Budapest, 1889). Sections of the first and fourth songs went into the symphony, and the experience of hearing these passages in orchestral sonorities may have induced Mahler to give the cycle orchestral garb. The scoring, which includes a harp and glockenspiel, and limits the use of the trombones only to the third song, is generally modest and transparent.

Mahler's important stylistic traits are evident in this song cycle: the folksy melodic quality, the diatonic disposition, the instrumental economy, and the gentle lyricism. The interval of the fourth plays an important role in the melodic delineation:

The harmonic treatment foreshadows the later Mahler. The first song begins in D minor and ends in G minor. The second, which furnished the thematic material for the first movement of the first symphony in D major opens in D major and closes in F sharp. The "stormy and wild" third song reveals one of the most characteristic traits of Mahler's symphonic elements: violent outbursts and vehement emotions. The song begins in D minor and concludes in E flat minor. The last line of the poem dictated this choice: "I wish my bed were a funeral bier, I never would waken thereafter." The wayfarer wishes to be dead, and the song dies away in a fourfold piano (*pppp*). The fourth song alludes to this musically; it commences in the mood of a funeral march. Sorrow and resignation expressed in E minor later yield to consolation and redemption. The gentle and simple melody in G major was also used by Mahler in the third movement of the first symphony.

It suggests the spiritual recovery of the wayfarer. But the sorrowful past seems still to reverberate in his thoughts. The motif of the funeral march in F minor which sounds in the concluding measures clearly indicate this. The decisive overcoming of the "wayfarer mood" is reflected by the triumphant conclusion of the finale of the first symphony and its sonorous apotheosis of the interval of the fourth.

MARCELLO, Alessandro (c. 1684—c. 1750)
Concerto in C minor for Oboe and Strings
Allegro moderato; Adagio; Allegro

Johann Sebastian Bach developed a keen interest in the concertos of Antonio Vivaldi which he played and studied when he presided over the musical establishment of the Duke of Anhalt-Cöthen (1717-1723). Vivaldi's music was available only in parts and not in score. Bach, according to Johann Nicolaus Forkel his first biographer, "conceived the happy idea of arranging them [the concertos] for the clavier." These arrangements were, to use a familiar term, piano scores adapted to the style of keyboard setting and technique. Sixteen of these transcriptions were published by the *Bachgesellschaft* in volume 42 of the *Complete Works*. Yet research carried out at the beginning of our century reduced Vivaldi's authorship of these concertos considerably: the third item of this series in the Bach edition was attributed to the Venetian Benedetto Marcello (1686-1739) by Arnold Schering, a noted Bach scholar and specialist in baroque instrumental music. His sources were manuscript copies, one of which preserved in Darmstadt bears the heading: *"Concerto di B. Marcello, accomod'e au Clavessin de J. S. Bach."*

Benedetto Marcello, the scion of a prominent Venetian family, studied law and embarked on a political and governmental career. He became *Provveditore*, a highly placed administrator, in Pola at the Adriatic coast—a port of the Austrian Navy until 1918—and Papal Chamberlain in Brescia. His musical output included vocal and instrumental works. An astute observer of the operatic scene, he wrote the satire *Il teatro alla moda*, a biting diatribe against contemporary opera (1720). It aroused great interest and a second edition was brought out in 1722.

Benedetto Marcello's authorship of the oboe concerto later transcribed by Bach was seriously challenged, in 1950, by the findings of a British author, the late Frank Walker. He located a collection of concertos for oboe and strings by Vivaldi, Albinoni, Veracini, Alessandro Marcello, and others, printed in 1737 in Amsterdam. The piece attributed to Alessandro Marcello, a brother of Benedetto, is identical with the third item of Bach's assortment, ascribed to Benedetto by Schering. Present day opinion is inclined to regard Alessandro as the composer of the piece.

Alessandro Marcello (c.1684-c.1750) was an extraordinarily versatile man. He played several instruments, was a singer, poet, and painter, and concerned himself with mathematical and philosophical problems. His oboe concerto clings to the three-movement structure perfected by Vivaldi. The oboe, which alternates with the orchestra in the first movement, is the dominating factor in the Adagio in which the orchestra is assigned a purely accompanying function. The finale is a dance movement. In it the oboe alternates with the first violin. The model used by Bach differs on two points from the version heard tonight. It is in the key of D minor, and the first Allegro is six measures shorter. The practice of the baroque allowed the performer to embellish solo parts, in a concerto or a sonata, through melodic decoration, or ornamentation. Bach availed himself of this practice in his transcription of the Marcello concerto, and his ornamentation is applied to the solo part in tonight's reading.

MARTIN, Frank (1890—
Concerto for Seven Winds, Percussion, and Strings
Allegro; Adagietto; Allegro vivace

Frank Martin was born in Geneva in 1890, the son of a Protestant minister, and was reared in a tradition rooted in the teachings of Calvin. Geneva has always maintained a distinctly conservative political outlook, although it did produce Rousseau, and its intellectual and artistic circles, in spite of the city's proximity to the French border, have remained aloof from controversial new concepts and daring experiments in French music. As Martin's early musical training was guided by a very conservative musician, Joseph Lauber, he was not affected by the contemporary musical trends and idioms as espoused by Debussy, Schönberg, Bartók, Hindemith, and Stravinsky until his stay in Paris between 1923 and 1925. Further influenced by Ernest Anser-met, the famous Swiss conductor and tireless champion of contemporary music, Martin completely changed his artistic physiognomy and in time emerged as the musical avantgardist of Switzerland. True, Arthur Honegger (1892-1955), his famous confrère, was also of Swiss parentage, but he is considered a French composer because he was born in France, with the exception of a few years spent his whole life there, and studied at the Paris Conservatory.

Martin was associated for a time with the Institute Jaques-Dalcroze and later taught in Amsterdam and Cologne. It was in particular his works created after 1938 that made him an outstanding figure of contemporary music and won him international acclaim. Although he cannot be associated strictly with a certain school or group, he did not hesitate to assimilate into his own musical language significant contemporary features such as the twelve-tone method, which is strikingly manifest in the concerto offered tonight.

The Concerto for seven winds, percussion, and strings was commissioned by and dedicated to the Bernische Musikgesellschaft. Martin began the composition in March of 1949 in Amsterdam and finished it on August ninth in a suburb of Geneva, La Petite Grave Genève. The Bernische Musikgesell-schaft performed it on October 25, 1949; the first American reading was given by the New York Philharmonic Society on December 28, 1950, under the direction of George Szell.

The seven soloistically treated wind instruments are flute, oboe, clarinet, bassoon, horn, trumpet, and trombone. The task Martin had set himself was to demonstrate the virtuoso qualities of the individual wind instruments of the symphony orchestra. He says, "I did not spare them any technical difficul-ties in order to bring out the quality of display."

Martin chose the time-honored three-movement design of the traditional concerto as his medium, without following the principles of the concerto grosso or the classical concerto; the wind instruments, therefore, do not alternate with the strings either as a group or as soloists. The oboe, clarinet, horn, trumpet, trombone, and flute enter successively in the first movement, like characters in a play, and engage in animated conversation. The bassoon joins later, and the kettledrum once cuts in vigorously. The second movement (its designation, Adagietto, is rather modest in view of its length) is characterized by a constantly maintained march rhythm and a prolonged solo passage of the trumpet that reflects the influence of jazz. The movement seems to depict a solemn and even somber procession that after a sonorous climax disappears far off.

The mood of the Adagietto is sharply contrasted with that of the finale, which clearly displays the familiar A (3/4)—B (4/4)—A (3/4) design. This formula can be roughly interpreted as waltz-march-waltz. The rhythmical diversity is highlighted by the participation of the *batterie*—snare drum, bass drum, and cymbals. The tympanist, who must handle four kettledrums and often change their tuning, is favored with an extended solo passage that puts him on an equal footing with his fellow soloists.

MARTINU, Bohuslav (1890-1959)
Concerto for Piano No. 2
Allegro moderato; Poco andante; Poco allegro

Bohuslav Martinu began his artistic career as an orchestra musician, as did Antonin Dvořák and Paul Hindemith. He was enrolled in the Conservatory of Prague, but left it to become a violinist in the Prague Philharmonic in 1913. With an increase in his compositional activities, he felt the necessity of continuing his theoretical schooling and once more entered the conservatory as a student of Josef Suk (1874-1935), Dvořák's son-in-law and, incidentally, a fellow violinist who played second violin for over a score of years in the famous Bohemian String Quartet that made Dvořák's chamber music known all over Europe. Martinu moved to Paris in 1923, where he studied for a time with Albert Roussel (1869-1937). His steadily growing creative output at that time attracted favorable attention; his orchestral pieces and chamber works were performed in European and American concert halls and programmed at the festivals of the International Society for Contemporary Music.

Alas, the political developments in the late 1930s were detrimental to his career and life. The Vienna premiere of his now well-known Concerto grosso was prevented by the *Anschluss,* a performance in Paris could not take place because the score and parts could not be obtained from Vienna, and a rendition in Prague had to be canceled because of the Munich crisis. At the outbreak of World War II Martinu was still in Paris, but in 1940 he fled to southern France and finally succeeded in getting a visa for the United States. Here he joined a host of renowned European composers, such as Arnold Schönberg, Igor Stravinsky, Paul Hindemith, Ernst Křenek, Bela Bartók, Jerzy Fitelberg, and others. Martinu settled in New York and taught at the Mannes College of Music. After the war he taught briefly at the Prague conservatory and in 1957 was resident composer at the American Academy in Rome.

His Piano concerto No. 2 was written in Paris and dedicated to Germaine Leroux, a devoted interpreter of his work. The first performance took place in Prague on November 13, 1935, with Rudolf Firkusny as soloist and Vaclav Talich (formerly a violinist) at the helm of the Philharmonic Orchestra. Martinu re-orchestrated it in 1944 (Christmas, New York), and this version was played by Firkusny on April 13, 1945, in Philadelphia. The composer regarded this reading as "a quasi-first performance."

Reared in the tradition of Dvořák, Martinu upholds in this concerto the classical three-movement pattern, but deviates from its uniform tonal order. The first movement is in B flat major, the second closes in G major and the finale closes in C major. Although the solo part is studded with technical difficulties and endowed with brilliancy, the concerto is not a pianistic display piece. The striking glitter of the piano provides a coloristic element that is blended into the symphonic fabric of the orchestra; the dazzling piano passages are woven around or into the symphonic manipulation of the themes and motifs. There are no cadenzas in the traditional manner of the nineteenth century. The flavor of the Czech idiom, particularly in the finale, will not escape the listener.

Rhapsody-Concerto for Viola and Orchestra
Moderato; Molto adagio—Allegro

Martinu's impressive output includes works for all musical media: opera, ballet, film and radio scores, numerous orchestral works (seven symphonies), chamber music, choral pieces, and songs. Reared in the tradition of Dvořák, he showed an inclination to neo-classicism, with stress on modern contrapuntal techniques, but he also revealed a determination to infuse native melodic and rhythmic features into the contemporary idiom. Untouched by the currents of serial and electronic music, Martinu was a rather conservative composer who wanted to please both the audience and the performer. The Rhapsody-Concerto for viola and orchestra, composed in 1952 in New York, is a case in point.

The unusual title indicates the salient formal and technical features of the work. It displays the irregularity of a rhapsody and at the same time the concept of the time-honored three-movement concerto design. The rhapsodic character is reflected by frequent changes of the tempo and meter, which create in the first movement a division that broadly corresponds to the thematic dualism of the classical sonata. That is to say, the appearance of new melodic material differing in meter and tempo from the opening statement suggests the second theme in a sonata sense. Thus the first movement is divided into five sections that can be described as Theme I—Theme II—Theme I—Theme II—Coda built on Theme I.

Martinu's lyricism is manifest in the Adagio, which also exhibits the rhapsodic quality in the frequent metrical changes; it closes with a cadenza that leads into the finale (2/4). Spiced rhythmically and instrumentally through such devices as *sull ponticello* (playing with the bow close to the bridge), *coll legno* (tapping the strings with the stick of the bow), and the conspicuous use of the small drum, it hurries along in perpetual motion.

When the drive is spent, the soloist, left in the company of the small drum, finally turns to a lyrical melody of the second movement to conclude the work tenderly and peacefully.

MENDELSSOHN BARTHOLDY, Felix (1809-1847)
Concerto for Piano and String Orchestra in A minor
Allegro; Adagio; Allegro non troppo

The piano concerto in A minor of Felix Mendelssohn Bartholdy is not a "discovery." Very far from it, for its existence has been known through references in the Mendelssohn literature and letters for almost eighty years. It belongs to a substantial collection of unpublished compositions which were given in trust to the Royal Library in Berlin by the Mendelssohn family in 1878. This great library, now called the Deutsche Staatsbibliothek, is situated in East Berlin. The International Felix Mendelssohn Society in Basel secured photostatic copies of Mendelssohn autographs in the Berlin holdings and now owns an almost complete collection of Mendelssohn's unpublished works. We are indebted for this information to Professor Eric Werner, author of an exhaustive Mendelssohn biography. The Mendelssohn Society acted very wisely and in time: the whereabouts of many a precious manuscript, e.g. twelve Mozart concertos formerly kept in Berlin, is shrouded in impenetrable darkness.

The first public reading of our concerto since the days of Mendelssohn with Rolf Kuhnert as soloist and Mathieu Lange conducting took place on November 27, 1960, in Berlin in the historic Singakademie where Mendelssohn had resurrected Bach's St. Matthew Passion in 1829. Mieczyslaw Horszowski, tonight's soloist, played it with the Lucerne Festival Strings, led by Rudolf Baumgartner, on September 3, 1961, in the church at Zermatt, the famous Swiss climbing center. Sponsored by the Mendelssohn Society, the presentation was joined to the Master Courses that, directed by Pablo Casals, have called many musicians to the foothills of the Matterhorn in recent years. Tonight's offering of the concerto is the first in the United States.

The question of whether the very early works of great composers, withheld from publication, should be publicly performed was and is still a matter of discussion. Brahms, for instance, argued strongly against it, and Weber held that first operas and puppies should be drowned. True, a concert is not a composition class or a session in a musicological seminar. Nonetheless these early works offer glimpses of the development of a genius and this arouses the interest of the public at large. Mendelssohn's clavier concerto in A minor belongs to a group of boyhood essays that includes thirteen symphonies for strings, a concerto for violin (D minor), and two for two pianos (A flat major and E major). These works were played in Mendelssohn's paternal home, where a small string body could be easily assembled. It is interesting to note that all Mendelssohn concertos for one solo instrument are in the minor mode and their respective keys correspond to the tuning of the violin: E (violin concerto), A (piano), D (piano, violin), and G (piano).

Mendelssohn's models were the concertos of Beethoven and to a certain degree the clavier works of Weber. The A minor concerto of the thirteen-year-old boy is a very ambitious piece, particularly its first Allegro. Running through 498 measures, it exceeds all Beethoven's first movements in length, save that of the E flat major concerto. Of perfect formal construction, it gives the pianist ample opportunities to display his proficiency and it reveals certain pianistic features that appear in Mendelssohn's mature works, such as alternating chords of sixteenth-notes. Yet the most interesting movement is the Adagio in E major. The orchestral prelude of the muted strings leads to a Recitativo. The instrumental recitative is a heritage of the baroque. Models by Torelli, Vivaldi, Bonporti, and Locatelli were not accessible in 1822, but Mendelssohn certainly knew the recitative passages in Johann Sebastian Bach's Chromatic Fantasie and in Philipp Emanuel Bach's first Prussian sonata. He also knew the recitative passages in Beethoven's D minor sonata (Opus 31, No. 2) and perhaps those of Haydn's quartet in G major (Opus 17, No. 5). The experiment with the recitative in this concerto is the most important hint at things to come. For Mendelssohn used recitatives in his violin sonata (Opus 4), clavier sonata (Opus 6), string quartet in A minor (Opus 13), Fantasy on "The Last Rose" (Opus 15), and F minor sonata for organ (Opus 65). And there is in the Adagio also a remarkable episode of a dramatic quality: the middle section in B minor with the excited piano part, accompanied by the tremolo of the violin and violas, now without mutes, and the agitated interjections of the plucked basses. This truly romantic passage points to Weber, whose resounding successes as opera composer and pianist in Berlin Felix witnessed. The gentle ending of the Adagio, presaging the conclusion of the Notturno of the music to *A Midsummer Night's Dream* (1843), is contrasted sharply with the entry of the finale. Save for two short orchestral passages, the solo instrument dominates from the beginning to the end.

One closing remark: The performance of the concerto in Zermatt, a village surrounded by mighty glaciers and the loftiest peaks of Switzerland was also a proper tribute paid to Mendelssohn, the enthusiastic hiker who loved the Swiss Alps so dearly.

Concerto for Violin in E minor, Opus 64
Allegro molto appassionato; Andante; Allegretto man non troppo—
Allegro molto vivace

Mendelssohn's violin concerto in E minor was composed as a gift to his close collaborator and great friend, the violinist Ferdinand David (1810-1873), whose eminent artistry he wished to honor. When Mendelssohn assumed the conductorship of the Gewandhaus Orchestra in Leipzig, he secured the appointment of David as concertmaster. A student of Spohr, David strove to raise the technical and musical standard of the orchestra; under the baton of Mendelssohn and the leadership of David, it became one of the best in Germany. Among the host of violinists who enjoyed the tutelage of David were Joseph Joachim and August Wilhelmj, the concertmaster of the first Bayreuth Festival in 1876.

The idea of composing a violin concerto had been in Mendelssohn's mind for years. The group of boyhood essays composed between 1821 and 1824 includes a violin concerto in D minor (1822) that was rediscovered and published in 1952, having been previously played for the first time from the manuscript by Yehudi Menuhin in New York. Mendelssohn was not only averse to the publication of juvenile compositions, but also maintained a very critical attitude toward his mature works. His refusal to publish the "Italian Symphony" illustrates this point. Thus, for practical purposes, the violin concerto of 1822 did not exist.

In a letter to David, dated August 30, 1838, Mendelssohn wrote: "I should like to make a violin concerto for you next winter, one in E minor is in my head and its beginning gives me no rest." But six years were to elapse before the work materialized. In July, 1839, Mendelssohn once more assured David of his great eagerness to write this concerto and promised to bring it if he should have a few "good-humored days." He added: "But the task is not light, however. You want a brilliant piece and how should one of us accomplish that?"

It seems that Mendelssohn did not tackle the job until 1844, completing it on September sixteenth; he then sent the score to David and asked for his opinion and technical advice. Proposed changes by David in the solo part and cadenza and certain details that vexed the composer were discussed in their correspondence. David confessed that the concerto was much more difficult than he had at first believed and suggested he edit the solo part carefully. Pointing to his own experience with the works of Bach and Beethoven, he said he wanted to refrain "from sending a violin piece without bowings and fingerings in the uncultivated violin world."

Naturally David had the honor of being the soloist at the first public rendition of the concerto on March 13, 1845, in Leipzig. As Mendelssohn was on leave at the time, his student Niels Gade (1817-1890), the Danish composer, directed the Gewandhaus Concerts for the master. David informed Mendelssohn on March twenty-seventh, in a judgment that has been confirmed by posterity, of the great success of the concerto: "The audience liked it immensely and unanimously declared it one of the most beautiful pieces of this kind. Actually it meets all requirements of a concerto to the highest degree and the violinists cannot thank you enough for this gift." David played the concerto again in Leipzig on October 23, 1845, with Mendelssohn presiding over the orchestra. The third presentation occurred in Dresden on November 10, 1845 and was an improvised affair. Clara Schumann was supposed to have been the soloist in a concert conducted by Ferdinand Hiller (1811-1885), who had assisted Mendelssohn in the 1843-44 Leipzig season; but Clara fell ill, and a boy of fourteen consented to play the new violin concerto by his great mentor. The young violinist was Joseph Joachim.

Basically conforming to the classical three-movement pattern of Mozart and Beethoven, Mendelssohn's violin concerto displays two outstanding new features. It dispenses with the orchestral exposition of the melodic material, introducing the soloist from the opening in a twofold capacity—as a structural factor through presentation of the widely-spanned arch of the main theme, and as a virtuoso through execution of brilliant passages. The second novelty is the treatment of the cadenza in the first movement. Beethoven had given much thought to the problematical nature of the cadenza, and his ultimate solution to the problem is illustrated by the following statement, written into the first movement of the E flat concerto (Opus 73): "Non si fa una cadenza" (No cadenza should be played). The historical place of the cadenza was at the end of the movement, a practice which often led—and still leads—to very disturbing misuses. Rejecting this concept, yet wanting to give the soloist some time in the limelight, Mendelssohn inserted the cadenza between the middle section and recapitulation as a transitional passage with a structural and harmonic function. In other words, while the customary cadenza was superimposed on the structure, Mendelssohn's innovation made it an organic part of the whole. He also required that all three movements be played without a break, a truly romantic device that he had used in his clavier concertos in G minor and D minor (1831 and 1837 respectively) and also in the Scotch Symphony (1842).

The virtues of the violin concerto are characteristic of Mendelssohn's artistry—appealing melody, gentle lyricism occasionally tinged with darker passages (second movement), well-balanced form, transparency of texture, and brilliant orchestral treatment that never puts the soloist to a disadvantage yet makes the orchestra a contributing partner. The concerto had an electrifying effect on Mendelssohn's contemporaries; Schumann, good-natured as he was, was prompted to tell David: "See, that is the concerto you always wanted to compose."

"Calm Sea and Prosperous Voyage
Third Concert Overture for Orchestra, Opus 27

Mendelssohn's sister, Fanny, wrote on June 16, 1828, to Felix's friend Carl Klingemann, in London: "Felix is writing a large instrumental piece *Meeresstille und Glückliche Fahrt* after Goethe. It is worthy of him. He wanted to avoid an overture with introduction and divided the piece into two juxtaposed pictures." *Calm Sea and Prosperous Voyage* was completed in the summer of 1828 in Berlin and played in a "Sunday Music" in Mendelssohn's paternal home on September 7, 1828. The first public performance took place in Berlin in the auditorium of the Singakademie, under the composer's direction. He revised the piece in the winter of 1833/34 in Düsseldorf, where he officiated as Municipal Music Director. On February 16, 1834, he wrote to his friend Eduard Devrient: "I must put my *Meeresstille* in order which means I have to recast nearly the whole Allegro." Three months later he confirmed that the composition was "an almost different piece." A tryout was arranged on October 4, 1834, in the Gewandhaus auditorium in Leipzig, which Mendelssohn entered for the first time on this occasion. He included the *Meeresstille* in the program of the concert on October 4, 1835, that opened his brilliant career as conductor of the Gewandhaus Concerts. Parts and score of the work were published in the same year in Leipzig under the title (given here in English) "Calm Sea and Prosperous Voyage, Third Concert Overture for Orchestra, Opus 27."

Goethe's two short poems entitled "Meeresstille" and "Glückliche Fahrt," which appeared in 1796 in Schiller's *Musenalmanach,* evoked three important musical settings. Schubert composed the eight-line "Meeresstille" in June

1815, and Beethoven wrote a choral setting of both poems in the same year. It was performed on December 25, 1815, half a year after Schubert had penned his song, which was not published until 1821. Mendelssohn may have known the settings of both Schubert and Beethoven. His work, like Beethoven's, is also in D major, but Beethoven's *Glückliche Fahrt* proceeds in 6/8 meter while Mendelssohn's sails along in common time.

Today's traveler prays for calm waters and still winds, but the sailors of yore dreaded quiet air because they needed wind to move the boat. Goethe had little seafaring experience—he sailed from Naples to Palermo—but he observed the disadvantage of the calm that held the boat in the harbor for a time. It may be noted parenthetically that the accepted translation of *"glückliche Fahrt"* as "prosperous voyage" does not render the meaning adequately. "Happy voyage" would express it better.

What Schubert and Beethoven attempted to express with the human voice, Mendelssohn tried to portray by means of instrumental music in a medium for which he coined the term "concert overture." Patterned after the first Allegro of a symphony, it reflects clearly defined programmatic, descriptive, and poetic notions, and constitutes for these reasons a musical category that in essence anticipates the concept of Liszt's symphonic poems. Mendelssohn depicts the calm sea in the introductory Adagio; at the same time the Adagio indicates the rhythmical contour of the main idea of the Allegro, which illustrates the quiet voyage. The arrival at the destination is heralded by trumpet flourishes, and the three concluding measures fading away in pianissimo are interpreted as the docking of the ship at the pier.

"The Hebrides" or *"The Fingal's Cave"*
Second Concert Overture, Opus 26

The history of Mendelssohn's overture *The Hebrides*, the "Scotch" Symphony in A minor, and the Fantasy in F sharp minor, *Sonate éccosaise*, strikingly illustrates the effect of external impression on the creative spirit and its influence on the shape and character of musical creations. After the historic performance of the *St. Matthew Passion* in Berlin in March, 1829, which Mendelssohn conducted, he journeyed to England in the spring and triumphed in London as pianist, conductor, and composer. Mendelssohn set out in July for a pleasure trip to Scotland. In Edinburgh he visited Holyrood Castle and the chapel where Mary was crowned Queen of Scotland. "I believe I found today in that old chapel the beginning of my Scotch Symphony," he wrote to his family. Mendelssohn traversed Scotland and reached the West coast. He visited Mull, Lona, and Staffa, the island with the famous Fingal's cave, which Carl Klingemann, his traveling companion, described as the interior of a tremendous organ.

From "one of the Hebrides" Mendelssohn wrote to his family on August 7, 1829: "In order to make you understand how extraordinarily the Hebrides affected me, the following came to my mind." The "following" is the beginning of *The Hebrides* overture, and twenty-one measures of it in a short piano score are entered in this letter. The passages correspond to the first ten and a half measures of the version we know, in which the note values of the sketch are reduced to half. Actually, Mendelssohn had already composed more than he indicated in the letter. Without taking into account the "etc." at the end of the musical example, the quote contains numerous indications for the orchestration. Noteworthy are the *pianissimo* entrance of the kettledrum in measure seven and the coming in of the trumpet in measure twenty-one; such fine detail work is generally not included in the first stage of the creative process.

Mendelssohn continued to work on *The Hebrides* during his stay in England, but interrupted the work when he set out on the journey to Italy. Despite the multifarious experiences and impressions that sunny Italy bestowed upon him, the memories of Scotland lingered on, and *The Hebrides* was not forgotten. He worked on the piece in Rome in 1830, and Mendelssohn informed his father he intended to make himself a birthday present of "his old overture to *The Solitary Island,*" and a few days later he reported: "*The Hebrides* [is] finished at long last and [has] become a peculiar thing." He was still not satisfied, however, and wrote from Paris on January 21, 1832: "The so-called development section does smack more of counterpoint than of train-oil, seagulls, and salt cod, and it should be the other way around." He revised the score, which received the first reading by the London Philharmonic Society under the direction of Thomas Attwood (1765-1838), at one time a student of Mozart in Vienna and always helpful to Mendelssohn. The program also included the first presentation of the cantata *Die erste Walpurgisnacht* (first version). After the performance, Mendelssohn cast the piece once more and conducted it in Berlin on January 10, 1833.

The overture was published under the title "*Second Concert Overture* 'The Hebrides' or 'Fingal's Cave.'" The term *concert overture* indicated that the piece was not tied to a theatrical performance. The type of overture that Mendelssohn created and patterned after the first Allegro movement of a symphony reflects clearly defined, programmatic, descriptive, and poetic notions. It constitutes, for these reasons, a musical category, which in essence anticipates the concept of Liszt's symphonic poems. Mendelssohn, who knew very well how to handle the brush, was, as Wagner once wrote, a first class musical landscapist. Particulary praising *The Hebrides,* Wagner stated that "wonderful imagination and delicate feeling are here presented with consummate art."

Overture to Die schöne Melusine, Opus 32

The overture to the fairy tale of the beautiful Melusine has a curious history with interesting ramifications. In 1833 Mendelssohn heard in Berlin the opera *Melusine* by Konradin Kreutzer (1780-1849), based on a libretto by Franz Grillparzer (1791-1872), Austria's greatest poet. Grillparzer had originally written it for Beethoven who, after several meetings with the poet, abandoned the plan in 1826. Later Grillparzer turned the libretto over to Kreutzer, who was conductor at the court opera in Vienna. Mendelssohn was displeased with Kreutzer's overture, but attracted by the subject matter he felt stimulated to compose a better musical prologue to the opera. It stands to reason that he never thought of replacing Kreutzer's overture with a composition of his own, but rather had in mind the creation of a piece that dealt adequately with the fairy tale of Melusine.

The story of Melusine, the mermaid who must leave her husband, the count Lusignan, because he breaks his promise not to ask who she is and whence she comes, is of French origin but exercised great appeal for German poets from Hans Sachs on. The parallel with the tale of Lohengrin is obvious. It was not the dramatic conflict alone, however, that kindled Mendelssohn's creative fancy, but the very nature of Melusine the mermaid and the sea that attracted Mendelssohn the landscapist. By 1833 he had already assembled a gallery of his exquisite musical paintings—the overtures *A Midsummer Night's Dream, Calm Sea and Prosperous Voyage,* and *The Hebrides,* and the Italian Symphony—and the Scotch Symphony was begun.

The first performance of the *Melusine* overture, with Ignaz Moscheles conducting, took place on April 7, 1834, in London's famous Hanover Square Rooms, where Haydn, Liszt, Berlioz, Wagner, and also Mendelssohn had appeared. There were some difficulties in the formulation of the title: Mendelssohn was afraid of British unfamiliarity with the story and submitted a variety of headings, such as "Overture to Melusine, the Mermaid," "German Mermaid," "The Knight and the Mermaid," or, "The Tale of the Fair Mermaid." The success of the piece was moderate.

After a private tryout in Düsseldorf in July, 1834, Mendelssohn decided to revise the overture and even wanted to burn the original version. Apparently he had more confidence in the remodeled form, since he included it in the program of a concert in the Gewandhaus in Leipzig on November 23, 1834, shortly after he had taken over the direction of that renowned institution. Yet he was unable to preside over the orchestra on this occasion because of his father's sudden death. He led a repeat performance on December 3 of that year. It was reviewed in the *Neue Zeitschrift für Musik* by Robert Schumann, whose poetic and fantastic interpretation did not meet with the approval of the composer.

The overture is pattered after the symphonic Allegro in which three musical ideas are manipulated. The poetic or programmatic connotation of the first theme

is clearly perceptible. Obvious also is the very close resemblance to one of the most important leitmotifs in the Nibelungen tetralogy, and *Rheingold* in particular. This is not a case of "borrowing": the kinship of these two motifs testifies to the affinity of the romantic composers, also apparent in the invention of what Wagner called "plastic nature motifs" *(plastische Naturmotive).* The "Melusine motif" is sharply contrasted with

which leads to the second theme in the sonata sense:

There are no formal anomalies. The overture closes softly with the Melusine theme in the major mode in spite of the tragic ending of the story. It is perhaps not out of place to recall that Mendelssohn was, in the last months of his life, occupied with an opera whose main figure was akin to the beautiful Melusine—Lorelei, the fairy of the Rhine.

Ouverture to "Die Heimkehr aus der Fremde"

When the silver wedding anniversary of Abraham and Lea Mendelssohn approached, Felix gave the matter much thought, for he wanted to contribute something special to the event that would please both his parents and their children. He decided to present his parents with an operetta that could be staged at home by the family and friends. He, of course, would conduct. Mendelssohn asked his friend Karl Klingemann (1798-1862), a cultivated man and a member of the Hanoverian legation in London, to supply the libretto. Klingemann had a pleasing poetic gift, and being a close friend of the Mendelssohn family, he was excited by the composer's idea.

Klingemann wrote the libretto in the spring of 1829, while Mendelssohn was making his first and tremendously successful concert appearances in England, which were to win him the lasting esteem and affection of the British musical public. That summer Klingemann accompanied Mendelssohn on his famous tour of Scotland where the A minor symphony ("Scotch") and the *Hebrides* Overture were conceived. On this trip Mendelssohn also worked on the silver anniversary operetta, whose title, *Die Heimkehr aus der Fremde,* translated roughly, means "The Return from Abroad."

Finished in the fall of 1829, the composition went into rehearsal about a week before the big day. Extensive letters to Klingemann, from Mendelssohn's mother and his sister Rebecca give a vivid account of these exciting days. The play was directed by Felix's friend Eduard Devrient (1801-1877), a professional baritone and actor, who had sung the part of Christus in Bach's *St. Matthew Passion* when the work was resurrected by Mendelssohn in the historic performance of March 11, 1829. The cast of the *Heimkehr* included Mendelssohn's sisters Fanny and Rebecca and Fanny's husband, the painter Wilhelm Hensel. Hensel was not musical, but Felix ingeniously arranged that he would sing in only one number and composed the part of the note F, to be repeated ninety-one times. The only deviation, a single *e*, did not present too great a risk, for even if Hensel did miss the note, he could be drowned out by Devrient. Being the only professional, Devrient had a hard time attempting to fashion actors out of these amateurs, who were like sticks of wood on the stage. When a change involving Devrient in the repertory of the Royal Theatre threatened to thwart the project, it was decided to advance the performance.

On December 26, 1829, about 120 guests gathered in Mendelssohn's home.

The orchestra included the best musicians in Berlin. The audience and performers had a very good time, and *Die Heimkehr aus der Fremde* scored a great success. In a letter to Klingemann of February 10, 1830, Mendelssohn contended, "I consider it the best piece I have composed thus far." Nevertheless he withheld the operetta from publication and public performance. It was presented in London in the Haymarket Theatre on July 7, 1851, under the title "Son and Stranger." A private performance had been previously arranged by Mathilde Graumann, who, under her married name, Marchesi de Castrone, became known as one of the greatest vocal teachers of the nineteenth century.

Mendelssohn designated the *Heimkehr* a *liederspiel*, a term that technically applies to plays in which the spoken word alternates with folklike music. The virtues of Mendelssohn's score are freshness, lightness, transparency, and a streak of humor. An example of this humor is the scene of the night watchman with his familiar call, "Hört ihr Leute ...," foreshadowing Wagner's night watchman in the second act of the *Meistersinger*. The overture uses musical ideas of the *liederspiel* in its opening Andante and in the beginning of the Allegro di molto. The young composer's masterly handling of the orchestra is displayed in the balance of sonorities and the delightful use of winds. The first public performance of the overture was given only after Mendelssohn's death: it was played from the manuscript in Leipzig on October 26, 1848, directed by Mendelssohn's friend Julius Rietz (1812-1877), the editor of his complete works.

Symphony in D major
Adagio-Allegro; Adagio; Minuetto: Allegro molto; Finale: Allegro molto

In 1878 the Royal Library in Berlin (now the German State Library in East Berlin) received in trust about fifty volumes of Mendelssohn's works. Included were autographs and copies, published and unpublished, carefully inscribed with both date and place. At present only thirty-nine volumes of this precious material are extant in the holdings of the Berlin library. Astonishingly enough, during eighty years they have never been sifted thoroughly or described precisely. This explains why Mendelssohn's first symphonic essays remained unknown until recent years. This particular unpublished group includes eleven three- and four-movement symphonies for strings, and one for full orchestra (not counting another, the C minor symphony of 1824, which was published by Mendelssohn in 1834), which is offered tonight for the first time on this side of the Atlantic. Musica Aeterna is very much indebted to the International Felix Mendelssohn Society in Basel, which secured photostatic copies of the composer's early and unpublished works, and to its director, Max F. Schneider, for the transmission of the filmed score from which the material for tonight's presentation was prepared. This writer also thanks Mr. Schneider who kindly supplied him with pertinent information.

Mendelssohn was fortunate enough to hear his juvenile symphonic essays at the musical parties held on alternate Sundays in the large dining room of his paternal home in Berlin. Here a small ensemble of string players could easily be assembled. It seems that Felix exercised the function of *maestro al cembalo* at these occasions and accompanied the quartet or quintet symphonies at the piano. The first in this series was composed in 1821. Felix was so fond of the eighth, in D major, which he composed in November, 1822, that he decided to rework it for full orchestra with a scoring equal to classical models such as Haydn's last symphonies or Beethoven's first, second, fourth, seventh, and eighth. Mendelssohn presented his credentials as symphonist to the musical world with the C minor symphony, finished in the spring of 1824, but published only in 1834 as Opus 11. However, there can be no doubt that our D major piece, which bears the number 9 in the series, constitutes Mendelssohn's first symphony in the true sense. Reared with a reverence for the classical masters, it was quite natural that in matters of form he should follow classical models in this first large-scale orchestral attempt. His familiarity with the contrapuntal science is demonstrated in the fugal middle section of the finale and suggests the study of Mozart's "Jupiter" symphony.

Although Mendelssohn's melodic genius is not yet in evidence in this youthful composition, it nevertheless shows a striking gift in formal and structural respects and a remarkable skill in orchestral treatment. Two interesting details may be singled out. The minuet deviates radically from the eighteenth century model and represents a rather scherzo-like type that Mendelssohn later cultivated with liveliness and craftsmanship. Note the extended transition from the trio to the main section. Another uncommon and interesting feature is exhibited in the orchestration of the Adagio, which not only silences oboes, trumpets, and kettledrums, but also dispenses completely with violins. An interesting precedent may have come to Mendelssohn's attention, namely the opera *Uthal* (1806) by Ètienne-Nicolas Méhul. In order to achieve the dark and melancholy mood of Ossian (the basis of the libretto) Méhul excluded the violins from this work. It was staged in Berlin in 1808. This writer ventures the assumption that Mendelssohn, if he had not seen Méhul's opera, must have heard of this extraordinary experiment. Intent on achieving a gentle quality and a dark color, the young and thoughtful composer deemed the exclusion of the oboes, trumpets, kettledrums, and violins insufficient. To realize his aims fully he employed the flutes and clarinets only once, but not in a melodic capacity.

Viewed biographically and technically the D major symphony, with its admirable transparency and astoundingly expert orchestration, marks the starting point of a development that led to the C minor symphony (1824), to the so-called Trumpet Overture of 1825, which uses one motif from the finale of the D major symphony, to the Octet for Strings (1825), and ultimately to the overture to *A Midsummer Night's Dream* (1826).

Symphony No. 1 in C minor

Allegro di molto; Andante; Minuetto: Allegro molto; Allegro con fuoco

Mendelssohn wrote this symphony in Berlin between March 3 and 31, 1824 when he was a boy of fifteen. The autograph numbers the work as Symphony XIII. It belongs to a group of boyhood essays that, among others, include thirteen symphonies for strings and two for full orchestra. The wish of the youthful composer to hear his creations explains the great number of string symphonies, as a small ensemble of string players could be assembled easily in his paternal home for this particular purpose. But the boy sought higher goals and, with the blessings of his mentor Karl Friedrich Zelter, Felix tried his hand at a symphony for orchestra whose scoring equaled that of the standard classical symphony, e.g., that of Beethoven's first, second, fourth, seventh, and eighth.

A conjecture has been advanced that Felix succeeded in having the symphony played in a concert given by the violin virtuoso Ludwig Maurer in Berlin in 1825. Yet the first documented performance took place on February 1, 1827, at the historic Gewandhaus in Leipzig. Of decisive importance for Mendelssohn's career, however, was the second reading, in London on May 29, 1829. It was given by the London Philharmonic Society in the Argyll Rooms, the favorite concert hall during the first decades of the nineteenth century before its destruction by fire in 1830.

Felix sent an interesting and charming report of this event to his family. In those days the direction of a concert was not in the hands of the conductor but of the "leader" (concertmaster), who indicated the tempi and sometimes used his bow as baton. The conductor sat at the piano, read the score, and sounded a few chords if the situation seemed to become serious. The leader of the London Philharmonic Society was Franz Cramer, the son of the famous pianist Johann Baptist Cramer. At the rehearsal Mendelssohn, armored with a white stick, was introduced by Cramer to the orchestra and they bowed to each other. "Some perhaps laughed a little that this little fellow with the stick should now take the place of their regular powdered and bewigged conductor." Then the rehearsal began. Everything went well and the audience, as well as the orchestra, applauded. After the finale "they made a great noise, and as I had to make them repeat it, because it was badly played, they made the same noise once more." Then started an exhausting handshaking tour of more than two hundred people.

The enthusiasm was even greater at the concert. The audience wanted the Adagio *da capo* but Mendelssohn, who sat at the piano, went on with the Scherzo. The applause was then so strong that he felt obligated to repeat the movement. However, it was not the one we hear tonight but the Scherzo of the famous Octet for strings, which Mendelssohn had set for orchestra. The enthusiasm after the finale knew no bounds and continued while Mendelssohn showed his gratitude to the orchestra by shaking each member's hand.

After his return home he addressed a letter to the London Philharmonic Society and once more expressed his thanks for the "brilliant execution of the orchestra." The Society, which elected Mendelssohn as honorary member in November, 1829, repeated the symphony under Sir George Smart in 1830, and Mendelssohn conducted it in Munich in October, 1831, in a concert for the benefit of the poor. Here, too, he had to repeat the Scherzo (of the Octet).

With the C minor symphony, published in 1834, Mendelssohn presented his credentials as symphonist to the musical world, which accepted him immediately. He had been reared in the true musical belief and reverence of the classical masters and it was quite natural that in matters of form he followed classical models in his first large-scale symphonic attempt. However, what he calls a *menuetto* does not represent the Haydn type but approaches rather the *scherzo*. But at the same time he added an extended coda to the trio with a very brief reference to the minuet at the ending. Looking to the baroque past, Mendelssohn, in the finale, occasionally indulged in a "learned" or fugal style of writing while an extended pizzicato passage stretching over twenty-eight measures testifies to the young romantic composer's highly developed sense of effective orchestral writing.

One usually speaks of the overture to *A Midsummer Night's Dream* of the seventeen-year-old Mendelssohn as of a miracle. Yet this miracle did not happen with an elemental suddenness. It was the product of a logical development and its astounding skill in orchestration and admirable transparency was contingent on two preceding works: the Octet for strings and the C minor symphony.

Symphony No. 4 in A major ("Italian")

Allegro vivace; Andante con moto; Con moto moderato; Saltarello: Presto

The London Philharmonic Society at a general meeting on November 5, 1832, passed a resolution: "That Mr. Mendelssohn-Bartholdy be requested to compose a symphony, an overture and a vocal piece for the Society, for which he be offered the sum of one hundred guineas..."

Mendelssohn enthusiastically accepted the commission and informed the society that he would lose no time in writing the requested pieces. Actually he had done a great deal of work on a symphony in the preceding years, and these efforts stood him in good stead now. This symphony had come into being during his Italian journey in 1830/31 as the result of experiences and impressions on Italian soil. In a letter to his family he called it the "Italian symphony" and remarked that it was becoming the merriest piece he had yet composed. Completed on March 13, 1833, it was first performed two months later under Mendelssohn's direction in the famous Hanover Square Rooms. The audience had then the good fortune to admire Mendelssohn as a composer, a conductor, and also as an interpreter of Mozart's piano concerto in D minor.

Mendelssohn later revised the symphony. He did not, however, consider the revision final, and this was the reason why he did not perform the symphony again or publish it. The revised version was played only after his passing, in Leipzig on November 1, 1849, and published in 1851 as Opus 50. To speculate on what Mendelssohn considered faulty or inadequate would be futile. The symphony seems to us a symbol of perfection in its architectural balance, the elaboration of its musical ideas, the transparency of its texture, and its enchanting orchestration.

While the opening movement reflects the serenity and pleasant atmosphere of the Tuscan countryside, the second movement has been generally interpreted as a kind of pilgrim's song, a suggestion, enhanced by the steadily moving eighth-notes (walking bass), heard throughout the piece in all voices. Mendelssohn wisely refrained from calling the third movement (Con moto moderato) a minuet. True, it is cast after the minuet pattern, but it displays a very remote relationship to the familiar type. On the other hand, it is a far cry from the characteristic and unique Mendelssohn scherzi that adorn his chamber music for strings (quartets, quintets, octet) and orchestral works ("Scotch" symphony, *Midsummer Night's Dream*). Italian impressions are most strikingly displayed in the finale, entitled Saltarello, derived from *saltare* ("to spring"). Mendelssohn actually combines here the saltarello with the wild tarantella, which uses constantly running triplets (second theme), while in the saltarello triplets and longer notes occur (opening idea). This boisterous movement with its conspicuous ending in A minor is the southern counterpart to the northern dance finale of Beethoven's A major symphony.

Symphony No. 3 in A minor ("Scotch")

Andante con moto—Allegro un poco agitato—Vivace non troppo—
Adagio—Allegro vivacissimo—Allegro maestoso assai

The year 1829 initiated one of the most important stages in Felix Mendelssohn's artistic career. He reached his twentieth birthday on February third, and on March eleventh he conducted the historic performance of the *St. Matthew Passion* in Berlin, an event of far-reaching repercussions for the appreciation of Johann Sebastian Bach and the rescue of his works from oblivion. On a trip to England in the spring Mendelssohn triumphed in London as pianist, conductor, and composer. Elated by this resounding success, he set out from London in July for a pleasure trip to Scotland with his friend Karl Klingemann (1798-1862), secretary to the Hanoverian Legation. He traveled to the Highlands, Glasgow, the Isle of Staffa, Abbotsford, where he met briefly with Sir Walter Scott, and Edinburgh, where he visited Holyrood Castle. "We went," he reports home on July 30, 1829, "in the deep twilight to the Palace of Holyrood, where Queen Mary lived and loved. There is a little room to be seen there, a winding staircase leading up to it. There the murderers ascended, and finding Rizzio drew him out; about three chambers away is a small corner where they killed him. The chapel is roofless; grass and ivy grow abundantly in it; and before the altar, now in ruins, Mary was crowned Queen of Scotland. Everything around is broken and mouldering, and the bright sky shines through. I believe I found today in that old chapel the beginning of my Scotch symphony."

This passage eloquently testifies to the importance of external impressions to Mendelssohn's creative spirit. He was not only a musical landscapist, but also delighted in illustrating his letters with pen and ink drawings and knew, as well, how to handle the brush. However, by the "beginning" we do not know if Mendelssohn meant the melancholic melody that opens the symphony or the basic mood of the introductory Andante con moto. Be that as it may, the plan of composing a "Scotch symphony" had taken firm root in his mind, for after his return to London he informed his sister Fanny on September tenth that the Reformation Symphony, the Scotch Symphony, and the Hebrides Overture were "shaping themselves gradually."

An extended trip Mendelssohn took to Italy the following year, 1830, did not encourage work on the Scotch Symphony. We can understand how the young man of twenty-one, when exposed to the irresistible spell of serene and sunny Italy, could not be carried back into the foggy mood of Scotland. Thus he put the Scotch Symphony aside and concentrated on the Italian Symphony, which he described in a letter to his family as the merriest piece he had ever composed. He completed the Italian Symphony in March, 1833, and bestowed the privilege of the first performance upon the London Philharmonic Society. This turned out to be an extraordinary privilege because Mendelssohn later withheld the symphony from performance and publication, as he had revised it and was dissatisfied with the remodeled version. It came to light only after his death.

Even after the completion and revision of the A major symphony ("Italian"), Mendelssohn did not concern himself with the A minor symphony ("Scotch"). Why he hesitated to continue working on it is unanswered, although his attitude was caused by psychological inhibitions rather than outer circumstances. No doubt he must have thought of the symphony on his subsequent visits to England in 1833 and 1837, but he did not resume work on it until 1841. He completed the symphony on January 20, 1842, in Berlin and on March third conducted the première in Leipzig.

The audience, though well-disposed to Mendelssohn, did not receive the symphony enthusiastically. Afterwards he made several changes in the score, and the new version was played two weeks later, with Karl Bach, Kapellmeister at the theatre in Leipzig, leading the orchestra. This time the symphony was accorded such hearty applause that the conductor was compelled to disregard the composer's wish to have the symphony played without pausing between the movements. Mendelssohn presented the symphony in London on June 13, 1842, and dedicated the published version (Leipzig, February, 1843), to "H.M. Queen Victoria of Great Britain and Ireland."

Although Mendelssohn called the symphony "Scotch" in his letters and conversations, he never authenticated this title in the score, parts, piano arrangements, or printed programs of early performances, so neither the general public nor the professional musicians were conscious of the Scotch background of the symphony. Robert Schumann made an amusing mistake when he reviewed the work in 1843. He learned from an erroneous thirdhand source that Mendelssohn had begun the symphony during his stay in Rome in 1831, but had completed it recently. Schumann, therefore, assumed that lovely Italian memories had kindled Mendelssohn's fantasy. He remarked that while listening to this gentle tone picture one could only suppress the sorrow of never having seen that blessed country. Thus misled, Schumann, the fanciful writer, characterized the symphony in geographical terms. Only after the discovery of its Scottish background did the discussion begin about how strongly—or if at all—Mendelssohn had been influenced by indigenous songs and bagpipe tunes.

However, Schumann, the analytical critic, has much to say that is to the point, as his observation on the melodic relationship between the chief ideas of the individual movements. For example, the theme of the A major epilogue (Allegro maestoso assai, 6/8) is rhythmically related to the Allegro un poco agitato of the first movement. The epilogue, though, contrasts markedly with the melodic ideas of the main body of the finale, which was originally designated as Allegro guerriero (warlike), and it is interesting to note Schumann's remark that the ending will not be to everyone's satisfaction. Actually this A major epilogue to the A minor symphony gives the composition a remarkable relationship to the A major ("Italian") symphony, whose boisterous finale closes conspicuously in A minor.

Richard Wagner chose the symphony for the commemoration of the deceased composer in a concert of the Dresden Royal Orchestra on March 8, 1848, and also conducted it in London on May 26, 1855. He remarked in his autobiography that even the joyous passages of the A minor symphony seem to be affected by a basically melancholic and sorrowful mood. As late as 1879, in a conversation with Hans von Wolzogen, the editor of the *Bayreuther Blätter*, Wagner characterized Mendelssohn as a first-class landscape painter and professed his particular liking for the first movement of the A minor symphony. In fact, its opening motif is used, though altered rhythmically and harmonically, in the moving scene from the second act of *The Valkyrie* where Brünnhilde tells Siegmund of his impending doom. The same melody also appears in Heinrich Marschner's once-famous opera *Hans Heiling* (1833), which Wagner knew very well, but as the Scotch Symphony was not completed in 1833, the influence of Mendelssohn on Marschner must be ruled out. Thus the Wagnerian melody stems from both sources.

Mendelssohn

Marschner

Wagner

The Scotch Symphony is usually listed as Mendelssohn's third symphony, while actually it is his fifth and last, not counting the unpublished D major symphony of 1823. The posthumous publication of the Italian and Reformation symphonies as numbers four and five is responsible for the confusing numbering.

Music to "A Midsummer Night's Dream," Opus 61
Overture; Scherzo; Intermezzo; Notturno; Wedding March

The plays of Shakespeare attained enormous popularity in Germany because of the translation of the brothers August Wilhelm and Friedrich von Schlegel, Dorothea Tieck, her father Ludwig, and Wolf Graf Baudissin. One usually speaks of the Schlegel-Tieck translation although Ludwig Tieck (1773-1853), one of the leading figures of German Romanticism, acted chiefly as an editor. The impact of this translation on the German stage cannot be overestimated. Shakespeare became a naturalized citizen of the realm of German literature, and many lines from *Hamlet, Julius Caesar, Othello, The Tempest,* and other plays became familiar quotations. Mendelssohn grew up with this translation although he was proficient enough to read Shakespeare in English. A passage in a letter of July 7, 1826, seems to indicate that he was toying with the idea of expressing musically impressions he received from *A Midsummer Night's Dream*. "Today or tomorrow, I shall begin to dream the *Summernight's Dream*." The title of Shakespeare's play is rendered in German simply *Ein Sommernachtstraum*.

The "dream" to which Mendelssohn alluded became a musical reality as the Overture to *A Midsummer Night's Dream*, an orchestral prologue that portrays the essential elements and the setting of the play. It depicts the realm of Oberon, includes the Dance of the Clowns (Act V), realistically imitates the braying of an ass, and alludes to the frolics of Puck and the sentiments of the lovers. Having completed the Overture on August 6, 1826, Mendelssohn, then only seventeen years of age, tried it out in a four-hand piano arrangement with his sister Fanny, and also played it for Ignaz Moscheles (1794-1870), an eminent pianist and teacher of Mendelssohn. The first orchestral rendition took place in Stettin on February 20, 1827, under the direction of Karl Löwe (1796-1869), the highly regarded composer of many popular German ballades. Mendelssohn appeared on that evening in manifold capacities: as composer, pianist, and orchestra musician. In addition to the Overture, one of his concertos for two pianos was presented (with the composer and Löwe as soloists). Mendelssohn also played Weber's famous *Concertstück* in F minor, and then he took a violin and joined the orchestra for the performance of Beethoven's Ninth Symphony.

The second and third readings of the Overture took place in London on June 24 and July 13, 1829, under the composer's leadership. The parts appeared in 1832 and the score in 1835 under the significant title: *Erste Konzert-Ouvertüre zu Shakespeare's "Sommernachtstraum."* The term *concert overture* conveys a meaning similar to that which Beethoven had in mind when he wrote in one of his sketchbooks "Overture for every occasion or for concert use." This entry reflects Beethoven's intention to broaden the scope of the overture. He had written an overture to *Coriolanus,* a play by Heinrich von Collin (1771-1811), and the remark quoted above referred to an independent overture that was not tied to a theatrical performance and could be played in the concert hall whenever and wherever such a piece was needed.

Yet the overture type that Mendelssohn created and patterned after the first allegro movement of a symphony reflects clearly defined, programmatic, descriptive, and poetic notions, and constitutes for these reasons a musical category which in essence anticipates the concept of Liszt's symphonic poems. Thus Hans von Bülow, throwing a barb at Liszt, once declared Mendelssohn's concert overtures as *"his* symphonic poems."

In 1843 Mendelssohn was asked to write the incidental music for the production of *A Midsummer Night's Dream* at the Royal Theater in Berlin. Although occupied with the organization of a conservatory in Leipzig and the work on music to *Athalia* (Racine) and *Oedipus at Colonos* (Sophocles), he completed the score for Shakespeare's play in the spring of 1843, and held eleven rehearsals for the first performance, which took place in the Neue Palais in Potsdam on October 14, 1843, for an audience of invited guests. He also conducted the first three public presentations at the Royal Playhouse on October 18, 19, and 20. One of the first conductors to whom the study and direction of Mendelssohn's incidental music was assigned was Richard Wagner (1813-1883), who then (1844) officiated as Royal Conductor in Dresden.

The music that Mendelssohn wrote sixteen years after the Overture, consists of twelve numbers, instrumental, vocal, and melodramatic (instrumental background to spoken lines), and utilizes the material from the Overture. The pieces offered tonight are: the Overture, the Scherzo, the Intermezzo, the Notturno, and the Wedding March. The Scherzo preludes Act II, the dialogue between Puck and a fairy. In the Intermezzo that precedes Act III, generally interpreted as Hermia's vision of the absent Lysander, the Allegro appassionato (6/8) at the beginning abates and leads to the appearance of the six amateur actors who wish to rehearse their play. Then the character of the music changes completely (Allegro molto commodo, A major, 2/4). The Notturno follows the close of Act III when the weary lovers lie down to sleep. The E major tonality of the Overture is once more used here to depict the romantic spell of a summer night. (Wagner availed himself of the same tonality to express the enchantment of *Johannisnacht* in *Die Meistersinger.*) The Wedding March is played in Act V in connection with the festivities after the wedding of the Duke of Athens and the Queen of the Amazons.

Lauda Sion

An extraordinary event in the Roman Catholic world provided Mendelssohn with a particular commission: he was invited to contribute a composition for the six-hundredth anniversary of the feast of Corpus Christi, which was commemorated with great pomp in the Belgian city of Liège in June 1846.

This feast originated in Liège. It was St. Juliana who, in the thirteenth century, fulfilling her religious duties in a nunnery near Liège, fervently advocated the special celebration of the institution of the Holy Eucharist. She made her idea known to Robert de Thoret, bishop of Liège, and to the Archdeacon Jacques Pantaléon, who later ascended to the papal throne as Urban IV. In 1246 Robert convoked a diocesan synod to discuss and organize the liturgical proceedings for the feast. The celebration of the feast of Corpus Christi was for several years an event solely in the liturgical calendar of Liège, but in 1264 Pope Urban IV ordered the entire Catholic world to celebrate the feast of Corpus Christi on the Thursday after Trinity Sunday.

He also charged the great Catholic philosopher St. Thomas Aquinas with the writing of special texts for the office and mass of the new high feast. Thomas's contribution for the mass was the sequence *Lauda Sion Salvatorem.* The commemoration of the Holy Eucharist on Maundy Thursday falls in the saddest of all weeks, while the celebration on Thursday after Trinity Sunday is a joyful feast. St. Thomas Aquinas refers to this antithesis in the third stanza of the *Lauda Sion.*

A sequence is a rhymed religious text sung prior to the Gospel readings. A substantial literature of sequences had accumulated from the end of the ninth century, but all were discarded in the liturgical reforms of the Council of Trent (1545-1563) except four: *Lauda Sion, Victimae Paschali Laudes;*

Veni Sancte Spiritus; and the famous *Dies Irae,* which became a part of the *Requiem.* A fifth sequence was sanctioned in the eighteenth century: the revered *Stabat Mater.* It is interesting to note that the *Lauda Sion, Dies Irae,* and *Stabat Mater* were all written in the thirteenth century.

Mendelssohn received the commission in April 1845 in Frankfurt and declared his readiness to accept it. In January 1846, he informed Ignaz Moscheles that he had composed a *Lauda Sion,* but, since it was not finished at that time, this is presumably a reference to the first sections of the work. The completed score was actually dispatched to Liège on February 23, 1846. The first performance took place on June 11, 1846, in St. Martin's church at Liège. Mendelssohn was in the audience. The work was led by a wealthy amateur musician, Henri Magis-Ghysens, and the performance left much to be desired because the church authorities failed to provide funds for sufficient rehearsals. The soli were sung by members of the chorus. The work was liked, however, and a repetition took place three days later.

In his exhaustive book on Mendelssohn (1963), Eric Werner points to the two problems that confronted Mendelssohn in the composition of the Corpus Christi sequence. One was spiritual, the other material. The Protestant musician, grandson of the great Jewish philosopher Moses Mendelssohn, had to set to music a text that deals with the dogma and mysteries of the Catholic church. His Jewish background was known, and it reflects admirably on the humanitarian spirit of the church authorities in Liège that they did not bestow the commission upon a Belgian Catholic composer, but upon the Jewish-born German Protestant. They were aware, of course, that Mendelssohn outranked the contemporary Belgian composers. (A native of Liège who was to become one of the foremost musicians of the nineteenth century emerged from obscurity only at the time Mendelssohn was already working on the *Lauda Sion.* It was *César Franck,* born 1822, whose biblical elogue *Ruth* was performed in Paris in January 1846.)

Nor was Mendelssohn a novice in the field of Catholic sacred music in 1846. He had entered it in his boyhood and written a number of pieces. In 1830 he composed three pieces for the nuns of the Roman Sacré-Coeur convent, which is attached to the church Santissima Trinità dei Monti, and in 1837, as a composer of stature, he recast and published this triptych under the heading "Three Motets." Now applying his creative genius to the sequence *Lauda Sion,* Mendelssohn created one of the important works of nineteenth-century Catholic liturgical music.

The second problem that confronted Mendelssohn was the poem itself. It consists of twelve strophes in trochaic dimeter. There are some irregularities, however. Stanzas I through IX consist of six lines, of which the third and sixth lack one syllable. Some lines have extra syllables (III, 4, 5), and others are wanting one (IV, 4, 5). The tenth and eleventh stanzas have eight lines, and the last stanza has ten. Mendelssohn, however, commanded an excellent knowledge of Latin. He was the best, perhaps the only, philologer among the great masters. In order to document his remarkable ability, his tutor Karl Ludwig Heyse published his German translation of a play by Terence in the original meter, done in 1825, when Mendelssohn was sixteen years old. He possessed the skill to grapple with the intricate meters of St. Thomas Aquinas, and he succeeded splendidly.

He deviated from the given text only once—in the omission of the last four lines of the eleventh strophe, which deal with the prefigured types of the "angelic bread." The omission does not imply any critical evaluation of this passage but was motivated by musical considerations. The musical treatment of the first part of the stanza constitutes a modification of the opening of the work and effects, at the same time, the transition to the closing section. Mendelssohn presumably felt that music set to the other four lines would overextend the transitory passage.

More than twenty rhymed versions of the poem have appeared in English. The prose translation chosen for this program was made by the American Benedictine scholar Dom Matthew Britt, who wanted an expression as literal as possible and also to give it an exegetical touch.

Mendelssohn organized the work into eight sections, which flow into each other. There is only one break, between the fifth and the sixth divisions. The piece is a cantata for solo quartet (soprano, alto, tenor, and bass), four-part chorus, and orchestra. The soprano is favored with short solo passages in No. 2 and an aria in No. 6. The scoring conforms to the classical standard but is augmented by three trombones. A certain concentration of the musical contents was necessary, for the composition had to be performed within the rites of a mass. Generally speaking, Mendelssohn exercised great restraint in the application of the "learned" style of the baroque and avoided the complexities of renaissance vocal polyphony. Although there are canonic passages and imitations (Nos. 1, 2, and 4), there are no fugal sections like those in the sacred music of Cherubini, Rossini, Gounod, Verdi, and Bruckner. In the alternation between solo soprano and chorus in the third section, Mendelssohn revived the ancient technique of responsorial psalmody.

The work is unified thematically through a motif developed from the interval of the fourth. Appearing in the short orchestral prologue, it occurs in both the slow and the fast sections of the opening chorus (Exs. a and b), in the quartet (No. 4, Ex. c), in the ensuing chorus (No. 5) in two versions (Grave and Andante, Exs. d and e), in the quotations of the opening passage in No. 7 and in the final chorus (Ex. f).

The melodic coherence also achieves the spiritual unification of a work that displays a variety of musical contrasts. Note for example the juxtaposition of the canonic style of the quartet (No. 4) and the compact block harmonies proclaimed by the vocal and instrumental forces in the ensuing chorus (No. 5). Witness the striking difference between the tender and lyrical soprano aria (No. 6) and the unison exclamation of the following choral section, with its accentuated rhythms. Rudolf Werner, a German author, pointed out in a study on Mendelssohn's church music (1932) that in this section the master moves close to the emotional and spiritual sphere of the *Dies Irae* and the Last Judgment. Accepting this thought, Eric Werner draws attention to the *Rex Tremendae Majestatis* in Mozart's *Requiem*. Mendelssohn's setting of this section parallels Mozart's treatment of the *Rex Tremendae* in the adoption of the same key (G minor) and the use of the incisive dotted rhythm.

The musical treatment of the last stanza is rather in the spirit of the German Protestant composers. Compact choral harmonies are juxtaposed with orchestral figurations. In the soft ending Mendelssohn repeats the first lines of the twelfth stanza: "Jesus have mercy upon us: feed us and defend us: make us see good things in the land of the living." This is perhaps his conception of the feast he has glorified musically.

Three Motets for Women's Voices and Organ, Opus 39

These three pieces were not written consecutively. The work on numbers two and three is separated from the composition of the first item by seven years. The triptych has an interesting history. Mendelssohn was stimulated to composition on a beautiful December day in 1830, when he chanced to enter the church Santissima Trinità dei Monti above the Piazza di Spagna at the *Ave Maria*. From one of his interesting and charming Roman letters (December 20), we gather that he was not attracted by the paintings of Daniele da Volterra, Michelangelo's favorite pupil, but by the musical offerings presented by the nuns of the Sacré-Coeur convent to which the church is attached.

The music as such was "ridiculous," the organ playing "even more absurd"; nevertheless, Mendelssohn was charmed by the singing of the nuns. "They have the sweetest voices in the world," reports the enthusiastic listener, then twenty-one years old, "quite tender and touching, more especially when one of them sings the chant in her melodious voice. We are accustomed to hear the chant in a loud, harsh, and monotonous tone, but this impression is very singular; moreover, it is well known that no one is permitted to see the fair singers. I have, therefore, formed a strange resolution. I am composing something to suit their voices which I know now very well, and I shall send them the piece which I have various means to accomplish. I am quite certain that they will sing it and it will be pleasant for me to have my chant performed by persons whom I never saw, as they in turn must sing it to the *barbaro Tedesco* whom they also have never beheld."

Music for the Roman Catholic liturgy was not an unfamiliar matter to Mendelssohn; he had entered this field in his boyhood. By 1821 he had composed a *Kyrie*, a *Gloria*, a *Salve Regina*, a *Te Deum*, and a *Magnificat* (for soli, chorus and orchestra). For the French nuns Mendelssohn selected texts that are used in Advent (No. 1), in the Vesper service (No. 2), and in the period before and after Easter (No. 3). Although there is no evidence in his later correspondence that he had realized his idea as outlined to his family in the lines quoted above, he certainly did not forget these pieces and in 1837 he resolved to publish them. He was then a composer of stature and, as conductor of the Gewandhaus orchestra and *Doctor philosophiae honoris causa,* a musician of tremendous prestige.

Mendelssohn took a hard look at these pieces and eliminated the second item, replacing it with the first two verses of Psalm 113 (King James) and the first verse of Psalm 128. At the same time he recast and considerably expanded the third piece. Mendelssohn had to decide upon a title for publication. He chose to call the pieces *motets* though he knew that being of a simple texture with accompaniment they have nothing in common with the highly contrapuntal motets of the renaissance composers, nor with the complex creations of Bach. Mendelssohn's guiding factor was the sacred text, which provided a spiritual link to the true and historic motet. He was also concerned with the German translation and since he was excellently grounded in the classical languages he resolved to tackle this task himself. In a communication to the publisher Simrock he confessed that this job had posed great difficulties, but he prided himself upon the result.

The first motet, which commences with a solemn invocation, is a three-sectioned piece whose middle division displays responsorial singing. The second motet consists of two textually independent and stylistically different pieces, of which the first part also discloses a three-sectional design. The opening section is polyphonic, while the second is homophonic in nature. For the latter the organ provides a kind of harp accompaniment. The final section combines the elements of the preceding divisions. Mendelssohn called the second piece (of the second motet) *Terzetto.* Based on the first verse of Psalm 128 it is treated antiphonically. That is to say, a group of three solo voices alternates with the chorus while the organ offers a restrained accompaniment.

The third motet is, in fact, a little cantata. It begins with a pastoral Andante in which a solo quartet (two pairs of sopranos and altos) alternates with the four-voice chorus. After a duet for two sopranos, a solemn passage for alto solo announces the resurrection of Christ and leads to the final chorus, which concludes with a remarkable Alleluia passage stretching over no less than sixty-nine measures. It forms a very impressive peroration and revives a synagogal practice of old that was retained in the Gregorian chant. Viewed as a whole the triptych that Mendelssohn, the mature master, submitted to publication went far beyond the idea he had conceived in his Roman days while listening to the invisible nuns of Santissima Trinità dei Monti.

Die erste Walpurgisnacht

In Germany the night of the 30th of April is called *Walpurgisnacht* and is dedicated to Walpurgis, a female saint of the eighth century. According to an old popular tradition, it is this night when witches meet on the Brocken, also called Blocksberg, the highest peak (3600 feet) of the Harz mountains in northwestern Germany. There the witches carouse with the devils. Goethe twice treated the *Walpurgisnacht* theme: in a poem that he designated a "dramatic ballade" and in *Faust,* part one. In 1799 Goethe conceived of using the folklore of the Walpurgisnight for a "dramatic ballade." This plan was soon realized, and the poem was sent to his friend the composer Karl Friedrich Zelter (1758-1832) in August. Though the *Walpurgisnacht* scene was not originally included in *Faust,* and does not appear in the fragment published in 1790, Goethe, in February 1801, seriously considered the inclusion of it in the drama. This became known when the final version of *Faust,* part one, reached the public in 1808—one year before Mendelssohn was born. Thus, *Die erste Walpurgisnacht* (The First Walpurgisnight) as the title of the "dramatic ballade" appears to reflect this chronology.

When Goethe transmitted the poem to Zelter, whom he regarded as his musical consultant, and whose lieder he preferred to those of Beethoven and Schubert, he had this to say: "This production came from the idea that one might develop dramatic ballades in such a way that they would give the composers material for a larger vocal piece . . . " Zelter found the poem "very original" and the verses "musical and singable." He actually started to set them to music, but gave up because he felt he could not "reproduce the atmosphere of the whole thing." After a lapse of thirteen years, Zelter made a new attempt, and requested from Goethe information about the Walpurgisnight and the popular traditions. Goethe obliged, and imparted to him the following: "Now one of the investigators of the German antiquities wanted to justify the witches' and devils' ride on the Brocken, which has been known in Germany for ages, by giving it a historical origin. It seems that the German heathen priests and patriarchs, after they had been driven out of their sacred groves and Christianity had been forced on the people, retreated with their faithful disciples, to the wild and inaccessible Harz Mountains, in the early days of Spring. There, according to ancient custom, they offered up their prayers and their fires to the incorporeal God of Heaven and earth. To protect themselves against spying armed missionaries, they thought it good to disguise several of their number, in order to frighten away their superstitious opponents; and, thus protected by devils' masks, they carried out the purist service of God . . ."*

This commentary was of no avail, and Zelter abandoned the project. We should be grateful for his decision because it is doubtful that Mendelssohn would have composed the poem if Zelter, his respected teacher, had already done so. Mendelssohn would have been reluctant to place himself in a position of competing or even outdoing him.

We know only approximately when Mendelssohn took up the composition of the ballade. This, according to a letter to his sister Fanny Hensel (dated Rome, February 22, 1831), was an "old favorite plan" of his. On the first leg of an extended journey to Austria, Italy, Switzerland, Paris, and England (1830-1832), he visited Goethe in Weimar and conceivably determined to realize "the old favorite plan." After a substantial part of the composition was completed, Mendelssohn informed Goethe: "What has been occupying me almost exclusively for several weeks is the music to Your Excellency's poem entitled *Die erste Walpurgisnacht*: I want to compose it with orchestral

* Eric Werner, *Mendelssohn, A New Image of the Composer and His Age* (London, 1963), p. 202.

accompaniment, as a sort of grand cantata . . . I do not know whether I shall succeed, but I feel how great the task is and with what concentration and awe I must undertake it."

He received a very encouraging reply, and Goethe included comments on the poem. Felix also revealed the new project to Fanny in the aforementioned letter: "Listen and wonder! Since I left Vienna, I have partly composed Goethe's *First Walpurgisnight,* but I have not yet had the courage to write it down. The composition has assumed a form, it has become a grand cantata, with full orchestra, and may turn out well." The doubt expressed in the letter to Goethe has been dispelled in the optimistic lines to Fanny. He expressed himself in a similar vein in a letter to his friend Eduard Devrient (1801-1877), actor and singer, who had undertaken the part of Christ in the historic Berlin performance of the St. Matthew Passion on March 11, 1829, conducted by Mendelssohn. "I have written a grand piece of music which will probably impress the public at large—the *First Walpur- gisnight* of Goethe. I began it simply because it pleased me and inspired me. I see that is it quite suitable for a great concert piece, and you must sing the bearded pagan priest at my first subscription concert in Berlin . . ."

The *Walpurgisnight* is frequently mentioned in Mendelssohn's correspond- ence from Italy. However, Rome offered so many distractions, particularly on beautiful days, that he once cried out for bad weather to be able to concentrate on his work. Taking advantage of a spell of bad weather in Naples, he took up the *Walpurgisnight* with zeal. "This thing," he wrote on April 27, 1831, "had interested me more and more so that I use every free minute to work on it." From Milan he reported to his family (July 14, 1831): "I tackled the eternal *Walpurgisnight* with *rabbia* (fury), to finish the thing. It will surely be ready tomorrow except for the overture. I do not know yet whether I shall compose a great symphony or a short "Spring transition" (*Frühlingseinleitung*). The first person for whom he played the work was Carl Mozart (1784-1858), the master's elder son, who was an Austrian civil servant in Milan. His enthusiasm for the composition affected Mendelssohn so that the "familiar matters caused him fun once more."

Felix announced the completion of the overture from Paris on February 4, 1832, and one week later he reported that an introduction "in which it thaws and Spring arrives was also done." At the same time, *the seven numbers* of the score were overhauled a little. After a private performance in Berlin on October 16, 1832, Mendelssohn presented the *Walpurgisnight* on January 10, 1833, in the Singakademie. Both the poet and Mendelssohn's teacher had passed away in the preceding months: Goethe in March and Zelter in May of 1832. The performance failed to satisfy Mendelssohn, and he withdrew the score to revise it later. Seven years elapsed before he concerned himself seriously with this task. Broaching this subject in a letter to his friend Carl Klingemann in London he once more indicated his plan to fashion the *Walpurgisnight* as a symphony with a choral finale. For this idea, he confes- sed, he had lacked the courage because he felt that three movements would be too long for an introduction; an introduction alone would not be suffi- cient. Now he wanted to take up the old plan and have the *Walpurgisnacht* preceded by three symphonic movements and then submit the piece to the public.

He reiterated this idea in a letter to his mother on November 28, 1832, and told her on December 11 that: "The *Walpurgisnight* will be resurrected, but garbed with a different habit than that before which was lined too warmly with trombones and was somewhat crude for the singers. For these reasons, I was compelled to rewrite the score from A to Z and to insert two new arias (?) and wrestle with the remaining tailor work. But if the thing will not turn out to be alright with me, I swear, to give it up for the rest of my life."

Testifying eloquently to Mendelssohn's self-critical attitude, this letter also explains the discrepancy in the numbering of the two versions. According to Mendelssohn (in a letter of February 13, 1832), the original version contained seven numbers while the final version, not counting the overture, is comprised of nine. Thus the "insertion of two new arias" would account for the total of nine. At the same time, the "two new arias" would imply the composition of music to an additional text. This was obviously not the case, because Mendelsson had set the entire ballade to music. Consequently, Mendelssohn's remark about the "arias" refers to the remodelling of portions originally projected for the chorus and were now to be sung by soloists. These passages are short and the soloists do not appear as sharply delineated dramatic characters, but represent the people portrayed by: an old woman (alto); the Druides (tenor, bass, and baritone); the Christians (tenor). In the process of revising the score, the original numbering of the individual pieces was also changed.

Mendelssohn finally abandoned the idea of a symphonic cantata. He finished the revision of the *Walpurgisnight* at the beginning of 1843, and set out to compose the incidental music to *A Midsummer Night's Dream*. But he lost no time in bringing the *Walpurgisnight* before the public. The first performance took place in Leipzig on February 2, 1843, one month after the premiere of *The Flying Dutchman* in Dresden. Berlioz, who attended the last rehearsal, "felt ... spellbound by wonder from the first moment through the beautiful timbre of the voices, the intelligence of the singers, the precision and verve of the orchestra, and above all by the marvelous composition." Mendelssohn and Berlioz had not seen each other since the days in Rome (1831). The enthusiastic Frenchman asked for Mendelssohn's baton, who in turn requested that of Berlioz. Berlioz received "Mendelssohn's scepter," and sent him on the following day "his heavy piece of oak wood." Mendelssohn conducted the *Walpurgisnight* in London on July 8, 1844. It was received "with incredible enthusiasm." *The First Walpurgisnight* was also presented in Dresden on July 28, 1844, by Richard Wagner, and published in the same year as Opus 60.

Mendelssohn was strongly attracted to both the spiritual and material elements of the poem. We have two pertinent comments by Goethe regarding the spiritual component: in the letter to Zelter of 1812 (quoted above) and in the communication sent to Mendelssohn upon partial completion of the composition (1831). At that time Goethe said about the poem: "Really, it [the poem] is intended symbolically. For, in world history, it must occur again and again that something old, well-established, well-tried, and comforting is pushed aside, and, if not extirpated, cramped into the least possible space, by innovations that crop up. The intermediate period, where hate still can, and does have its countereffect, is presented here pregnantly enough, and a joyous, indestructible enthusiasm flames up once more in glory and truth."

Two different spheres are projected in the poem: that of bigotry and that of enlightenment. Eric Werner in his exhaustive and absorbing Mendelssohn biography refers to the poem: "born of the spirit of the Enlightenment, the work surpasses the limits of superficial Rationalism, and in its own way, foreshadows the ideas of Nietzsche. It is a humanistic poem in the deepest sense." Like his forebears Moses and Abraham Mendelssohn, Felix upheld the ideals of humanism.

The lines which dealt with supernatural characters, witches, werewolves, and she-dragons and the horrors of Walpurgisnight must have kindled Mendelssohn's spark of fancy. He had been familiar with these elements of German romanticism ever since he attended the première of Weber's *Freischütz* in 1821. The description of nature and landscape in Goethe's poem was irresistibly appealing to Mendelssohn, the drawer and painter. He took musical and poetic liberty and added another scene of nature to the poem by prefacing it with an overture portraying bad weather (Winter) and the transition to Spring. This was a stroke of genius. The transitional section established the mood expressed in the opening lines of the poem, and at the same time provided a strong effect for the entrance of the human voice and the chorus.

The overture was completed in Paris in the Winter of 1832. Just as the melancholy of Scotland puts its stamp on the A minor symphony ("Scotch"), and the vivid life of Italy is mirrored in the Italian symphony, so the overture to the *Walpurgisnacht,* in this writter's opinion, reflects a severe storm of catastrophic proportions which Mendelssohn witnessed in Switzerland in 1831.

The cantata including the overture consists of ten numbers organized in the manner of an operatic finale: all numbers are connected and follow each other without a break. The harmonic current flows from A minor to C major (conclusion). There are no pages filled with "learned music," fugues or contrapuntal complexities. The piece is imbued with a distinct motoric quality. There is no Adagio section and the music constantly moves evenly in three Andante maestoso portions in which the Druid priest speaks. The core of the piece is undoubtedly the chorus (No. 6) which depicts realistically the happenings on the Blocksberg (Brocken) during the Walpurgisnight, for which the owls provide the music. Mendelssohn employs here a rich orchestral palette with piccolo, trombones, bass drum, and cymbals, and spiced the music with biting dissonances. He first hesitated to use the big drum and piccolo, but felt "that at any rate a big noise has to be made"; and if he would dispense with the piccolo, he would be the only composer who "composed the Blocksberg" without piccolo. He finally decided to employ both the big drum and the small flute, but only for the dark side of the story. They are excluded from the apotheosis in the shining C major—the hymnic praise of the power of light.

MENNIN, Peter, *Fantasia for String Orchestra*

Peter Mennin, born in 1923, studied at the Oberlin Conservatory and Eastman School of Music, where he received a Ph.D. in 1947. In the same year he was awarded a Guggenheim Fellowship. Mennin taught at the Juilliard School of Music from 1947 to 1958. He was then appointed director of the Peabody Conservatory in Baltimore. In 1963 he became president of the Juilliard School of Music. Mennin is one of America's leading composers. The impressive list of his works includes seven symphonies, concertos for violin, for piano, chamber music pieces, choral works, and songs.

Mennin's *Fantasia* for string orchestra, composed in 1946, reverts to the late 16th century instrumental forms of contrapuntal texture. It comprises two movements, a canzona and a toccata, which are contrasted in tempo, color, and mood. Historically speaking, the multi-sectioned canzona of the Renaissance is one of the preforms of the fugue. Its imitation technique and organization stem from the polyphonic motet of the 16th century. Mennin's canzona reveals only two themes which appear in an altered form by means of increased and diminished note values. The themes are given fugal treatment by the muted string orchestra. There is a dynamic climax when the two ideas appear, projected without mutes, in contrapuntal combination. After a gradual diminuendo the piece fades away with a brief reference to the opening theme in the basses.

The canzona is contrasted sharply with the energetic toccata that is not, however, a specimen in the manner of Buxtehude or Bach. The 18th century toccata is a rather rhapsodic piece with a conspicuous virtuoso quality. This particular trait provided the point of departure for composers of the 19th and 20th centuries. One may recall Schumann's fast C major toccata (Opus 7) and Debussy's toccata that concludes the suite *Pour le piano* in *moto perpetuo* fashion.

Mennin's toccata goes back to 16th and 17th century models which, as Egon Kenton has demonstrated are not rhapsodic, but organized on a plan. Mennin's piece is built on two themes. The first is stated in unison, then developed and repeated in the bass. The second theme is treated fugally, after which themes I and II appear in augmentation in a lyrical passage. After a development we hear a passage of the opening section as well as the lyrial episode with the augmentation of the fugal subject. Thus the piece discloses the traits of the sonata design. Utilizing the opening idea, the coda completes the circle with forcefulness.

MONTEVERDI, Claudio (1567-1643),
"Lamento d'Arianna"

Claudio Monteverdi was a boy of fifteen when his early creative efforts, a group of sacred songs for three voices, reached the public in 1582. He was only sixteen when a collection of *Madrigali spirituali* was brought out in 1583. In the following year his *First Book of Madrigals* appeared. Five others followed between 1590 and 1614. As a composer of highest repute, he was appointed *maestro della musica* in 1603 to Vincenzo Gonzaga, the art-loving duke of Mantua. One of Monteverdi's duties was the composition of operas and his first fruit in this new field was *Orfeo*, in 1607.

The next opera was *Arianna* (1608), which met with resounding success. Monteverdi's poetic collaborator was Ottavio Rinuccini, who had written the libretto of Jacopo Peri's *Dafne* (1597), the first opera, whose score is lost. The same misfortune befell *Arianna*, for which, incidentally, Peri had supplied recitatives. Only one portion of the opera has come down to us, the "Lament of Arianna"—a piece of melodic beauty, harmonic boldness, and dramatic expression. A chronicler of the time relates that the discriminating audience was so deeply moved by the lament that "none of the ladies remained without tears." The composer decided later to convert the piece, which originally had an instrumental accompaniment, into a five-voice madrigal which he included in the *Sixth Book of Madrigals* in 1614. This version, which comprises four sections, differs from the original in the harmonic treatment and the insertion of striking dissonances.

Madrigali guerrieri e amorosi
Altri canti d' amor; Hor che' el ciel; Così sol d' una chiara fonte; Ardo avvampo

Claudio Monteverdi entitled this eighth book of his madrigals published in 1638, "madrigals of war and love." Some of the verses he selected for this series had great significance at the time of their publication, the second decade of the Thirty Years' War (1618-1648). This circumstance may also explain his intended dedications to Emperor Ferdinand II, a great music lover, who died in 1637. His son Ferdinand III was a professionally trained musician and composer, and was known as such among his contemporaries. Yet he had to continue, politically, spiritually, and militarily where his father left off, and take to the sword.

Monteverdi realized the difficult mission that his crowned fellow composer had to accomplish. This is clearly reflected in the first madrigal, the poet of which is not known. This madrigal is a hymn to Emperor Ferdinand III in the *stile concitato,* which the composer discussed in the elaborate preface to the *Madrigali guerrieri e amorosi.* The "excited" style was to complement the expressions of temperance and humility, and here Monteverdi underlines his claim to having discovered "the style of warlike expression" that he applied to the war madrigals. In contrast to Monteverdi's earlier books of five-voice madrigals, the seventh (1620) and eighth books contain pieces for six and eight voices with orchestra accompaniment; this new arrangement approaches the cantata.

The opening item of the madrigals of war and love, *Altri canti d'amor,* is for six voices, strings (violins, violas, viola da gamba, and bass viol), and figured bass accompaniment. Prefaced by a short instrumental introduction, it discloses the following disposition: a three-voice choral setting; a six-part setting with programmatic instrumental effects in the *stile concitato;* a bass solo, *Tu cui tessuta han di Cesare,* in both recitative and arioso manner (coloraturas) with discreet accompaniment; and the entry of the entire ensemble. This last section is a modification of the first. It will be noted that the poem refers not only to Mars but also to his female counterpart Bellona, the goddess of war.

The contrast of tutti and soli, characteristic of the cantata, is evident in *Hor che' el ciel e la terra* (from Petrarch's *Canzoniere*) in the antithesis of nature, calmness, and beauty, on the one hand, and the fury of war on the other. *Così sol d'una chiara fonte,* for six voices with violin and figured bass accompaniment, comes from the second part of Petrarch's sonnet. The spiritual connection is obvious.

Ardo, avvampo, for eight voices with violin and figured bass accompaniment, also displays the two-sectional design. The first is in triple time and is characterized by overpowering realism and sound. The element of contrast is represented by the comparison of a destructive conflagration with the fire burning in the human heart.

"Nigra sum"; "Tempro la cetra"; "Con che soavità"

Monteverdi's circumstances changed considerably before his publication of the *Sixth Book of Madrigals* in 1614 because of his appointment as *maestro di capella* at Saint Mark's. He remained at the helm of the musical establishment of this church until his death in 1643. His productivity during the thirty-year tenure in the service of the *Serenissima Repubblica* encompassed music for the church, the stage, and also for the proficient amateur singer (madrigals). The fifth book marked the transition from renaissance to the baroque madrigal by means of the introduction of the figured bass accompaniment. This new setup approached the cantata. This stylistic change appears more pronounced in the seventh book of 1620, from which two outstanding pieces are examined here.

Monteverdi entitled the seventh book *Concerto.* This is presumably less a reference to the original meaning of the word, derived from *conserere* (to join together) which implied playing together, but rather indicates that the book is comprised of instrumentally accompanied pieces. Monteverdi in preceding madrigal books defined the accompaniment as *concertato nel clavicembalo.* The seventh book actually includes madrigals for one, two, three, four, and six voices with figured bass and even with orchestra accompaniment.

The first piece, *"Tempro la cetra,"* serves as a prologue. Its four stanzas are framed by a sinfonia and separated from each other by a ritornello. The material of the ritornello is taken from the sinfonia, which is considerably expanded at the conclusion.

"Che soavità" ranks as one of Monteverdi's finest achievements on account of its melodic sweetness, the novelty of its orchestral treatment, and its richness of colors. The orchestration is in some respects reminiscent of that of *Orfeo,* although the size of the orchestra and the assortment of the instruments as employed in the madrigal are smaller than that of the opera. The instrumental body of the madrigal is organized in three groups, the first employing bass lutes (*chitarone*) and harpsichord, the second, violins and violas, and the third, violas da gamba, bass, and organ. The prevalence of dark "colors" is conspicuous. Ingeniously devised, the score is unquestionably ahead of its time and offers, according to Hans Ferdinand Redlich,

the first example of orchestral writing in modern coloristic sense.

"Nigra sum," based on the Song of Solomon, chapters 1 and 2, was included in a volume of sacred music, masses, motets, etc., which was published in 1610 in Venice. It bears a dedication to Pope Paul V, a member of the famous Borghese family, who ascended to the throne in 1605. *"Nigra sum"* is the only item for one voice in this collection. It clearly reveals the influence of the Florentine innovators and their melodious declamatory style which, first appearing in the fourth madrigal book of 1604, became an essential feature in Monteverdi's musical language.

MOZART, Wolfgang Amadeus (1756-1791)
Adagio in E major, K. 261, for Violin and Orchestra

The autograph of this piece bears the heading *Adagio. Di Amadeo Wolfgango Mozart* 1776. Mozart wrote it for Antonio Brunetti, the soloist of the Salzburg orchestra, who was supposed to play the composer's violin concerto in A major (K. 219, 1775) but found its Adagio too long and elaborate. Mozart showed his good will toward his colleague by consenting to write another movement for Brunetti. The replacement piece is considerably smaller than the original Adagio (55 compared to 128 measures), but the process of simplification did not entail a change of style or lessening of the musical standard. Although Mozart refused to insert it permanently into the A major concerto, this sensitive piece adorned with delicate musical ideas set against a discreet orchestral accompaniment merits well its separate rendition.

Rondo in C major, K. 373, for Violin and Orchestra

Like the Adagio in E major, the Rondo for violin in C major is a composition rarely included in the usual concert repertory. Dated April 2, 1781, Vienna, it is the last work Mozart created in his line of duty as an employee of the archbishop of Salzburg, Count Hieronymus Colloredo. It was written for Brunetti, who played it in Vienna on April 8, 1781, at the home of Count Rudolf Colloredo, father of the archbishop. Simple in texture and provided with a charming orchestral accompaniment, it gives the soloist good opportunities for the display of his talents and pleases the audience through the imaginative use of the attractive main theme.

Six German Dances, K. 509

As early as the era of enlightened absolutism under Emperor Joseph II (1780-1790), Vienna was a fertile breeding ground of dance music. Around the turn of the eighteenth century and later, Viennese composers wrote a prodigious amount of it. In terms of musical history these two eras coincided with the glorious period of the Viennese classical school. Haydn, Mozart, Beethoven, and their lesser contemporaries, who occupied conductors' posts at the court theaters and important churches, did not consider the task of furnishing music for the ballroom either beneath their official dignity or detrimental to their artistic prestige. They did not run this risk because, as Carl Ferdinand Pohl, Haydn's biographer, once aptly put it, they set their pens in motion for the imperial dance halls, which august purpose a priori ennobled their dance music. Emperor Joseph favored masked balls as a means of bringing the upper strata of society together with the less privileged classes, and the court ball administration made a point of commissioning the ball music from renowned composers. Either commissioned or written in the line of duty, the dance music of Haydn, Mozart, and Beethoven was considered marketable by both authors and publishers. These ballroom dances of the classical composers were scored for a small band, and in some instances for violins (I and II) and bass only. Piano arrangements of the music were brought out in the wake of the carnival at which these pieces were played for the first time in the Redoutensaal. This last is not a hall of large dimensions and serves now as a branch theater of the Vienna State Opera for the staging of Mozart's operas.

Mozart's main duty as imperial chamber composer was not the creation of music for the court chapel or concerts, but the contribution of dances for the court masked balls. This modest task happily met a particular trait of his personality, for he was an enthusiastic dancer. Putting aside the very early dance pieces (many minuets) and taking into account the output of his Viennese years, Mozart penned one hundred dances in 3/4 time and twenty-eight in 2/4 time. But sly publishers, taking advantage of Mozart's fame, put his name to dance collections of dubious authenticity.

The *German Dances* (K. 509) originated in February, 1787, in Prague. Mozart had gone to the Bohemian capital to conduct *The Marriage of Figaro* and to appear in a concert for which he wrote the D major symphony known as the "Prague" Symphony (K. 504). His stay in Prague coincided with the carnival, and this circumstance led to the composition of these dances. They were a contribution to the balls held by the Prague aristocracy, a group in which Mozart had many admirers.

The *Deutscher Tanz* (German dance), often called a *"Deutscher,"* is a forerunner of the waltz. In contrast to the Viennese usage, Mozart employed for these dances a full symphony orchestra with pairs of flutes, oboes, clarinets, bassoons, horns, trumpets, kettledrums, and the string complement without violas. Each dance has an alternativo, (trio) and is connected with the following dance through a bridge passage that also functions as a modulatory agent, for the dances are in different keys (D, G, E flat, F, A, C). There is an extended coda with a remarkable crescendo passage, which must have driven the dancers into a kind of frenzy.

Three German Dances, K. 605

This charming group of three German dances was written in 1791. For two (D major and G major) we have the exact date: Mozart entered them as *2 Teutsche* (two German dances) on February 12, 1791, in his own thematic catalogue. The third dance, known as "The Sleigh Ride," appears with the other two in an old manuscript, which caused Köchel to combine the three under number 605. However "The Sleigh Ride" differs markedly from the other two in design and particularly in orchestral treatment.

The D major dance is scored for flutes, oboes, bassoons, trumpets, kettledrums, and strings (violin and basses); the G major item employs the same woodwind combination, horns, and strings. (Note the exotic quality of the trio of the G major piece.) The third dance came into being for a special occasion for which information is lacking. In addition to a piccolo, oboes, bassoons, trumpets, kettledrums, and strings (without violas), the score calls for little bells in five different tunings and two post horns. This simple brass instrument was used by the mail coachmen to announce their arrival in the villages and towns on their routes. Mozart had elevated it into the sphere of art music in the "Posthorn Serenade" of 1779 (K. 320). The sound of the posthorn invokes nostalgic feelings: Gustav Mahler ingeniously used it in his third symphony for a sentimental folk melody blown backstage.

Mozart may have portrayed childhood memories in this dance and the melody of the trio certainly points to the Alpine *ländler.*

After repeating the opening section, Mozart deviates considerably from the common dance pattern by appending an extended coda. It opens with trumpet flourishes and restates the *gemütliche* melody of the trio with the sleigh bells which then fade away with the sound of the trumpet in the distance. Mozart, the mature man, has left the ballroom and has gone back in his thoughts and feelings to past days.

Divertimento in D major, K. 131
Allegro; Adagio; Minuetto—Trio I—Trio II—Trio III; Allegretto;
Minuetto—Trio I—Trio II; Adagio—Allegro molto

The divertimento in D major, K. 131, scored for two violins, two violas, bass, flute, oboe, bassoons, and four horns, originated, according to the autograph, in Salzburg in June 1772. It is not known who commissioned the work. One could term it a study in orchestral diversity. Mozart, then sixteen years of age, had already acquired considerable experience in matters of orchestration: he had composed no less than thirty symphonies (of which four are lost) and had written five operas, among them the voluminous score of *Ascanio in Alba* (Milan, 1771), which runs through almost five hundred pages. The divertimento heard tonight combines both orchestral and chamber music with a distinct preference for the horn. This clearly points to certain local conditions and the availability of fine players, a circumstance that Mozart skillfully took into account.

The instrumental opulence of the opening Allegro is contrasted with a gentle Adagio for strings. The following Minuet displays a gradual increase in the sonorities: first, it employs the strings only; the first trio is a horn quartet; the second (G major), a woodwind terzet; and the third (D minor), a septet for all the wind instruments. The ensuing Allegretto is a piece for strings, flute, and oboe. The second Minuet matches the first in instrumental diversity: flute, violins, and bass cooperate in the first trio (G major); oboe, violas, and bass in the second (A major); the coda employs the full instrumental complement. The spirited finale (4/4) is prefaced by a slow introduction, in which the horns are dominant once more. The movement closes surprisingly with an extended, very speedy section in 3/8 time. Thus Mozart even provided the listener with an entirely unexpected encore.

Divertimento for Strings in D major, K. 136
Allegro; Andante; Presto

The contribution of entertainment and dinner music was a frequent task of the eighteenth-century composer, an obligation that did not tarnish his artistic reputation. The musician who did not hold a church position was economically dependent on a court or the patronage of the wealthy aristocracy—such was the relationship of Haydn to Prince Esterházy, for whose court Haydn had to furnish a vast amount of music. Austrian, Bohemian, and Hungarian noblemen employed small bands that played in their palaces in Vienna and Prague during the winter, and their castles in the country in the spring and summer. The primary obligations of the musicians were not always of an artistic nature: the house personnel of an aristocrat sometimes included only musical servants, valets, and secretaries, who had to be proficient enough on their instruments to play in the princely orchestra.

The social conditions that prevailed in the archbishopric of Salzburg in the 1770s were of decisive influence on Mozart's creative work and account for a large number of his compositions that are usually defined as "social music." Such music was to be played on social occasions in aristocratic circles or at festivities arranged by wealthy burghers. This musical category includes the divertimento, serenade, notturno, and even piano concertos, which Mozart wrote in Salzburg for proficient aristocratic ladies.

What is a divertimento? If we begin with the meaning of the Italian word *divertimento* (pleasure), we attach the term to a type of music, which pleases and entertains. This quality obviously precludes music in the minor mood and the application of contrapuntal devices, or, in short, "learned music." No exactly-defined formal design was attached to the term "divertimento." Haydn enumerated more than 260 divertimenti in his list of compositions, called *"Entwurfkatalog,"* but among them are sonatas, trios, and quartets with a varying number of movements. The number of movements in the classical divertimento ranges from two to eight. Mozart wrote divertimenti for three, four, five, and more instruments: for strings, for wind instruments (wood and brass), for many combinations of strings and winds, and even joined together two flutes, five trumpets, and four kettledrums.

The *divertimento* (K. 136) was composed in Salzburg during the winter months of 1772, after Mozart returned from his second Italian journey. It belongs to a set of three (K. 136, 137, and 138) for which, however, the denomination is not authenticated because the title *divertimento* on the autograph of all three pieces is not by Mozart's hand. Yet Köchel's classification *Divertimento for two violins, viola, and bass* became, so to speak, official and was retained in the latest edition (1964). From the scoring that indicates the fourth part with *basso*, not with *violoncello*, we can assume that Mozart had an orchestral execution in mind—although Mozart scholars differ on this point.

The Italian influence is evident in the three-movement design, like that of the Italian type of symphony, and in the lightness and songfulness of the Andante. The spirited finale and its contrapuntal episode in particular point to the symphonies of Joseph Haydn and his brother Michael. The latter was a member of the Salzburg court chapel from 1762 until 1806, and Mozart knew his works well. Alfred Einstein regarded this piece and, of course, its two sister works as symphonies for strings, composed by Mozart for the impending third trip to Italy, in anticipation that symphonies might be demanded from him.

Divertimento in D major, K. 334

Allegro; Andante (Theme with Variations); Minuetto; Adagio; Minuetto—Trio I, Trio II; Rondo: Allegro

The divertimento in D major was composed in Salzburg in the summer of 1779. Mozart called it *Musique vom Robinig*. Georg Josef Robinig von Rothenfeld was a respected Salzburg businessman, scythe manufacturer, and arsenic producer, whose son and three daughters were friends of Wolfgang and his sister Nannerl. The Mozarts were welcome guests both in Robinig's Salzburg home and his spacious house in the suburb of Gnigl. The composition of this divertimento was prompted by a social affair arranged by Robinig, and the piece was intended for an "open air" reading.

"Divertimento" means "entertainment," and the divertimento as a musical category emerged in the classical period—along with the serenade and the cassation—as an important form of music in a light vein for social occasions. It was the popular correlate of chamber music and the symphony. There were divertimentos or serenades for small ensembles and some with orchestral scoring and of considerable length. Generally speaking, the divertimento was a piece of several movements of simple texture, devoid of contrapuntal complexities, in the major mode. These characteristics appear logical, for the minor mode and counterpoint seem to preclude entertainment. Mozart deviated from this tradition only once, in the C minor serenade for wind instruments (K. 388), which was written in Vienna. We lack, however, any information about the circumstances that caused Mozart to abandon the gay spirit of the serenade for a more serious mood.

The divertimento was not written for orchestra, but for single players: that is, the part of each instrument was usually played by one musician. However, as compared with the eighteenth century, the technique of orchestral playing has achieved such perfection today that the rendition of classical divertimentos by chamber orchestras is warranted.

The D major piece is scored for strings and two horns and comprises six movements. The first Allegro, which follows the sonata design, shows concerto-like violin passages and radiates playfulness. Yet the ensuing Andante in D minor, a series of six variations, definitely leaves the divertimento mood. The first two variations are display pieces for the first violins; the third accentuates the rhythmical element; the fourth, in D major, places the horns in the foreground. Rhythmical diversity is the characteristic of the fifth variation, which re-establishes the minor key; and the first violin once more reasserts itself in the sixth, to which a short coda is attached.

The *ländler* melody of the first minuet is contrasted with the virtuoso treatment of the first violin in the trio. The trio is a display piece, which ties in with the glittering violin passages of the first Allegro. Devoid of any dance qualities, these runs and broken chords in sixteenth-notes are a far cry from the customary trio. The minuet has become a favored encore item of recitalists and is always heartily welcomed by the audience. The fourth movement, an Adagio in A major, could be called a coloratura aria for violin. The following minuet has two trios in the minor mode (D minor and B minor), which cast dark clouds over the serene atmosphere. It it interesting psychologically that Mozart chose a dance movement for this deviation, which the listener hardly expects. But the dark colors of this episode are swept away by the buoyancy of the melodious and delightful Rondo finale.

Concerto for Flute, Harp, and Orchestra in C major, K. 299
Allegro; Andantino; Allegro

Dissatisfied with the conditions prevailing in Salzburg, Mozart quit his position with the musical establishment of the archbishopric in the fall of 1777 and, accompanied by his mother, journeyed via Munich, Augsburg, and Mannheim to Paris in quest of a more suitable employment than the one offered in his home town. When he arrived in the French capital in March 1778 he was faced with an unfavorable situation. Musical circles were absorbed in a tug of war that pitted the champions of a French-style opera, as represented by the creations of Gluck, against the partisans of the Italian opera. The favorite of the latter was Niccolò Piccini, drawn into this "querelle célèbre" against his wishes and convictions. Mozart managed to avoid this controversy, which ruled out any possibility of his receiving an operatic commission.

Instead, he tried to make connections with influential people who might be helpful in securing a position. Thus he renewed his acquaintance with Friedrich Melchior Grimm (1723-1807), a German publicist, who had settled in Paris in 1747 and had befriended the Mozarts on their first visit to Paris in 1763. As editor of a newsletter that dealt with philosophical, literary, and aesthetic topics, he knew Rousseau, Diderot, and other prominent intellectuals and moved in influential artistic circles.

Grimm introduced Mozart to the Duke of Guines, a music-loving diplomat who achieved notoriety by his conduct as French ambassador in London and had to be recalled. Nevertheless, the duke stood in high favor with Queen Marie Antoinette, an Austrian princess who had known Mozart since her girlhood when little Wolfgang as a lad of six had played for the imperial family in Vienna. Leopold Mozart, who followed closely from Salzburg Wolfgang's movements in Paris, implored him to "do his best to gain the friendship of the duke." The queen was expecting a child and the practical-minded Mozart senior, thinking of the festivities in connection with the impending event wrote his son, "You may get something to do and make your fortune." Leopold was thoroughly mistaken, for after the child was born Wolfgang failed to receive a commission.

Meanwhile, he realized that he could gain the good will of the duke by writing a composition for flute and harp; the duke was a very good flutist and his daughter played the harp "magnificently." But Mozart did not like these instruments. Dr. Josef Frank, a renowned Viennese physician who was for a time Mozart's piano student, relates that the master detested both flute and harp. Nonetheless he suppressed these inhibitions and wrote a concerto to meet the circumstances. In acquiescence to the nature of the instruments and the taste of both the performers and the audience, the concerto is cheerful. Devoid of contrapuntal complexities, it abounds in beautiful melodies. Designed to please the aristocratic French society of the eighteenth century, it has not lost its charming qualities with the passage of time.

Mozart and the Clavier Concerto

Mozart's fertility in the concerto field left not only a large number of master-pieces to posterity, but also was of great historic importance. He created the formal structure of the modern concerto, which combines the principle of the baroque concerto whith the concept of the classical sonata form and symphonic orchestration. The clavier concerto is a child of the violin concerto: the latter an Italian achievement. In particular it was the ingenious and prolific experimenter Antonio Vivaldi (1678-1741) who created a clearly defined formal pattern that served not only as a model to the baroque com-posers but also as a source from which the classical sonata design was to evolve.

Bach was a very diligent student of Vivaldi's concertos and, since they were not available in score, he took the trouble to arrange nine violin concertos (for one, two, and four solo parts) by the Italian for harpsichord and organ for his personal use and pleasure. These arrangements were piano scores adapted to the style of keyboard setting and technique. Yet the lasting fruit of Bach's Vivaldi studies are his own violin concertos, of which only three (one for two violins) are extant, while others have come down to us in the transcriptions for harpsichord and string orchestra. Lack of time and personal circumstances may have prevented Bach from cultivating the piano concerto; nevertheless the converted violin pieces for harpsichord stimulated the interest and creative abilities of his splendidly trained sons.

Wilhelm Friedemann (1710-1784), Carl Philipp Emanuel (1714-1788), and Johann Christian (1735-1782) were outstanding performers at the keyboard but moved musically in different directions. Wilhelm Friedemann was deeply rooted in his father's style, while Philipp Emanuel was given to experiments. The latter wrote close to fifty concertos for one and two harpsichords. These works follow the firmly established three-movement pattern, employ horns and flutes in the orchestra, and reveal a predilection for dynamic contrasts, sudden change of forte and piano, and a rather dramatic juxtaposition of solo and tutti. This attitude is significant of the north German type of piano concerto: the basic conception of the relationship between tutti and solo is not that of coexistence, as indicated by the original meaning of *concerto*, as derived from *conserere* ("to play together"), but rather that of competition, as expressed by *concertare*.

Johann Christian Bach, who in Italy as Giovanni Cristiano completely forsook paternal traditions and enthusiastically adopted the new developing classical style, emancipated himself from the north German type of the harpsichord concerto. Preferring the modern hammerklavier to the cembalo, he discarded the contrapuntal-polyphonic setting of the baroque in favor of that simple, transparent, and melodious style which swept Europe after the eighteenth century had passed its halfway mark. Logically, he cast aside the principle of competition in the concerto: soloist and orchestra don't oppose each other, but alternate peacefully. Johann Christian Bach's influence on the young Mozart was considerable.

Another fertile ground for the cultivation of the piano concerto was Vienna, where momentous developments in the symphonic and chamber music field took place. Vienna, with its large Italian colony, was always open to southern influences. However the prominent Viennese composers, Matthias Georg Monn (1717-1750), Georg Christoph Wagenseil (1715-1777), Leopold Hoffmann (1730-1792, whom Mozart was to succeed as conductor at St. Stephen's), and Johann Baptist Wanhal (1739-1813), all predecessors and important contemporaries of Haydn, developed both the symphony and the concerto independently. The Viennese concerto type upheld the three-movement design with the sonata pattern in the first Allegro and a minuet as finale. It displays arpeggios, diatonic scales, and richly ornamented melodies, elements that anticipate Mozart's pianistic style. The tutti shares the thematic elaboration with the solo instrument. The concerto (concerto grosso and solo concerto) was the chief type of ensemble music in the baroque period, and was supplanted by the classical symphony. This development logically affected the function and importance of the concerto. Mozart's historic mission was to adapt the concerto, this heritage of the baroque, to the changing style of the time and to create a framework that secured its future development.

The first clavier concertos that came to little Wolfgang's attention in the paternal home were those of the Viennese Georg Christoph Wagenseil; however the young Mozart received stronger impressions and stimulating suggestions during the long journey from 1763 to 1766 and the extended sojourn in Paris and London. In the French capital he was attracted by the works of a German composer, Johann Schobert (1720-1767), who represented stylistically the Mannheim school. His piano music—passionate, serious, and filled with emotional contrasts—revealed a language the lad of eight had not heard before. In London it was Johann (John) Christian Bach who artistically and also personally made a deep impression on the boy. The elegant man of the world and the small child prodigy became friends.

It was realized then that the clavier concertos would make useful additions to the repertory of the traveling Mozarts, and Wolfgang sat down and converted, with fatherly advice, three piano sonatas of the London Bach into concertos with the accompaniment of strings (violins, violoncello, and bass). One of the essential features of the post-Bach piano concerto is the participation of the solo clavier as a continuo instrument in the orchestral sections. Naturally the boy followed this procedure, which the mature composer applied even to his masterpieces. The sonatas adapted from Johann Christian Bach, once regarded as original concertos by Mozart, slipped with the Köchel number 107 into the complete works. The same holds true of four clavier concertos, K. 37, 39, 40, and 41, which are based on sonata movements of four now forgotten composers (Johann Gottfried Eckardt, Leontzi Honauer, Hermann Friedrich Raupach, and Johann Schobert), who enjoyed a great vogue in Paris in the 1760s. Mozart provided for these adapted sonatas an orchestral accompaniment after the model of the London Bach (strings, two pairs of oboes and horns), which he applied often to his mature concertos.

The true source of these four clavier concertos was revealed only in 1912 by the French Mozart scholars Théodore de Wyzewa and Georges de Saint-Foix, who placed Mozart research on a new foundation. With K. 37, 39, 40, 41, and 107 eliminated, the D major concerto, K. 175, composed in Salzburg in December 1773, is Mozart's first true clavier concerto. At that time he already had fifteen string quartets and about thirty symphonies to his credit. In Salzburg five more clavier concertos came into being (one for three, and one for two pianos); seventeen were created in Vienna. The great piano concertos originated in the period when Mozart's craftsmanship had reached its peak in chamber music (quartets and quintets) and the symphony. The artistic maturity and technical mastery were, so to speak, the prerequisites for the solution of the classical concerto problem—the fusion of the baroque principle of instrumental dualism (tutti and solo) with the symphonic concept and thematic dualism of the sonata.

The function and composition of the orchestra underwent important changes as well. To the string ensemble of the baroque, wind instruments were added: first a pair of oboes and horns, later flutes, clarinets, trumpets, and finally, kettledrums. Thus the clavier appears in the symphonic commonwealth not as a ruling factor, but rather as a prominent member with a special task.

Although Haydn had written a considerable number of concertos for various instruments in the 1750s and 60s, he evinced less interest in this category the more he progressed artistically as a symphonic and quartet composer. He was not a virtuoso and had no personal reasons to write concertos for his own appearances. Mozart, the concertizing pianist, had as a creative artist to concern himself with the concerto problem, which he ultimately solved in an ideal manner.

Concerto for Piano in E flat major, K. 271

Allegro; Andantino; Rondo: Presto

This concerto in E flat major, scored for two oboes, horns, and strings, was composed in January of 1777 in Salzburg. It was the most important work Mozart created before he set out on a journey to Munich, Augsburg, Mannheim, and Paris in the hope of securing an appointment preferable to his Salzburg post. He wrote the concerto for a French pianist, Mlle Jeunehomme, whose name appears in Mozart's letters in the quaint spelling "Jenomi." The work is the first concerto in the key of E flat major: three more were to come (K. 365 for two pianos, 449, and 482).

We know very little about Mlle Jeunehomme, her personality or artistic stature. However, if a conclusion on the basis of the intrinsic value of this concerto is permissible, she must have been an extraordinary young lady and pianist. Thus there is a marked difference between the Jeunehomme concerto and its immediate predecessors, K. 242 in F major for three pianos, and K. 246 in C major, of 1776. They were written for ladies of the Salzburg nobility, in a gallant style to suit the taste and enjoyment of Salzburg society, but the Jeunehomme concerto tells a different story.

Mozart offered it together with K. 238 and K. 246 to an engraver in Paris but demanded immediate cash payment. Naturally, the deal never came through: the E flat concerto would never have found many customers, because it was not written to ingratiate the public with amiable melodies and glittering passages. The concerto is a work of a serious crisis and shows an audacity and a concept that anticipates that of the great Viennese concertos. Einstein, referring to the momentous importance of the *Eroica* in Beethoven's development, comments, "This E flat major concerto is Mozart's *Eroica*."

The opening of the first Allegro is striking. After the first measure the piano surprisingly injects itself and completes the phrase. This happens twice before the orchestra has a chance to go on with the exposition. This is matched at the end of the orchestral prologue when the clavier enters with an extended trill, which, however, adds a new color to the orchestral palette. In the recapitulation the main theme is built up in the reverse order: the clavier begins and the orchestra continues, but the original order reappears before Mozart's cadenza.

The Andantino, the first of Mozart's concerto movements in the minor mode, anticipates the C minor Andante of the sinfonie concertante in E flat major for violin and viola (K. 364, 1779) in several respects: the time signature (3/4), the emotional quality, and the orchestral treatment (muted strings). Note the recitative-like phrases that point to Mozart the dramatist. Wyzewa and Saint-Foix expressed themselves strongly about this trait in their stylistic analysis of the concerto by suggesting that "one could almost mistake the Andante for a tragic recitative from some opera of Gluck's and transferred from the voice to the first violin and piano." The slow movements of many a baroque concerto are arias for violin and suggest operatic scenes. The dramatic quality in Mozart's Andantino is strongly emphasized in the dynamics of the concluding measures, where the violins discard the mute, and the closing C minor chord sounds with incisive force.

The final rondo, which commences with an extended clavier solo, deviates conspicuously from the emotional sphere of the preceding movements. Although this jubilant Presto offers the soloist good opportunities for his pianistic gifts, it does not aim at virtuosity for its own sake, but rather at quick motion in the manner of gay comedy. And in the course of it Mozart comes up with an amazing surprise: the interpolation of an elegant, and at the same time expressive, minuet in A flat major. Mozart duplicated this feature exactly in the great E flat major concerto (K. 482, 1785). This episode, adorned with highly ornamented variations, is the domain of the pianist. A short but brilliant cadenza leads to the return of the rondo refrain, which contains the thematic germs of Monostatos's aria in *The Magic Flute*:

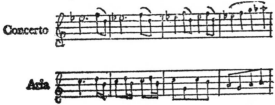

It seems, however, that Mozart borrowed this idea from a C major symphony by the Bohemian composer Josef Mysliveczek (1737-1781). He had heard the symphony in Milan in 1770. Both Leopold and Wolfgang were very much impressed and wanted to include it in the repertory of the Salzburg orchestra. Leopold actually inquired whether the symphony were in the music archives of the Salzburg chapel, because he was determined to acquire it if it were not.

The recapitulation proceeds without improvisatory interruption or startling turns, yet Mozart has a surprise in store for the very end. The frequently repeated main motif dominates the conclusion of the movement, which, gradually becoming softer (pianissimo), ends abruptly with two forceful strokes. This passage foreshadows exactly the ending of Beethoven's violin concerto, and must in all probability have left the audience of 1777 in a state of bewilderment.

Concerto for Piano in A major, K. 414
Allegro; Andante; Allegretto

This concerto belongs to a group of three that Mozart composed in the fall of 1782 for a series of subscription concerts to be given in Lent of 1783, after the carnival season. Alfred Einstein has presented convincing arguments to the effect that our piece, which according to Köchel was supposedly the second of the triptych (K. 413, 414, and 415), was actually the first. Consequently, in his revision of Köchel's catalogue, he assigned to the A major concerto the number 386a (K. 414), and listed the others as 387a and b (K. 413 and 415). These three are among the seven concertos that were published in Mozart's lifetime (1785 in Vienna) and appeared actually in the order of Einstein's revised listing.

Thus the A major piece is the first clavier concerto Mozart wrote after a pause of six years, if we leave the concerto for two pianos in E flat major (1779/80) out of consideration. The first of the Viennese series of seventeen, the A major concerto was preceded by *The Abduction from the Seraglio* and the *Haffner Symphony*, while the G major string quartet (K. 387), which opens a set of six dedicated to Joseph Haydn, is one of its important chronological neighbors.

Mozart characterized the three concertos in a letter to his father as "a happy medium between what is too easy and too difficult; they are very brilliant, pleasing to the ear, and natural without being vapid. There are passages here and there from which connoisseurs alone can derive satisfaction; but these passages are written in such a way that the less learned cannot fail to be pleased without knowing why...."

Offering these pieces to the Parisian publisher Johann Georg Sieber, an enterprising musician of German extraction, Mozart pointed to the possibility of their execution "merely *a quattro*," i. e., as clavier quintets (clavier plus four strings) at home. This method was often applied to the clavier concertos of Johann Samuel Schröter (about 1750-1788), a protégé of Mozart's friend Johann Christian Bach in London, and his successor as music master of the queen. These "very fine" pieces aroused Mozart's sincere interest. They were simple in their structure, but appealing melodically and provided with a thin orchestral garb. The rendition as a piano quintet of both the Schöter pieces and Mozart's concertos was possible or permissible because the soloist, playing the parts of the wind instruments, participated in the tutti portions and lent more tonal body to the string ensemble. Yet only the presentation in accordance with the score fully reveals the beauty of these concertos.

The melodic charm and the suavity which dominate the first Allegro are akin to the emphasis of pure melody which is characteristic of Mozart's violin concertos of 1775. This trend also accounts for the absence of a symphonic manipulation of the themes in the development section which, conforming to this attitude, introduces a new idea. The beauty and poetry of the Andante requires no particular comment. Georges de Saint-Foix has drawn attention to the source of the solemn opening theme which Mozart had taken from an overture of Johann Christian Bach. The French Mozart scholar surmises that the use of the theme was an act of homage to Bach, who had died on January 1, 1782, and whose passing Mozart termed "a sad day of the world of music." The final rondo has been aptly characterized as music of "the gracious gaiety that smiles but never bursts into a laugh." The cadenzas played tonight are by Mozart.

Concerto for Piano in E flat major, K. 449
Allegro vivace; Andantino; Rondo: Allegro ma non troppo

Mozart wrote this concerto for his gifted pupil Barbara (Babette) Ployer, the daughter of a prosperous financier who had moved from Salzburg to Vienna and often entertained musical connoisseurs at his home in the suburb of Döbling. The piece came into being in a period of amazing creative activity. Within ten weeks Mozart composed the clavier concertos in E flat major, B flat major (K. 450), D major (K. 451), and G major (K. 453), and also the quintet for piano and woodwinds in E flat major (K. 452), which he termed in a letter to his father the best work he ever composed.

In these busy, if not hectic, weeks he gave three *Akademies* and presented the brand-new concertos. The E flat piece is dated February 9, 1784. It is the first item that Mozart entered in a little notebook of forty-four leaves, in which he listed all completed compositions with the date and the opening measures. He kept up these entries almost until his death, and we can only regret that he failed to institute this procedure earlier, as it would have aided immensely the Mozart chronology.

Scored for two oboes, horns, and strings, this concerto follows in the orchestration the pattern of most of the Salzburg concertos and of K. 413 and 414 (1782), which could be played as piano quintets with five musicians only, or *a quattro*, to use Mozart's language. This procedure conforms to the concerto concept of Johann Christian Bach and Johann Samuel Schröter, who regarded the orchestra as an "accompanist," an attitude completely at variance with Mozart's. Thus it seems strange that he suggested execution as a quintet for the C major concerto (K. 415), whose orchestra includes oboes, bassoons, horns, trumpets, and kettledrums. If he conceded a rendition *a quattro* also for our concerto, it should not be taken as a rule but rather as a makeshift solution. Mozart knew that the concerto was to be played in Babette Ployer's home, where there was not enough room to seat an orchestra with six or more wind instruments. The limitation to four wind players, and beyond that a performance *a quattro,* took care of this difficulty. But the exclusion of the oboes and horns, even if their parts are played by the clavier, deprives the concerto of characteristic sonorities and instrumental colors. The present work is actually the last with a small wind unit; the later concertos employ a large wind section, which definitely precludes the rendition *a quattro.*

Mozart played the E flat major concerto in the first of three subscription concerts he gave on consecutive Wednesdays in Lent, in March 1784. The concerts took place in the salon of the residence of the court printer and publisher Johann Thomas von Trattner, whose wife Therese, a fine pianist, was dedicatee of Mozart's great sonata and fantasia in C minor (K. 457 and 475). The list of the 176 subscribers to those *Akademies* reads like the social register of Vienna at the turn of the eighteenth century. We find here the names of the most influential aristocratic families, who played an important part in the life of both Haydn and Beethoven. The E flat concerto, though heartily acclaimed, was published in parts only in 1792, in Offenbach (near Frankfurt) by Johann André, whose son had acquired from Mozart's widow the master's musical estate.

The first movement is one of the three opening Allegros in the twenty-three concertos that are in triple time, the others being K. 413 in F major and the great C minor concerto. It has been suggested that the movement reflects an element of unrest and that this quality makes the Allegro a forerunner of the first movement of the C minor concerto (1786). Einstein puts it this way: "One is tempted to say that it [the Allegro of K. 449] seeks to express in E flat major what a later movement in the same meter completely realizes," namely the opening piece of K. 491. Mozart provided a cadenza (played tonight), which may have been primarily intended for Babette Ployer. The movement closes as a baroque concerto does with the concluding portion of the opening tutti.

The middle movement is a prototype of a "singing" Andantino in which, after the orchestral prelude, the clavier has the dominant voice. The orchestral interludes are brief, not exceeding four measures. The piano part is studded with trills, turns, and ornamental figurations. It is an instrumental coloratura aria devoid of any rhetorical trait or sentimentality.

The Andantino is effectively contrasted with the perpetual motion of the Rondo which, nonetheless, leaves room for contrapuntal elements, as the opening statement reveals. The close collaboration of solo and orchestra is astonishing, and there is only one stretch over fifteen measures that interrupts the steady flow of eight- and sixteenth-notes and triplets. This circumstance explains why the movement does not abound in tunes, as do Mozart's other rondos. In several respects it is related to the finale of the E flat major concerto (K. 271): both movements have a *moto perpetuo* quality, and a coda in 6/8 meter, and both end abruptly after a gentle and transparent passage.

Concerto for Piano in B flat major, K. 450
Allegro; Andante; Rondo: Allegro

In the year 1784 Mozart's mind and creative urge were centered on the piano concerto. No less than six came into being between February 1 and December 11: the concertos in E flat major, K. 449, B flat major, K. 450, D major, K. 451, G major, K. 453, B flat major, K. 456, and F major, K. 459. There were two other larger works as well: the string quartet in E flat major, K. 458, and the quintet for piano and winds in E flat major, K. 452, which Mozart affectionately termed the best piece he had written in his life. The quintet and the series of piano concertos, K. 449, 450, and 451, were composed for concerts he gave during Lent.

Mozart had made arrangements for three subscription concerts, scheduled for the Wednesdays of March 17, 24, and 31, in the salon of the court printer and bookseller Thomas Johann von Trattner, whose wife, Therese, was one of Mozart's piano students. Mozart felt a strong attachment to her, and dedicated the C minor sonata, K. 457, and Fantasy, K. 475, to this very musical lady. The price of the three concerts was six florins, about $36 in terms of 1966. The list of 174 subscribers represented a Who's Who of Austria's high aristocracy, government, and scholarly and financial worlds. It included foreign diplomats and all the wealthy patrons of music encountered in the biographies of Haydn and Beethoven.

Before this exclusive audience Mozart played the B flat concerto, K. 450, in all probability on March 24. According to the entry in his own thematic list, the D major concerto, K. 451, was completed on the same day. In a letter of May 26 of that same year to his father, Mozart discussed the various piano concertos that the had composed in the preceding months. Declaring his inability to make a choice between the concertos in B flat and D major (K. 451), he wrote: "I regard them both as concertos that make me sweat. In point of difficulty the one in B flat has the edge on the one in D major. Furthermore I am very anxious to know which of the three [K. 450, 451, and 453] pleases you and my sister best. I am curious to see whether your judgment agrees with the general verdict here and with my own. Of course, you have to hear all three well performed."

The autograph of the B flat concerto is preserved in Weimar as a donation of Grand Duchess Maria Paulovna, Liszt's supporter in the years of his conductorship in Weimar. The manuscript reflects the hectic days that preceded the completion and performance of the concerto. There are changes in all movements. In the Andante Mozart altered several measures of the theme after the parts of the piano, the first violin, and the bass had already been written down. Eight measures were inserted in the finale just fourteen measures before the close.

In his travels Mozart carried only the orchestra parts of his concertos in his bag. For the solo part he used music paper on which he had jotted down only the main ideas, some indications for ornamental passages, and the figured bass. He relied completely on his memory, which never failed him, and therefore he could leave the score at home, thus protecting himself against thievery and misuse on the part of ruthless copyists and publishers. Only seven of his twenty-three concertos are known to have been published in his lifetime. The B flat piece might be the eighth, since recent researches do not exclude the possibility that F. A. Hoffmeister published or prepared an edition in Vienna around 1786.

The piece shows Mozart on the road to the symphonic concerto in which he fused the baroque principle of alternation between tutti and solo with the classical concept of thematic dualism. In the preceding E flat concerto, K. 449, the participation of the two oboes and two horns is optional, and the work can be performed as a quintet for piano and strings. The orchestration of the B flat concerto, demanding a flute, two oboes, bassoons, and horns, conforms to the more symphonic quality of the work. The first version of the great G minor symphony of 1788 has the same scoring.

Although Mozart depended on the support of a very exclusive audience, he refrained from writing a concerto that was purely social music. Nonetheless, a certain eighteenth-century elegance and brilliance appear in some pages of the B flat piece. The technique of variation is applied to the second movement, upon which Mozart also bestowed a most delicate orchestral garb and tender ornamental piano embroidery. Concerning the tempi of the middle movements, Mozart wrote on June 12, 1784: "In no concertos should they be Adagio, but always Andante." Yet he deviated from this maxim in his last concertos and wrote Larghettos and even an Adagio (K. 488). The concluding movement is a spirited rondo in 6/8 time. Mozart chose this meter for the finale in his two later B flat concertos (K. 453 and 595). These movements are musically and technically akin to our rondo finale and have identical features.

The B flat piece heard tonight and Beethoven's B flat concerto, Opus 19, reveal amazing parallelisms. Their metrical design is similar: 4/4, 3/8 (3/4 in Beethoven), and 6/8, both have a middle movement in E flat and both show the same orchestration.

Concerto for Piano in D major, K. 451
Allegro assai; Andante; Allegro di molto

Mozart played the concerto in his third subscription concert on March 31, 1784. According to the entry in his own thematic list, it was completed on March 22, two days before the second concert in the series, which probably featured the concerto in B flat major (K. 450).*

The concerto in D major displays a richer orchestral palette than the preceding sister works in E flat major (K. 449) and B flat major (K. 450). Scored for flute, pairs of oboes, bassoons, horns, trumpets, kettledrums, and strings, it foreshadows the orchestration of the later symphonic concertos,

---

* See note on the Concerto in B flat, (K. 450)

such as K. 466, 467, and 503, and the scoring of the "Jupiter" symphony. Although Mozart depended on the support of a very exclusive audience, he steadfastly refrained from composing a concerto that was purely social music. At the very beginning the incisive march rhythm and vigorous fanfare seem to fit an overture to a pompous opera. The orchestral ritornello sounds the keynote of the first Allegro, which is devoid of long lyrical passages, and Mozart excludes them even from the cadenza he had provided for the concerto.

The rich sonorities of the Allegro are contrasted with the tenderness of the Andante (4/4, G major), in which not only trumpets and kettledrums are silenced, but to achieve the utmost delicacy and transparency, the wind section is reduced to three players. The delightful interplay of flute, oboe, bassoon, and piano anticipates instrumental combinations of the quintet for wind instruments and piano in E flat major (K. 452), which Mozart completed only eight days after he had finished the piano concerto heard tonight.

The final rondo (Allegro di molto, 2/4) keeps up the incessant speedy motion. It is dominated by the spirit of the opera buffa, leaving no room for lyricism. Mozart also shows his sense of humor in a curious way, by including a short fugal passage in the cadenza. He does not really mean to become involved in counterpoint and springs a surprise after the cadenza, changing the meter from 2/4 to 3/8 and forming the coda as a break-up dance. Remembering the solemn beginning as we reach the gay ending, elated and refreshed, we realize that we have traveled far.

Concerto for Piano in G major, K. 453
Allegro; Andante; Allegretto

This concerto was completed on April 12, 1784. It was written for Barbara Ployer, according to the autograph which once was housed in the Prussian State Library in Berlin. Barbara was the daughter of a prosperous broker from Salzburg who moved to Vienna and took up residence in the suburb of Döbling. Concerts were given in the Ployer home, and Mozart reported to his father that Barbara, one of his most gifted students, played the new G major concerto there, and that he joined her in a reading of the D major sonata for two pianos (K. 448). One of the guests was the famous opera composer Giovanni Paisiello (1740-1816), whom Mozart took to Döbling in his carriage "in order that he might hear my compositions and my pupil." The concerto is one of the seven for which he was able to secure a publisher (1787, Speyer, Germany).

Scored for flute, two oboes, bassoons, horns, and strings, the work does not aim at virtuoso brilliancy but rather at the integration of the solo instrument into the orchestral fabric. Intimacy is the keynote. Once more we find the marchlike quality in the main theme of the first movement, yet it enters not in a military spirit but rather gently, and the entrance of the solo instrument after the orchestral exposition conforms to the tender opening. An interesting feature of the solo exposition is the introduction of a new melody while the second theme of the orchestral prologue assumes the function of a closing theme in the solo exposition. The development does not concentrate on the elaboration on the material previously stated. Instead it abounds in broken chords and arpeggios, and therefore has the earmarks of the so-called fantasia development. It slides inconspicuously into the recapitulation which closes like a baroque concerto, after the cadenza (by Mozart), with the concluding passage of the opening statement.

The Andante combines serenity and sadness. The basic mood is conveyed in the extended orchestral opening. The clavier dominates either alone or in a tender dialogue with the woodwinds. The third movement is a series of five variations with a symphonically expanded coda termed "finale," which exceeds even slightly the previous music in length (174 as opposed to 170 measures). The theme, which Mozart's pet starling was taught to whistle, actually anticipates the *lied* of the bird catcher Papageno in *The Magic Flute*. The starling may have whistled the tune off key, but was forgiven by his master, who combined in the Allegretto witticism and fun with consummate artistry. This amazing efficacy paired with unique imagination is evident in the diversity of the variations, in the setting of pianistic figurations against the original melody (variations II and III), in the harmonic and rhythmic complications in the G minor section (variation IV), and in the imagery and inexhaustible variety of instrumental combinations and surprising turns in the finale.

Concerto for Piano in B flat major, K. 456

Allegro vivace; Andante un poco sostenuto; Allegro vivace

Mozart wrote the B flat concerto for piano K. 456 in September of 1784. In that year no less than six piano concertos came into being: K. 449, 450, 451, 453, 456 and 459. Two of this remarkable group, K. 449 and 453, were composed for his pupil Babette Ployer, three, K. 450, 451 and 459, for Mozart's own appearances and our piece according to a remark in a letter of Leopold Mozart was intended for the blind piano virtuoso and composer Maria Theresa von Paradis (1759-1824). Consequently the piece is often referred to as the *Paradis Concerto*. The blind lady was a student of the Bohemian composer Leopold Anton Kozeluch (1752-1818) who had achieved a considerable prestige as a piano teacher in aristocratic circles in Vienna. He held a record in the mass production of piano concertos (about 50) and driven by envy and ill-will, he antagonized Haydn, Mozart and Beethoven. The latter called him "miserabilis" and, ironically enough, it was Kozeluch who succeeded Mozart in the position of the Court Chamber Composer. It testifies to Mozart's magnanimity that he, overlooking Kozeluch's unpleasant behavior, favored with a concerto the blind pianist who excelled in the playing of her teacher's compositions.

The generally accepted notion that Mozart's B flat concerto was played by Maria Theresa von Paradis in Paris in 1784 has been proven erroneous by recent investigations. She stayed in Paris in the first half of the year and the concerto was according to Mozart's entry in the autograph completed on September 30, 1784, thus long after the young lady had left the French capital. The programmes of her Parisian recitals contain works by Kozeluch,

Haydn and others but nothing of Mozart. Emperor Joseph II acclaimed the B flat concerto with a loud bravo when Mozart played it on February 12, 1785, in a concerto given by the Italian soprano Luisia Laschi, who created the roles of the countess in *Le Nozze di Figaro* and Zerlina in *Don Giovanni*.

The concerto is scored for flute, two oboes, bassoons, horns, and strings. The opening tutti of the first Allegro vivace exposes all the musical ideas of the movement. The marchlike quality of the main theme is a characteristic element in the first movement of several Mozart concertos. We find it in K. 415 (C major), 451 (D major), 453 (G major), 467 (C major), and 537 (D major). We also hear drum rhythms that, however, do not disclose a quality that could be defined as military. The marchlike main theme enters softly, and its gentle dynamic grade is never increased in order to build up a climax in the manner of Beethoven. (Witness the concertos in C major and E flat major). The basic character of Mozart's Allegro is mildness and serenity.

The Andante in G minor is a variation movement whose emotional content points to Mozart the opera composer. In fact the piece has been linked by Alfred Einstein to Barbarina's cavatina in the last act of *Le Nozze di Figaro*. Yet the gentleness and melancholic mood are seriously threatened by the dramatic character of the third variation, which in turn contrasts sharply with serenity of the fourth, in G major. The theme whose two strains may be indicated by A and B in the following chart is proclaimed by the orchestra. The structural pattern of the variation series can be described as follows:

Variation I	piano alone
Variation II	A (tutti), then piano, accompanied
	B (tutti), then piano, accompanied
Variation III	A (tutti), then piano alone
	B (tutti), then piano alone
Variation IV (G major)	A (tutti), then piano, accompanied
	B (tutti), then piano, accompanied
Variation V	theme (tutti) and variation (piano) simultaneously
Coda	tutti and piano

The melancholic turn apparent in the gentle ending of the Andante is contrasted with the gay main idea of the final rondo stated by the clavier and repeated by the orchestra. The movement charms the listener through its melodic flow. It is interrupted by an episode in the distant key of B minor in which a recitative-like passage of the piano in 2/4 is set against the 6/8 accompaniment of the orchestra. But soon the gay mood returns and obliterates the traces of crisis in the delightful interplay of the clavier and orchestra.

Concerto for Piano in F major, K. 459
Allegro—Allegretto; Allegro assai

According to the autograph, preserved in the Westdeutsche Bibliothek in Marburg, Mozart completed this concerto on December 11, 1784. We have no information about a Viennese performance in the 1780s, and only a post-humous edition—the piece was not published in Mozart's lifetime—contains a notice to the effect that the concerto was played by the author in Frankfurt at the coronation of Leopold II in October 1790. Mozart had expected that as Imperial Chamber Composer he would go to Frankfurt in the entourage of the emperor. His hope was not fulfilled. Antonio Salieri (1750-1825), with Ignaz Umlauf (1756-1796) as his now totally forgotten deputy, and fifteen other musicians were sent to Frankfurt. Mozart decided to undertake the journey at his own expense, hoping for a financial success from the receipts of one or two concerts. He had to pawn his silverware to meet the traveling expenses.

Mozart gave one *Akademie* in Frankfurt on October 15 that brought him much applause and honor, but a meager financial harvest. On this occasion he played two concertos, K. 459, which we hear this evening, and one in D major, K. 537, generally known as the Coronation Concerto. The latter was apparently completed in a rush, for Mozart left the clavier part in a very sketchy state and often omitted the music for the left hand. But he knew what he had to play, and since he never had the opportunity to publish the work, he had no incentive to edit it. At any rate he considered it an effective piece, and he doubtlessly also entertained a high regard for the F major concerto, which was meant to show him in a favorable light both as composer and pianist before the distinguished audience assembled at the coronation. Its rendition at that occasion warrants for it also the designation of "Coronation Concerto" which can be found in the Mozart literature.

The concerto in F major is scored for flute, two oboes, bassoons, horns, and strings and displays the same qualities as its five sister works of the blessed year 1784 (K. 449, 450, 451, 453, and 456). Their scoring is by and large identical, except for K. 451 which calls for trumpets and kettledrums. The persistent march motif that opens the first movement and is heard about a hundred times links this Allegro to those of K. 451, 453, and 456, as well as to the C major concertos K. 467 and 503 and the other coronation concerto in D major. Marchlike melodies and motifs are evident in all these concertos.

The concerto has no slow movement, but rather an Allegretto, which designation Mozart probably substituted for a somewhat quicker Andante. In an F major piece one would expect a middle movement in B flat, but this one is in the festal key of C major, which is, however, sometimes darkened in that the second theme appears in G minor and C minor. The general mood and the transparent orchestration, particularly of the wind section, foreshadows Susanna's aria *Deh vieni, non tardar* in the last act of *The Marriage of Figaro*.

Space forbids a detailed discussion of the Rondo finale, which authors of consequence such as Einstein and C. M. Girdlestone consider the strongest part of the work. The buffonesque rondo theme is introduced by the clavier, which appears not so much as a solo instrument but rather as a member of the orchestra in order to add a particular color to the extended tutti, whose length amounts almost to a fifth of the finale.

After the *buffo* theme is stated, the course veers to the opposite direction in subjecting a new idea to fugal treatment. Einstein points out that the finale contains "a few rhythms that are to be found note for note" in a carnival pantomime that Mozart had penned in 1783, of which only fragments survive. The use of this material in the finale seems very appropriate. Mozart infused this quick-paced movement with sharp witticisms, and cleverly combined homophony with fugal techniques. The application of the counterpoint has some mocking overtones and anticipates the jests of the F major divertimento (K. 522), known as *A Musical Joke*. Yet there is no insignificant passage work, and the scales and arpeggios sustain the incessant motion that carries us irresistibly along.

Concerto for Piano in D minor, K. 466

Allegro; Romance; Allegro assai

This concerto, whose autograph is one of the precious manuscript treasures owned by the Gesellschaft der Musikfreunde in Vienna, was completed on February 10, 1785. We learn about the circumstances that surrounded the first performance, on the following day, from a letter by Leopold Mozart addressed to his daughter Nannerl, since 1784 Baroness Berchtold zu Löwenburg. The concert, the first of a series with more than 150 subscribers, took place in the ballroom of the Hotel zur Mehlgrube, located on the Mehlmarkt, today called Neuer Markt. (Close to the Mehlgrube stood the palace of Prince Schwarzenberg where Haydn's oratorios, *The Creation* and *The Seasons* received their first reading.) When the Mozarts arrived at the Mehlgrube on the day of the concert (February 11) the copyist was still busy writing out the parts for the finale. Naturally there was no time to rehearse it, and the Rondo had to be played at sight. Evidently it went off without derailment, since Leopold Mozart commended the orchestra, which played without a conductor, as "excellent." The new concerto was judged by this severe critic as "incomparable" and "excellent." Wolfgang programmed it again at the second subscription concert given at the Mehlgrube on February 15, and Leopold notified his daughter that "your brother played the big new concerto in D [!], magnifique...." One year later he informed her of a Salzburg performance of the concerto by his pupil Heinrich Marchand, aged fifteen, assisted by Joseph Haydn's brother Michael who "had the pleasure of seeing with what art it is composed, how delightfully the parts are interwoven and what a difficult concerto it is."

Scored for flute, two oboes, bassoons, horns, trumpets, and kettledrums, it was Mozart's first concerto in the minor mode, although he had previously composed thirty for clavier, violin, and wind instruments. This makes it a landmark and constitutes a break with a then prevailing concept: a concerto was considered social music, and the society of the *ancien régime* and the rococo wanted to be entertained. They eschewed crises and conflicts. This point of view precluded the use of the minor mode for the basic key, but Mozart negated the validity of this concept in the D minor concerto, and spoke his musical language convincingly in it. He was understood, as the utterances of Leopold Mozart testify.

Viewed historically, Leopold's enthusiastic response seems surprising if one recalls that he had advised Wolfgang strongly against taking the path of Gluck, but rather suggested he follow the Italians instead. More than the preceding concertos, the D minor piece is in the nature of a symphony with the clavier as an obbligato instrument and not a virtuoso vehicle with orchestral accompaniment. A work of consummate artistry, it speaks the "language of the heart," as the aesthetes of the period phrased it.

The beginning, with its persistent syncopation and growling bass motif, prepares us for serious things to come. A violent outburst makes us fully aware of the conflict we will have to face. The movement is a drama with occasional mild episodes. The argument (summary of the contents) presented in the opening tutti leaves the outcome uncertain, but the gradually waning coda with an ominous bass motif, dying in pianissimo, reflects a tragic ending.

Mozart called the second movement, in B flat major, a Romance. Formally speaking, this denotes a three-sectional pattern whose middle portion is in a different key and states new melodic material. Peace and tranquility seem to reign supreme in the first section; yet the situation is altered radically in the violent and tumultuous middle section in G minor. The piano, singing at first, now produces raging passages against cries of the wind instruments. The storm abates and there is a return to the peaceful mood of the beginning.

The Rondo finale reverts to the passionate mood and agitation of the first Allegro. But there are passages that seem to presage a more optimistic turn of events, and this change really occurs after the cadenza: Mozart leaves the minor mode and breaks into the major. But he did not accept this solution as final, as the endings of the C minor concerto and G minor symphony prove so emphatically. Beethoven greatly admired the D minor concerto and wrote cadenzas for the first and third movements that are used in tonight's presentation.

Concerto for Piano in C major, K. 467

[Allegro maestoso]; Andante; Allegro vivace assai

The concerto was composed in February of 1785 and completed on March 9: this we learn from the autograph, which reposes in the collection of the Heineman Foundation in New York. The work came into being shortly after the string quartet in C major, K. 465, known as the "Dissonances Quartet" (January 1785), and the great clavier concerto in D minor, K. 466, which Mozart had played on February 11, 1785, and repeated four days later. He must have commenced the C major concerto soon after these appearances. A greater contrast than that offered by the concertos in D minor and C major can hardly be imagined. There passion, conflict, and storm; here resoluteness, calmness, and optimism. Mozart played it at an *Akademie* he gave on March 12, 1785, which netted him 559 florins, to the great satisfaction of his father who was deeply moved by the beauty of the new concerto and the applause Wolfgang received. It is characteristic of the conditions prevailing in those days that only three days elapsed between completion and performance; there was very little time for copying the parts and rehearsal.

The concerto is scored for flute, two oboes, bassoons, horns, trumpets, kettledrums, and strings. This is the same as Beethoven's orchestra, minus clarinets. Mozart omitted the tempo indication for the first movement. Most editions give it as Maestoso, which is appropriate to a certain extent. The movement is dominated by a marchlike quality that is emphasized in the symphonic tutti exposition, and the rhythm is driven home by the wind instruments and kettledrums. The movement discloses a richness of musical ideas, some of which are subjected to contrapuntal treatment. To illustrate the symphonic breadth of this movement it should be pointed out that its 417 measures exceed in length the first Allegro of the Jupiter Symphony by more then 100 measures.

The second movement, in which the trumpets and kettledrums are silent, violins and violas muted, and violoncellos and basses plucked except for ten measures out of 104, is, to borrow an expression of C. M. Girdlestone, a "dream Andante." It is also a "singing" Andante, whose symphonic conception is reflected by the modulatory richness of the middle section. The very fast Rondo finale, animated by buffo spirit, upholds the symphonic unity in thematic allusions and almost literal references to the first movement. From this great concerto a road leads to the C major concerto, K. 503, and on to the Jupiter Symphony.

Concerto for Piano in E flat major, K. 482
Allegro; Andante; Allegro

The road that Mozart had taken in his six piano concertos written in 1784 (K. 449, 450, 451, 453, 456, and 459) led inevitably to the creations in D minor, K. 466, and C major, K. 467, composed in February and March 1785. These two works represent the culmination of Mozart's achievement in the concerto field. The evolution of the piano concerto from social music to a medium of highly personal expression and symphonic depth was effected over a period of four years, beginning in 1781 when Mozart settled in Vienna. The emotional contents and passion of the D minor concerto—Mozart's first in the minor mode—definitely removed the concerto from the sphere of social and entertaining music, and the symphonic breadth of the C major piece inaugurated a development that was to produce the great C major concerto, K. 503, and the "Jupiter" Symphony.

The E flat major concerto, K. 482, came into being at the end of 1785, when Mozart's creative mind was concentrating on *The Marriage of Figaro*. He composed the concerto for his subscription concerts to be given in Lent of 1786, but he gave the piece a tryout in an *Akademie* in the Burgtheater on December 23, 1785, and received such a hearty acclaim after the Andante that he consented to repeat it.

The concerto is scored for flute, two clarinets, bassoons, horns, trumpets, kettledrums, and strings. The absence of the oboe from the orchestral palette is noteworthy. This significant feature links this concerto to the sister work in A major, K. 488, which Mozart wrote for the same subscription series. The energetic opening of the first movement discloses a certain similarity to other pieces in the same key: the sinfonia concertante for four wind instruments; the sinfonia concertante for violin and viola, the concerto for two pianos, and the piano concerto, K. 449. The first tutti does not expose all the material utilized later in the solo section, and the soloist enjoys the benefit of presenting the "singing theme."

The Andante, in C minor, combines the rondo design with the variation technique. It treats the solo part not as a dominating component of the instrumental commonwealth, but more as a *primus inter pares,* the first among equals. The wind instruments are given conspicuous preference and play through one section alone, performing a septet in E flat major for flute, two clarinets, bassoons, and horns. This section is the counterpart to the opening statement of the muffled strings that introduces the theme. The following chart demonstrates the structural design of the Andante, in which the trumpets and kettledrums are silent:

Theme in C minor	Orchestra
Variation I	Piano and strings
Episode in E flat	Wind instruments
Variation II	Piano and strings
New Episode in C major	Orchestra
Variation III (expanded)	Piano and orchestra

A similarity to *The Marriage of Figaro* is felt in the Andante, particularly in the woodwind episodes—compare the cavatina of the Countess in Act II— and touches us once more in the finale. The finale also shows a certain resemblance to the earlier E flat major concerto of 1777, K. 271. In the finale of the latter there is a change of tempo and meter from Presto, 2/4, to Minuetto cantabile, 3/4, in A flat major. The same situation occurs in the finale of K. 482, when, after a cadenza, we expect to hear the engaging main theme, and instead a new melody is projected by the wind ensemble in the soft key of A flat major, in an Andante cantabile, in 3/4 time. This episode is a dialogue between the wind instruments and the strings, assisted by the piano, which Mozart treats here as a member of the orchestra. The piano regains its prominence only with the re-entry of the basic tempo, but is submerged once again in the orchestral fabric of the briskly ending coda.

Concerto for Piano in A major, K. 488
Allegro; Adagio; Allegro assai

The A major concerto (K. 488) is the thirteenth of the monumental series of seventeen concertos which Mozart wrote in Vienna between 1782 and 1791. His symphonic production had been more extensive during the years spent in Salzburg and travelling abroad, but when he settled down in Vienna in 1782, the concerto became increasingly important. Mozart needed concertos for public appearances in a series of a subscription concerts. During the same period, Mozart composed only five symphonies. There is still no certainty that the last three in E flat major, G minor, and C major, were ever performed by him.

The concerto in A major, the preceding E flat major piece (K. 482), and the following concerto in C minor (K. 491) were written for a concert series which took place during Lent of 1786. In that hectic winter, Mozart was preoccupied with the composition of the opera *Le Nozze di Figaro,* and also had to compose the one-act *singspiel The Impresario (Der Schauspieldirektor),* staged on February 7, 1786. The A major clavier concerto was completed on March 2 and the concerto in C minor three weeks later. The autograph of the C minor piece reveals the strain under which Mozart then worked. It shows many corrections and alterations and some passages are only sketched.

Apparently, Mozart had also given a great deal of thought to the concerto in A major. In the manuscript collection of the Mozarteum in Salzburg, there are several fragments of concerto movements (which Mozart later abandoned) related to the work on the concerto heard tonight. C. M. Girdlestone has pointed out in his excellent book on Mozart's piano concertos that Mozart has used the A major tonality in only a very few larger works in his Viennese period. But these are creations of the first order: the string quartet (K. 464), the quintet for clarinet and strings (K. 581), the piano concerto in A major, and the concerto for clarinet (K. 622). The last three pieces in this group have one important element in common—the employment of the clarinet. The elimination of the oboe and its replacement with the clarinet is a very significant feature in the orchestration of the A major concerto, which is geared to the formation of more gentle sonorities and excludes the incisive trumpets and kettledrums.

Mozart's great piano concertos originated in the period when his craftsmanship had reached its peak in both chamber music and the symphony. Artistic maturity and technical mastery were the prerequisites for the solution of the classical concerto problem: the fusion of the baroque principle of the instrumental dualism (tutti and solo) with the symphonic concept and the thematic dualism of the sonata. This was Mozart's great historic achievement. The A major concerto combines structural perfection, richness of musical ideas, and beauty of sound. Sir Donald Tovey the noted British scholar termed it a "study in euphony." The euphony is the result of the superb blending of the clavier timbre with the orchestral sonorities. Yet Mozart employs only seven wind instruments: flute and pairs of clarinets, bassoons, and horns.

The gentle beginning of the Allegro sets the keynote for the movement which is devoid of dramatic developments but displays an abundance of musical ideas. The Allegro closes as gently as it opens. The Adagio in F sharp minor in the Siciliano rhythm (6/8) is set in a melancholy mood that was foreshadowed to a certain extent in the elegiac quality in the middle section of the first movement. In discussing the Adagio, authors of consequence such as Sir Donald Tovey and Professor Girdlestone refer to it as the *Andante* in F sharp minor. In doing so, they are the victims of corrupt editions that are full of nonsensical phrasings, incorrect dynamic signs, and wrong notes and tempo indications. The autograph of the A major concerto, preserved in the Bibliothèque du Conservatoire Nationale de Musique in Paris, indicates *Adagio* for the slow movement and *Allegro assai* for the finale, which is given the heading *Presto* in numerous editions containing arbitrary alterations and adaptations passed on from generation to generation, with uncritical eyes, for 150 years.

The Rondo-Finale is the mode of expression for gaiety and merriment. This becomes apparent with the entrance of the sparkling rondo theme. Mozart seems to have aimed for a *moto perpetuo* (perpetual motion) movement. He achieved the quality less through an incessant motion of runs in sixteenth-notes than through the character of musical ideas. These ideas do not retard the motion even in the absence of runs and quickly moving motifs. Such motifs are an essential element in the building up of ensembles and finales in the *opera buffa*. It is actually the *buffo* (comic) spirit that dominates the Allegro assai. This may not come as a surprise to the listener. The effervescent movement convincingly reflects the interdependence of Mozart's creative activities. During the winter of 1786, when his mind and energy were greatly occupied with *Le Nozze di Figaro,* the *buffo* spirit was too strong to be restricted to the stage. It penetrated other spheres and brought to them playfulness, exhilaration, and gaiety—qualities which always find a receptive audience.

Concerto for Piano in C minor, K. 491
Allegro; Larghetto; Allegretto

Mozart composed the great C minor concerto also for his Lenten subscription concerts, at the end of the winter of 1786. The autograph—now owned by the Royal College of Music in London but housed in The British Museum—gives March 24 as the date of its completion. Composition of this concerto and two others (K. 482 and 488) interfered with work on *The Marriage of Figaro* (K. 492), which was produced on May 1, 1786. Mozart played the concerto in a subscription concert on April 3 and repeated it in an *Akademie* on April 7 in the Burgtheater, where *The Marriage of Figaro* was to be staged.

The autograph reveals that this concerto, too, was written in haste: it shows many corrections and alterations and three and even four versions of one passage written above one another. Some passages are very difficult to read; others are only sketched. This naturally posed no problem to Mozart the pianist, but presents difficult questions to a conscientious editor or interpreter, whose supreme aim is to play the work in a version that faithfully reflects the intentions of the composer.

The C minor concerto is scored for flute, two oboes, clarinets, bassoons, horns, trumpets, kettledrums, and strings. Beethoven, to whom this work was particularly dear, applied the same scoring to his concertos in C major and G major. The first Allegro of the concerto, 523 measures long, is a movement of extraordinary symphonic dimension. In fact, it is, in terms of measures, the longest in sonata form before the "Eroica" (1804). Its outstanding trait is the preponderance of the rugged main theme, a feature that links this classical creation to the baroque concerto. The characteristic rising seventh recalls similar motifs in the works of Bach, Handel, Vivaldi, and other baroque composers. Despite occasional bright rays, the tragic mood, which Mozart faces with what H. Abert called "titanic defiance," is maintained throughout.

The basic mood reflects pessimism, even desperation, and the attempt to conquer these seems to have been in vain, in view of the clearly noticeable diminishing strength in the coda and the *pianissimo* ending. The emotional content of the concerto did not fit the image the romantic aesthetes had of Mozart, and nineteenth-century editors tried to soften the rugged passages by presenting them *legato.* They are also guilty of many mutilations of the original phrasings and dynamic indications, and they allowed numerous false notes to creep in. In his own thematic list Mozart indicated the scoring of the strings as follows: *Violini, 2 Viole ... e Basso.* The division of the violas is of great significance because it increases the potentialities in the low register of the string body, foreshadowing an important device of the romantic composers.

The lyrical Larghetto, in which the solo passages of the clavier are combined with either the strings or the woodwinds, marks a short digression from the passionate seriousness and emotion that pervade the first movement and that return in the variation series of the finale. The marchlike theme of the finale is a striking antithesis to the pleasing light march melodies that open the first movements of other Mozart concertos (e. g., K. 453). Alfred Einstein defined it aptly as an "uncanny revolutionary quickmarch," which is truly out of step with the mentality of the *ancien régime.* The following chart indicates the disposition of the theme and variations among tutti and solo.

Theme	Orchestra
Variation I	Clavier, theme in orchestra
Variation II	Orchestra (theme) and clavier (variation) alternating
Variation III	Clavier (theme) and orchestra (theme) alternating emphatic accentuation of the march tune
Variation IV	Interlude in A flat major, wind instruments and clavier alternating
Transition	
Variation V	Clavier dominating (C minor)
Variation VI	Dialogue of woodwinds and clavier, the only section in C major in the work
Variation VII	Clavier (variation) against orchestra (theme)
Cadenza	
Variation VIII	Finale (6/8)

Concerto for Piano in C major, K. 503

Allegro maestoso; Andante; [Allegretto]

This concerto was completed on December 4, 1786, as Mozart's own thematic list informs us. It is the last in a series of twelve which, commencing with the E flat concerto (K. 449), came into being within the span of only four years. The autograph, now held in trust by the University Library in Tübingen, reflects in changes, cancellations, and insertions the results of second thoughts. In this context a few brief remarks on the procedure Mozart followed when he committed his works to paper may not be amiss.

The writing was in the most cases the last, almost mechanical, stage which complemented the creative act. The composition was already complete in his head when he set out to write it down. If the piece or a passage was of simple texture he indicated the leading voices and the bass, while the harmonic framework was to be filled in later. But he went into a detailed scoring in cases of a more complex setting. In this concerto the dominating voices are entered with black, and the others with brown, ink. The first entrance of the clavier was originally of less virtuoso character. At one place Mozart made such substantial changes that the insertion of a new leaf was necessary. No doubt during the composition Mozart faced psychological problems that we will discuss shortly.

The concerto was published in parts in Bonn in November 1797, at a date when Beethoven's B flat concerto, Opus 19, had been already performed publicly (1795) and his C major concerto, Opus 15, was also completed. In 1798 Constanze Mozart had the concerto engraved with a dedication to Louis Ferdinand, the musically gifted Hohenzollern prince, brother of Friedrich II, who fell on the battlefield during the Napoleonic wars. Constanze served notice on the title page that the edition was brought out at the expense of the widow of the late composer. The purpose of this badly engraved edition and the dedication was probably to arouse the interest and good will of the Prussian prince who, incidentally, was honored by Beethoven through the dedication of the C minor concerto.

Information on the work under discussion, be it documentary or from letters, is very scarce and the only exact date we know is the entry in Mozart's thematic catalogue of December 4, 1786. It assumes particular significance, however, if we bring it in relation to another entry, that of December 6, 1786, which records the completion of the D major symphony (K. 504), known as the Prague Symphony.

It is obvious that Mozart did not compose the symphony within forty-eight hours, and it is also clear that his creative mind was working on two tracks simultaneously for a considerable time. In these forty-eight hours that elapsed between the completion of both the clavier concerto and the symphony, his task was chiefly a mechanical one, that is to say to complete the writing of the score. The creative process for the symphony was in the main concluded. Summing up, Mozart worked simultaneously on the concerto and the symphony but this did not cause an ambivalence of his creative mind, since he did not follow two diverging, but rather parallel, running tracks. The symphony and the concerto (which is thoroughly symphonic in nature) have several out-standing features in common: the monumentality of the conception, the maestoso character of the first movement, the appearance of the *buffo* spirit in the finale in the same meter (2/4), and the scoring which demands flutes (one in the concerto) oboes, bassoons, horns, trumpets, kettledrums, and strings. Yet in spite of this, the occupation with two works, in some instances, created difficulties to which the numerous changes in the autograph score of the clavier concerto bears witness.

The monumental character of the concerto is determined by the choice of the key and the breadth of the symphonic orchestral exposition, in which a short motif enters and is later expanded to a triumphant march tune. Its rhythmical relationship to the head motif of Beethoven's Fifth is obvious. Note that the clavier enters not with a theme of its own but in collaboration with the orchestra. Mozart matches this in the recapitulation: there he weaves the clavier part into the orchestral fabric.

The middle movement, in spite of the marking Andante is decidedly an Adagio. It is a calm and lofty piece of deep feeling with a few serious moments in the short middle section and a very delicate ending. The final rondo, whose refrain is stated by the clavier, is devoid of heroic accents. As C. M. Girdlestone has pointed out, the theme is an almost literal replica of a gavotte from the ballet music of *Idomeneo*. The tapping of this source of 1781 is by no means an accident, since Mozart thought of a revision of the opera in 1786. The preliminary work led to the composition of a soprano aria with a piano obbligato (K. 505), which instructively reflects the interdependence of the works Mozart created in December of 1786. Propelled by a gay spirit, the rondo never falls into boisterous laughter. Upholding the loftiness of the preceding movements, it completes the artistic unity of this great concerto, the superb forerunner of the C major string quintet and the great C major symphony (Jupiter).

Concerto for Piano in D major, K. 537, "Coronation"

Allegro; Larghetto; Allegretto

The piano concerto in D major, completed on February 24, 1788, is the sixteenth in the shining galaxy created in Vienna. It is the only work of major proportions composed between *Don Giovanni* (October 28, 1787) and the symphony in E flat major (June 26, 1788). Information about the history of the piece is scanty. It is not known if Mozart wrote it for an appearance in Vienna or if he had an opportunity to play it there. However, a performance in Dresden on April 14, 1789, is documented.

The piece is generally referred to as the "Coronation" Concerto, a nickname prompted by events that followed in the wake of the coronation of Leopold II in Frankfurt, in October 1790. *

Mozart was very careful in the selection of the concertos that he wanted to present. He realized he had to choose compositions that would fit the prevailing mental climate of this particular occasion. This precluded the selection of works in the minor mode, and of two of his greatest works, the concertos in D minor and C minor. By the same token, he found that the symphonic breadth of the C major concerto, K. 503, would certainly not be to the liking of the princely and aristocratic audience, who wanted to be entertained. He also ruled out the concertos in E flat major, K. 482, and in A major, K. 488, because of their middle movements in minor keys. Finally, he chose the F major concerto, K. 459, of 1784 and the D major piece of 1788. The first editions of both bear the following remark on the title page: "This concerto was played by the author in Frankfurt on Main at the coronation of Leopold II." Thus we have actually two "coronation" concertos, but the denomination is usually applied to the D major piece. Mozart gave an *Akademie* in Frankfurt on October 15, 1790, and played both "coronation" concertos. He received much applause but had to be content with a meager financial result.

The autograph of the D major concerto, which is now in the collection of the Heineman Foundation in New York, reveals that the work was completed in a rush. Mozart left the clavier part in a very scanty state and often omitted the music for the left hand: the measure total of the piece is 906, and for 452 measures there is no music for the left hand; it is entirely lacking for the second movement. Mozart knew what he had to play, and because he

* See note on the Concerto in F major, K. 459

never had the opportunity to publish the concerto, he had no incentive to edit it.

When Johann André in Offenbach (near Frankfurt) decided in 1794 to publish the concerto, he faced a difficult situation. If he did depend upon the deficient original manuscript or a copy of it, a great deal of editing and filling in of the lacunae had to be done in order to make the piece marketable. However, the source of his edition is not known, and the assumption that he had acquired an edited copy cannot be entirely ruled out, especially since he brought out the other "coronation" concerto in F major, K. 459, shortly before issuing the D major concerto. Being a prolific composer himself, André was capable of shouldering the editorial responsibility and filling in the empty spaces in Mozart's score. Nevertheless, André's edition of 1794 was the textual basis of all later editions with their numerous false notes and arbitrary phrasings and dynamics. The evil started right in Mozart's autograph, into which somebody entered the tempo markings "Larghetto" and "Allegretto" for the second and last movements.

Mozart discriminated perceptively between the musical pleasure-seeker and the serious connoisseur. When he set out to write the D major concerto in 1788, he must have thought of a particular audience assembled at a festive occasion. He deemed it wise to satisfy the music lovers of the aristocracy, whose support he needed. The result of this was a piece that displays brilliancy as well as simplicity. The "Coronation" concerto marks to a certain extent a return to the earlier concerto type that, devoid of tension and emotional stress, found favor with the aristocratic audiences and those listeners who were looking for playfulness, lightness, and gaiety.

Although the "Coronation" Concerto failed to bring Mozart the desired reward, it scored a success he could never have imagined, for alas, it was not in his lifetime. The concerto achieved enormous popularity with nineteenth-century audiences, who in this case seemed to agree with the society of the *ancien régime*. This concerto was a must for the serious piano student as well as for the concert artist. When Carl Reinecke, who in the 1870s and 1880s attempted to revive Mozart's concertos for concert life, published a booklet "Concerning the revival of Mozart's concertos," he drew the musical examples only from the "Coronation" Concerto. Things have changed considerably since then. The monopoly of the "Coronation" Concerto is a matter of the past, and we are now familiar with all facets of Mozart's piano concertos. We admire and are moved by the works that reflect storm and stress, but we also love those that, like the serene concerto in D major, emanate gaiety, melodic freshness, gracefulness, and appealing simplicity. Mozart was great even when he wished to write "popularly."

Concerto for Piano in B flat major, K. 595
Allegro; Larghetto; Allegro

Mozart wrote his twenty-three piano concertos, six in Salzburg and seventeen in Vienna, either for appearances in the *Akademies* which he gave on his own account, or for some of his advanced students. Viewed artistically, the Vienna concertos represent a line moving steadily upward; the climax is reached in the stormy, dramatic, and passionate C minor concerto, K. 491, of 1786 and the great and symphonically conceived piece in C major, K. 503.

For almost two years, Mozart apparently had no reason to write a piano concerto, but in the fall of 1789 he went to Frankfurt to concertize at the festivities connected with the coronation of Emperor Leopold II. For this purpose he wrote a concerto in D major that was nicknamed the "coronation" concerto. As the year 1790 drew to a close, Mozart was faced with the task of composing another piano concerto. We do not know who commissioned it; in fact, all events related to the concerto in B flat major are shrouded in darkness. He worked on it presumably in the last days of the year, and completed it on January 5, 1791.

There are no records regarding where and by whom it was first played. We know only of one instance in which Mozart himself was the soloist: he appeared as an "assisting artist" in a concert given by the clarinetist Joseph Beer (1744-1811), who had the distinction of having been the first travelling clarinet virtuoso. He appeared with Mozart in the dining room of a restaurant belonging to the *Hoftraiteur* (court chef and caterer) Ignaz Jahn. A man of enterprising spirit, Jahn wanted to give a cultural air to his restaurant, adjacent to one of Vienna's outstanding baroque palaces, now the Ministry of Finances. Beethoven also played in Jahn's restaurant where Mozart performed the B flat concerto on March 4, 1791. Published in Vienna in August of that year, it is one of the seven that appeared in his lifetime. A second printing in Amsterdam in 1792 suggests a warm reception of the work.

Our concerto follows, of course, Mozart's well established pattern. It has been said that the piece emanates the feeling of resignation. It is true that it lacks the passion and accents of tragedy of the C minor concerto. Its deftness and lyricism are a far cry from the monumental concerto in C major, K. 503, the superb forerunner of the "Jupiter" symphony. Mozart avoids here the accentuation of contrasts, harmonic clashes, and contrapuntal complexities. He aims at clarity and serenity. Interesting are reminiscences in the first movement of the finale of both the "Jupiter" and G minor symphonies. The gentle ending of the first Allegro seems to correspond to the general character of the movement which is devoid of tension and firmness.

The middle movement, entitled Larghetto, shows the same emotional attitude as the preceding Allegro. Cast in the ternary song form with the modified repetition of the first part, it reflects peace and tranquility. There are no sharp harmonic turns or striking contrasts. The finale is in 6/8, in the 18th century associated with the hunt. Mozart employed it in three of his four B flat concertos and also in the E flat piece, K. 482. But there is no wild hunting and running in our finale. Steadily flowing and couched in gaiety, serenity, and mildness it smilingly concludes the splendid row of Mozart's piano works.

Concerto for Violin in G major, K. 216
Allegro; Adagio; Rondeau: Allegro

The popular image of Mozart invariably associates him with the piano.

Begotten by many accounts of miraculous feats accomplished by the child prodigy as a pianist and composer for that instrument, this image is also enhanced pictorially. In a Viennese painting the six-year-old Mozart is shown in gala dress standing at the piano, and most of the artists who portrayed the mature Mozart considered the piano an indispensable accessory. Teaching piano was an important source of income for Mozart during his years in Vienna (1781-1791), and his clavier concertos were written primarily for his own public appearances or for his advanced students.

This image is far from complete. Mozart was not only a master at the piano, he was also a violin virtuoso. His father was seriously concerned with the development of his son's great violinistic talent, and the violin became the second medium of Mozart's virtuoso career. He was not even fourteen years old when he received the appointment as concertmaster of the musical establishment maintained by the Archbishop of Salzburg.

Leopold Mozart once wrote to Wolfgang: "You don't even know how well you play, and if you would only do yourself the honor and play with fire, determination, and high spirit, you would be Europe's first violinist." This should not be understood as the expression of fatherly benevolence. Leopold was always a severe and unrelenting critic of his son's musical activities, and he was one of Europe's foremost experts in matters of violin playing and the author of the famous treatise on the subject.

Mozart's activities as a concert violinist were also artistically productive. In 1775 at Salzburg he wrote five violin concertos in quick succession between April and December; the autograph of the G major concerto, the third in the series, bears the 12th of September as the date of completion. Mozart had come to grips with the formal problems of the concerto in 1773, when he wrote his first original piano concerto (D major, K. 175). The violin concertos must be regarded therefore both as a very important proving ground for the manipulation of the concerto form and as a technically progressive phase in a development that culminated in the seventeen clavier concertos created in Vienna.

The three-movement construction of Mozart's violin concertos stems from baroque models developed by the outstanding Italian violinist-composers Antonio Vivaldi, Pietro Locatelli, and Giuseppe Tartini. A great deal of Italian violin literature was certainly available to Mozart in his paternal home and from Antonio Brunetti, the soloist of the Salzburg chapel, and during his stay in Italy undoubtedly some works of these composers must have come to his attention. Mozart also adopted the baroque pattern of alternation between tutti and solo and combined it with the sonata design and its thematic dualism.

His violin concertos display a transparent texture and a delicate setting in the songful slow movements. In the Adagio of the G major piece the accompanying violins are muted, and the bass part is plucked except for a few measures. Mozart also replaced oboes by flutes, which were capable of a gentler tone production than the eighteenth-century oboe.

The finale, entitled Rondeau, offers a variety of musical ideas and national characteristics: the main theme (3/8), with an *acciaccatura alla Lombarda*, points to Italy; the short G minor passage (4/4) seems to be of French descent; the succeeding melody in G major (Allegretto) emanates the flavor of a German folk tune. In the treatment of the solo instrument of the Allegretto melody Mozart achieves the so-called musette effect. "Musette" was actually the name of an instrument of the bagpipe family. A violinist can achieve the musette quality by playing the melody on one string and producing the drone on the adjacent lower, open string. The use of this device in the G major concerto foreshadows a similar passage in the finale of the Major concerto, (K. 218). There is no animated coda and the piece ends gently as do the later sister works in D major and A major.

Concerto for Violin No. 4 in D major, K. 218
Allegro; Andante cantabile; Rondeau: Andante grazioso

Mozart's great talent for the violin became evident when he was seven years old and his father, the author of the famous *Violinschule,* did not fail to develop it. Thus the violin became the second medium of Mozart's career as a virtuoso. It was chiefly in his capacity as violinist that he was appointed a member of the musical establishment of the archbishopric of Salzburg. He served as concertmaster and also as organist.

The concerto for violin in D major was composed in October 1775 in Salzburg. The first Allegro discloses the basic elements of the sonata form with its three-sectional design.

Songfulness and grace are the characteristics of the Andante cantabile in A major. Mozart entitled the finale Rondeau; using this term the composer alludes to French models. Here he offers a variety of pictures: first an Andante grazioso which introduces the rondo theme, and then an Allegro section (6/8). Alternating constantly, these two ideas frame an episode which commencing with a simple gavotte-like melody continues with a Musette passage.

Mozart coupled the bagpipe effect with a melody of folklike quality. After this episode we hear twice the alternating play of the Andante grazioso and sparkling Allegro. There is no bright and animated coda—on the contrary, the movement fades away into a whispering pianissimo.

In a letter to his father written from Augsburg in October 1777, Mozart referred to this work as the "Strassburger-Concert." This was explained by the similarity of the Musette theme, with the Musette designated as "Ballo Strasburghese," in a symphony by Mozart's successful contemporary Carl von Dittersdorf (1739-1799). Obviously, Mozart availed himself of a folklike tune of Alsatian origin in the concerto and also used it in a series of dances (K. 269b) probably written in January 1777.

Concerto for Violin in A major, K. 219
Allegro aperto; Adagio; Tempo di Minuetto

The violin concerto in A major, dated Salzburg, December 20, 1775, is the last in a series of five that Mozart composed in comparatively quick succession during that year.

The autograph of our concerto, once in the possession of Joseph Joachim, is now preserved in the Library of Congress. The first movement displays some unusual features. The opening entrance of the solo violin occurs in a somewhat improvisatory passage which has no thematic connection with the preceding statement of the orchestra. Only after this interposed episode does the sonata design with exposition, development, and recapitulation definitely unfold. Although the composer offers the soloist a good chance to show his proficiency in runs and broken chords, he also stresses the singing element: witness the Adagio in E major, which is akin to those appealing pieces that Culberth Girdleston in his fine book on Mozart's clavier concertos characterized as "dream andantes." The solo part displays no brilliancy, but rather an enchanting melodic richness and depth of feeling.

Although bearing the heading *Tempo di Minuetto*, the finale is by no means a minuet. It shows a clearly defined three-sectional structure whose opening portion (6/8, A major) is followed by, and markedly contrasted with, an Allegro in A minor, whereupon the first section returns. The whole is a mosaic of attractive musical ideas. The most interesting features of the finale are disclosed in the middle section, which contrasts with the preceding passage in key (A minor), tempo (Allegro), meter and rhythm (2/4), dynamics (note the frequent use of the *fp*), and chromaticism. It is music *alla turca*, anticipating the rondo of the well-known piano sonata in A major (1778, K. 331) and, of course, the Turkish flavor of *The Abduction from the Seraglio*. The "Turkish" episode in the finale of our A major concerto became a problem of Mozart research. Mozart took the melodic material from sketches of an intended ballet *Le Gelosie del seraglio*, supposedly contemplated for his opera *Lucio Silla* (Milan, 1772-1773). The sketches (autograph) are preserved in the Mozarteum in Salzburg and are duly listed as No. 135a in Köchel's catalogue. Yet most recent researches established a surprising and at the same time puzzling fact. Some of the pieces of this ballet were identified as compositions of the once very popular Viennese ballet composer Josef Starzer (1726-1787), and Mozart's authorship of others appears questionable. Be that as it may, the effect Mozart obtained with this "Turkish" episode is extraordinary. The audiences of the 1770s must have grown uneasy listening to this "gruesome sounding gypsy music" but Mozart was gracious enough to provide for a happy end by the return to the gallant rococo music of the beginning.

Kirchensonate No. 14 in C major, K. 317a

In accordance with an old Salzburg custom, an instrumental piece, a *sonata al epistola,* was played in the high mass between the recitation of the Epistle and the reading from the Gospel. This is the liturgical background of Mozart's seventeen church sonatas, which stylistically and technically have nothing in common with the baroque *sonata da chiesa,* its four-movement structure, and the "slow-fast-slow-fast" design. On the contrary, they are one-movement pieces. Devoid of the fugal passages and contrapuntal complexities of the baroque church sonatas, they display the scheme of the first allegro of the classical sonata and its thematic dualism.

Mozart, who practically grew up in the church as the son of a church musician, wrote his first church sonata for two violins, bass, and organ in 1766 as a boy of ten, and the others after 1772 in his capacity as organist. (The omission of the viola in the string body was a Salzburg custom.) There was, however, no particular part for the organ in the first nine sonatas: the organist played from the figured-bass part and fulfilled a function similar to that of the harpsichordist in the duo or trio sonata; that is to say, he improvised his part. Only from 1776 on did Mozart supply a written part for the organ.

Three of the later sonatas were endowed with richer orchestration, and the piece under review is a case in point. It was composed in March 1779, after Mozart's return from Paris, and is scored for pairs of oboes, horns, trumpets, kettledrums, violins (I and II), bass, and organ. It has been observed that the piece fits the mood of the well-known "Coronation" Mass completed on March 23, 1779, which is also in C major and parallels the scoring of the sonata except for the use of trombones. It stands to reason that the position of the *sonata al epistola* demanded brevity and precluded an extended thematic elaboration of the melodic material (development) in the middle section.

Mozart wrote the last *sonata al epistola* in 1780. After he left the service of the Archbishopric the church sonata was banished from the rite and replaced by a Gradual.

Overture to "La Clemenza di Tito"

Although occupied with the orchestration of the first act of *The Magic Flute*, Mozart received a commission that he could not decline. He was requested to write an opera for the coronation of Emperor Leopold II as King of Bohemia. The communication reached him in the middle of July 1791, and the coronation was scheduled for September 6. He had to stop working on *The Magic Flute* and also to put aside the *Requiem,* for which he had received an advance payment. The libretto of the coronation opera, *La Clemenza di Tito,* was based on a play by Pietro Metastasio but altered by the Saxonian court poet Caterino Mazzolà. Like most of Metastasio's libretti, it had been set to music several times before.

After having made the most needed preparations, Mozart left Vienna accompanied by his wife Constanze and his student Franz X. Süssmayer, who, it is said, wrote the secco recitatives for the new opera. Mozart worked on it in the coach and elaborated on the sketches in roadside inns and lodging houses. He completed the opera in eighteen days. The exclusive audience that attended the première on September 6 was not very enthusiastic, and the Empress Maria-Louise dismissed Mozart's work as *porcheria tedesca* (German swinishness). Nevertheless the opera was not a failure and was later produced in Vienna, London, Germany, Italy, and Russia. It is ironic that Mozart at the end of his career was compelled to return in *La Clemenza di Tito* to the stereotyped *opera seria* that he had considered outdated after his *Idomeneo* (1780). But in 1791 this operatic type was still regarded as a traditional element in the ritual of coronation festivities.

The overture was supposedly written by Mozart at the last moment—the same way in which he had composed the overture to *Don Giovanni* in 1787 at Prague. It sounds a festive and pathetic note like the overture to *Idomeneo*. The overture displays the appropriate orchestral splendor, with pungent dramatic accents, and reveals the composer as a symphonist in the contrapuntal manipulation of the principal ideas.

Overture to "The Impresario"

In February of 1786 a festive reception in honor of the Governor Generals was held in the imperial palace in Schönbrunn, the Versailles of Vienna. It featured a command performance of the actors of the Burgtheater and the singers of the German and Italian ensembles of the court opera. The Italians appeared in a work of the powerful court conductor Antonio Salieri (1750-1825). They presented his opera buffa *Prima la musica e poi le parole,* a theme treated 150 years later by Richard Strauss in his last opera *Capriccio.* The German ensemble of the court opera entertained the exclusive audience with Mozart's one-act *singspiel Der Schauspieldirektor (The Impresario).* The double bill was mounted on February 7, 1786, and Mozart's work of only four numbers was repeated twice.

Goethe became interested in a textually similar opera *L'impresario in angustie* (The Impresario in Trouble) by Domenico Cimarosa (1749-1801). He did a German adaptation entitled *Theatrical Adventures,* that incorporated Mozart's entire music to *Der Schauspieldirektor.* This concoction was given in Weimar in 1797, and was much applauded. Later, in 1845, a new version of the text in which Mozart appeared as a character, was adapted to his music. Since four numbers did not suffice to fit the new text, additional Mozart pieces (lieder and others) were tapped to meet the situation. In 1896 the Mozart specialist Rudolf Genee produced a *singspiel Der Kapellmeister* using the music of *Der Schauspieldirektor* and other Mozart pieces, and also introduced Mozart as an acting character. Mozart never would have imagined that his little *singspiel* could attract Goethe and provide material for an opera to be staged more than a century later.

The libretto of Mozart's singspiel is a travesty of the problems of a theater manager who has to deal with the rivalry of female singers. It is a play without psychological development of the leading characters. Mozart, who had considerable experience with the whims and weaknesses of theater people, underlined the most easily parodied features. This is apparent in the overture. It is a movement of symphonic design filled with a mixture of seriousness and playfulness, pathos and merriment—a speedily moving instrumental prologue to the play which depicts essentially the strange nature of Thalia's servants.

Overture in B flat major, K. 311a

This composition, unknown to Jahn, Köchel, and other Mozart scholars of the nineteenth century, is not included in the edition of the collected works published between 1876 and 1886 and referred to as the *Alte Gesamtausgabe* (old complete edition) to differentiate it from the monumental new edition now in progress. When Mozart arrived in Paris in March 1778, he was introduced to Joseph le Gros (1730-1793), a former tenor of the Royal Opera and famous interpreter of Gluck's heros. Le Gros had quit the stage in 1777 to succeed the famous violinist Pierre Gaviniès as director of the Concert spirituel. Founded in 1725, these concerts took place around Easter and on holidays when the Opéra was closed. Since twenty-four concerts were given during the year a sizable amount of music, instrumental and vocal, was presented, and the connection with the director held out a definite prospect for Mozart.

Of the four choral pieces he was first commissioned to write, only two were performed. In addition, a sinfonia concertante for flute, oboe, bassoon, and horn was never put on because of the intrigues and double dealings of le Gros. Humiliated and disappointed at the loss of such a good opportunity, the frustrated composer broke off his relationship with le Gros.

Sometime later Mozart chanced to meet him in the company of the tenor Anton Raaff who, incidentally, was to become the first Idomeneo in 1781. Le Gros proffered his humble apologies and, to make up with Mozart, asked him to write a symphony for the Concert spirituel. Mozart was satisfied with this challenge and, accepting it, wrote the D major symphony, K. 297, generally called the Paris Symphony. Its first performance on Corpus Christi day (June 18, 1778) was a triumph, and as a result le Gros asked Mozart for another symphony.

We learn from a letter to his father, dated September 11, 1778, that Mozart had written two symphonies in Paris which did him much honor. Yet accepting this as a fact, we know only one of these two symphonies, namely K. 297 in D major; the other has not survived. The expression "survived" is in this case particularly appropriate if we remember the fate of the autographs of the works Mozart composed for the Concert spirituel. All are lost, including the choral pieces for a *Miserere* by Ignaz Holzbauer, the Sinfonia concertante for wind instruments in E flat major, the D major symphony, and the second Paris Symphony. The latter was performed on September 8, 1778, three days before Mozart wrote the above mentioned letter. The *Journal de Paris* announced it as a *Nouvelle symphonie de la composition del Signor Amadeo Mozart*. The reading on September 8, 1778 was probably not the only one in Paris. Georges St. Foix, the eminent French Mozart scholar, has pointed out that symphonies by Mozart were included in the programs of the Concert spirituel three times in 1779. However, the wording of a passage in Mozart's letter of October 3, 1778, to his father confused the matter. In this letter he reports that he has sold both *overtures* and the Sinfonia concertante to le Gros. Mozart evidently meant both *symphonies*. But where is the second of these symphonies? No trace of it has been detected so far.

Around 1900 Julien Tiersot (1857-1936), a pupil of Franck and Massenet, a prolific author who was then assistant librarian of the Paris conservatory, came across a lot of orchestra parts of a piece in B flat major bearing the heading: *Ouverture à grand orchestre par Mozart*. It was brought out as the eighteenth publication by *L'Imprimerie du Conservatoire*. The activities of the printing plant began in 1800 and the overture appeared probably in

1802. A performance by the student orchestra on September 3, 1803 is recorded but there are no records of later performances. The piece was shelved and quickly forgotten.

The importance of Tiersot's find was recognized although in some quarters the question of the authenticity was raised, particularly in view of the orchestration. The overture is scored for two flutes, oboes, clarinets, bassoons, horns, trumpets, kettledrums, and strings. This instrumental setup links the piece closely to the D major Paris Symphony. Yet the treatment of the orchestra is different from Mozart's technique in the late 1770s. Probably some "editing" was applied to the original score. This calls to mind the case of the Parisian Sinfonia concertante for wind instruments which did not come down to us in its original setting. Yet it is hard to believe that the printing plant of the conservatory would have consciously committed a falsification.

Other voices were heard that welcomed the discovered overture as the lost second Paris symphony. Proceeding from this assumption the overture was discussed in the second edition of Köchel's catalogue (1905) in the section "Lost Compositions" (Appendix I, No. 8). While it is true that the main body (Allegro) of the overture displays symphonic qualities it is difficult to acknowledge this one-movement piece as the lost symphony which was certainly as long as the D major symphony.

Serenade in B flat for thirteen Winds, K. 361

Largo—Allegro molto; Minuetto—Trio I—Trio II; Adagio;
Minuetto—Trio I—Trio II; Romanze: Adagio—Allegretto—Adagio;
Tema con Variazioni; Rondo: Allegro molto

Mozart's contributions to entertainment music constitute a most lovable facet of his work. His more than thirty cassations, divertimenti, notturni, and serenades, generated by social events, are the product of an old Austrian tradition. A British traveler, Dr. E. Brown, reported in 1684 that during his stay in Vienna he had enjoyed almost every evening a performance of a serenade in front of his windows. An account of the late eighteenth century stresses the fact that the Viennese serenades had practically nothing in common with the Italian and Spanish practice of singing with guitar accompaniment; instead of being designed to express the feelings of one individual to another, the Viennese serenades were offered by groups, small or large, who sang ensemble pieces from operas, or played orchestral and even symphonic music. This Viennese custom gave a strong impetus to art music, with which Mozart had ample opportunity to become acquainted through his father's compositions and also those of Joseph Haydn's brother Michael (1737-1806), who had joined the musical establishment of the Archbishopric in Salzburg in 1762.

While the serenade was basically intended for open-air performances, the stylistically related divertimento was meant to entertain a company dining indoors. *Divertimento* actually means "entertainment"; such a piece included two dance movements (minuets) and was supposed to be light fare. Yet that this form can transcend its usual surroundings and reach the highest artistic sphere is illustrated by Mozart's Divertimento for string trio in E flat major,

K. 563, which was composed in 1788, at the time of his last symphonies, and is one of his greatest creations. Mozart also intentionally moved in this direction in his serenades, which he sometimes designated *Finalmusik*. A concert may have begun with a symphony, continued with a concerto and vocal offerings, and concluded with a serenade as *Finalmusik*.

Mozart's output of serenades and divertimenti is a dazzling kaleidoscope of instrumental combinations. There are pieces for wind band, for strings, and for symphony orchestra. The famous "Haffner" serenade, K. 250, is an example of an orchestral work, and the well-known *Eine kleine Nachtmusik*, K. 525, would represent a piece for strings. Two of his most significant works for wind instruments are the Serenade in B flat major, K. 361, and the Serenade in C minor, K. 388. The latter, called by Mozart "Nacht Musique . . . auf Harmonie," departs from a well-established tradition in its four-movement form and in its dark instrumental colors and strong emotionalism.

In sharp contrast is the earlier B flat serenade, an unusual piece, whose autograph is now in the Library of Congress. Mozart aptly designated the serenade "Gran Partita." The Italian expression *partita* means a "lot" (of goods) and our serenade indeed offers a "lot" of pieces: a symphonically conceived first movement, two minuets with two trios each, an Adagio, a Romanze, a variation series, and a Rondo finale. The history of the piece is shrouded in darkness. We do not know who commissioned it, nor what circumstances may have prompted Mozart to choose this particular scoring. It is assumed that Mozart began the composition at the end of 1780, a period when his creative mind was focused on *Idomeneo*. One important influence on the opera—the excellence of the orchestra in Munich, where *Idomeneo* was to be produced—could have provided a stimulus for the composition of the serenade.

Mozart knew that the quality of the Munich court orchestra could hardly have been matched anywhere, for it was composed chiefly of members of the Mannheim orchestra, considered the best in Europe. Familiar with the Mannheim musicians from his stay there in 1778, Mozart knew that he could count on four horns, and *Idomeneo* is actually the only one of his seven major operas scored for four horns. He was also aware that the technical standard of the Munich woodwind players was high, which the scoring of *Idomeneo* convincingly reflects. Therefore, the assumption that Mozart conceived the "Gran Partita" with the excellence of the Munich wind players in mind has a solid foundation. We do not know how long it took him to compose the serenade. Alfred Einstein places its completion in the first half of 1781, after Mozart had moved to Vienna. We know of a reading that took place in Vienna in 1784 at a concert given by the excellent clarinetist Anton Stadler, who became an intimate friend of Mozart. The playwright Johann Friedrich Schink notes, "I have heard a piece for wind instruments by Herr Mozart today. Magnificent! It employed thirteen instruments and at every instrument a master. The effect was grand and magnificent beyond description."

The mastery of orchestration in *Idomeneo* is also manifest in the "Gran Partita," where Mozart for the first time employs the basset horn, the alto of the clarinet family, which had been constructed in 1770 and later improved by Stadler. The absence of the flute in this large ensemble is not surprising: Mozart did not love the instrument, and the scoring of the "Gran Partita" is actually an enlargement of the standard eight-piece ensemble, consisting of one pair each of oboes, clarinets, bassoons, and horns. Mozart charms the listener by the delicate and diversified grouping of instruments, and holds the attention of the audience by the astounding variety of movements.

In the first movement the slow and pompous introduction alerts the listener to the more serious things to come. The main body of the movement (Allegro molto, 4/4) proceeds along symphonic lines. There ensues a sprightly minuet, which is then contrasted with the gentle sonorities of the first trio in E flat major, executed by the clarinets and basset horns, as well as to the minor mode of the second trio (G minor). The Adagio (E flat major) evolves around the steadily moving broken chords of the bass line and a characteristic rhythmic motif, incessantly repeated:

A poetic interpretation of this Adagio, which is not equaled in all serenade literature, is left to the listener.

The serenity we associate with a serenade is repressed again in the first trio (B flat minor) of the second minuet. This episode over, Mozart soothes any disturbed listener with the *ländler* of the second trio (F major), which foreshadows those delectable tunes of the "Sleigh Ride" or of the great E flat major symphony. The fifth movement is a typical Romanze—a three-section piece with a sharply contrasting middle division. In the center section the Allegretto tempo is set against the Adagio of the other divisions; the 2/4 meter is in opposition to the basic 3/4; and the C minor key offers a tonal contrast to the E flat major key of the preceding and following sections. The third section, a restatement of the first Adagio, is amended by a coda. In the next movement a series of six variations, in which oboes, clarinets, and basset horns are favored, provides splendid and rewarding opportunities for the players. Musically the variations correspond to a set which appears in the Andantino of the quartet for flute, violin, viola, and violoncello in C major, K. 285 b (Einstein), composed presumably in January or February 1778 in Mannheim. The pleasant tone of the serenade is once more abandoned in the fourth variation (B flat minor). Yet Mozart obliges the listener by closing with the major chord to cancel the potential harmonic contrast at the beginning of the fifth variation, the tenderness and charm of which recall the Adagio. The sixth and final variation, an Allegretto in 3/4 time, prepares the listener for the sparkling and humorous Finale (2/4).

Serenade for Winds in E flat major, K. 375
Allegro maestoso; Minuetto; Adagio; Minuetto; Allegro

We are well informed about the history of this work through a letter that

Mozart wrote to his father on November 3, 1781. The pertinent paragraph reads:

> It happened to be my name day (October 31), so I performed my devotions in the morning, and, just as I was going to write you, a whole crowd of congratulating friends literally besieged me. At 12 o'clock I drove out to Baroness Waldstädten at Leopoldstadt, where I spent my name day. At eleven at night I was treated to a serenade performed by two clarinets, two horns, two bassoons—and that too of my own composition—for I wrote it for St. Theresa's Day [October 15] for Frau von Hickel's sister, or rather the sister-in-law of Herr von Hickel, court painter, at whose house it was performed for the first time. The six gentlemen who executed it are poor beggars who, however, play quite well together, particularly the first clarinet and the two horns. But the chief reason why I composed it was in order to let Herr von Strack, who goes there every day, hear something of my composition; I wrote it rather carefully. It has won great applause too and on St. Theresa Night it was performed in three different places; for as soon as they finished playing it in one place, they were taken off somewhere else and paid to play it. Well, these musicians asked that the street door might be opened and, placing themselves in the center of the courtyard, surprised me, as I was about to undress, in the most pleasant fashion imaginable with the first chord in E flat."

Herr von Strack was not a nobleman, but a valet of Emperor Joseph and an amateur cellist who was in charge of the regular musical meetings in which the Emperor participated. Strack, who also took care of the program, exercised a certain influence in the choice of pieces to be played. Mozart's anxiety to win this man over is understandable. His efforts, however, were of no avail, not because of the lack of good will on the part of the imperial musical valet, but because of the very conservative attitude of the Emperor, who was not touched by the music of Haydn or Mozart.

To put the serenade in the proper biographical perspective, it should be recalled that Mozart penned it while his mind was focused on the opera *The Abduction from the Seraglio.* Nevertheless, as he worked on the opera, he did not forget the serenade and converted it from a sextet into a wind octet, by adding parts for two oboes. In doing so, he gave the piece the instrumental garb customary for groups that performed dinner music. Mozart provided a classic example of such an ensemble in the dinner scene in the second act of *Don Giovanni.*

Did Mozart receive a commission that would account for the conversion of the original for an eight-piece ensemble? It has been suggested by Alfred Einstein that the octet version was solicited by Prince Alois Liechtenstein, the son of the reigning prince, who wanted to organize a little wind band for which Mozart would provide the repertory. Yet the project came to naught. The octet version was published in 1792, after Mozart's death, while the sextet, though printed in 1804, faded completely into oblivion. It was resurrected in 1955, without important practical results.

Mozart's statement that he wrote the E flat major serenade "rather carefully," is another way of saying that he intentionally deviated from the usual pleasant atmosphere surrounding social music. This is particularly evident in the opening Allegro maestoso, which is very similar to the beginning of the Allegro maestoso of the sinfonia concertante for violin and viola in the same key (1779, K. 364). By giving the first movement a more serious air and dispensing with the customary repeat of the first section (exposition), Mozart clearly aimed at conciseness. The trend to brevity is also apparent in the first short minuet.

The Adagio is not entertainment either. Permeated with noble lyricism and tenderness, it is appealing because of the beauty of its sound. Although Mozart used ideas of folklike quality in the spirited rondo finale, he did not hesitate to include a short passage of "learned music" and a contrapuntal play with a simple horn signal. This, too, is one of the features he had in mind when he said that he composed the serenade "rather carefully."

Serenade for Winds in C minor, K. 388

Allegro; Andante; Minuetto in canone; Allegro

At the end of July 1782, Mozart was requested to write another serenade for the Haffner family, Salzburg patricians whose name he made immortal among music lovers through the well-known "Haffner" serenade (K. 250) of July 1776. Mozart was not very happy about the Salzburg business. *The Abduction from the Seraglio* had packed houses in spite of the "terrible heat," as Mozart put it, and he was very busy arranging this new successful opera for wind-band. He also had another matter to attend to—a commission for a serenade about which no facts are known. Mozart, however, could not decline the request from Salzburg, so he informed his father, through whom the commission had been arranged, that he would send the requested serenade piecemeal. Explaining the situation to his father in a letter dated July 27, 1782, Mozart contended that he had no other alternative because he had quickly to write another *Nacht Musique,* but only for wind instruments, and that he could not use it for Salzburg. The second "Haffner" serenade was not published for 180 years, but we know it in a revised and reduced version as the "Haffner" symphony in D major (K. 385). The other *Nacht Musique . . . auf Harmonie* is the serenade heard tonight.

Its history is shrouded in darkness. We do not know who commissioned it nor the circumstances that compelled Mozart to concern himself first with this piece, while postponing the order from Salzburg. The missing information would shed light on this remarkable work, which contradicts the concept of the serenade in spirit and letter.

Who was the mysterious personage who wanted a serenade for wind instruments on such short notice? According to the 1964 edition of Köchel's catalogue, it was Prince Alois Liechtenstein, the son of the reigning prince of the tiny state. The Liechtensteins resided in their palaces in Vienna, where their magnificent painting collection was kept. The young prince, interested in music for wind instruments, wanted to organize a band for which Mozart would supply music. Mozart demanded an appointment for life, a condition that the prince declined to meet. The only tangible results from this abortive project were presumably the octet version of the E flat serenade for six instruments (K. 375) and the work under discussion.

Were there personal circumstances that led Mozart to abandon the customary form and qualities of the serenade in the C minor piece? Gone are the multi-movement structure with two dance movements, the concerted rondos, the delightful Andantes, the sweetness, the jocular passages—in short, all the pleasantries of entertaining music. Breaking fully with an already well established tradition, Mozart wrote one of his most serious works, charged with strong emotionalism, and garbed with dark instrumental colors. The four-movement C minor serenade has hardly more in common than the name with its extended sister works of seven or eight movements. In one respect only does the C minor piece keep with tradition, namely in the scoring: pairs of clarinets, oboes, bassoons, and horns form the standard eight-piece band for dinner music, which Mozart has immortalized in the dinner scene in the second act of *Don Giovanni*.

The C minor serenade is a work of almost symphonic conception, of eminent tonal balance and consummate craftsmanship, which is displayed prominently in the *Minuetto in canone* with the *Trio al rovescio*, a contrapuntal achievement of the first order. There are two melodic units; the second voice answers the melody sounded by the first, by producing its intervals in inversions. The finale is a chain of variations akin to the last movement of the piano concerto in C minor (K. 491). The fourth variation is a double variation. That is to say, each of the two sections of the theme is varied twice. Then follows an episode in E flat major, with bright colors in marked contrast to the serious main key. The minor mode returns with the fifth variation, which, like the sixth, is also a double variation. Events then take an unexpected turn in the bright C major coda.

This remarkable work, which in spite of its title cannot be placed in the category of social music, has been interpreted as a manifestation of an emotional and spiritual crisis. It must have been dear to Mozart, because he decided to arrange it for string quintet to make it performable in the home of the average amateur and musician. Köchel gave the quintet version the number 406 and dated it 1784. This was an error. Mozart converted the serenade into a string quintet in 1787, the year of *Don Giovanni*, when he prepared for publication his two great string quintets in C major (K. 515) and G minor (K. 516). Einstein numbered it K. 516b. The fact that Mozart considered the quintet version worthy to be combined with two such extraordinary achievements as the aforementioned quintets reveals how highly he thought of the C minor piece. It is clear that only the scoring prompted Mozart to call it *"Nacht Musique."* For the quintet version he could dispense with this denomination without the slightest scruple.

Eine kleine Nachtmusik, K. 525

Allegro; Romance: Andante; Minuetto; Rondo: Allegro

Mozart entered *Eine Kleine Nachtmusik* (K. 525) in his own thematic catalogue as No. 65 on August 10, 1787. From this date, we can conclude that he composed the piece while his mind was focused on *Don Giovanni* (K. 527). The première of the opera, which was written for Prague, was originally scheduled for October 15, and Mozart had to work hard in August to complete a substantial part of the opera before he set out for the production in Prague. Yet he put aside *Don Giovanni* to work on *Eine kleine Nachtmusik* and a violin sonata in A major (K. 526), both of which were probably commissioned by an amateur or a connoisseur. Compared to the large "Haffner" serenade (K. 250), the "Posthorn" serenade (K. 320), and the Gran Partita for wind instruments (K. 361), the *Nachtmusik* is a small work indeed, but in the opinion of Alfred Einstein "a most enigmatic one." Who commissioned it? Did the mysterious unknown want a short piece and one for strings only? And why was it published only as late as 1827?

The publication added another puzzle. Mozart's entry in his catalogue reads "*Eine kleine Nachtmusik*, bestehend [consisting of] in einem Allegro, Menuett und Trio—Romance, Menuett und Trio, Finale. 2 Violini, Viola e Bassi." Thus we learn that *Eine kleine Nachtmusik* originally consisted of five movements and included two minuets. Yet for the first edition, one minuet was inexplicably discarded. Mozart's entry also indicates that the piece was not conceived as a string quartet, but as an orchestral composition, which required "*Bassi*," violoncello and double bass.

Eine kleine Nachtmusik is the last in Mozart's series of serenades and displays the outstanding features of the series: the transparent texture and absence of contrapuntal complexities, the predominance of the major mode, the serene and joyful mood. The appearance of the minor mode is limited to the middle section of the Romanze. This is a structural and harmonic requisite of the Romanze (Romance, or Romanza in Italian), which many a listener has observed in the Romanze in Mozart's piano concerto in D minor (K. 466). The C minor passage in the *Nachtmusik* Romanze—a canonic dialogue between the first violin and the bass—is only a fleeting episode; the clouds soon disappear, and serenity, pleasantness, and delight stay with us throughout the minuet and the animated Rondo finale.

Sinfonia concertante in E flat major for Violin, Viola, and Orchestra, K. 364

Allegro maestoso; Andante; Presto

One of Mozart's great delights was playing chamber music, particularly string quartets in which he took the viola part. Thus he approached the composition of the sinfonia concertante for violin and viola with the expert knowledge of the solo instruments and their potentialities. It is assumed that the sinfonia concertante was composed in the summer of 1779 in Salzburg. The loss of the autograph, which Mozart usually dated, and the absence of other documentary evidence precludes the exact determination of the time of composition. The virtuoso demands of the viola part, at a time when there was a lack of violists, suggests that Mozart played it himself.

He seems to have had a great interest in the sinfonia concertante as a form, because shortly after completion of the E flat major piece, he decided to try his hand at it once more in the sinfonia concertante for violin, viola, and violoncello in A major. His official duties and his work on the opera *Idomeneo* interfered with the completion of this sinfonia concertante. Later no occasion arose that might have induced Mozart to take up this project again. Technically, the sinfonia concertante was superseded by the Mozartian concerto type, which combines the baroque principle of instrumental dualism, tutti, and solo with the thematic dualism of the classical sonata and symphony.

The symphonic element in this work is accentuated in the outer movements, specifically in the impressive opening¹ tutti of the Allegro maestoso. Here Mozart, the symphonist, speaks with supreme command over the orchestral forces, notably in the extended crescendo of the remarkable trill chain, a passage that anticipates the language of the great E flat major symphony of 1788 (first movement). The symphonic spirit is also evident in the first entry of the solo instruments: tutti and solo are not separated, and the entrance of the latter occurs rather unobtrusively. Running through 382 measures, the first Allegro of this sinfonia concertante exceeds in length the first movements of Mozart's last four symphonies, D major ("Prague"), E flat major, G minor, and C major ("Jupiter"), which are in length 302, 309, 299, and 313 measures respectively. The proportions of the structural design link the work to Mozart's great symphonies as well as to the outstanding creations of the Viennese piano concertos.

The concerto element naturally required the inclusion of cadenzas. Mozart was particularly concerned with the cadenza for the Andante and wrote three for it. This movement, in the fateful key of C minor, is perhaps the most intense and introspective music Mozart had created thus far. Its serious mood is in sharp contrast to the serene finale, which teems with musical ideas. The latter movement is a melodic kaleidoscope, to which the entire ensemble, the soloists and their confrères in the orchestra—especially the oboists and horn players—happily contribute.

Sinfonia concertante in E flat major, K. Anhang C. 14.01, for Oboe, Clarinet, Horn, Bassoon, and Orchestra
Allegro maestoso; Andante; Presto

In 1777 Mozart obtained a release from his appointment at Salzburg and, accompanied by his mother, journeyed to Munich, Augsburg, and Mannheim in search of a better position than the one he had held in his home town. Mannheim, the seat of the Elector of the Palatinate, appealed strongly to Mozart. No wonder—Mannheim prided itself upon an excellent orchestra that in the 1760s and 1770s was considered Europe's outstanding instrumental organization. Mozart became very friendly with the conductor, Christian Cannabich, and several first-desk men, the flutist Johann Baptist Wendling, the oboist Friedrich Ramm, and the bassoon virtuoso Georg Wenzel Ritter. The latter three, who were about to leave the organization to undertake a concert tour to Paris, invited Wolfgang to join them as accompanist and composer. At first he declined, but after his attempts to obtain a good position in Mannheim came to naught he decided to try his luck in Paris.

He arrived there in March, 1778 at a very unfavorable moment. How could the young man of twenty-two attract the attention and interest of musical and intellectual circles in the French capital then engulfed in an aesthetic tug of war? It was the feud between the French faction, the admirers of Gluck, and the Italian party, which favored Piccini. Mozart steered clear of this controversy. He soon realized the impossibility of receiving an operatic commission and gladly accepted an offer to contribute something to the program of the Concert spirituel, conducted by Joseph le Gros. Instituted in 1725 these concerts were given in the Tuileries during the period before and after Easter and on certain days when the Académie de Musique was closed. Mozart was introduced to le Gros by his Mannheim friends Wendling, Ramm, and Ritter who had been joined by the splendid Bohemian horn virtuoso, Johann Wenzel Stich, who preferred to be called by his Italian nom de plume, Giovanni Punto.

Le Gros wanted Mozart to replace certain sections of a *Miserere* by the Austrian composer Ignaz Holzbauer (1711-1783), conductor in Mannheim. Though Mozart expressed satisfaction with his contributions in letters to his father, he was frustrated by le Gros who, in the performance, omitted two of Mozart's choral pieces and "thus left out the best." The composer had to be satisfied with the applause accorded him at the rehearsal. Nor did he fare better with the second commission, a sinfonia concertante for flute, oboe, bassoon, and horn.

With excellent musicians at his disposal, Mozart went to work with enthusiasm. Punto, the horn virtuoso, had no rival. His artistry was admired by Beethoven who wrote him a sonata (Opus 17) and appeared with him on the concert stage at its reading (1800). Mozart composed the Concertante in "greatest hurry" and handed over the score to le Gros. Only four days were left for writing out the parts. Two days before the concert Mozart found the score hidden by other music in le Gros' place. Asked whether he had ordered the copying of the parts, le Gros answered: "No, I forgot about that." Mozart realized the situation. The soloists, who were "enamoured" with the work, became furious, but their anger was of no avail, for le Gros did not want to perform the composition. Mozart suspected Giovanni Cambini (1746-1825), an Italian composer, as the wire-puller behind the scenes.

The fate of the manuscript is shrouded in darkness. Mozart failed to retain a copy, and some years later wanted to reconstruct the composition from memory, but there were evidently no compelling circumstances to set his pen in motion. Köchel listed the work in his thematic catalogue, published in 1862, as "entirely lost" (gänzlich verschollen), yet in the estate of the great Mozart scholar, Otto Jahn (1811-1868), a nicely written copy of a sinfonia concertante in E flat major was found. Considered Mozart's lost sinfonia concertante of 1778, the find posed, nonetheless, an intriguing puzzle—the solo instruments are not flute, oboe, bassoon, and horn as in Mozart's original composition, but oboe, clarinet, bassoon, and horn. In other words, the version we know is an arrangement that is no way authenticated. These circumstances prompted the later editors of Köchel's thematic catalogue, now already a centenarian, to list our sinfonia concertante in the appendix (*Anhang*). This does not amount to final judgment of authorship. It simply refers to unsatisfactory sources.

The sinfonia concertante emerged from the attempts of the early composers in the classical style to infuse the concerto principle, one of the most significant features of baroque instrumental music, into the outstanding structural achievement of the classical style—the symphony. The example under review discloses a variety of elements characteristic of both the baroque and classical styles: the three-movement structure points to the baroque solo concerto and the Italian and early classical symphony, including works by Haydn and Mozart; the scoring, which provides for a concertino of four wind instruments and a larger body (strings, oboes, horns), stems from the concerto grosso; the inclusion of a cadenza for all solo instruments at the end of the first movement, sporadically found in the baroque, is a feature of the classical concerto; the design of the first movement conforms to the classical sonata and symphony. All these elements are blended together with a craftsmanship that also mirrors Mozart's observation of the devices of the Mannheim composers.

The symphonic quality is accentuated in the opening Allegro of our Concertante in the energetic main idea that anticipates the first theme of the piano concerto in E flat major, K. 482. The slow middle movement represents the type of "singing" Andante that offers the solo instruments ample opportunity to "sing." The finale, a set of ten variations, deviates somewhat in structure from the symphonic principle, yet it must be pointed out that this procedure did not remain an isolated case since Mozart later applied the variation technique to the final movements of the piano concertos in G major (K. 453, 1784) and C minor (K. 491, 1786). In our special case Mozart, wanting to oblige the Parisians, presented as a theme a simple gavotte-like melody in the manner of the popular round with refrain, which as *vaudeville* became an essential feature of the opéra-comique.

The melody is introduced by the concertino while the orchestra adds the refrain. In the variations all solo instruments get a chance to display their technical proficiency. There is no refrain after the last variation but a recitative-like passage that leads to a short finale (Allegro, 6/8). Here, suddenly, a solemn passage is heard, seemingly an admonition to the audience to take the composer seriously in spite of the light fare he offered them in the finale.

Symphony in C major, K. 200

Allegro spiritoso; Andante, Minuetto; Presto

After the return from his third Italian journey in March 1773 and a short trip to Vienna in that same summer, Mozart resumed his obligations as a member of the musical establishment of the Archbishop of Salzburg. There he produced a number of instrumental works for the evening concerts that took place daily from seven until eight-fifteen. The program would include a symphony, two arias, and a concerto or another symphony. A large quantity of music was required to meet these demands, which accounts for the immense productivity of both Mozarts—Leopold was also a composer to the Salzburg court (1757-1787)—and Michael Haydn, who entered the service of the Archbishop in 1762. (The same conditions prevailed in Esterház where Joseph Haydn had to bear the burden as Kapellmeister for thirty years.)

The influences to which Mozart was exposed in Italy and Vienna are manifest in his early symphonic output. Some of his symphonies follow Italian models in their three-movement design and melodic quality, whereas others are patterned after the four-movement Viennese type that includes a minuet. To this group belongs the C major symphony, K. 200, presented tonight. It forms with its sister works in G minor, K. 183, and A major, K. 201, a remarkable trilogy, which anticipates on a smaller scale the monumentality of the triad of 1788—E flat major, G minor, and C major. The C major symphony was completed on November 12 or 17, 1774, in Salzburg, a date established as a result of investigation of the manuscript undertaken for the 1964 edition of Köchel's catalogue.

The first movement, Allegro spiritoso, displays the thematic dualism of the more advanced symphonic type and also a real working out of the main theme (Ex. 1).

The movement also has a coda, a feature Mozart had found in the symphonies of Joseph Haydn's brother Michael. The Andante in F major introduces a tune in the spirit of the German lied, which displays delicate orchestration with the muffled violins. The minuet is devoid of rustic or ceremonious elements, and one feels the composer's intention to elevate it to a higher plane. Witness the romantic character of the horn call and the contrasting qualities in the trio. The crown of the work is the finale in which not only symphonic workmanship and the *buffo* spirit are harmoniously blended together but also a thematic integration with the first movement is splendidly achieved. The theme of the finale is a changed version of the theme of the opening Allegro (see 1 and 2).

The motif of the running eighth-notes given out by the second violins

proves to be a thematic factor of great importance and hurries through the piece in a *moto perpetuo* fashion. The obstinate repetition of motif *3a*, as well as the crescendo passage built upon it, anticipates, technically and emotionally, passages in the overture to *The Abduction from the Seraglio*.

Symphony in A major, K. 201

Allegro moderato; Andante; Minuetto; Allegro con spirito

This symphony, written in Salzburg presumably in January 1774, originated during the period when the influence of Joseph Haydn became manifest in Mozart's string quartets and symphonies. Throughout the nineteenth century the standard orchestral repertory included only the symphonies of Mozart's Viennese years, 1782 to 1791. The preceding symphonies were neglected although they had been made readily accessible when the complete works were issued between 1876 and 1886. Only in our century were the intrinsic values of our symphony recognized, much to the enrichment of concert programs and the pleasure of audiences.

The work combines fine orchestral writing with a delicate chamber style. The first Allegro captivates the listener through the richness and diversity of its musical ideas. The tender Andante, in which the violins are muted, is the domain of the first violins, which "sing" charming melodies and playful coloraturas that betray Mozart the opera composer. The mildness of the Andante is contrasted with the dotted rhythms of the energetic minuet, which is remote from the graceful French court dance. Yet the courtly *menuet* was originally a rustic dance before Pierre Beauchamp, the dancing master of Louis XIV, refined it. Though conflicting with the prevailing fashion, the classical composers inadvertently restored the original quality of the minuet in numerous instances. In our case Mozart reserved the elegant and fashionable manner for the ensuing trio.

The quick finale reflects the spirit of the opera buffa, notably in the middle section. The alternation of the opening motif by the first violins and the basses seems to portray a lively argument of an insistent young woman (soprano) with a grumbling old man (basso). In 1782 Mozart begged his father to dispatch the symphony from Salzburg to Vienna, as he wanted to include it in the program of one of his Akademies. He must have been fond of this symphony. Twentieth century audiences share this sentiment.

Symphony in C major, K. 338

Allegro vivace; Andante di molto; Allegro vivace

In the first half of 1780, before Mozart concerned himself with the opera *Idomeneo,* he wrote three important works in C major: the mass, K. 337, the symphony, K. 338, and the vesper, K. 339. The symphony completed a triptych composed of the pieces K. 318 (G major), K. 319 (B flat), and K. 338 (C major), which show a distinct stylistic kinship. They are the last symphonies he created in Salzburg. Lacking the minuet, they represent the three-movement Italian symphonic type that was still the preferred one in Salzburg, while in Vienna, Germany, and France the four-movement symphony had become established. When Mozart selected K. 319 and K. 338 for performances in Vienna, he deemed it necessary to provide them with minuets to comply with the accepted pattern. A sketch for a minuet is actually jotted down in the autograph of K. 338, dated Salzburg, August 29, 1780.

A Viennese reading of this symphony may have been given a year after its composition; the following passage is from a letter Mozart dispatched to his father on April 11, 1781: "I forgot to tell you the other day that at the concert the symphony went *magnifique* and had the greatest success—40 violins played—the wind instruments all doubled—10 violas, 10 doublebasses, 8 violoncellos, and 6 bassoons."

A ninety-piece orchestra could be assembled only on special occasions in Vienna in Mozart's time, and this concert was offered by the *Tonkünstler Sozietät,* a professional welfare organization. The *Sozietät* gave four concerts yearly, on days when theatrical productions were prohibited on religious grounds, such as during Holy Week or Advent. Naturally, every musician felt morally bound to donate his services, and the concerts took place in the Opera and later in the Burgtheater.

In 1781 the concerts were directed by the court composer and conductor Joseph Bonno (1710-1788), who was on friendly terms with Mozart. Bonno gave Mozart a splendid chance. He included a symphony in the program on April 3 and featured Mozart as pianist. Whether the symphony in C major was actually played then has not been determined on the basis of documentary evidence, but the assumption that Mozart chose it is not farfetched, since it was his most recent symphony, and he may have thought it would raise his stature as a symphonist.

The late Eric Blom, editor of the monumental fifth edition of Grove's *Dictionary of Music and Musicians,* considered K. 338 "the earliest of Mozart's symphonies to achieve any degree of permanence, as far as concert practice goes." This may be debated, but it is certain that the symphony no longer leads a Cinderella existence as it did thirty and forty years ago. It always finds a delighted and grateful audience. The parts of the symphony were first published in 1797, and the score only in 1828.

The first movement, which lacks the customary repeat of the first section (exposition), sounds a festive note characteristic of the Italian opera overture. There are no tense or emotional episodes. The gentleness, however, yields to vigor and energy in the forceful coda. The Andante was originally scored for strings only. Mozart later added a bassoon part, not for color but to reinforce the bass line. The movement is a tender piece, light and transparent, which enraptures the listener through the simplicity and charm of its musical ideas. The rapid finale, which displays the mood and motion of the tarantella, races along in *moto perpetuo* fashion. It represents the union of the spirit of the *opera buffa* and German symphonic technique.

Symphony in D major, K. 385, "Haffner"

Allegro con spirito; Andante; Minuetto; Finale: Presto

At the end of July 1782 Mozart was requested by his father to write a serenade for the festivities arranged to celebrate the nobilitation of the highly esteemed, patrician Salzburg family Haffner. The request came at a most inconvenient time. *The Abduction from the Seraglio* had packed full houses in the Burgtheater despite the "terrible heat" described by Mozart, and he was very busy arranging this new and successful opera for wind-band. This business could not be postponed. Mozart feared that someone would get the jump on him and "reap the profits." In addition, he had quickly to write another *"Nacht Musique,"* but for wind instruments only. This was the serenade in C minor whose history is shrouded in darkness. Mozart could not use this piece for Salzburg because it is one of his most serious works, charged with strong emotionalism, and garbed in dark instrumental colors. It is music which can not be offered at gatherings where the guests had to be entertained in the spirit of merriment.

Mozart's situation in those days was further aggravated by his impending marriage to Constanze Weber; a marriage of which his father disapproved. Mozart, therefore, wanted to avoid exasperating his father for any reason.

In view of the friendly relationship between the Mozarts and the socially prominent Haffner family, Wolfgang could not turn down his father's request. He had no other alternative than to burden himself with the composition of another Haffner serenade.

Mozart had already written a serenade, in July 1776, for the marriage of Elisabeth, a daughter of Sigmund Haffner a former mayor of Salzburg. The wedding serenade (seven movements and a march) had immortalized the name of the rich Salzburg family in the music world. The serenade which Mozart contributed to the later nobilitation festivities is of smaller dimensions than the earlier one. Like its predecessor of 1776, K. 250, it is also in D major, and consisted of a March (K. 408, No. 2), an Allegro, Andante, two Minuets, and a Finale. The guests who gathered in the garden of the Haffner mansion must have liked the serenade because it met the generally gay atmosphere of the occasion. One particular feature was probably not understood: the allusion in the Finale to Osmin's aria *"Ha wie will ich triumphieren"* from the *Abduction*. It added an autobiographical note and, perhaps, reflected Mozart's high-spirited conviction that he was going to surmount all his current difficulties. He did. He fulfilled his commission on time, was married on August 4, and received on the following day, the paternal consent.

In the Winter of 1783 Mozart begged his father to send him the score of the second Haffner serenade. He wanted to convert it into a symphony to be played in one of his Viennese concerts in March. Upon receipt of the piece he expressed his astonishment about the work in a letter to his father: "I did not remember a word of it, and it must be very effective." Removing the serenade character by excluding the march and one minuet, Mozart reduced the work to four movements. He altered the scoring (two oboes, bassoons, horns, trumpets, kettledrums, and strings) through inclusion of flutes and clarinets. (Strangely enough, the first printed edition of the symphony [1832] presents the piece in the Salzburg orchestration without flutes and clarinets.) The autograph of the Vienna version once in possession of King Ludwig II of Bavaria, the patron of Richard Wagner, is now owned by the National Orchestral Association of New York. The manuscript of the second Haffner serenade has disappeared.

In its shortened and orchestrally revised version, the *Haffner Symphony* acquired a firm place in the orchestral repertory. It was first heard in Vienna on March 23, 1783.

Symphony in C major, K. 425, "Linz"

Adagio—Allegro spiritoso; Poco Adagio; Minuetto; Presto

In July of 1783 Mozart and his young wife Constanze journeyed to Salzburg, hoping to achieve reconciliation with his father, who had strongly opposed Wolfgang's marriage. Wolfgang assumed that Constanze would make a good impression and his father would not overlook that his artistic prestige had risen considerably since the resounding success of *The Abduction from the Seraglio*. Yet Mozart was deeply disappointed. His father was unrelenting and his sister Nannerl treated Constanze coolly. Constanze felt deeply hurt, and Nannerl's attitude alienated her brother. It was not a pleasant visit, and

Mozart certainly left his father's house with some relief, after a stay of about three months, without having accomplished his purpose. One bright spot in these unhappy days was the performance of the great mass in C minor, K. 427, which, however, has come down to us only in a fragmentary stage.

Mozart left Salzburg in a gloomy mood and arrived on October 30 in Linz, heartily welcomed by Count Thun, a prominent Austrian nobleman. It seems that the visit was planned but Mozart arrived later than expected, for he was faced with the task of composing a symphony for an *Akademie* scheduled for November 4. On October 31 Mozart wrote his father of his involvement in this concert and added: "And because I have not a single symphony with me I am writing a new one head over heels and must finish it by that time [November 4]."

We know from Mozart's letters that the day of the *Akademie* was a Tuesday, and the period between October 31 and then included a Sunday and All Saints Day, November 1. Church attendance and a certain minimum of social obligations toward his host must have kept Mozart away from his work for a time. The symphony must have been completed the night of November 3 so that the task of copying the parts could be undertaken on the fourth in the hours before the concert. The whole situation foreshadows the story of the composition of the overture to *Don Giovanni*: the copyists of the theater in Prague had to write out the parts of the overture of 291 measures on the day of the première of the opera. The men in Linz had to copy 863 measures under the same trying circumstances. If this were actually accomplished in one day, one must ask: was there any time left to play through the symphony before the *Akademie*? Did Mozart succeed in finishing the symphony in time? Only the autograph could answer the question since Mozart entered such dates in his manuscripts, but the autograph of the symphony was lost with many others.

The matter assumes a still more puzzling aspect because of its connection with the history of the G major symphony, listed as No. 444 by Köchel and published in the complete edition of Mozart's works. Earlier Mozart biographers did not know that this symphony was actually the work of Michael Haydn (1737-1806) and considered it the piece that was played at the *Akademie* on November 4. Mozart did provide a slow introduction (twenty measures) to the first Allegro and began to copy the parts. When Köchel investigated the material, the fact that the manuscripts were partly in Mozart's handwriting prompted him to regard this as a composition of Mozart. The true author was identified by the French Mozart scholar Georges St. Foix in 1908. One wonders about the reason that would have caused Mozart to burden himself with editing this symphony in four days. Perhaps he did not finish the C major symphony and worked on the Haydn piece as a makeshift solution. If he actually occupied himself simultaneously with the two works in these four days, the inescapable conclusion is that the C major symphony was in his mind and the creative process was practically finished before Mozart began to commit the symphony to paper.

With the C major symphony Mozart re-entered the symphonic field after a pause of three years. To be sure, in March 1783, he converted a serenade composed in 1782 into a symphony, commonly referred to as the "Haffner"

Symphony. It was preceded by the three-movement symphony in C major, K. 338, dated Salzburg, August 28, 1780. In his Viennese period (1781-1791) Mozart wrote only five symphonies: the C major piece, nicknamed the "Linz" Symphony, the so-called "Prague" Symphony, K. 504, of 1786, and the great triptych of 1788 in E flat major, G minor, and C major, K. 543, 550, and 551. There is an interesting coincidence: the last Salzburg symphony is in C major, the first in the Viennese period is in C major, and Mozart's very last symphonic creation is in the same key.

Mozart's Viennese years coincided with Haydn's third and last decade in the employ of Prince Esterházy. The symphonies Haydn created in the years 1773-1792 had spread his fame all over the Continent and England. Mozart fell under his influence, and this is evident in the "Linz" Symphony: in the four-movement design; in the slow introduction to the initial Allegro, a device frequently applied by Haydn; in the gentleness of the slow movement and in the siciliano rhythm, which we encounter often in Haydn; in the rustic quality of the minuet; and finally in the humorous air of the last movement.

The close relationship to the C minor mass is also evident in this C major symphony. The splendid beginning recalls the pomp displayed in certain sections of the Gloria and Credo. The fanfare-like motifs in the Allegro spirit are reminiscent of similar passages in the mass. The Adagio in F major, 6/8, discloses a certain affinity with the *Et incarnatus est* (Andante), which is in the same key and meter. Naturally, in the minuet we enter a more earthly sphere, and the finale sustains it. Mozart's gay spirit and Haydn's sense of humor join in a lively piece, free of dramatic accents and contrapuntal problems, and in playing with good-natured dynamic contrasts and a witty handling of small motifs, manipulations that bring about surprising turns and delightful combinations.

Symphony in D major, K. 504, "Prague"
Adagio—Allegro; Andante; Finale: Presto

In January 1787, Mozart, accompanied by his wife, journeyed to Prague to attend the performance of *The Marriage of Figaro* and to give a concert in the Bohemian capital. In his bag he had a new symphony, whose autograph, once owned by Franz Liszt, is dated December 6, 1786, Vienna. It was his first symphonic creation after a pause of four years. Performed in Prague on January 17, 1787, it was later nicknamed "the D major symphony without minuet." The propriety of this christening is more than questionable, since Mozart wrote a number of minuet-less symphonies—four in the key of D major, among which is the well-known Paris Symphony (K. 297). Theodor Kroyer, a German author, argued that the dramatic accents and moments of tension, significant in this symphony, may have caused the exclusion of the minuet. Yet the famous G minor symphony of 1788 reveals sharper dramatic, even tragic, accents and greater emotional strains, but it includes, nonetheless, a minuet. Alfred Einstein explains the absence of the minuet by contending that the symphony "says everything it has to say in three movements," an explanation that will not satisfy everybody. The omission of the minuet has presumably a great deal to do with the circumstances that surrounded the simultaneous origin of the C major piano concerto (K. 503) and the symphony under discussion.

Mozart's own thematic catalog, begun unfortunately as late as 1784, contains records for December 4 and 6, 1786, the dates of completion of the C major piano concerto and our D major symphony. It is obvious that Mozart did not compose the symphony within forty-eight hours, and it is also clear that his creative mind was working on two tracks simultaneously for a considerable time. In these forty-eight hours that elapsed between the completion of both the piano concerto and the symphony, his task was chiefly a mechanical one, that is to say to finish the writing of the score of which a substantial part must have already existed. The creative process for the symphony was in the main concluded. Working under pressure Mozart presumably postponed the composition of the minuet. Whether he added one later which was lost or he substituted one at hand we do not know. Summing up, Mozart worked simultaneously on the concerto and the symphony but this did not cause an ambivalence of his creative mind, since he did not follow two diverging, but rather parallel running tracks. The symphony and the concerto (which is thoroughly symphonic in nature) have several outstanding features in common.

The symphony, scored for two flutes, oboes, bassoons, horns, trumpets, kettledrums and the customary strings, is a creation of monumental design. This is conspicuous in the Adagio introduction to the first movement, which has no counterpart in symphonic literature up to Beethoven's second symphony in D major (1802). Mozart's introduction is even a bit longer (36 as opposed to 33 measures). The main theme of the Allegro is unfolded on two levels. It commences in the middle and lower voices (second violin, viola, and bass) and rises to the first violins and woodwinds. The vivid phrase proclaimed by the first violins anticipates the fugal subject of the overture to *The Magic Flute*. Contrapuntal treatment is one outstanding feature displayed in the Allegro. A few years ago, sketches in which Mozart had elaborated on the contrapuntal combinations for the development section came to light.

The apparent ease with which Mozart overcame contrapuntal problems has become almost a legend, but we have documentary evidence to the effect that even Mozart was sometimes confronted with difficulties of a contrapuntal nature. We have a number of fragmentary sonata movements that break off before the development section, or in it, because, as Einstein points out, "Mozart had neglected to prepare for the surmounting of this obstacle by making a contrapuntal sketch." Taught by experience, he made such a draft when the situation tended to become difficult, as was the case in this symphony. He shows his miraculous workmanship in the development section, which is one of his finest, and according to Einstein also "his most serious and most aggressive." It is clear that the tender melodious second theme is not used in the contrapuntal and "aggressive" passages. The preparation of the recapitulation through a pedal point on *A*, stretching over twenty measures and interrupted only once by the B flat chord, closes fittingly these remarkable pages. The recapitulation enters with a striking melodic alteration of the chief theme, which provides interesting harmonic consequences

(D—F sharp—A sharp instead of the D major chord).

The pastoral Andante in G major follows the sonata design and displays songful passages as well as thematic manipulation, in conformity with the tendency that dominates the first movement. The listener is not led into a musical Arcadia, for here, too, serious episodes are unfolded. A conspicuous anticipation of a phrase in the duet of Zerlina and Don Giovanni in Act I (*Andiam, andiam mio bene*) will certainly be noted.

Mozart provided this symphony with a finale that is remarkable in several respects. In the first place, its head motif of only four notes resembles rhythmically the basic motif of Beethoven's C minor symphony, and Mozart manipulates it in a manner similar to that employed by Beethoven about twenty years later. Note that the trend to polyphonic elaboration and canonic treatment of the chief theme, strongly evident in the preceding movements, is also present in the last. Finally the head motif itself stems from the duettino of Susanna and Cherubino (No. 14) which is, despite its brevity, one of the most original of the *Figaro* score.

There Mozart developed the short duettino from a small thematic organism. Now he proves anew its generating potentialities by making it the germ cell of an expanded symphonic movement. One closing remark: while the monumental Adagio introduction seems to anticipate the language of the serious scenes of *Don Giovanni*, the Presto Finale—the canonic episodes notwithstanding—certainly hails from the world of the *opera buffa*. Even comedies have their anxious phases and moments of suspense.

Symphony in E flat major, K. 543

Adagio—Allegro; Andante con moto; Minuetto; Finale: Allegro

The symphonies of Haydn and Mozart created during the decade from 1786 through 1795 constitute the crowning accomplishment of the eighteenth century symphony. It is estimated that the industrious composers of this century produced about ten thousand symphonies. Yet how many of these have withstood successfully the ravages of time and the unavoidable process of aging? Perhaps fifty, if we take a realistic view and use the current repertory as a yardstick. Mozart's symphony in E flat is one of those rare creations blessed with eternal youth. With its sister works in G minor, K. 550, and C major, K. 551 ("Jupiter"), it forms the great symphonic triptych Mozart wrote in the summer of 1788 for a series of subscription concerts that were several times postponed and never materialized. This was a financial disaster for Mozart and, in the long run, a tragedy for posterity because with these three works, which apparently were never performed in his days, Mozart's career as a symphonist ended abruptly.

As a lad of eight he had composed in London his first symphonic essay, one in E flat major. All the boy could do then was to emulate the popular models, specifically the works of Johann Christian Bach and Carl Friedrich Abel, whose symphonies he had heard or copied in London and whose friendship he had gained. The works of these German musicians represented the Italian type of symphony that stemmed from the three-sectional Italian opera overture, called *sinfonia*. Mozart's later symphonies reflect the influences to which he was exposed during the periods of their creation. Stimulated by experiences he had in Italy, he wrote symphonies in the Italian manner, and impressed by the orchestral achievements of the Mannheim composers, he amalgamated their techniques with his symphonic style, as, for example, in the Paris Symphony of 1778. Finally, under the influence of Haydn, he adopted the four-movement symphony, by now a firmly established form. He had written two three-movement symphonies (K. 319 and K. 338) in Salzburg in 1779; wishing to present them in Vienna after settling there in 1781, he adjusted them to the Viennese symphonic form through the inclusion in each of a minuet.

When Mozart occupied himself with the E flat major symphony in June, 1788, about a month after the unsuccessful presentation of *Don Giovanni* in Vienna, he was working simultaneously on five compositions. He finished the symphony on June twenty-sixth and on the same day entered in his list the violin sonata in F major, K. 547, as completed. For June twenty-second he recorded the trio for piano, violin, and violoncello in E major, K. 542, and the arrangement of the piano fugue in C minor, K. 426, for strings, with the addition of a newly composed Adagio introduction, K. 546. The piano sonata in C major, K. 545, a must for every piano student, came into being at the same time. These dates, given by Mozart, present a puzzle of miraculous proportions; when he committed to paper the two sonatas, the trio, the introduction to the fugue, and the symphony, the creative process was almost completed. Richard Wagner characterized this phenomenon in his article, "A Happy Evening," published in the *Gazette Musicale,* Paris, 1841: "It is impossible to assume that Mozart did not conceive the plan of a symphony of which not only its themes, even its entire structure as we know it, lived already completed in his head."

Another amazing fact to be deducted from the history of the E flat major symphony is the discrepancy between its basic mood and the conditions under which it was created. The symphony reflects in no way the sad and nearly desperate tone of the letters Mozart had written to his friend Michael Puchberg on June seventeenth and twenty-seventh, describing his severe economic situation. Yet he was capable of leaving everyday anxieties and fleeing to the lofty and serene spheres of his creative fancy. In this instance it is not the symphony alone that reveals this amazing psychological phenomenon: its companion pieces, the sonatas and the trio, also being in the major mode, do not convey what Mozart called "black thoughts" *(schwarze Gedanken).*

Despite the symphony's moderate scoring—one flute, pairs of clarinets, bassoons, horns, trumpets, and kettledrums, and the customary strings—it emanates rich sonorities, a particularly opulent sound being achieved by the long stretches of unison playing in the combined violin sections. The first movement is a creation of monumental design, conspicuous in the slow introduction, which in spirit is related to the Adagio that prefaces the first movement of the D major symphony ("Prague") of 1786. These two powerful, solemn, and dramatic introductions have no counterparts in the symphonic literature until Beethoven's second symphony in D major (1802). The lyrical aspect of the second movement is emphasized by the elimination of the trumpets and kettledrums from the orchestral palette, producing a gentle chamber music character, especially in the tender treatment of the wind instruments. The minuet returns to the festive quality of the first movement, while the gentle, ländler-like trio reveals Mozart as Imperial Chamber Composer whose official duty was to provide dance music for the court balls. In the quickly moving finale Mozart pays homage to "Papa" Haydn in spirit and also technique by constructing a humorous and exhilarated piece from the animated main theme.

Symphony in G minor, K. 550
Allegro molto; Andante; Minuetto; Allegro assai

Documentary evidence of the biographical circumstances surrounding the composition of Mozart's last three symphonies, in E flat major, G minor, and C major ("Jupiter"), is very scanty. The only available factual information are the dates that Mozart entered in his thematic list. From this we know that the E flat major symphony was completed on June 26, 1788, the G minor piece on July 25, and the "Jupiter" symphony on August 10 of the same year. The symphonies may have been commissioned or written for a series of concerts which, apparently, never took place. However, we do have three pieces of information which, though they are vague and can not be specifically connected with any one of the three symphonies, may refer to this symphonic triptych.

In the Spring of 1789, Mozart undertook a trip to Northern Germany, and gave an *Akademie* in Leipzig on May 12. The program included the piano concertos in B flat major (K. 456), C major (K. 503) and a symphony. We are told that Mozart had taken the tempo of the first Allegro of the symphony very fast, and became angry because the orchestra did not follow him. If this incident can be brought into relationship with the symphonies of 1788, one has to choose between the Allegro vivace of the "Jupiter" symphony and the Allegro molto of the symphony in G minor. In 1790 Mozart traveled to Frankfurt to the coronation of Leopold II hoping to benefit from the concerts arranged in connection with the festivities. He gave an *Akademie* on October 15 that "began with a new great symphony of Herr Mozart" and concluded with a symphony. The "new great symphony" could refer to one of the symphonic items of 1788. Lastly, the performance is recorded of a "great symphony of Mozart" on April 16 and 17, 1791, in a concert given by the Viennese *Tonkünstler Sozietät*, a charitable organization of professional musicians.

The autograph of the G minor symphony, once owned by Johannes Brahms and now in the collection of the *Gesellschaft der Musikfreunde* in Vienna, presents an interesting element in this veiled chapter of Mozart's life story. The symphony was originally scored for flute, two oboes, bassoons, horns, and strings. Later Mozart decided to add two clarinets. This modification necessitated the alteration of the oboe parts. A score including only the new clarinet and altered oboe parts was appended.

The question arises: was the change of orchestration motivated by second thoughts or practical experience—by observations made at a performance or try-out of the symphony? If this is true, the possibility that the clarinet version was played in the concerts on April 16 and 17, 1791, can not be ruled out entirely. Although the clarinet version seems to represent the composer's definite ideas, the printed 19th century editions of the G minor symphony offer the first version. Tonight's performance follows the later version with clarinets.

Only two of Mozart's almost fifty symphonies are in the minor key: the "little" G minor symphony of 1773 and the work under discussion. Though separated by fifteen years the compositions are closely related, spiritually and emotionally. The earlier work, written when Mozart was only 17, is because of its passion, pessimism, and expression of despair, an amazing precursor of the great symphony created by the mature artist in 1788. The use of the G minor tonality offers fascinating aspects of Mozart's aesthetics of key relationships. Proceeding from the "little" G minor symphony we pass Constanze's moving lament (*The Abduction from the Seraglio*, Act II, 1782), the forceful *Qui tollis* of the C minor Mass, 1783, the wild and almost frenzied first movement of the G minor quartet for piano and strings (K. 478) of 1785, and the unique G minor quintet (K. 516) of 1787. The quintet despite its gay finale, stands together with the G minor symphony as one of the most profound and melancholy pieces Mozart penned. There is also the expression of deepest sorrow and hopelessness that permeates Pamina's G minor aria in *The Magic Flute* (Act II, 1791) and, finally, the last stop on the road through the G minor sphere of Mozart's music: the *Rex tremendae* and the Offertory of the *Requiem* that also signifies the end of Mozart's earthly pilgrimage.

In the G minor symphony the basic emotional quality is enhanced musically by means of thematic unification, imitation techniques, and rhythmical accentuation. All four movements begin with the up-beat. The opening theme of the Andante reveals an amazing feature. The basic melodic line of the first half of the theme shows the familiar Gregorian phrase that was used frequently before by Mozart, and reappears again in the finale of the "Jupiter" symphony.

In his treatise *On Conducting* (1869) Richard Wagner expressed himself poetically about the Andante and interpreted the conclusion as "happiness of a death through love." Here speaks the creator of *Tristan and Isolde* rather than the adoring conductor of Mozart.

The Minuet is a far cry from the gentle dance of the aristocratic society. It is a rugged piece, spiced with metrical irregularities and contrapuntal treatment. It is contrasted sharply with the gentle trio and its dreamy horn passages. The finale reflects the feelings and emotions expressed in the first movement to an even higher degree and emphasizes them with "merciless consequence." Mozart was, no doubt, fully aware of a serious emotional crisis in which he found himself during the dark July days of 1788, and he may have been determined to overcome this painful situation creatively. The "Jupiter" symphony with its triumphant finale was the solution.

The Great C minor Mass

Mozart's two greatest religious compositions, the Mass in C minor, K. 427 (417a according to Einstein), and the Requiem, K. 626, remained unfinished. Their history discloses interesting similarities and their fragmentary state posed absorbing questions to the scholar and editor. Great names in music became involved in the controversies and problems centering around these torsos. Johannes Brahms was the editor of the Requiem for the Complete Works and Philipp Spitta, the most learned Bach biographer, took charge of the C minor Mass.*

Mozart planned it in 1782 as a votive offering for his wife Constanze and conceived it as a *cantata mass*. This type is characterized by a considerable expansion of the individual sections, particularly of the *Gloria* and *Credo*, which are not treated as musical entities but split in numerous autonomous sections. Today the most familiar example is Bach's B minor Mass which Mozart has not known. But there were several Austrian models by Florian Gassmann (1729-1774), Georg Reutter Jr. (1708-1772) and Joseph Haydn at hand. The architectural design of Haydn's *Missa Sanctae Caeciliae*, composed between 1768 and 1773, was perhaps not without influence on Mozart in 1782. Yet he was already familiar with the *cantata mass* in his teens when he wrote his remarkable Mass in C minor, K. 139 (114a) in Salzburg in 1772. It is in some respects a forerunner of the Mass under consideration.

The circumstances which surround the first performance of the great C minor Mass in the Peterskirche in Salzburg on August 25, 1783, are shrouded in mystery. Our source of this date is the Mozart biography by Georg Nikolaus Nissen (born 1761), a former Danish diplomat who had married Constanze in 1809. He collected documents and letters and gathered information from Constanze and Mozart's sister Nannerl. Nissen died in 1826 and it fell to Constanze to see the book through the press in 1828. Evidently from her he received the information that Constanze sang one of the soprano solo parts (2) in that performance. When Johann Anton André, composer and publisher, who had acquired the bulk of Mozart's manuscripts from his widow in 1800, examined the C minor Mass, he discovered that it was incomplete. It included the *Kyrie, Gloria, Sanctus* and *Benedictus* and only two sections of the *Credo* with incomplete instrumentation. The *Agnus* was entirely lacking. André asked Constanze for an explanation. She suggested to "make inquiries in Salzburg where it [the Mass] was composed and performed." The phrase "it was composed" could only mean that Mozart had put the finishing touches on the work in Salzburg. For we know from a letter to his father, dated January 4, 1783, that "the score of half a mass ... was waiting to be finished." Thus we are confronted with an intriguing puzzle. The Mass was performed but it has come down to us as a torso. What was actually

---

* This writer is indebted to Vox Productions Inc. for the kind permission to quote extensively from his introduction to the recording of Mozart's Mass in C minor (1958).

played on August 25, 1783? There are two answers to this question: either Mozart has, as Constanze indicated, completed the Mass, and the part of the autograph, written in Salzburg, was lost, or the missing sections were filled with the textually corresponding divisions of Mozart's earlier masses.

The first possibility depended solely on the time factor. Mozart reached Salzburg at the end of July and the rehearsal took place on August 23. Were three weeks sufficient to complete the work and have the orchestral and singing parts ready for the performance? Two-thirds of the Mass were already in existence. Still to be done was the completion of the *Credo* and the composition of the *Agnus*. The overriding task was, of course, the work on the *Credo*, textually the largest section of the Mass. But conforming to the tradition, Mozart planned the *Credo* as a far less expanded complex than the *Gloria* which runs through 734 measures. The extant autograph reveals that Mozart had reached almost the half way mark in the *Credo*. This portion required, interestingly enough, only 235 measures which total hardly equals a third of the *Gloria*. Taking Mozart's miraculous productive capacity into account, it is safe to conclude that three weeks gave him sufficient time to complete the score and to have the material ready for the rehearsal and performance.

Let us consider the second possibility, namely the filling of gaps with portions from Mozart's earlier masses. H. C. Robbins Landon, the renowned Haydn scholar, condemned this procedure as "a dreadful compromise" in the very informative preface to his excellent new edition of the score (C. F. Peters, New York). He argues that "there is hardly anything in Mozart's earlier, and often conventional even superficial, church music which compares in emotional scope and musical maturity to the present work." This writer disagrees with Landon's point of view inasmuch as he firmly believes that the *Credo* and *Agnus* of the C minor Mass, K. 139 (114a) presented and even still present an acceptable makeshift solution for liturgical performances. The recent edition of Köchel's thematic catalog, however, gives October 23 as the date of the rehearsal and October 26 as the day of the performance. Thus Mozart had ample time (about fourteen weeks) to complete the mass and under these circumstances there was no need of stuffing the score with pre-existing material. The matter becomes even more puzzling if we consult the diary of Mozart's sister. Nannerl records 50 church attendances between August 23 and October 26 but does not say one word about the presentation of a mass by her brother in the Peterskirche.

Two years later Mozart was commissioned to compose an oratorio entitled *Davidde penitente* for the Lent concerts of the *Wiener Tonkünstler Societät*. The text was contributed by Lorenzo da Ponte. Mozart adapted to it the music of the *Kyrie* and *Gloria* of the C minor Mass and added two arias to it. Performed on March 13 and 15, 1785, *Davidde penitente* was heartily acclaimed and maintained itself not only in Vienna but appeared at music festivals in other cities up to the middle of the 19th century. The success of *Davidde penitente* and Emperor Joseph's II austerity edict in matters of church music explain why Mozart did not concern himself with the C minor Mass later on. Would he have lived longer and assumed the conductor's post at St. Stephen's which was secured for him, he would have undoubtedly introduced the complete Mass in Vienna.

The torso fell into oblivion. André brought out the fragmentary score in 1840. It was reprinted in the Collected Works in 1882, but at that time the autograph, preserved in the Royal Library in Berlin, had become still more defect: of the *Sanctus* only a short score of wind instruments and kettle drums was extant and the *Benedictus* had disappeared. The editor (Spitta) could close these gaps by using the score published by André.

Around 1900 Alois Schmitt, founder and director of the Dresden Mozart Association, undertook "to patch up the torso," to borrow a phrase of Alfred Einstein. Schmitt used various portions from Mozart's earlier church music. His version, first performed on April 3, 1901, in the Martin-Luther-Kirche at Dresden, was later published by Breitkopf & Härtel. Schmitt, however, was not the first musician who had seriously wrestled with this difficult problem. An earlier attempt, made in Vienna back in 1847 by Joseph Drechsler (1782-1852), conductor at St. Stephen's Cathedral, remained almost unnoticed. A modest footnote in Alfred Schnerich's study on *Mass and Requiem since Haydn and Mozart* records this event. Drechsler employed Mozart's thematic material taken from the torso. Drechsler conducted his version on November 15, 1847, in St. Stephen's. (A detailed report was published in the Wiener Allgemeine Musik-Zeitung.) Schmitt used for his reconstruction eight different sources, Masses, two individual Kyrie compositions and a Lacrimosa fragment. The latter was recently (1954) identified as a composition of Johann Ernst Eberlin (1702-1762), Domkapellmeister in Salzburg. Mozart had copied it and it slipped as a genuine Mozart autograph into the Complete Works.

Regardless of the shortcomings of Alois Schmitt's edition he must be credited with the introduction of the C minor Mass into the musical life. His edition secured for the work a certain popularity. Thus his version has fulfilled its high mission: Mozart's great C minor Mass was revived. Yet our generation has become more and more *Urtext conscious.*

Mozart combined in the C minor Mass the operatic brilliance of the Neapolitans and their followers with the severe choral polyphony of the German masters of the North. The operatic element is represented in the highly ornamented soprano solo in the middle section of the *Kyrie,* the soprano aria *Laudamus te,* the duet for two sopranos *Domine Deus,* the terzet *Quoniam to solus sanctus,* and in the soprano aria *Et incarnatus est.* The latter is richly endowed with coloratura embroidery and also includes a "concerted cadenza" in which the voice is joined by a flute, oboe and bassoon. The influence of the baroque masters shows up in the four-, five- and eight-part choral settings. Note the allusion to Handel's *Alleluia* in the *Gloria*

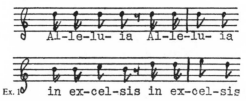

Ex. 1

and the application of the ostinato technique in the *Gratias* and *Qui tollis.*

The fugue *Cum sancto spiritu* is preceded by a four times chanted invocation *Jesu Christe*. The fugal subject also appears inverted.

Ex. 2

Recent performances follow the edition of H. C. Robbins-Landon who closed some gaps in the orchestral parts of the *Credo* and reconstructed the double chorus texture of the *Sanctus* and *Osanna*. We will always deeply regret the turn of events which befell this work. Conceived on a lofty plane, it was destined to become one of Mozart's greatest creations. But even as a torso the C minor Mass communicates overwhelmingly religious conviction and sincere devoutness, marvelous grandeur and sublime Mozartian beauty.

Vesperae solennes de confessore, K. 339

As a member of the musical establishment of the archbishopric of Salzburg, Mozart was a church musician both as a performer (organist) and composer. True, his close ties to the organ loft ceased when he settled in Vienna. He had, however, striven to secure a position in Vienna with the court chapel and St. Stephen's cathedral. In his petition for the vice-conductorship of the court chapel Mozart stressed the fact that he had acquired full mastery of the church style in his youth. No wonder, for he was the son of a church musician, and grew up with an intimate knowledge of the Salzburg repertory and the models penned by the expert local craftsmen. Among his sacred works, which number about sixty, are two Vespers, K. 321 of 1779 and K. 339 of 1780. Both are in C major, evidently a preferred key in Salzburg. Nine of Mozart's complete Masses are in C major.

The Vesper (*Officium Vesperarum, Vesperae*) is the evening service of the Roman Catholic Church. It comprises the singing of antiphons, five psalms (110, 111, 112, 113 and 117) and the *Magnificat*. Each psalm concludes with the Lesser Doxology, a short liturgical formula in praise of God. The title of *Vesperae solennes de confessore* indicates that it was written for a saint venerated as a confessor. Musically, Mozart observed an established Salzburg tradition in the general character, the contrapuntal treatment, and the orchestration of this Vesper. He employs trumpets and kettledrums, trombones to support the chorus, and a three-voice string body without viola. This setup (violins I and II and bass), called *Kirchentrio*, is a baroque feature and stems from the trio sonata. The psalms are, except for one, quick movements. This is also true of the concluding *Magnificat* which, however, commences with a short Adagio introduction. The exclusion of slow sections reflects the Salzburg taste—their preference for vigor and brilliancy.

Mozart displays extraordinary ingenuity in the amalgamation of the psalms and the Lesser Doxology. The latter never appears as an appendix, but always as an organic part of the psalm. Of greatest interest is the fourth item (*Laudate pueri*, Psalm 113), on account of the severe contrapuntal treatment and the use of the old baroque fugal theme with the characteristic step of the descending diminished seventh.

Lau- da-te pu-e-ri Do-mi-num

Ky-ri-e   e- le-i- son

We find it in Bach, Handel, Philipp Emanuel Bach, Haydn, in previous Mozart compositions, and finally in the *Kyrie* fugue of the *Requiem*. Interestingly enough, Mozart retains the minor mode of this psalm also in the Lesser Doxology. The somber quality of the piece is contrasted with the pastoral mood of the ensuing psalm. Trumpets and kettledrums, silent since the opening piece, join the orchestra in the concluding *Magnificat*. Naturally Mozart had to limit himself to a very concise treatment of the text, which he did in a spirit of firm confidence and optimism, expressed in a clear and vigorous musical language.

PERGOLESI, Giovanni Battista (1710-1736)
Concertino No. 2 in G major for Strings
Largo; A capella, non presto; Andante affetuoso; Allegro

This piece is one of a series of six concertini published in the *Opera Omnia* of Pergolesi edited between 1939 and 1942 by Don Filippo Caffarelli in Rome. The history of this series is shrouded in darkness. Caffarelli does not reveal his source, speaking only of an *antico manoscritto*, once owned by the German musicologist Franz Commer (1813-1887) and auctioned after his death. He adds, however, that two exact copies are extant, one in the Paris Conservatory and the other in the Library of Congress. This implies that he must have compared them with the mysterious Commer manuscript. However, the Library of Congress revealed to me the astonishing fact that the Washington manuscript bears the stamp of F. Commer. Thus Caffarelli's information in the *Opera Omnia* is fictitious.

In 1949 C. L. Cudworth, a British writer, discovered that the six Pergolesi concertini were anonymously published in 1740 in The Hague as "Six Harmonic Concertos" at the expense of Carlo Ricciotti, "Music Master and Citizen of The Hague." Cudworth also disclosed that Handel's publisher, John Walsh, printed them in London several years later under the same title, as compositions by Ricciotti. These concertos (not concertini) are also held by the Library of Congress, listed under Ricciotti, while the same compositions in score are catalogued under Pergolesi. Who, then, is the composer—the famous Pergolesi or the unknown Ricciotti? If it is the former, how did the latter come into possession of the manuscript, why did he wait until four years after Pergolesi's death to publish it, and why did he first issue it anonymously? If the mysterious Ricciotti is really the composer, then we have an unrecognized genius. But first we must find convincing proof to deny definitely Pergolesi's authorship of the concertini.

The plot thickens. Fred Blum of the Library of Congress's music division informed me that in November of 1952 a reader of the Washington manuscript copy of Pergolesi's concertini noticed the thickness of the title page and observed that it consisted of two leaves glued together. Their separation revealed an inner title page with the following startling inscription:

6 [Concertini] Septetti Per 4 Violino, Alto, Violoncello e Basso continuo in partitura del. F. G. Handel [N. B. Pergolesi]

The bracketed words appear, according to Mr. Blum, to be a later addition in a different hand. Obviously the scribe of this copy (Cafarelli's *antico manoscritto*) worked from a manuscript that bore the name of Handel. When the manuscript changed hands, the new owner did everything he could to obliterate the ascription to Handel.

To add to this confused situation, Hans Joachim Moser, Berlin author of thirty musical books, named a new candidate for the authorship—the German violinist Johann Adam Birkenstock (1687-1733), who had composed twelve concertos for four violins, viola, violoncello, and figured bass, of which no copy has survived. The similar manner of scoring in our concertini prompted Moser to consider Birkenstock. The situation can best be characterized by an adaptation of the title of Pirandello's play: "Six concertini in search of an author."

The attractive piece in G major is representative of the series in style and musical language. The composer still clings to the "slow-fast-slow-fast" design of the church sonata and also reverts occasionally to the concerto grosso treatment, as, for instance, in the Andante affetuoso, where a solo quartet alternates with the entire ensemble. The tempo signature *a capella* for the second movement is an obsolete indication for *alla breve*; thus the half note rather than the quarter note is the time unit. The virtues of the piece—fine workmanship, melodic freshness, rhythmic variety, and sonorous sound—testify to the high artistic caliber of its author.

Concerto in G major for Flute and Strings
Spiritoso; Adagio; Allegro spiritoso

Giovanni Battista Pergolesi, born at Jesi near Ancona, showed symptoms of tuberculosis in early infancy and also limped all his life because of a maimed leg. In 1726 he entered the *Conservatorio dei Poveri di Gesu Cristo* at Naples, one of the four historic conservatories of that ancient city. The students had a hard time all year round. The school's rigorous routine kept them awake from as early as 4:30 a.m. until 10:00 or 11:30 at night, according to the season. The quantity of food was small and the discipline iron. Records disclose that rods and handcuffs were used against offenders. It stands to reason that these conditions, which Pergolesi had to endure for five years, had an effect on his weak constitution. Actually his life as a practical musician and creator lasted only five years. His fecundity is astonishing.

Pergolesi's fame rests mainly on his delightful *opera buffa, La serva padrona* (1733), and the *Stabat mater*, which he completed only a few days before he passed away at Pozzuoli, near Naples. Dead of consumption at twenty-six, he was laid to rest in a common burial pit for the poor. After his death, numerous forgeries and misattributions were committed and spurious pieces even slipped into the *Opera Omnia* (1932). In addition to his operas and vocal works (masses, oratorios, cantatas) he left a sizable number of instrumental compositions. The two flute concertos were discovered in connection with the researches for the *Opera Omnia*. The only bibliographical reference pointing to the existence of *due concerti per flauto traverso con accompanimento di violini e basso continuo* was drawn from an old catalogue of the Leipzig publishing house Breitkopf and Härtel, which started its music printing business in 1756. Two pieces of this kind were finally located in the library of the Royal Academy in Stockholm. They were probably written for a flutist in the service of Pergolesi's patron, the Prince of Stigliano, equerry to the Viceroy of Naples. Pergolesi wrote most of his instrumental compositions for the ensemble employed by the prince.

In this work Pergolesi adopted the Vivaldian concerto pattern with three movements: an opening Allegro with alternation of tutti and solo, an "aria" for the solo instrument with orchestral ritornellos for the slow middle movement, and a dancelike finale. The absence of the viola in the orchestra points to the trio sonata, the favorite ensemble of baroque chamber music, to which Pergolesi had contributed a remarkable series in 1731.

POULENC, Francis (1899-1963), *Organ Concerto*

Francis Poulenc received his pianistic training from the Spaniard Ricardo Vines and studied composition with Charles Koechlin, an eminent pupil of Fauré. Poulenc was thrust into the limelight at twenty-one when the Parisian music critic Henri Collet introduced in a newspaper article six young composers whom he grouped together as "Les Six Français." "Les Six," as they were often called, included Poulenc, Arthur Honegger, Darius Milhaud, Georges Auric, Louis Durey, and Germaine Tailleferre. Although they went their own artistic ways and seldom appeared together on the concert stage, the sobriquet stuck.

Poulenc, who pursued a line of sophisticated entertainment in his early works, developed particularly in his piano pieces a contemporary style. He created in all fields of music: he wrote operas, ballets, incidental music to plays and film scores, orchestral and chamber music, numerous piano pieces, sacred choral compositions, and songs. He was interested in the French clavecinists of the baroque, whose ideas he revived in a modern vein. Poulenc wrote a concerto for harpsichord, and his Organ Concerto in G minor is a contribution to a literature that had not been enriched since the days of Handel.

The combination of organ and orchestra was not known in Italy, Germany, and France before Handel and failed to become popular later because it was too closely associated with Handel's practice of appearing as an organist at the performances of his oratorios. Poulenc followed Handel's model by joining the organ, which represents a combination of wind instruments, to the strings; however, he added kettledrums. Thus, with regard to the tone production, Poulenc's assortment comprises all elements that form the orchestra: winds, strings, and kettledrums.

Formally speaking, the concerto is freely constructed and rather rhapsodic in the frequent change of slow and fast sections. The rhythmic irregularity of the opening Andante, caused by the succession of 6/4, 3/4, 4/4, 3/4, and 5/4 meters is very conspicuous. It actually forecasts things to come and appears as a characteristic trait of the piece, which discloses seven sections in the order "slow-fast-slow-fast-slow-fast-slow." There is a return to the mood of the Allegro initial and to the musical material of the introduction in the conclusion.

The concerto was composed in the spring and summer of 1938. It was published in 1939 and played for the first time in Paris on June 10, 1941.

RAVEL, Maurice (1875-1937)
Introduction et Allegro for Harp, Strings, Flute, and Clarinet

The event that caused the composition of Maurice Ravel's *Introduction et Allegro* was the invention of the chromatic harp, and the subsequent commission of Debussy by the manufacturing firm of Pleyel to write a piece for it. This provoked the Érard piano company, the leading maker of the double-action pedal harp, to counter Pleyel's move by commissioning Ravel to do a piece with prominent use of the customary harp. Ravel had already an impressive list of works to his credit.

Ravel, at that very moment, was about to embark with a group of friends on a yachting trip to Holland, and the commission almost interfered with his participation. After eight days of feverish struggle and several sleepless nights he completed the score, which he wanted to polish during the cruise. His friends had meanwhile sailed, but he found that he could catch up with them at the lock of Soissons. Hurrying to a haberdashery store, he purchased some articles but left the manuscript on the counter, to the delight of the *chemisier* who happened to be an amateur musician. The manuscript was later recovered.

The piece received its first performance in Paris on February 22, 1907, and was first heard in America in New York on January 15, 1927, at an all-Ravel program in the composer's presence. Though the title page bears the wording *pour harp avec accompagnment de quatuor à cordes, flute et clarinette,* it also lists among the different editions the *partition d'orchestre* (orchestral score), which clearly indicated that Ravel contemplated both kinds of execution—as a septet and with a chamber orchestra. Marcel Grandjany, tonight's soloist, plays it with string orchestra as he did once under the direction of the composer.

The slow introduction alludes to the material used in the Allegro, chiefly to

which is contrasted rhythmically with

Besides the prominent use of the harp there is a wealth of startling instrumental combinations that produce a surprising volume of sound. In the Allegro a three-sectional pattern roughly conforms to the customary division into exposition, development, and recapitulation. The latter is preceded by the virtuoso cadenza of the harp, alluding to the introductory passage, and closes with a stirring coda.

Ma Mère l'Oye

Pavane de la belle au bois dormant; Petit poucet; Laideronette, impératrice des pagodes; Les entretiens de la belle et de la bête; Le jardin féerique

Maurice Ravel, who was very fond of children, wrote the suite *Ma mère l'Oye* for piano duo in 1908. He subtitled it *Cinq Pièces Enfantines* and dedicated it to the children of his friend Eduard Godebski. When the piece was first played publicly in Paris, the pianists were two little girls, aged six and ten. Ravel then conceived the idea of converting the suite into a little ballet that was mounted at the *Théatre des Arts* in 1911. To place the piece in its historical perspective it must be noted that a number of now famous works of Ravel were already in existence or performed. They were the *Pavane pour une Infante défunte, Alborada del gracioso,* the string quartet, *Rapsodie espagnole,* and the opera *L'Heure espagnole.*

Ma Mère l'Oye has nothing to do with Mrs. Goose of Boston and her *Mother Goose's Melodies.* Ravel's literary source was the assemblage of eighteen tales entitled *Contes de ma Mère l'Oye* (1697) which Charles Perrault (1628-1703) published under the name of his infant son Perrault d'Armancourt. The suite consists of five movements. The first *Pavane of a Sleeping Beauty,* a short and very gentle piece in which not even a mezzoforte occurs, leads us into a fairyland. The second tells the story of Hop-O-My-Thumb who "believed that he would easily find his path by means of his bread crumbs which he had scattered wherever he passed; but he was very much surprised, when he could not find a single crumb, the birds had come and eaten everything up." This is a delicate piece of rhythmical piquancy that begins and closes with the conglomeration of four different meters: 2/4, 3/4, 4/4, and 5/4.

The tale of the snake and the girl cursed with horrible ugliness, and the disenchantment is narrated in the third movement. It reveals Ravel as an orchestral magician of the first rank in the kaleidoscopic employment of instrumental colors and delicate use of percussion instruments, xylophone, glockenspiel, celesta, and harp. The story of the conversation of a "Belle" and a beast, and its broken enchantments, is depicted in a delicate waltz. The finale, that depicts a magnificent fairyland garden once more displays Ravel's superb art of orchestration and his mastery of achieving rich sonorities with comparatively modest means. His orchestra is that of Haydn's *Military Symphony* complemented by a glockenspiel, celesta, and harp.

Le Tombeau de Couperin
Prélude, Forlane, Menuet; Rigaudon

In the summer of 1914 Ravel conceived the idea of composing a Suite française for piano, but World War I interfered with his intentions. Ravel served in the French army from 1916 until early 1917. After his discharge he immediately plunged into creative work and wrote three of his most popular compositions: *La Valse,* the ballet-masque *L'Enfant et les sortilèges,* and the suite for piano, which he now entitled *Le Tombeau de Couperin.* Consisting of six pieces, it is dated "July 1914; June-November 1917." Each item is dedicated to one of Ravel's friends who had died in the war.

In choosing the term *Tombeau* (tomb) the composer went back to an old French custom that can be traced to the first half of the seventeenth century, specifically to Denis Gaulthier (c. 1600-1672), the famous lutanist in whose creations French lute music of the seventeenth century culminated. His ornamentation influenced the style of the composers for the claveçin (harpsichord), while the fanciful titles of his pieces were musically suggestive to Couperin le Grand. One of these titles, *Le tombeau,* was applied to pieces that were composed as dirges to the memory of friends or outstanding persons. Proceeding from this basic idea, Couperin went further and wrote extended suites in homage to Lully and Corelli, which he entitled *Apothéose.*

Ravel took a similar line in his *Tombeau de Couperin.* In his words this piece was conceived as a tribute "less, in reality, to Couperin himself, than to eighteenth century French music," or to be more specific, in the period during which music for harpsichord flourished. In this connection it is not amiss to recall that he had written a piece in the true French tombeau tradition long before the work under discussion, namely the *Pavane pour une Infante défunte* (1899). The serious *tombeaux* of the seventeenth century were in the style of the pavane.

Shortly after the completion of the original piano version, Ravel orchestrated four pieces of it, which were performed for the first time in Paris in 1920. The orchestral suite reached America in the same year through the good offices of Pierre Monteux who conducted it in Boston on November 19, 1920. The score calls for two flutes, two oboes, English horn, two clarinets, two bassoons, two horns, trumpet, harp, and strings. The suite was very well received; choreographers lost no time applying their imagination to Ravel's delicate music. A choreographic presentation was given in Paris in 1920 by the Ballet Suédois a few months after the first orchestral rendition.

ROSSINI, Gioacchino (1792-1868),
Overture to "La scala di seta"

Gioacchino Rossini who has born on February 29, 1792, entered the Liceo Filarmonico in Bologna in 1807. At the Liceo the tradition of Padre Giambattista Martini, the greatest musical scholar of the 18th century, was duly perpetuated by the teaching methods of his favorite pupil, Padre Stanislao Mattei, who became the counterpoint teacher of Rossini. Longing for operatic laurels, Rossini left the Liceo prematurely in 1810 and succeeded in receiving a commission for a one act opera for the Teatro Giustiniani a San Moisè in Venice, a small playhouse with a seating capacity of 800 and an orchestra of 27 musicians. Here Rossini's apprenticeship as an opera composer began on November 3, 1810, with the production of *La cambiale di matrimonio.*

Weber once said that first operas and puppies should be drowned but Rossini, apparently, had quite different ideas. In 1812, barely twenty years old, he received five commissions. Among these operas was *La scala di seta* (The silken ladder) which, billed as *farsa comica* (comic farce), was staged on May 9, 1812, in San Moisè. The story concerns a secret marriage, a topic familiar to the audience through Cimarosa's very successful *Il matrimonio segreto*. The silken ladder is the means by which Dorvil the husband climbs to the chamber of his wife Giulia.

Rossini's farces show all the salient musical and technical virtues characteristic of his later works which made him the most famous Italian opera composer in the 1810's and 1820's: inexhaustible melodic inventiveness, rhythmic verve, mastery in the building up of ensembles and finales, irresistible witticism, and finally, effective orchestration. The last trait is, of course, also evident in his overtures. These have not been affected by the ravages of time, and are still played in symphonic, popular, and garden concerts, though the operas to which they belong have mostly disappeared from the boards.

The overture under review is a case in point. Its opening slow introduction is preceded by a quick run that may portray the falling down of the silken ladder. We then hear a typically Rossinian device in the soloistic passages of several wind instruments (oboe, flute, horn). The air of expectancy permeating the introduction is swept away by the entry of the sparkling Allegro which assures the listener or spectator that he can look forward to a pleasurable experience. Once more the woodwind instruments succeed in leading the musical conversation. They also contribute to the famous Rossinian crescendi that earned the composer the nickname "Monsieur Crescendo."

Ouverture to William Tell

The opera *Guillaume Ieu* was first performed on August 3, 1829 in Paris, during the reign of Charles X. The libretto is based on a legend that glorifies the uprising of certain Swiss territories located around Lake Lucerne against the rule of the Hapsburgs and their governors. Although Rossini was the most famous living Italian in the 1820s, Italy's political climate in those days was not favorable to operatic plots hailing revolutionary events. In order to pass the censorship of the reactionary governments, the libretto of Rossini's work had to be changed completely, its innuendos obliterated. The opera fared much better in the German orbit where Schiller's play *Wilhelm Tell* enjoyed immense popularity. Surmounting the formidable barriers of Metternich's police censors, Rossini's work scored well in Vienna and reached a total of 422 performances between 1830 and 1907. This figure may equal (if not exceed) the total of all presentations of the work in Italy during the same period. Nonetheless, its revival at the Maggio Musicale Fiorentino in 1939 was a revelation to many people.

William Tell was Rossini's last dramatic creation. It eloquently testifies to his remarkable artistic development from such one-act farces as *La cambiale di matrimonio* (1810) and *La scala di seta* (1812) to the very demanding works of his Paris period, characterized by powerful choral numbers, mass scenes, and elaborate orchestration in the tradition of French grand opera. In *William Tell* the plotting scene particularly revealed a new intense musical language that even an astute listener might not have ascribed to the witty creator of the hilarious scenes in *The Italian Lady in Algiers* or *The Barber of Seville*. In fact, the grandiose *giuramento* in the second act of *William Tell* was the model for the "consecration of the swords" in Meyerbeer's *Les Huguenots* (1836), the conspirator scenes in Verdi's *Ernani* (1844) and *La battaglia di Legnano* (1849), and the oath of the monks in *La forza del destino* (1862).

The instrumental prologue to *William Tell* deviates radically from the familiar Rossinian overture pattern. Usually the slow introduction is followed by a quick movement designed after the sonata scheme, without a manipulating middle section, yet spiced by orchestral witticism and Rossini's famous crescendo passages. In the *Tell* overture Rossini set out to portray musically certain features of the landscape where the events took place. Hector Berlioz, who wrote an elaborate study on this opera in *Gazette Musicale de Paris* in 1834 (which he, unfortunately, failed to include in his collected writings), speaks of the overture as "a symphony in four distinct parts." He saw in the opening section (Andante, 3/4, E minor) "the calm of a profound solitude, this solemn silence of nature when the elements are at rest." The composer achieves this mood through the imaginative and highly original handling of the orchestra, which is reduced to five soloistically treated celli, the basses, and the kettledrum. As the scene changes we witness the breaking, raging, and abating of a violent storm (Allegro, 4/4, E minor). Uproar and excitement over, we enjoy the tranquility and peace of a Swiss Alp where the shepherd sounds the *ranz des vaches* to call the scattered cattle. The frolicking flute above the melody of the English horn, the gentle accompaniment by the plucked strings, and the occasional strokes of the triangle mirror Rossini's masterful handling of the orchestral palette (Andante, 3/8, G major). Rapid, incisive fanfares of the trumpet break the idyllic mood and the scene changes once more. The rhythmical structure of the Allegro theme (2/4, E major) is derived from a military march, written in Vienna in 1822, and anticipates the famous *Radetzky March* of Johann Strauss, Sr. To quote Berlioz, this section of the overture is treated with fire and verve that always excite the emotion of the listener. Rossini injects here the element of virtuosity with violin passages that are reminiscent of Paganini's *Moto perpetuo*.

Petite Messe Solennelle

The abrupt end of Rossini's spectacular career as an opera composer has stunned his contemporaries, the public, managers, singers and musicians alike, and has intrigued his biographers as well as the serious student of the phenomenon called Gioacchino Rossini. At eighteen years of age he had made his first successful steps on the lyric stage (1810). Three years later after the first performance of *Tancredi* in Venice he was talked about as the greatest living Italian composer and after the triumphant international success of the *Barbiere,* Rossini was regarded as the greatest living opera composer of the world. In 1823 he settled down in Paris, the operatic world capital, and climaxed his activities with the production of *Guillaume Tell* (August 3, 1829). Nobody and particularly Rossini himself would have imagined that the internationally celebrated and adored maestro would cease to enrich the operatic repertory.

The fact that a highly successful and very famous composer in the prime of his life—Rossini was thirty-seven years then—would put a stop on his creative work is unique in the history of music and impossible to comprehend particularly if Rossini's incredible and also proverbial inventive facility is taken into account. In the search for the motivation of Rossini's artistic withdrawal the phrase "the great renunciation" was introduced and became an indispensable term in articles, essays and writings dealing with the master from Pesaro. There is no point in dealing here with this particular facet of the literature on Rossini.

It seems, however, as if certain facts were deliberately played down in accordance with a Victorian moral code. The true reasons for Rossini's withdrawal from the lyric stage were known to his physicians, close friends and early biographers. For example S. Silvestri says in his life of Rossini (1874) that the master was in the 1840's plagued by an illness of the bladder which made him suffer not only bodily but also mentally. He had to live more or less in solitary confinement in Paris for three months. Yet even after the illness receded the seclusion and physical pains seriously aggravated his frame of mind. There is more to it than it meets the eye as we will hear presently. References to Rossini's illness can be found frequently in Giuseppe Radiciotti's monumental Rossini biography (1927-29) and also in Francis Toye's *Rossini* which is biographically based on Radiciotti. In a chapter designated as "The Great Renunciation" Toye has marshalled facts to dispose of several opinions, conjectures and allegations which should account for Rossini's retirement in 1830. Yet after the appearance of Toye's book in 1947 an important document was unearthed which in connection with letters written between May, 1839, and June, 1843, by Olympe Pélissier, the master's second wife, sheds full light on the clinical side of the case.

The document is a medical report written in French on four leaves by an unnamed physician of Bologna and addressed to Dr. Civiale in Paris whom Rossini was to see in May, 1843, about his bladder condition after the doctors he had consulted in Bologna had considered a chirurgical operation as mandatory. Excerpts from this medical report are included in a fascinating essay *A Medical-Psychological Profile of Gioacchino Rossini* by Bruno Riboli published in *La Rassegna Musicale,* 1954. This writer gratefully acknowledges his indebtedness to Riboli's penetrating study. We have already heard about Rossini's confinement which, ordered by Dr. Civiale, had a terrific impact on him. He was seized by the idea of death which caused him terrible torments. It stands to reason that under these conditions, aggravated by chronic intestinal difficulties and hemorrhage, the master whom we usually visualize as a happy go lucky man, would not think of engaging in creative work.

Yet the force of circumstances compelled him to do so. The case concerned his famous *Stabat Mater* which Rossini had written in 1832 in collaboration with Giovanni Tadolini (1785-1872), conductor at the Théâtre Italien in Paris. He had composed it for a Spanish prelate and stipulated that the piece was never to go into print. The heirs of the prelate sold the work to a Paris publisher. Rossini started a law suit to prevent the circulation of the piece and to establish a copyright on the *Stabat Mater* he had to replace the sections contributed by Tadolini by music of his own. The numbers he wrote in 1839 are inferior to those of 1832 with one notable exception which significantly conforms to his state of mind of these years. It is the finale, an extended fugue on the words "In sempiterna saecula, Amen," a highly impassioned piece which sharply contrasts with the idea of the paradisean glory to which the last stanza refers. The conspicuous avoidance of a consoling note is understandable in view of the tragic circumstances under which the *Stabat Mater* was completed. Rossini followed a similar line of thought twenty-three years later in the concluding passage of the *Petite Messe Solennelle*.

Considering the sad state of affairs, we must also take into account the standard of medical science in the 1840s when neither the causes of many illnesses were fully known nor medication available to cure them or to mitigate the sufferings of the patient. Yet in the case of Rossini, the chronic illness alone does not fully explain why he fell into a physical and psychical prostration which lasted almost twenty-seven years. Modern psycho-analysis provided the key to the understanding of Rossini, the man, and disclosed the very nature of the psychopathological phenomenon that almost destroyed his life.

The unexcelled master of the opera buffa, the personification of fun and laughter, was beset by cyclo-thymia, a temperament, characterized by alternation of lively and depressed moods, of euphoria and times of depression, moral and physical sufferings, of extreme difficulty in doing mental (creative) work. It predisposes the individual toward manic-depressive insanity and suicide. Observations recorded by Olympe Pélessier and statements made by her most unfortunate husband reveal a very sad picture. Madame Olympe once remarked that Rossini had changed morally more than physically. Rossini whom the popular image always portrayed as a man ever ready to smile, to joke and to show his wit, deplored his mental impotence and physical infirmity in letters to his friends.

A painful symptom was the sensation of hearing any music simultaneously with the upper major third. This crisis generated a profound melancholy and a longing for the death. Sometimes he had set a knife on the throat and crying, he cursed his cowardice which kept him from taking his life. It is obvious that a composer spending many years under such unbearable strain is, of course, incapable of creative work. To be sure Rossini has written a few insignificant pieces in these years for the sake of convenience but it was the routine, not the intellect which guided his pen. It is also clear that the hollow catchword of the "great renunciation" is without factual foundation. It is known that Rossini, after the production of *Guillaume Tell*, was expecting a libretto which centered on Jeanne d'Arc. But his neuro-psychic troubles increased and so did the painful disease stemming, as the medical report states, "from youthful excesses."

In time he was mentally and physically a wreck.

Summing up, Rossini has not renounced activities as stage composer. He was invalidated by circumstances beyond his control. But for the devotion and care of his second wife he would have taken his life, or worse, ended up in an institution. Thanks to Madame Olympe he was able to live through a painful quarter of a century until, cured of his physical illness, the torments of melancholy, the affliction and depression which blocked his creative efforts, began to disappear. In the spring of 1857 Rossini's serene spirit which begot *L'Italiana in Algeri, Barbiere, La Cenerentola* and *Le Comte Ory* returned and with it the pleasure as well as the urge to write music. He composed about 200 smaller pieces, vocal and instrumental; but the major work of the last years of his life, the period of the regeneration, as we may regard it, is the *Petite Messe Solennelle*.

The History of the "Little Missa Solemnis"

Rossini's contributions to the musica sacra are small in numbers. He wrote a few pieces and a mass for male voices, organ and orchestra in his student years. In 1820 he was approached by the Neapolitan Archconfraternity of San Luigi to compose a mass for the Feast of the Seven Dolors of the Virgin Mary which is celebrated nine days before Easter. Although hard pressed by work, Rossini consented but laid down the condition that the composition had to be a joint undertaking with a fellow composer. He asked Pietro Raimondi (1786-1853), a master craftsman of counterpoint, to help him out. Raimondi who finished his musical career as maestro di capella at St. Peter's cathedral in Rome agreed. The mass was performed on March 19, 1820, in San Ferdinando, which is located across the famous San Carlo Theater to which Rossini was attached as musical director and composer. The score of the mass is lost and, thus, we do not know the share of Raimondi in the work.

Glowing reports as well as biting criticism from a German listener have come down to us. The service started with an overture by Simon Mayr (1763-1845) which was dominated by a dance theme. The choice is significant because Mayr cultivated the extended crescendo which became a stock in trade of Rossini. This he immediately demonstrated by conducting his overture to *La gazza ladra*. Now the congregation was ready for the *Kyrie* which is described as very sad. But Rossini made up for it with the *Gloria* which was much applauded. The *Credo* was dismissed by the German critic as a ragout of phrases from Rossini's operas. This was probably true since Rossini is said to have written his share in three days. The rest, *Sanctus, Benedictus* and *Agnus Dei*, probably contributed by Raimondi, was judged by our German listener as not of much value. The local papers extolled the mass while a priest is said to have declared that it will secure to Rossini the absolution from his sins. . . .

We have already alluded to the strange story of the *Stabat Mater* which in its original version as a joint undertaking duplicated the Neapolitan Mass of 1820. The "ragout" of phrases from Rossinian operas in the *Credo* found later a companion piece in the *Messe de Rossini*, a concoction from *Tancredi, Semiramide, Barbiere* and *La Cenerentola* for which the French author, critic and composer Francois Castil-Blaze (1784-1857) is responsible. Rossini was unable to stop Castil-Blaze but the matter may have been one of the reasons that prompted Rossini to compose a mass. He was hatching the project for a long time and materialized the idea in the summer of 1863. During these months he showed once more great irritation, was very pensive, taciturn and extremely impatient. Madame Olympe exercised every possible precaution to prevent any interference with her husband's work which was carried out in the suburb of Passy. The very extended title reads as follows:

"*Petite Messe Solennelle* in four parts, with accompaniment for two pianos and a harmonium, composed for my summer stay in Passy. Twelve singers of three sexes, men, women, and *castrati,* will suffice for its performance; that is to say, eight for the chorus and four for the solos; twelve Cherubim in all. May God forgive me the following comparison. Twelve in number also are the Apostles in the celebrated fresco by Leonardo called *The Last Supper.* Who would believe it? Among Thy disciples are some capable of singing wrong notes! Lord, be reassured, I guarantee that there will be no Judas at my luncheon, and that all mine will sing accurately and *con amore* Thy praises, as well as this little composition, which is, alas, the last mortal sin of my old age.— Passy, 1863."

There is also a postscript:

"Dear God—Well, this poor little Mass is completed. Have I for once written real Sacred Music or merely damned bad music? I was born for *opera buffa,* as Thou knowest! Little skill, but some heart! that about sums it up. So blessed be Thou, and grant me paradise."

It would be a mistake to see in these lines fun only. It is a mixture of humor and seriousness, self-irony and truth, wisdom and experience. Rossini had found his inner peace after many years of suffering and torment. He dedicated the mass to Countess Pillet-Will whose father in law had counselled him in financial matters. She requested the privilege of having the mass first performed in her palace.

The performance was carefully prepared. Jules Cohen, professor at the Conservatoire and chorus master at the Opéra, coached the chorus whose members were selected by Auber, venerated director of the Conservatoire. Leading singers of the Théâtre Italien were asked to assist: the sisters Carlotta and Barbara Marchisio, Italo Gardone (tenor) and Luigi Agnesi (Bass). All were artists of European fame. Georges Mathias, a student of Chopin, sat at the piano and young Albert Lavignac who later distinguished himself as educator, musicologist and encyclopaedist, played harmonium. The first performance took place on Sunday, March 14, 1864, in the afternoon. Rossini stood at the first piano, indicated the tempi and acted as a page turner. Very few listeners were admitted: Auber, Meyerbeer, Thomas, Rossini's close friend Michele Caraffa, a veteran of Napoleon's Russian campaign, and some prominent Parisians.

The impression the mass created was profound. Meyerbeer was deeply moved and embraced Rossini so warmly that the latter admonished him to calm down because he was concerned about Meyerbeer's impaired health. He was aware that Meyerbeer had left his sickbed to attend the performance. Yet the latter remained unperturbed, gave a little speech and closed with the word: "He [Rossini] is the Jupiter of our time and holds us all in the hollow of his hand." The mass was repeated on the following day for a larger audience. Meyerbeer, despite his sickness, neglected Rossini's warning and came also to the second performance which was attended by the Papal Nunzio and prominent people from government, literary and musical circles.

The critics did not write reviews but hymns and panegyric essays. Jacques-Léopold Heugel, founder of the renowned music publishing house, commended the importance of the unknown harmonic treasures that make the Mass a whole treatise of new harmonies. Whereupon Rossini jokingly remarked: "It is true I did not spare the dissonances but I have sugar-coated them." He probably derived the most satisfaction from a short note by Meyerbeer which reached him shortly after the repeat performance:

"To Jupiter Rossini
Divine Master:

I cannot let the day go by without thanking you once more for the immense pleasure I derived from the two readings of your last and sublime creation; may the heaven bestow upon you a hundred years to create other similar master works and may God grant me also a high age to enable me to hear and admire the new creations of your immortal genius.

As ever your admirer and old friend

Paris, March 15   G. Meyerbeer"

Jupiter Rossini may have often remembered the advice he gave the agitated Meyerbeer at the first reading of the mass, for Meyerbeer died seven weeks later.

The possibility of setting the piano and harmonium parts for full orchestra was probably discussed among some listeners. One critic remarked that if the mass would be orchestrated it would emanate a fire which would burn cathedrals of marble. Rossini occupied himself with the orchestration of the mass in 1865 but abstained from including in the orchestrated version the Prélude Religieux (for harmonium or piano) which written as music for the Offertory preceded the *Sanctus* in the original score.

We are told that after the completion of the orchestration Rossini had expressed his preference for the original version. And he contended that he undertook the orchestration only in order to prevent somebody else from doing it and perhaps even employing saxophones. Did Rossini really mean it? There are humorous elements connected with the mass. See the preamble and the prostscript. The title is a joke because the *Petite Messe Solennelle* is longer than the last great masses of Haydn and exceeds in length the masses of Beethoven, Schubert and Bruckner.

Rossini's "little" mass is monumental in concept and design. An ensemble of twelve "cherubim" plus the six hands of the accompanying keyboard players will never suffice to bring out the monumentality of the *Gloria* and *Credo* and the dramatic character of the concluding pages if the mass should be sung in a church of larger architectural proportions. Rossini was anxious to hear the orchestral version in a great church. His wish was never fulfilled. After his passing on November 13, 1868, it was decided to perform the orchestral version as a memorial service on his birthday. Since Rossini was born in a leap year on February 29, 1792, the 28th of February, 1869, was chosen as the day closest to his birthday. The memorial concert took place in the Théâtre Italien which the late composer once directed. The chorus and orchestra of the theater was joined by a solo quartet of famous singers such as Marietta Alboni (Soprano), Gabrielle Krauss (alto), Nicola Nicolini (tenor) and Luigi Agnesi (bass). Then the inevitable happened: the mass was commercialized and presented by a travelling company in many cities.

Some Analytical Observations

What were Rossini's models? He had two alternatives to chose from: either the 18th century Neapolitan type or the classical model created by Haydn and also adopted by Beethoven, Schubert and Cherubini. The former type is known as the cantata mass in which the sections of the ordinary with the greatest wordage, *Gloria* and *Credo,* are split up in several self-contained divisions that are treated as arias, duets, terzets, etc. The classical mass eliminates the arias and uses a solo quartet which fulfills a function similar to that of the concertino in the concerto grosso. In addition *Gloria* and *Credo* show a three-sectioned design in which the musical material is manipulated along the lines of the sonata form. Rossini chose neither one but struck a balance of both possibilities and adopted the classical scheme for the *Kyrie* and *Credo* and upheld the Neapolitan tradition for the *Gloria.*

The *Kyrie,* cast in ternary form, displays two contrasted musical styles: homophony in the outer sections and strict a capella Renaissance polyphony in the middle portion (*Christe eleison*), a scheme which Verdi adopted for the *Kyrie* of the *Messa da Requiem.*

The *Gloria* is, except for the concluding fugue, the domain of the soloists. Consisting of six sections, it is organized like an operatic finale in which the individual self-contained units, contrasted melodically, harmonically and emotionally, are linked together by modulatory bridges. After the powerful

intonation the chorus recedes into the background and returns only after the fifth section (bass aria in A major) with a restatement of the Gloria intonation—

adapted to the words "Cum sancto spiritu in gloria Dei patris." It prefaces the extended fugue—

which leads to a third statement of the *Gloria* intonation preceding the concluding Amen. The repetitions of the *Gloria* intonation serve as a musical connecting link but also as a unifying spiritual factor.

The *Credo* shows a clear-cut three-sectioned construction in which the *Crucifixus* forms the middle division. Rossini comes up with a new tempo indication: *Allegro Cristiano,* whose real meaning is impossible to fathom.

A joke? The thematic development of the Credo is based on two small motifs:

which are manipulated in a symphonic manner. The movement begins in E major turns to the key of the lower third (C) and finally one more third down to A flat major, the tonality of the *Crucifixus* which is an aria for soprano. The main key re-enters with *Et resurrexit*. Here we reach, thematically speaking, familiar territory. The *Credo* concludes with an extended double fugue—

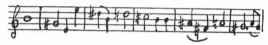

in which powerful dynamic climaxes are built up. One wonders about the effect if only eight or twelve singers are to bring out these passages in a triple forte (FFF).

The combined *Sanctus* and *Benedictus* are brief in length and as an a capella section restrained in sound. Note the pastoral quality—

and remarkable dynamic contrasts. The *Agnus Dei* is preceded by an alto aria *O salutaris hostia*. This is an Eucharist hymn which is normally sung as a benediction hymn but can be inserted at the appropriate place in the mass —before or after the *Agnus Dei*—i.e. as a communion hymn. It is not the practice to use it in the context of the proper or ordinary but it can be sung in addition to these. Rossini proceeded probably from a local custom as did Cherubini who included the benediction hymn in several of his masses. The three last numbers of Rossini's score have one conspicuous trait in common: the very loud ending after a soft (pianissimo) passage. The alto is also dominating in the *Agnus Dei* which contains three invocations and three statements of the *Dona nobis pacem*. The third statement is extended and discloses strong dramatic accents and a build up as in an operatic finale. This agitated passage whose musical language is akin to that of Verdi seems somewhat strange in connection with the text which calls rather for a peaceful and consoling mood. This unusual approach seems to point to Rossini's frame of mind and can perhaps be interpreted as an aftermath to the tragic crisis which overshadowed the second half of the composer's life.

Shortly after the performance of the mass Rossini was visited by Eduard Hanslick who expressed his regret for not having attended the reading. Rossini encountered: "This is nothing for you Germans. My most sacred music is only *semi-seria*." Self-irony? Perhaps but with a small dosis of truth. Rossini who was a subscriber to the Complete Edition of Johann Sebastian Bach's Works very well understood German musical thinking. Noting that he tried to belittle somewhat his *Petite Messe Solennelle*, we do not agree with the master on that score and take it seriously.

The mass shows the melodista of yore who knew how to write for the singers effectively. It shows at the same time the craftsman who gave in the fugues a superb proof of his studies in the contrapuntal tradition of Padre Martini and finally it shows in the *Agnus Dei* the great dramatist who as a septuagenarian has adopted the musical language of the contemporary opera of his homeland. Notwithstanding a few other pieces written later, the *Petite Messe Solennelle* is Gioacchino Rossini's musical testament.

ROUSSEL, Albert (1869-1937), *Concert pour petit Orchestre*
Allegro; Andante; Presto

Albert Roussel's career resembled that of Rimsky-Korsakov. As a youth, each served in the navy of his own country, and by traveling to different parts of the world—Roussel to North Africa and Indo-China and Rimsky-Korsakov around the world by clipper—they became acquainted with the indigenous music of other peoples, which left its mark on their works. Roussel resigned from the French Navy in 1894, when he was twenty-five, and began to study music. He became a pupil of Vincent d'Indy at the renowned Schola Cantorum in Paris and continued his studies until 1908, when he was thirty-eight years old. At the Schola Cantorum he was appointed an instructor of counterpoint. Among his students were Erik Satie and Edgar Varèse. During the First World War Roussel served as an ambulance driver with the Red Cross, and, after his health was undermined in the battle of the Somme, he was discharged in January 1918.

The *Concert pour petit orchestre* aims to combine the individual tone colors of soloistically treated instruments. It was first performed in Paris on May 5, 1927, and published in the same year. Its three-movement design points to the baroque, while the use of pairs of flutes, oboes, clarinets, bassoons, horns, one trumpet, kettledrums, and strings conforms to the classical orchestra.

The first movement (Allegro, 2/4) grows out of a simple motif from which the entire thematic development and the rhythmic impulse is derived. This little motif heard at the opening is ingeniously woven into the texture and dominates throughout the movement. The Andante in 6/4 time is a gentle and transparent concerted piece in which flute, bassoon, trumpet, and horn are prominently displayed. The Finale in 3/4 time is a humorous parody of a quick waltz spiced with dissonant chromatic harmonies. The conclusion is surprising: after a clamorous climax the music fades away in a gentle *pianissimo*. Roussel dedicated the piece to the French conductor Walther Straram (1876-1933) who, shortly after the premiere of *Concert pour petit orchestre*, led the first performance of Ravel's *Bolero*.

Sinfonietta for String Orchestra, Opus 52
Allegro molto; Andante—Allegro

Roussel's first creative efforts coincided with the rise of Debussy (born 1862) and the emergence of Ravel, who, born in 1875, was six years younger than Roussel. Roussel achieved notable success with his ballets and instrumental music in the 1920s. He attracted considerable attention and was recognized as an outstanding composer abroad; his third symphony was commissioned for the fiftieth anniversary of the Boston Symphony Orchestra. Roussel was at first susceptible to the influence of French Impressionism, but as a student of the music of the seventeenth and eighteenth centuries, he later leaned toward neoclassicism. He even occasionally showed an interest in jazz.

The Sinfonietta for string orchestra was composed in the summer of 1934, when Roussel was recovering from a serious attack of pneumonia. Yet the piece does not reveal any traits that would point to the physical weakness of the composer. On the contrary, it is saturated with youthful vitality and energy. Technically, it goes back to the three-movement baroque concerto and its "slow-fast-slow" order, which Antonio Vivaldi developed in his concertos and symphonies for strings. Roussel's piece was originally conceived as an introduction and Allegro; the Allegro molto, which now opens the piece, was added later. The Allegro molto shows the thematic dualism of the sonata Allegro in a concise manner. The dignified Andante is connected with the finale by an incisive motif, which is stated four times in the concluding measures of the Andante by the basses and appears in the entrance of the violins in the finale.

Basically homophonic and displaying in a nutshell the bi-thematic design of the sonata, the movement drives speedily along. The sinfonietta was first performed in Paris on November 19, 1934.

SCHUBERT, Franz (1797-1828)
Five Minuets with Six Trios

The Five Minuets with Six Trios originated in November 1813. This month was a turning point in Schubert's life. His voice had changed in 1812 when he was fifteen and therefore his days as an imperial chorister with free tuition, board, and lodging in the so-called Convict were numbered. The authorities let him stay on, but around the end of October, 1813, he left and entered the Normal-Hauptschule for a ten-month preparatory course for a teacher's license. This offered the best road of escape from Austrian military service, the duration of which was fourteen years.

The autograph of the five minuets is dated November 19, 1813. This is the only precise information we have. The minuets were not published until as late as 1886 in the *Complete Works*. It is safe to assume that Schubert wrote these pieces for the orchestra of the Convict (perhaps as a parting gift?), in which he had played at the second desk of the first violin section. The student orchestra was no doubt capable of the technical requirements of the minuets. The series is made up of three minuets with two trios each, and two minuets without trios. The order is as follows:

No. 1, C major, with trios in C major and C minor
No. 2, F major
No. 3, D minor, with trios in F major and D minor

No. 4, G major

No. 5, C major, with trios in C major

Haydn differentiated between the symphony or sonata minuet and that type he defined as *Tanzmenuett*. Schubert, who later wrote a great deal of dance music, here leans toward the symphony minuet. The old court dance appears in an astonishing melodic, rhythmic, harmonic, and dynamic variety, devoid of artificiality and sophistication. We hear simple melodies, but also one that encompasses nearly three octaves (No. 1, second trio):

We find themes of a rather rustic character in the first minuet, and those of a more brilliant quality in the second. We encounter the contrast between forcefulness (unison motifs) and gentleness, in combination with an imaginative orchestration. In this respect we may single out the second trio of the fifth minuet,

which strikingly demonstrates the gift of the sixteen-year-old composer for the effective handling of the orchestra, a virtue he brilliantly displayed in his first symphony which he had completed shortly before the composition of the minuets.

Overture in Italian Style

Late in the fall of 1817 Schubert wrote two overtures "in Italian style": one in D major and the other in C major. It seems that Schubert valued highly the introductory Adagio to the D major piece because he used it three years later for the overture to the incidental music for the play *Die Zauberharfe (The Magic Harp)*, commonly referred to as the overture to *Rosamunde;* a confusing situation we need not discuss here. The C major overture of 1817, unquestionably superior to its D major twin, received a reading by the amateur orchestra that played most of Schubert's early symphonies, in the apartment of Otto Hatwig, piano teacher and violinist of the Burgtheater orchestra. The leader, or concertmaster, of this group was Eduard Jaell who included in a concert he gave on March 1, 1818, "an entirely new overture by Herr Franz Schubert." This was in all probability the C major overture "in Italian style."

The review in the *Allgemeine Theaterzeitung* (March 14, 1818) read: "The second part began with a wondrously lovely overture by a young composer, Herr Franz Schubert, a pupil of our much-venerated Salieri, who has learned already to touch and convulse all hearts. Although the theme was surprisingly simple, a wealth of the most astonishing and agreeable ideas developed from it, worked out with vigor and skill. It is to be wished that this artist will quite soon delight us with a new gift." It may be judged that the piece was a clear-cut success because it was also reviewed in the Dresden *Abendzeitung*. This notice was the first critical mention abroad of any work by Schubert.

Striving for a wider circulation, Schubert made an arrangement for piano duo that was included in a program of a concert and recitation by the court actor Karl Friederich Müller. It drew much critical acclaim: "Profound feeling, disciplined yet spontaneous force and appealing charm mark his every work, large and small; once practice, that mother of all human perfection, has done her own work with him, they will without doubt find their favored place among the productions of the day." The overture was presented by four players at two pianos, and among the performers were Schubert and his friend Anselm Hüttenbrenner, a composer whose works are forgotten. (He lives on as the man who tucked away Schubert's unfinished B minor symphony for more than forty years.) The overture remained in manuscript for some time, and was not publised until 1866.

Why was it defined as an overture "in Italian style?" What are the criteria to justify this designation? It is not written in the vein of Salieri who was a follower of Gluck, nor in the manner of Cimarosa, Piccini, or Paisiello, the prominent representatives of the 18th century *opera buffa*; neither is it in the style of Cherubini nor does it show the features of the pompous and heroic opera of Spontini. No doubt Schubert was influenced by the then "modern Italian style." This was the musical language of Gioacchino Rossini, born in 1792, whose star shone brightly over Europe. Schubert was impressed by the sound of the colorful Rossini orchestra and its motoric quality that enthralled audiences everywhere. Strangely enough these features were not exactly Rossini's artistic property. Some were introduced by Simon Mayr (1763-1845), a Bavarian, who had settled down in Bergamo and italianized himself completely. The splendor of his instrumentation with its noisy crescendos captivated the Italians, and Rossini adapting these devices to his miraculous melodic facility pushed the operas of Mayr from the boards. In the piece of Schubert, significant features of the Rossinian type of overture are evident: the slow introduction, the rhythmically incisive principal idea of the main body (Allegro), the occasional shift to the minor mode, the absence of a thematic elaboration in the middle section, the woodwinds moving in thirds, boisterous double basses, and of course, the effective crescendo passages

Overture to "Die Zauberharfe," and Entr'acte and ballet music to "Rosamunde"

Two theatrical events in 1820 thrust Franz Schubert into the limelight of Vienna, his hometown, where he was still unknown to the public. First, his one-act *singspiel Die Zwillingsbrüder* (*The Twin Brothers*) was produced in the Court Opera on June 14. Two months later, on August 19, his name appeared on the posters of the Theater an der Wien as the composer of the incidental music to the play *Die Zauberharfe* (*The Magic Harp*) by Georg von Hofmann, the author of *Die Zwillingsbrüder*. Schubert owed the commission for *The Magic Harp* to the stage painter Hermann Neefe, a son of Christian Neefe, Beethoven's teacher in Bonn.

The play and the music did not fare well with the critics. There were laudatory reviews, but also very critical remarks. One paper dismissed the music as "often thin, insipid, and stale in taste." The correspondent of the important *Allgemeine Musikalische Zeitung*, Leipzig, found "talent here and there" in the score, but characterized much of it as "too long, ineffective, fatiguing, the harmonic progressions too harsh, the orchestration redundant, the choruses dull and feeble."

However, the *Zeitung* singled out as the most successful pieces the introductory Adagio (actually Andante) to the overture and a romance for tenor. (The latter was sung by Ferdinand Schimon, who became a successful painter, and to whom we are indebted for a famous portrait of Beethoven.) For the commended "Andante" Schubert raided his Overture "in Italian style" (D major, 1817) and remodelled its introduction to fulfill the same function in the overture to *The Magic Harp*. This overture has two features in common with the Rossini overture type: the absence of a thematic elaboration in the middle section and the effective crescendo passages with the frequent repetition of a small motif.

Rosamunde was billed as a "great romantic play in four acts, with choruses, music accompaniment and dances" by Helmine von Chezy (1783-1856), and was given first on December 20, 1823, in the Theater an der Wien. The authoress was a Berliner bluestocking, who achieved immortality thanks to her most unfortunate collaboration as a librettist with both Weber, for his opera *Euryanthe*, and Schubert. The production of *Euryanthe* brought her to Vienna, where she stayed for ten years.

Rosamunde was a failure and saw only two performances. Schubert's music, ten orchestral and vocal pieces, received a few good notices. Having been rushed into this work, he found no time to compose an overture and used instead the one to this opera *Alfonso und Estrella*, composed in 1821/22 and produced as late as 1854 in Weimar under Liszt's direction. The Viennese audience liked the overture very much and obtained an encore. Despite the fact that the piece was published in 1826 as the overture to *Alfonso und Estrella*, in an arrangement by Schubert himself for pianoforte duet, the *Collected Works* associated it with the music to *Rosamunde*, with which it has not the slightest musical connection. To top off this confusion, the overture to *The Magic Harp*, in spite of its melodic connection with the music to that play, is often referred to as "overture to *Rosamunde*." This is an arbitrary denomination historically and artistically.

The most popular selections from the music to *Rosamunde* are the Entr'acte and ballet from the fourth act. The first section of the Entr'acte is known to all friends of chamber music from the slow movement in the String Quartet in A minor (1824), and to pianists as the theme for variations in the third Impromptu of Opus 142. The well-known ballet music in G major, with the rythmically contrasting alternativo (trio), has been exploited in the Schubert musical *Blossom Time* by Heinrich Berte and Sigmund Romberg, and in its English version *Lilac Time* by George H. Clutsam.

Symphony No. 2 in B flat major
Largo—Allegro vivace; Andante; Minuetto: Allegro vivace; Presto vivace

Schubert penned his first symphony, in D major, when he was a boy of sixteen, a student at the Vienna Stadtconvict. The symphony may have been played by the student orchestra. He lost this medium for having his orchestral music performed when he left the Convict in November, 1813. Yet he refused to be daunted and, driven by his irresistible creative urge and youthful optimism, commenced his second symphony on December 10, 1814. He finished it in February 1815 during the time of the Congress of Vienna, which was to establish the new political order in Europe after the defeat of Napoleon. It stands to reason that a boy of seventeen had no chance to bring a symphony before a public then in a turmoil of festivities, gala performances, and balls. The new symphony was perhaps given a tryout by the student orchestra, but the work was probably beyond the capabilities of the players.

Actually not one piece of Schubert's symphonic output reached the Viennese public at large in his lifetime and the renditions of his first symphonies were strictly private affairs organized by amateurs. These readings did not take place in a spacious salon of an aristocratic mansion but in living rooms in apartment buildings. Chamber music was seriously cultivated in Schubert's paternal home. This amateur group also played symphonies in quartet arrangements. Wind players later joined the group: when a nucleus of an orchestra was formed the group moved to the house of the merchant Franz Frischling, and later to Otto Hatwig and to the Schottenhof, which still exists. Hatwig was a member of the Burgtheater orchestra, and a violin and piano teacher, and a composer. He directed the steadily growing amateur orchestra from 1815 to 1818. Later Anton Pettenkofer, a wholesale grocer and landowner, took over.

Many of the orchestra parts of Schubert's second symphony, dated 1816 and 1817, have turned up. This could be taken as an indication that the symphony was played by this amateur group under Hatwig's direction. The first public performance was given not in Schubert's hometown but in faraway London, on October 20, 1877, in the Crystal Palace conducted by August Manns. The inclusion of Schubert in these London concerts must be credited to Sir George Grove, the famous lexicographer, who had gone to Vienna in 1867 to search for Schubert manuscripts. The second symphony, the autograph of which is in the archives of the Gesellschaft der Musikfreunde in Vienna, was published in 1884 under the supervision of Johannes Brahms.

The road the young boy had to follow as a symphonic composer was foreordained. He had to take Haydn, Mozart, and the Beethoven of the first and second symphonies as his models, and to think in terms of the late eighteenth century symphony rather than of the revolutionary creations of his day (Beethoven's third, fifth, and seventh symphonies). Schubert's second symphony shows several familiar features: the slow introduction to the first movement, an Andante with variations instead of an expanded Adagio and a minuet. Yet the first Allegro discloses a tendency to extend the customary form, and a movement of more than six hundred measures is the result. The expansion of the framework is not achieved by thematic elaboration, however, but by repetition. Changes Schubert made in the process of composition were considered by Brahms as "significant evidence of the freshness and unconcern with which Schubert planned and even wrote his works."

The five variations of the Andante are akin to those of Haydn. The basic lyrical quality is temporarily abandoned in the agitated fourth variation in C minor, but the conclusion occurs gently in a typically Schubertian twilight. Although the usual editions designate the third movement as a minuet, the manuscript does not. It is a very vigorous and fast minuet contrasted with the gentle ländler of the trio. Matching the first Allegro in length and architecture, the finale is sparkling and vibrant and pulls effective dynamic surprises.

Symphony No. 3 in D major

Adagio maestoso—Allegro con brio; Allegretto; Minuetto; Presto vivace

Schubert's career as a symphonist is a sad chapter in his life story. Not one piece of his symphonic output reached the Viennese public during his lifetime (1797-1828). Only an amateur group gave him the opportunity of hearing his first six symphonies written between 1813 and 1818. These were in no way performances, but readings which took place in the living rooms of apartment buildings rather than in the spacious salons of aristocratic mansions.

Symphonies arranged for string quartets were played in Schubert's paternal home. Wind players later joined the group and formed the nucleus of an orchestra that moved to the home of Otto Hatwig, a violin and piano teacher and member of the Burgtheater orchestra. He directed the steadily growing ensemble from 1815 to 1818, and then Anton Pettenkofer, wholesale grocer and landowner, took charge. This event provides us with an illuminating glimpse of the state of musical affairs in the Austrian capital after the Congress of Vienna (1814-1815). Emperor Franz I (1768-1835) played string quartets with patrician generals and with the court conductor Joseph Eybler, under whose baton Schubert had sung as a chorister in the Court Chapel. But the private bands maintained by aristocrats were gone, and simple middle class people played under the direction of such conductors as Pettenkofer, the wholesale grocer. This orchestra numbered thirty-six players before it disbanded in 1820, and was sufficient numerically to play Schubert's early symphonies. We have no reports, however, which might enlighten us about the artistic standards of the orchestra. It was strictly a private affair. The lack of adequate performing media may have been the reason why Schubert abstained from orchestrating the sketch of the E major symphony of 1821 and from completing the B minor symphony.

It was in Hatwig's house that Schubert's creations probably received their tryouts. Presumably this was the case with the symphony No. 3 in D major.

According to the autograph preserved in Vienna (Gesellschaft der Musik-freunde) Schubert began the symphony on May 24, 1815, but interrupted his work during the first Allegro. He took up the symphony again on July 11, completed the first movement on the following day, and composed the other movements between July 15 and 19.

There are no records of a public reading in Vienna until December 2, 1860, and this performance limited to the Finale occurred under peculiar circumstances. The orchestra was led by Johann Herbeck (1831-1877), one of the best musicians Vienna produced in the 19th century. Later as conductor in the Court Chapel and director of the Court Opera, he exerted immense influence. He championed the cause of both Wagner and Bruckner, and resurrected from neglect and oblivion many works of Schubert, among them the unfinished symphony in B minor. Herbeck conceived of the idea of forming a symphony by combining individual movements from several Schubert symphonies still in manuscript. He chose the first and second movements of the fourth symphony (C minor), the Scherzo of the sixth (C major), and the Finale of the third, and called the assortment "Symphonic Fragments." The first complete reading of the third symphony took place in London in the Crystal Palace on February 19, 1881, under the leadership of August Manns. The inclusion of Schubert's six early symphonies in these London concerts must be credited to Sir George Grove the famous lexicographer who, accompanied by Arthur Sullivan, had gone to Vienna in 1867 to search for Schubert manuscripts.

The road young Schubert had to follow as a symphonist was predestined. He took Haydn, Mozart, and the Beethoven of the first and second symphonies as his models, and thought in terms of the late eighteenth century rather than of the revolutionary creations of his day (Beethoven's third, fifth, and seventh symphonies). The symphony No. 3 in D major reflects this approach. It is an easy-going creation blessed with the charm of youth. The listener who expects the *maestoso* introduction as a preparation for serious things to come will be surprised by the entrance of the playful Allegro which, however, ends up with a forceful and "massive" coda. The gently orchestrated second movement (Allegretto) seems to foreshadow the delight-ful melodies of the ballet music of *Rosamunde*, while the Minuet displays the rustic quality of peasant dances to which the gentle *ländler* of the Trio provides a marked contrast. The Finale is a rapidly moving perpetuum mobile in the manner of a tarantella.

Symphony No. 5 in B flat major
Allegro; Andante con moto; Minuetto; Allegro molto; Allegro vivace

Completed on October 3, 1816 the symphony was played by Hatwig's* group shortly afterward. The first recorded public performance took place on February 1, 1873, in London under the baton of August Manns, a German who after a humble beginning and activities as a military band-master in his home country made a brilliant career in England. The score of the fifth symphony which calls for one flute, two oboes, bassoons, horns,

---

* See notes on Symphony No. 8

and the customary strings, like Mozart's G minor symphony and many of his clavier concertos, fitted the capabilities of Otto Hatwig's players. In contrast to its four preceding sister works, it lacks a slow introduction. This function is fulfilled by the four opening measures which, however, are manipulated at the beginning of the middle section. The Andante con moto charms the listener through its typically Schubertian melodic sweetness. The minuet surprises us because of its seriousness, but this attitude is dispelled by the graceful *Ländler* melody of the trio. Haydn was the godfather of the spirited finale, a piece of exhilarating gaiety and peerless clarity, which Alfred Einstein termed "perhaps the purest, most polished and most balanced piece of instrumental music Schubert had yet written."

Symphony No. 6 in C major
Adagio—Allegro; Andante; Scherzo Allegro moderato

It was presumably in Hatwig's house that Schubert's sixth symphony in C major received its tryout. According to the autograph preserved in the Vienna *Gesellschaft der Musikfreunde* (Society of Friends of Music), Schubert began the symphony in October 1817 and, working on it with interruptions, completed it in February 1818. When the *Gesellschaft der Musikfreunde* rejected his great C major symphony of 1828 as too long and too difficult, he then offered the C major symphony of 1818, which was accepted. Alas, Schubert did not live long enough to attend the performance on December 19, 1828. He had died on November 19.

Another reading was given on March 3, 1829. There are no records of a third public presentation in Vienna until December 12, 1860, and this performance occurred under peculiar circumstances. The orchestra was led by Johann Herbeck (1831-1877), one of the best musicians Vienna produced in the nineteenth century. Later as conductor in the Court Chapel and director of the Court Opera, he exerted immense influence. He championed both Wagner and Bruckner, and resurrected from neglect and oblivion many works of Schubert, among them the unfinished symphony in B minor. Herbeck conceived of the idea of forming a symphony by combining individual movements from several Schubert symphonies still in manuscript. He chose the first and second movements of the fourth symphony (C minor), the Scherzo of the sixth (C major), and the Finale of the third (D major) and called the assortment "Symphonic Fragments." One wonders why such an eminent musician as Johann Herbeck resorted to a practice that cannot be defended on artistic grounds.

The first presentation of the sixth symphony outside of Vienna occurred in London in the Crystal Palace Concerts on November 21, 1868, under the leadership of August Manns. The inclusion of Schubert's six early symphonies in these London concerts must be credited to Sir George Grove, the famous lexicographer, who, accompanied by Arthur Sullivan, had gone to Vienna in 1867 to search for Schubert manuscripts.

Schubert designated the sixth symphony in the autograph "Grosse Sinfonie" as if he wanted to set it apart from the previous sister works. Yet it is usually called "the little C major symphony" in order to avoid confusion with "the great C major symphony" of 1828. Despite Schubert's classification it is no less easy-going than the preceding B flat symphony (No. 5). It is true that its orchestration is much richer and the structural proportions are greater. But viewed as a whole, it is blessed with the charm of youth and the spell of optimism. Like most of Schubert's symphonies, it follows tradition by prefacing the first Allegro with a slow introduction, which is not connected melodically with the main body but creates an air of expectancy. Schubert undoubtedly took Haydn's "Military" symphony as a model for the beginning of the Allegro, with a gentle announcement of the theme by woodwinds and its forceful restatement by the full orchestra.

In the Andante, Schubert indulged in a study of contrast. The graceful opening is followed by a portion rhythmically animated with triplets. The triplet rhythm, characteristic of this section, also has a bearing on the varied repetition of the opening. After a restatement of the rhythmically animated passage, the movement fades tenderly away. The Scherzo, the first in Schubert's symphonies (the previous ones included only minuets), foreshadows the Scherzo of the great C major symphony of 1828 in orchestral and harmonic treatment, the choice of key for the trio (in 1818, the upper third E; in 1828, the lower third A), and in the transition passage from the trio to the recapitulation of the Scherzo. The symphony, and the second and fourth movements in particular, reveals a kinship to the C major Overture in Italian style, also composed in the fall of 1817. The Finale shows typical Italianisms in the melodies and phrases, which move in thirds. The movement abounds in pleasing ideas, striking dynamic contrasts, surprising harmonic turns, and effective orchestral combinations. In short, it is a movement that entertains the listener immensely.

Gesang der Geister Ueber den Wassern

In Schubert's vast output of 567 lieder that were set to words of 39 poets, Goethe is represented with 57 poems of which eleven appear in very different versions. This latter group does not include a number of songs which are extant in several versions differing only in some details but not in their musical substance. The best known example is that of the *Erlkönig* of which four versions have come down to us. The reasons why Goethe's poems have attracted Schubert and many other composers (Mozart, Beethoven, Mendelssohn, Schumann, Loewe, Brahms, Liszt and Wolf) are obvious. Goethe's lyrical poetry is permeated with musical elements and their sheer sound generates a strong and often irresistible appeal to the musician. The universality of Goethe's poetry is impressively reflected by Schubert's songs. We find ballads and romances, love songs and lieder of a folklike quality, songs that mirror impressions derived from nature, and religious and philosophical songs. Among Schubert's unfinished works, sonatas, quartets, symphonies, choral works and operas, were also five songs set to Goethean texts and one of these constitutes Schubert's first attempt to compose: *Gesang der Geister über den Wassern* (Song of the Spirits over the Water).

Goethe wrote the poem on October 9-11, 1779, during his second jaunt through Switzerland. Like many travellers before and untold visitors of

Switzerland afterwards, Goethe went to Lauterbrunnen in the Berner Ober-
land to see the Staubbachfall which falls down perpendicularly about 1000
feet over vertical rocks. This spectacular sight generated very sublime thoughts
which Goethe converted into poetry. The original version of the poem which
Goethe dispatched on October 14 to his friend Charlotte von Stein in Weimar,
is conceived as a dialogue of two Spirits. The version on which Schubert's
composition is based was published ten years later (1789).

Two components are joined in the poem: pictoral and allegorical-philo-
sophical elements. Proceeding from the natural phenomenon, the unceasing
motion of the waterfall, the poet perceives the eternal contrast in human
life, the collision of lofty ideals with harsh realities, of composure and
passion, and the obstacles that beset man's path through life. As the wave
is a play of the wind, so is the soul a play of fate. The allegoric union of the
soul and fate, as well as of water and wind, symbolizes the unity of the
spiritual and material world.

Schubert took up the poem in September 1816 and left the composition
in a very fragmentary state in which the first two stanzas and the last significant lines are missing. Interesting in his treatment of the lines "ragen Klippen
dem Sturz entgegen" (over crags projecting from the deep it [the water]
falls) by means of a descending bass motif while the interval of the ninth in
the vocal lines is to depict the falling water. The conjecture seems not to be
far-fetched that Schubert left the song unfinished, because he felt that he was
not quite ready for it.

He returned to it in March, 1817, and set it for four-part male quartet.
Again, he was not satisfied with the result which, he probably felt, did not
bring out fully the symbolism of the poem. He set out once more to compose
Gesang der Geister über den Wassern in December, 1820. Meanwhile,
Schubert had grown intellectually as well as artistically and so did the scope
of the piece, which in this version calls for an eight-part ensemble with
piano accompaniment. The unfinished sketch of December, 1820, has been
preserved, while the complete composition was published only as late as
1897 in the Collected Works. Yet this version was not the last word.

Schubert once more concerned himself with the *Gesang der Geister* in
February, 1821. He wanted to include it in the program of a "Grand Concert
with recitations and tableaux" which was arranged by the Society of Ladies
of the Nobility. The concert featured three pieces of Schubert: *Erlkönig, Das
Dörfchen* (The Little Village) for four-part male ensemble and *Gesang der
Geister über den Wassern*. Schubert had revised the eight-part version and
provided it with an accompaniment of low string instruments: two violas,
two violoncellos and double bass.

The 7th of March, 1821, was a red-letter day for Schubert because his name
was projected into the limelight of a gala evening which featured such
illustrious names as Sophie Schröder, the greatest German actress of her time,
her daughter Wilhelmine, who was to become the foremost German dramatic
soprano during the first half of the nineteenth century, young Fanny Elssler,
the future Fanny I Queen of the Dance, and Johann Michael Vogl, the
admired baritone of the court opera, who championed the songs of Schubert.
Actually in the wake of this "Grand Concert" *Erlkönig* and 23 other Goethe

lieder were published. Alas, it is a different story with the *Gesang der Geister*. In the first place we do not know which version was sung. The poster gives only the name of six singers and adds "two choristers." Whether the accompaniment was provided by the piano or a string ensemble as required for the version of February, 1821, the poster does not say. The piece evidently was not sufficiently rehearsed and fared badly as we can gather from the following review which appeared in the Vienna *Allgemeine Musikalische Zeitung* (March 21, 1821)): "Herr Schubert's eight-voice chorus was recognized by the public as an accumulation of every sort of senseless, disordered and purposeless musical modulation and side-tracking. In such works the composer resembles a drayman who drives eight-in-hand, and swerves now right, now left—in other words, avoids collision—then turns back, and goes on with the same game without ever getting along the road." Similar judgments were meted out by other papers which in effect condemned the piece into the oblivion from which it was resurrected thirty-six years later by Johann Herbeck to whom we are also indebted for the resurrection of the Unfinished Symphony in B minor (1865).

Herbeck found the *Gesang der Geister* in the archive of the Viennese music publisher Karl Anton Spina and succeeded in having the parts printed. He lost no time in performing the piece and presented it in a concert of the Wiener Männer-Gesangverein (Viennese Men Singing Association) on December 27, 1857. Greeted by Hanslick as a work of overwhelming genius, it was so enthusiastically acclaimed that Herbeck saw fit to encore it. Now Spina published it with the arbitrary opus number 167 and a likewise arbitrary dedication to Schubert's friend, the painter Leopold Kuppelwieser. Herbeck and his men have redeemed the *Gesang der Geister* from the mistreatment on the part of the singers of 1821, and the public of 1857 rehabilitated it from the the ill-treatment by Schubert's contemporaries. Yet if we grant them the extenuating circumstances of the insufficient rehearsal and the bewildering musical language, it is plain that Schubert boldly penetrated into harmonic spheres that are characteristic rather of the 1840s and it is also plain that the public at large was not ripe for this harmonic idiom and failed to understand Schubert's musical language in its relationship to Goethe's lines.

The history of *Gesang der Geister über der Wassern*, spanning five years, clearly proves that Schubert had given much thought to the composition in order to achieve perfect harmony with the text and bring out its two components, the pictorial and philosophical elements. To create a mysterious mood and to avoid bright colors in the instrumental accompaniment he chose a string ensemble of violas, violoncellos and double bass. As for the formal organization, he proceeded not from the strophic design but rather from the content. Thus the first section (Adagio molto) which is based on his favorite dactylic rhythm:

comprises only the first two lines. The second (Piu Andante) encompasses the rest of the first and the entire second stanza (15 lines). It describes the waterfall. The illustration is continued in the third section (Un poco piu mosso) and refers to the roaring of the water over the crags. The musical means which Schubert employs here are syncopation and an obstinate motif in sixteenth-notes.

The fourth division depicts the flowing of the brook across a meadow. A new musical idea is introduced here. Lyrical in quality it anticipates one of Bruckner's favorite phrases.

The tempo quickens somewhat in the fifth part but slows down in the final portion which, referring to the human soul, resumes the musical material of the beginning. Richard Heuberger who wrote a life of Schubert designated *Gesang der Geister über den Wassern* as *Faust* among Schubert's compositions for men's chorus. Indeed, it not only holds a towering position among Schubert's output for male chorus, but in all choral literature. And, in fact, it is one of Schubert's most important works.

Mass in G major

This Mass was composed between March 2 and 7, 1815, and performed in that spring in the Lichtental church.* Schubert never succeeded in having the work published; yet a copy came into the possession of Robert Führer (1807-1861), organist at the cathedral in Prague, who had the effrontery to publish the Mass in Prague under his name. This outrageous plagiarism conformed to the notorious life of the perpetrator: Führer, a highly gifted organist who once competed with Anton Bruckner, committed a series of embezzlements, fraudulent transactions, and other criminal offenses that led him ultimately into prison.

Here are a few brief remarks about Schubert's work. The *Kyrie, Gloria,* and *Credo* reveal the three-sectional design of the sonata form. The *Christe eleison* with its soprano solo forms the modulatory middle section of the *Kyrie,* and the *Domine Deus* that of the *Gloria.* In the *Credo* the contrasting element is formed by the *Crucifixus,* in which the vocal forces are contraposed by the unison string body. The passage that follows (*Credo in Spiritum Sanctum*) is a modified replica of the opening section and corresponds to the recapitulation in the sonata sense. Note that the entire portion of the *Credo,* from the very beginning up to the entry of the recapitulation is an expanded crescendo ending in a powerful climax on the words *cujus regni non erit finis.* The recapitulation begins softly and dies away deftly with the *Amen.*

The *Sanctus* with the Handelian dotted rhythm recalls the baroque tradi-

* See Note on the Mass in E flat

tion of the court chapel, while the *Benedictus* seems to be influenced in several ways by the quartet *Mir ist so wunderbar* (Andante, G major, 6/8) in the first act of Beethoven's *Fidelio*. The resemblance between the two is not only evident in the identical tempo, key, and meter, but also particularly in the canonic setting, increased motion of the accompaniment, and parallelism in the endings (descending scales in triplets). The performance of Beethoven's opera in its third version in 1814, eight years after the presentation of the second version, and the publication of the vocal score, also in 1814, acquainted the younger generation with *Fidelio*.

Solo voices (soprano-bass-soprano) alternate with the chorus in the *Agnus Dei*, which consists of three equal passages, the second and third being harmonically modified repetitions of the first. It is music of a tender and lyrical quality, which explains the absence of the contrast in the musical treatment of the prayer for mercy (*Miserere nobis*) and in the appeal for peace (*Dona nobis pacem*).

Mass No. 6 in E flat major

The Vienna Court Chapel

On September 30, 1808, eleven-year-old Franz Schubert, accompanied by his father, went to the so-called Wiener Stadtkonvikt across from the old university, which is still standing now, to be auditioned as a chorister for the court chapel. The boy was hardly aware of how much was at stake on that afternoon, but his father, who had to provide for a large family, was. With admission to the court chapel came tuition-free education, upkeep, and clothing for several years, all of which would lessen the financial burden of the poor schoolteacher. The beautiful soprano voice of the lad and his musicality aroused the interest of the Hofkapellmeister, Antonio Salieri, on whose word hinged the decision. Although the role he played in Mozart's life is now viewed controversially, and his compositions are no longer popular, the Italian Salieri was nevertheless the one who opened the door to musical education for the greatest musician Vienna has ever produced.

The term court chapel (*Hofkapelle*) as used in Vienna has a twofold meaning. It refers to the small Gothic edifice which, built into the imperial palace, was the place of worship of the imperial family. It holds perhaps about 400 people. The music for the service was provided by the *Hofmusik-kapelle* (Court Music Chapel) usually called *Hofkapelle*. It was a unique musical institution. Founded in 1498 under Emperor Maximilian I, it recruited the country's best musical forces and exercised great influence because of the creative and performing activities of its members. A host of musicians of consequence emerged from the little group of generally ten boys, who, along with eight or nine men, formed the choir. We must imagine little Schubert clad in a uniform which consisted of an old-fashioned, low, three-cornered hat, a white neckerchief, an open coat of dark brown color with a small gilt epaulet on the left shoulder, light polished buttons, an outmoded waistcoat hanging down over the abdomen, knickerbockers with straps, buckled shoes, and no sword. In his attire the chorister Schubert walked on all Sundays and Holidays—and there were many in imperial Austria—from the Imperial and Royal Seminary (*Stadt-konvikt*) to the court chapel, climbed up to the small choir on the fourth floor, and sang under the direction of Antonio Salieri or his deputy Joseph Eybler through four years from October 1808 until July 1812. In hundreds of liturgical performances, and in the daily practice of the school orchestra, Schubert learned much that stood him in good stead later. Yet the liturgical repertory of the court chapel under Salieri's tenure, which lasted thirty-six years (1788-1824), was conservative and without the slightest consideration for his fellow Austrian composers who were enjoying European reputation. The most important masses created in the 1790s and in the years of Schubert's boyhood did not have their first reading in Vienna, but in the Bergkirche in the small town of Eisenstadt, which lay in the domain of Haydn's employer Prince Esterházy. For example, the last six great masses of Haydn, the three of Johann Nepomuk Hummel (1778-1837), Haydn's successor as Kapellmeister in Eisenstadt, and Beethoven's Mass in C major (1807) were taboo to the powerful Salieri. Although his activities reached far into the nineteenth century, and Beethoven outlived him by only two years and Schubert by three, he personified the eighteenth century and was not able to understand the musical language of Haydn, Mozart, and Beethoven. Nothing is more indicative of Salieri's musical and aesthetic credo than his statement, "The world should have stopped with Gluck." Schubert's friend, Franz Doppler, relates that in going over a mass by Schubert, Salieri crossed out all passages that seemed to him reminiscent of Haydn and Mozart.

However, in spite of his conservative attitude, Salieri was steeped in the counterpoint tradition of Padre Martini, regarded as an infallible authority, and was the right man to introduce young Schubert to the fundamental principles of composition and other basic theoretical instruction. It stands to reason that Schubert must have detached himself from Salieri when he became conscious of the talent that was leading him with sheer elemental force to artistic paths of which Salieri, because of his very nature, could never approve.

The masses, graduals, offertories, vespers, and requiem masses Schubert came to know intimately in the lustrum he spent as choir boy in the court chapel were chiefly by Salieri and the predecessors and contemporaries acceptable to him, such as Joseph Eybler, a favorite of Emperor Franz I, and Peter Winter, court conductor in Munich who turned out church music on a mass production basis. This literature certainly did not excite Schubert. Mozart's Requiem was banished from the court chapel by Salieri, not only for personal, but for professional reasons; Salieri contended that it went "beyond the rules." He expressed his opinion about Haydn's masses in a letter to Giuseppe Carpani, his compatriot and the author of a Haydn biography: he dismissed as mishmash ("*mescolanza di tutti generi*") and a grave sin against the church style Haydn creations that Beethoven adored as "inimitable masterpieces."

When Emperor Franz let it be known that he definitely did not wish to hear Haydn masses in the court chapel, Salieri was delighted to be supported in his repertory policy. The attitude of Franz is all the more significant as it was directed against the most patriotic Austrian composer, who was the creator of the Austrian national anthem. Schubert, as we will see presently, became a victim of the same imperial gesture. Nevertheless, Schubert had an opportunity to hear the masses banished from the court chapel, for they were performed in other churches of the Viennese diocese. Breitkopf & Härtel in Leipzig published Haydn's last five masses between 1802 and 1808, and when Schubert left the court chapel in 1813, the C major Mass of Beethoven was already in print. However, Schubert could not have taken these works as models as long as he was under the tutelage of Salieri.

Schubert and the Mass

Schubert wrote his first mass (F major) in 1814 for the centenary of the parish church in suburban Lichtenthal, which is the Schubert church par excellence. There he was baptized, there his beautiful soprano sounded for the first time in public, there he conducted his first mass, on October 16, 1814, his brother Ferdinand officiating at the organ, and there, probably, the ensuing masses in G major, B flat major, and C major were first heard.

As it was composed for a particular occasion, the F major work is not in the nature of a *missa brevis,* but is a creation of larger proportions and rich instrumentation. In addition to the customary strings Schubert employed oboes, clarinets, bassoons, horns, trumpets, three trombones, kettledrums, and an organ, the scoring he also used in his last mass, in E flat major. Salieri, who attended the service, was impressed by the work of his pupil, but because he had to follow the directive of the Emperor, he could not help Schubert by including the mass in the repertory of the court chapel. Yet presumably he did go out of his way by interceding on Schubert's behalf at the St. Augustin Church, the church of the parish district of the imperial palace. Only the representation of an influential person could have secured for an unknown, seventeen-year-old composer the honor of directing his own mass in such a distinctive house of worship. It is safe to assume that delegates to the Vienna Congress (1814-1815) were present at this occasion. In his following masses, G major, B flat major (both 1815), and C major (1816), practical considerations prompted Schubert to forego ambitious projects and to approach the style of the *missa brevis.* He was thinking of those churches whose *regens chori* commanded only small instrumental forces and lacked the necessary funds to reinforce the available means.

Then, late in the fall of 1819, Schubert began to compose a mass in A flat major that he conceived as a *missa solemnis.* For unknown reasons he lost interest in the work after the completion of the *Kyrie.* After three years he decided to finish the mass, as he intended to dedicate the work to the Emperor and Empress, hoping that by attracting their attention and gaining their favor, he could obtain a position. Schubert regarded the mass a good piece (*gelungen*). Would the Emperor have shared this opinion? Hardly so.

A directive conveyed to Beethoven in 1823 states clearly the wishes of the Emperor concerning the composition of the mass. Short soprano and alto solo passages were permitted; violin, oboe, and clarinet solos were acceptable. "His Majesty likes expertly worked-out fugues that should not be too long. *Sanctus* and *Osanna* should be very short in order not to hold up the Elevation." Schubert's Mass in A flat (completed in 1822) in no way conformed to such demands Its large-scale design and particularly the extended fugue of more than 170 measures that concludes the *Gloria* would have aroused the indignation of the Emperor, and the romantic orchestration, bold chord progressions, and subjectivism of Schubert's musical language would have frightened him. The Emperor actually exercised a censorship on liturgical music, and Salieri and other musicians gladly submitted to it. When the publisher Tobias Haslinger once discussed these things with Beethoven, the latter exclaimed with indignation, "Such spirits in the temple of the Lord of all Lords. O misery! (*O Miserabilität!*)." Schubert, who must have been aware of these conditions, could not have counted on a performance of the A flat major Mass either in the court chapel or in St. Stephen's Cathedral. Salieri, whom Schubert's friend Anselm Hüttenbrenner described as "the greatest musical diplomat and the Talleyrand of music," would not have lifted a finger to plead for a mass that did not harmonize with imperial opinions that were precisely his own.

When Salieri died three years later (1825) and was succeeded by Joseph Eybler (1764-1846), Schubert decided to apply for the position of the Vice-Hofkapellmeister vacated by Eybler. Schubert and Eybler were old acquaintances from Schubert's days as a choir boy of the court chapel. He paid a courtesy call to the new Hofkapellmeister and submitted the Mass in A flat for consideration. Eybler professed that he had never heard a composition of his former subordinate, a statement that was hard to take even for the modest Schubert. After all, about sixty compositions had appeared in print and about forty performances of vocal and instrumental works had taken place, among them the one-act singspiel *The Twin Brothers,* which was staged in the court opera (1820). After a few weeks he saw Eybler again and was told that the mass was a good work, but was not composed in the style the Emperor liked. Schubert went away and thought—as he related to friends—that he was not fortunate enough to have the ability of writing in the imperial style.

Eybler's attitude was not caused by malevolence. He certainly realized the high artistic qualities of the A flat major Mass, but regardless of its merits, Eybler was a tutor of imperial princes and a musician who played chamber music with the Emperor, and therefore had to deny the possibility of liturgical execution to a creation whose large dimensions, dramatic power, and romantic orchestration violated the concepts and commands of the emperor. Schubert's application failed, and the post was left vacant. There are no records of a liturgical performance in Vienna of the A flat Mass until 1863.

The experiences of Schubert as church composer parallel those of Mozart, who was impeded by the so-called Josephinische Verbote, the edicts issued by Emperor Joseph II between 1783 and 1784 that sharply curtailed the length of masses and specifically limited the use of instruments. The Josephinian church reform obliterated the musical splendor displayed in the great Austrian churches and was the reason why Mozart left the great C minor Mass, K. 427, unfinished. "One wonders," says H. S. Robbins Landon, the renowned Haydn scholar, "whether Haydn would (or could) have written his last six great masses if Joseph II had reigned into the next century." In the case of Schubert, it was the conservative tendencies of Emperor Franz that functioned as a brake; Beethoven had to resort to the shrewd subterfuge of smuggling sections of both the C major Mass and the *Missa solemnis* into concert programs, billed as "Great Hymns with Chorus and Soli," as the censor, in deference to the ecclesiastical authorities, did not permit concert performances of liturgical music.

The Mass in E Flat Major

Fortunately for posterity Schubert refused to be daunted by these conditions and within a period of eight months in the last year of his short life, 1828, he created the great C major Symphony (begun in March), the Fantasy in F minor for pianoforte duet (finished in April), the Mass in E flat major (begun in June), the songs that were published in a series entitled *Swan-Song*, the incomparable String Quintet in C major (September), and the triptych of piano sonatas in C minor, A major, and B flat major (finished in September). The fact that Schubert resolved to write a mass again, in view of his discouraging experiences and bitter disappointments, is intriguing.

The masses of Haydn, Mozart, and Beethoven were commissioned or written in the line of official duties. Their public reading within the liturgical service was assured before they were composed. That was not the case with Schubert except for his very first mass. The chances of an adequate performance of such a demanding work as the mass in E flat were practically nil. So were the prospects of finding a publisher in Vienna or elsewhere. Publishers are business men and none would have regarded the mass a marketable commodity. Considering Schubert's serious economic plight, the creative efforts he made for the mass would seem to be a labor of love from which no material gain, urgently needed, could ever accrue. Thus we must conclude that the composition of the E flat Mass was prompted by inward forces and an irresistible emotional compulsion that led Schubert to apply his creative power to the sacred words.

The history of the Mass in E flat is shrouded in darkness. The autograph, once in the possession of the Prussian State Library, gives no date. The only available documentary record is provided in a letter written by Schubert's friend Johann Baptist Jenger on July 4, 1828, to Marie Pachler, an accomplished pianist, who had played host to both Jenger and Schubert in Graz, the capital of Styria, in 1827. Stressing "the not very brilliant financial circumstances of friend Schubert," Jenger reports "that Schubert works diligently at a new mass." Thus we may assume that he began the mass late in the Spring and concluded it in July or August. As the mass is large-scale and the prospects of a performance in the court-chapel, St. Augustin, or in St. Stephen's Cathedral were nil., Schubert must in all probability have thought of a reading in a suburban church. The *Dreifaltigkeitskirche* (Church of the Holy Trinity), a church of the Minor Friars where, incidentally, the last rites for Beethoven were held, offered a distinct possibility for Schubert since his childhood companion, Michael Leitermayer (1799-1867) became *regens chori* there in 1827.

Schubert endeared himself to the parson, the friars, the parishioners, and to Leitermayer by composing a chorus for the solemn dedication of the church's recast bell. The chorus was sung on September 2, 1828.

The first performance of the Mass in E flat, on October 4, 1829, almost one year after Schubert's death on November 18, 1828, was indeed in this church. Leitermayer, who had rehearsed the mass, yielded the baton to Schubert's brother Ferdinand (1794-1859). The day of the performance was a festival for the Minorites (St. Francis Day), the name day of the Emperor, and last but not least, the name day of Schubert. Lacking accounts of this event, we hear indirectly about it from a report that appeared in the *Berliner Allgemeine Musikzeitung* on March 20, 1830. The Vienna correspondent says about the E flat major Mass: "The latest novelty in the field of religious music was a mass left by Franz Schubert, which the composer's brother has brought twice before the public. Although the performance cannot be judged as satisfactory (*gelungen*) a lasting impression could hardly be achieved even in a reading of highest perfection." The correspondent ventures the opinion that the late (*verklärte*) composer already bore death in his heart and head when he conceived the mass. If this statement implies that the mass reflects a premonition by Schubert of impending death, we can accept it. But if the correspondent contends that even an excellent performance could be of no avail because the mass shows declining creative power, we must reject the remark as an aberration of a listener lacking the faculty to perceive the technical qualities and emotional content of the work. Neglected for almost forty years, the mass was very dear to Brahms, who put considerable efforts into the adaptation of a piano score in 1865. Brahms's piano score, issued anonymously, contributed a great deal to the circulation of the mass prior to the publication of Schubert's collected works between 1887 and 1897. Nowadays Schubert's last mass is a pillar in the liturgical repertory in the great churches of Austria and other Catholic countries.

It has frequently been observed that in all of his six masses Schubert omitted the words "[Credo in] unam sanctam catholicam et apostolicam ecclesiam" (I believe in one, holy, catholic and apostolic church). Could the boy Schubert have intentionally skipped these six words in his first mass? Hardly so. Why did he disregard them in his later masses? Error, carelessness, or perhaps disbelief? Alfred Einstein offers "the most simple and trivial explanation" of the puzzle by suggesting that Schubert made a copy of the text of the mass in which he inadvertently omitted these six words, and that he continued to use this copy whenever he sat down to compose a mass. It was not as simple as that. In the first place, Schubert, who went through rehearsals and performances of masses week after week for four years, must have known the text by heart, as does every experienced church singer, organist, and choir director. Secondly, if he did not trust his memory and needed a written text of the mass, as Einstein assumes, then he must have made up a very bad copy, for all his masses show deficient texts and omissions that could exclude these compositions from liturgical use. In the E flat major Mass there are five omissions, two passages in the *Gloria* (21 words out of 77) and three in the *Credo* (18 words out of 163). These "sins" are in some instances oversights, occurring in the heat of the creative process, and in other cases they represent deviations committed for purely musical reasons. That is, when the musical development of a certain section was concluded, Schubert could not fit all the words into the texture.

A letter of July 25, 1825, in which Schubert refers to his famous *Ave Maria*, sheds light on his attitude to sacred texts. "People wonder greatly," he writes to his father, "at my piety which I have expressed in a hymn to the Holy Virgin, and [which], it seems, grips every spirit and turns it to devotion. I believe this is because I never forced myself to devotion and never compose hymns and prayers of that kind, except when I am involuntarily overcome by it. Then, however, it is usually the right and true devotion." In other words Schubert's fancy was not kindled by dogmatic and speculative factors but by the mystic and dramatic elements of the mass text. This approach accounts for the conflict between musical fancy and liturgical realities. Yet in spite of the textual deficiences which in compliance with a Papal decree are corrected in the liturgical practice, Schubert's music is inspired by and convincingly expresses true devotion.

In the E flat Mass Schubert speaks a language that often reflects tension and a highly agitated frame of mind. To intensify these qualities he uses bold harmonies and refrains from applying bright colors to the orchestral fabric by excluding the flute and avoiding the high register of the violins. In addition, he conspicuously employs the brass instruments, particularly the trombones, in important melodic passages. A few significant musical and technical details are pointed out in the following paragraphs.

This is mainly a choral mass. Solo passages occur only in the "Et incarnatus est" (*Credo*), *Benedictus* and the concluding *Dona* (*Agnus Dei*), in all only in 116 measures out of a total 1,686. The basically lyrical *Kyrie* displays a three-sectional design. The gentle opening is a marked contrast to the rather dramatic "Christe" that unfolds above incessantly running triplets with a harmonic and instrumental treatment that presages Anton Bruckner. Bold harmonies and chromaticism are also evident in the third division, which concludes tenderly.

The *Gloria* opens with an energetic exclamation of the chorus before the orchestra enters. There is a multitude of dynamic contrasts and surprising harmonic turns until the "Gratias agimus" is reached. Here Schubert exhibits a variety of sonorities by alternating the men's voices cast in a four-part chorus with the women, who sing as a three-part group. Schubert then takes the textual liberty of repeating the first lines of the *Gloria*, followed by changes in tempo, meter, and key (Andante con moto, 3/4, G minor). It is in this passage ("Domine Deus, Agnus Dei") where the omission of 21 words of the liturgical text occurs, an omission that can also be found in the Mass in A flat major. This striking parallelism, extending even to the musical treatment of the remaining lines, permits us to postulate, with some confidence, an explanation of Schubert's violation of the liturgical text. He could have been concentrating here on an anticipation of the text of the "Agnus Dei"; wanting these lines to stand out in bold relief, he disregarded words that preceded and followed them. The music is charged with emotion and grief portraying the suffering of the Redeemer, yet the outburst of a penitent soul is mitigated by a humble and tender prayer for mercy ("miserere nobis"). Schubert portrayed this episode three times to conform to the three invocations of the "Agnus Dei." The musical treatment of this passage in the A flat

Mass discloses an emotional restraint, subdued dynamics, and a transparent texture, but in the E flat Mass Schubert projects the spiritual idea of the "Agnus" with emotional vigor, dynamic force, and, evoking the potentialities of the brass instruments, with sheer explosive power. In "Quoniam tu solus sanctus" the original tempo, meter, key, and melodic material return. An extended fugue of more than two hundred measures, whose subject stems from the E major fugue of the *Well-tempered Clavier*, Book II,

Cum san-cto Spi-ri- tu in

concludes the *Gloria* with a prolonged "Amen."

In the beginning of the *Credo* a romantic spirit is prevalent in the pianissimo roll of the kettledrum and the mysterious intonation of the chorus that is answered by a deft horn call. This drum roll occurs seven more times, fulfilling a harmonic function. Schubert, the lyricist, devoutly speaks to God in the "et incarnatus est" (Andantino, 12/8, A flat major). A trio of two tenors and the soprano evolves gradually, prefaced by the cellos. After "homo factus est" the appealing charm of the music suddenly gives way with the entry of the six-part chorus to pain and sorrow depicting the ordeal of the crucifixion. The "et incarnatus est" and "crucifixus" episodes are repeated, the latter in harmonic and dynamic intensification. The main tempo is resumed with the drum roll that precedes the announcement of the resurrection, and like the *Gloria*, the *Credo* also concludes with an extended fugue.

The *Sanctus* startles the listener through the awe-inspiring sequence of the E flat major, B minor, G minor, and E flat minor chords, a striking progression that foreshadows the harmonic peculiarities of later romantic composers. To understand fully the psychological significance of this passage we must think of the liturgical importance of this phase of the mass. The *Sanctus* initiates the preparation for the mystery of the elevation. Most composers of the classical period treated the text with gentleness and restrained joy. Schubert's approach, anticipated to a certain extent in the A flat major Mass, discloses a striking deviation from the classical tradition. There is no gentleness and happy expectation but excitement and commotion instead. These feelings are mitigated only by the fugal *Osanna* whose conclusion, however, still reflects a certain tension. Seen in context, the *Sanctus*, too, is affected by the highly emotional atmosphere which permeates the work except the *Benedictus*. The tender *Benedictus* (Andante, 4/4, A flat major) is akin to the *Benedictus* in the same key and meter of Bruckner's great F minor Mass.

The *Agnus Dei* guides the listener, or rather the worshipping community, to another region. Two musical ideas in contrapuntal manipulation are used here. Both stem from the C sharp minor fugue of the *Well-tempered Clavier*, Book I, the first being identical to the main theme of Schubert's song "Der

Doppelgänger" (Heine) written in August of 1828.

Bach

Ag- nus De- i

A spiritual bridge connects the sorrow and despair of the *Agnus Dei* with the grief and violent emotion of the song. As pointed out in the discussion of the *Gloria*, the *Agnus Dei* parallels in texture, meter (3/4), tempo (Andante con moto), and feeling the "Domine Deus" of the *Gloria*. These two outstanding parts of the work are even melodically related:

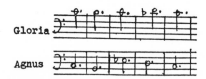

As in the "Domine Deus" Schubert applies to the three invocations of the *Agnus Dei* the same dyamic registration: the prayer for mercy is uttered in a low voice. With the entry of the "Dona obis pacem" (Andante) we are led into a peaceful and serene atmosphere that is, however, interrupted by the resumption of the text and music of the *Agnus*. But the grief and sorrow are ultimately alleviated by the re-entry of the "Dona" whose soft melodic strains and consoling harmonies bring about the peaceful and moving conclusion.

The E flat Mass carries for Schubert the same artistic importance and spiritual significance as the Requiem for Mozart. Yet while Mozart's incomplete work leaves us completely in the dark as to the conclusion he intended to give to his artistic and personal farewell, the ending of Schubert's mass leaves no doubt in this respect. It is a touching message of comfort, hope and peace.

SCHUMANN, Robert (1810-1856)
Concerto for Piano in A minor
Allegro affetuoso; Intermezzo: Andante grazioso; Allegro vivace

Schumann's only piano concerto has an interesting history. In 1841, after he had composed the First Symphony in B flat major and completed the D minor Symphony (later revised and published as No. 4), he wrote an Allegro affetuoso in A minor for the piano with orchestral accompaniment. He occupied himself with this piece in the summer; an entry in his diary says "The Symphony in D minor is almost finished and the Fantasy in A minor is put in order and ready for playing." Schumann did not lose time in subjecting the brand-new piano piece to a practical test: it received a tryout with his young wife Clara at the piano in a rehearsal of the Gewandhaus Orchestra on August 13, 1841. The results fully satisfied Schumann's expectations and he undertook to have the Fantasy published.

His attempts were of no avail. He even went so far as to offer the piece to the renowned Leipzig firm of Breitkopf & Härtel as a premium for the acceptance of the choral work *The Paradise and the Peri*. The publisher acted wisely in declining the offer; Schumann himself realized that a one-movement piano piece with orchestra was not marketable, but that there was considerable interest in clavier concertos. He drew the practical conclusion from the situation and acted accordingly. Adding two movements to the Fantasy, he created in 1845 a full-fledged piano concerto. He dedicated it to Ferdinand Hiller, who conducted the first performance in Dresden on December 4, 1845, with Clara Schumann as soloist. Richard Wagner, then royal conductor in the Saxon capital, may have been in the audience.

Subsequent performances were led by Mendelssohn (Leipzig, 1846) and by the composer (Vienna and Prague, 1847), with Clara proudly interpreting the creation of her beloved husband. The reception in Vienna was, as Eduard Hanslick recounts, somewhat cool, and the applause was apparently intended for Clara. But the concerto was published (as Opus 54) in 1846 after a triumphant performance in Leipzig on New Year's Day of that year. It gradually acquired a firm place in the repertory, which it has maintained thanks to its youthfulness and the appealing qualities that, typical of Schumann, mirror his concept of the Florestan-Eusebius relationship—daring and dramatic elements paired with meditative and poetic lyricism.

Schumann followed the road laid out by Mozart and Beethoven. Cast in the traditional three-movement design, the work represents the type of symphonic concerto in which the clavier and the orchestra complement each other. The listener not familiar with the history of this concerto could hardly guess that its second and third movements came into being only by the force of circumstances, for Schumann was completely successful in creating a unity of style for the entire work and he tied the three movements together thematically through a short motif of four notes. This motif is derived from the main theme of the first movement, i.e., the original Fantasy, or Allegro affetuoso.

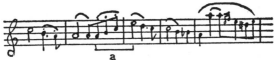

Although keeping the traditional structure of a sonata movement, the Allegro affetuoso also discloses individual features such as its distinctive beginning with rhythmically incisive chords (Grieg's model), the insertion of an Andante espressivo in A major in the middle section, and the written-out cadenza which prevents the soloist from superimposing brilliant pianistic fireworks upon the poetic and noble lines of the piano part. The main theme

and its derivatives

provide the melodic material for the Allegro affetuoso. The coda also stems from the main idea:

The ensuing Andante grazioso, entitled Intermezzo, symbolizes Eusebius— and Clara. The three-sectional piece opens with a deft dialogue of the clavier and the strings carried on with a short motif drawn from the Allegro affetuoso (see examples 1a and 2a):

A new idea, introduced by the violoncello and taken up by the viola, is presented in the middle section:

The extended repetition of the first dialogue leads straight into the finale (Allegro vivace in A major), which is linked thematically to the first movement (examples 1a and 2a):

The complex rhythmic quality of a second theme

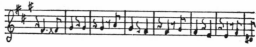

once gave the musicians a hard time and Schumann encountered almost unsurmountable difficulties at the first rehearsal. Midway the key changes to F major and a new idea appears:

The recapitulation does not enter in the tonic key but in D major instead. We return to A major in the restatement of the passage with the complex rhythm. There is a lengthy and brilliant coda that reveals a thematic connection with the intermezzo in the conspicuous falling fifths of the first violins.

Introduction and Allegro Appassionato for Piano and Orchestra, Opus 92

One wonders why Schumann, after his experiences with the A minor* Fantasie, set out once more in 1849 to compose a one-movement piano work. This composition, which he entitled Introduction and Allegro (*Concertstück für Pianoforte*) was sketched September 18-20, and completed September 25. Its purpose was to provide his wife with a new piece for her repertory, yet he did not conceive it in terms of a glittering virtuoso piece but as a work in which the timber of the piano was amalgamated with the orchestral sonorities. First played by Clara in the Gewandhaus in Leipzig on February 14, 1850, and repeated in Düsseldorf on March 13, 1851, with the composer conducting, it was published the following year. It must be borne in mind that Schumann was at this time an acclaimed composer and a musician of stature who encountered no difficulties in getting his works into print.

The title *Concertstück* denotes a one-movement piece of concerto character with alternation of the solo instrument and the orchestra. It was a type preferred by the romanticists since the appearance of Weber's famous F minor Concertstück, which even has programmatic connotations. We are struck with the romantic quality in Schumann's work in the delicately orchestrated introduction with the conspicuous horn call that assumes structural importance through its use in the Allegro. The piano, which in the introduction participates chiefly as a rather coloristic element, has ample opportunities for pianistic display in the Allegro, whose beginning discloses a spirited quality akin to that of the A minor concerto. Viewed as a whole, the Allegro clings to the sonata form. The neglect of this noble, brilliant, and effective composition is difficult to understand.

Concerto for Violoncello in A minor, Opus 129
Nicht zu schnell—Langsam—Sehr lebhaft

The idea of writing a concerto for violoncello must have occurred to Schumann before the summer of 1850, when he decided to leave Dresden and accept the position of municipal music director in Düsseldorf. The new post entailed the direction of orchestral concerts given on a subscription basis. Schumann's previous experience as a conductor was limited to the direction of choral groups. He owed the Düsseldorf appointment primarily to his prestige as composer, writer, and critic. After his arrival in Düsseldorf, Schumann had to find a suitable house, get settled, pay the necessary visits to the dignitaries and board members of the musical society, and prepare the first concert, scheduled for October 24, 1850. In spite of these distractions, his creative mind was restless and focused on the concerto for violoncello. It was sketched between October 10 and 16. The orchestration was finished on October 24, the day Schumann faced the critical Düsseldorf audience for the first time as conductor of the municipal orchestra.

In her diary on November 16, 1850, Clara Schumann noted that Robert had composed a concerto for violoncello during the months before. It was

---

* See note on the Piano Concerto.

written, she continues, "in true violoncello style." Another entry, of October 11, 1851, reads: "I have played Robert's violoncello concerto again [on the piano] and thus procured myself a truly musical and happy hour. The romantic quality, the flight, the freshness, and the humor, and also the highly interesting interweaving of cello and orchestra are, indeed, ravishing, and what euphony and deep sentiment are in all the melodic passages."

The composer himself viewed his work with a critical eye; he pronounced it fit to print only in November 1852. Schumann read the proofs in February 1854. At this time he was suffering a mental collapse that necessitated his confinement in an asylum at Endenich. The concerto was published as Opus 129 in August of that year. Thus far, no documentary evidence of a public reading in Schumann's lifetime has been discovered. A performance was planned in 1852, but we do not know if it materialized.

The dearth of good concertos for violoncello may have prompted Schumann to enter this sparsely cultivated field. He did not want to write a purely virtuoso piece; on the other hand, he was fully aware of the nature of the instrument and of the problems arising from it. The violoncello is effective in melodious and songful passages, but the player faces difficulties in projecting runs and quickly moving passages on the lower strings—problems all the more intensified when the violoncello is set against a symphonically treated orchestra. Though keeping the time-honored three-movement design, Schumann deviated from the classical concerto type of Mozart and Beethoven. First, he dispensed with the symphonic orchestral exposition and introduced the soloist immediately, as he did in his famous piano concerto in A minor (1841-1845). Second, in contrast to the classical concerto, he required all three movements played without a break. Mendelssohn had initiated this typically romantic device in his piano concertos in G minor and D minor. Schumann also used this scheme in his D minor symphony (1841).

Overture to "Manfred," Opus 115

After the completion of his only opera *Genoveva* in August 1848, Schumann soon went to work on the music to Lord Byron's *Manfred*. The choice of this subject matter was of particular personal significance for Schumann: the Manfred of the English poet is a restlessly-wandering human being plagued by terrible thoughts and an addiction to communicating with ghosts; it is this special trait of Manfred's mental nature that was also characteristic of Schumann's tragic illness. He developed an unbounded attachment to Byron's mentally-tortured figure. "Never have I devoted myself to a composition with more love and exertion of strength than to the work on *Manfred*," Schumann stated. Once when he read the poem to his future biographer Joseph von Wasielewski, his voice ceased to sound, he began to cry, and was seized with such emotion that he was unable to continue reading. The assumption that he saw in the gruesome life of Manfred a premonition of his own terrible fate is not-far-fetched.

Schumann did not take up Byron's drama in its original form, but used an adaptation. His music consists of an overture and fifteen larger and smaller numbers that are cast as melodramas (recitation with background music) and closed musical forms. He completed the overture at the beginning of November 1848 and the rest of the score within two weeks (November 23). The overture received its first performance in Leipzig on March 14, 1852, under the composer's direction. The first stage production of Byron's drama with Schumann's music took place in Weimar on June 13, 1852, under the baton of Franz Liszt, and was one of Liszt's historic achievements as a conductor. A concert version was presented in Hamburg on April 21, 1855, in the presence of Clara Schumann and the young Johannes Brahms (born 1833), fourteen months after Schumann's mental collapse and his subsequent conveyance to an asylum.

The overture was published in 1852, and the entire score posthumously, under the tile: "Manfred. A dramatic poem in three divisions by Lord Byron for Declamation, Solo voices and Orchestra." The overture was regarded as one of Schumann's greatest achievements, and its spiritual greatness towers over his other instrumental compositions. It reflects the melancholic and demoniac strains of the poem, the dissension in Manfred's soul, the somber glow of his feelings, and his final destruction.

Symphony No. 1 in B flat major, Opus 38, "Spring"
Adagio-Allegro vivace; Adagio; Allegro vivace; Allegro ma non troppo

In 1839, one year before her marriage, Clara Schumann, evaluating Robert's creative ability, entered the following passage in her diary: "It would be best if he composed for orchestra; his imagination cannot find sufficient scope on the piano. . . . His compositions are all orchestral in feeling . . . . My highest wish is that he should compose for orchestra—that is his field." Posterity does not fully agree with her on the last point. But Clara's wish that Schumann should devote himself to orchestral composition did materialize in 1841, when the symphonies in B flat major (No. 1) and D minor were composed. (The latter received the No. 4 because it was not published until 1851.)

Schumann sketched the first symphony in four days (January 23-26) and completed the orchestration on February 20. No time was lost in bringing it before the public. It was played by the Gewandhaus Orchestra in Leipzig on March 31, 1841, under the direction of Felix Mendelssohn. The composer also led performances in other cities, including St. Petersburg (1844) and Vienna (January 1, 1847). The Vienna performance was a fiasco. Clara played the piano concerto in A minor on this occasion. Schumann was an unknown quantity in Vienna and was spoken of as the "husband of Clara Wieck." Both the symphony and the concerto were received with respectful silence; this was noted by Eduard Hanslick, who also added that respect was accorded to Clara. But Schumann as the composer fared badly in the city of Haydn, Mozart, Beethoven, and Schubert—and so did other great musicians. The Viennese found their way to Schumann only after he had departed from the earthly scene. The second performance of the B flat symphony in 1856 resulted in only limited success because of the mistreatment by the conductor.

Schumann, the lyrical clavier poet and master of the lied, was fully aware of the difficult situation the post-Beethoven generation of composers faced in the symphonic field. A continuation from where Beethoven left off seemed impossible, and the road laid out in Beethoven's more lyric-epic symphonies (Nos. 4, 6, and 8) seemed the less problematical one. It was followed by both Mendelssohn and Schumann, who, taking a cue from Beethoven's *Pastorale,* attached poetic and programmatic connotations to some of their symphonies. Schumann's B flat symphony is a good example of this.

It is known that Schumann considered applying the following titles to the four movements: "Spring's Awakening" (Andante, Introduzione, and Allegro vivace); "Evening" (Larghetto); "Merry Playmates" (Scherzo); "Blooming Spring." In a letter written in 1843 to Wilhelm Taubert, conductor in Berlin, Schumann was more explicit: "Try to inspire the orchestra with some spring longing which chiefly possessed me when I wrote the symphony in February 1841. At the very beginning I should like the trumpet sound like a call to awaken. In what follows of the introduction there might be a suggestion of the growing green of everything, even of a butterfly flying up, and in the following Allegro, of the gradual assembling of all that belongs to spring . . . . Concerning the last movement, I only want to tell you I think of it as Spring's Farewell . . . . " Schumann added in this letter that these fancies came to him after the completion of the work. Nonetheless, as the "Spring" symphony, the work has acquired a firm place not only in the orchestral repertory, but also in the hearts of many music lovers. It is scored for a full-fledged romantic symphony or opera orchestra, employing a brass section of four horns, two trumpets, and three trombones, and requiring three kettledrums.

The opening signal of the introduction anticipates the chief idea of the Allegro molto vivace, which is of the sonata design, but uses new melodic ideas in the coda. The orchestral palette is reduced in the highly lyrical Larghetto: one pair of horns, the trumpets, and kettledrums are silenced. The trombones are called in for the concluding measures to gently anticipate the theme of the Scherzo, which follows without a break. Here Schumann deviates from tradition in adding a second trio. Thus the movement shows the following pattern: Scherzo (D minor, 3/4)—Trio I (D major, 2/4)—Scherzo—Trio II (F major, 3/4)—Scherzo (considerably shortened)—Coda (D major) using material of the first Scherzo and first Trio.

The beginning of the finale anticipates melodic components of the second theme derived from a piano work, the *Kreisleriana,* composed in 1838. The movement enraptures the listener through its imagery and romantic features, for example, the horn call about midway and the surprising virtuoso cadenza of the flute leading to the re-entry of the playful main idea. Ingenuity and sentiment, imagination and poetic feelings in this symphony combine to transplant us into the happy atmosphere of spring, even if we listen to it in winter.

SCHUETZ, Heinrich, *Dialogo per la Pascua*

Heinrich Schütz, the foremost German composer of the seventeenth century, was born in Kötritz in eastern Thuringia in 1585—exactly one hundred years before Johann Sebastian Bach. Though Schütz's musical ability had secured him an appointment as choirboy at the court chapel at Cassel (Hesse), he did not consider a musical career and entered Marburg University as a law student. When the Landgrave of Hesse offered him a fellowship to study music in Italy, Schütz accepted. He went to Venice in 1609 and became a pupil of Giovanni Gabrieli, the principal organist at St. Mark's cathedral. He stayed there until Gabrieli's death in 1612. The sojourn in the lagoon city had a decisive influence in forming Schütz's artistic individuality, and was therefore of great importance in the history of German music.

Under the tutelage of Gabrieli, Schütz familiarized himself with polychoral writing as practiced by Gabrieli and his school. He also learned of the recent achievements in the field of lyrical monody (*stile rappresentativo*) and the musical drama. That the Venetians were interested in these artistic currents is manifested by the appointment of Claudio Monteverdi as *maestro di cappella* at St. Mark's in 1613.

Schütz returned to Germany in 1612 and finally settled down as conductor at the court chapel in Dresden. His activities there were greatly hampered by the catastrophe of the Thirty Years' War. Schütz was able to escape this holocaust temporarily through extended visits to, and employment in, Copenhagen. He died in 1672 at the age of eighty-seven. It was his mission to transmit to Germany the technical novelties developed in Italy in the second half of the sixteenth century: the polychoral style and dramatic monody. He composed the first German opera, *Dafne* (1627), the score of which is lost. In his church music, psalms, and particularly in the Passions after the Evangelists, he appears as a forerunner of Bach. It is worth mentioning that Heinrich Schütz's collected works, eighteen folio volumes, were edited by Philipp Spitta, the great Bach scholar.

The *Dialogo Per la Pascua Del Nostro Salvatore Giesu Christon con Maria Maddalena a 4 Johannis 20 Capit* (title of the autograph) upholds stylistically the Gabrieli tradition. It is, in spite of its Italian title, a piece of music set to German words. Schütz has shortened the Gospel text somewhat. Dialogues for two voices were in vogue in Italy in the seventeenth century; to differentiate them from operatic dialogues, one spoke of *dialoghi fuor di scena*. Schütz availed himself of this medium by means of his expressive declamatory style, and bold harmonic writing which discloses chord progressions of Brucknerian quality. The realization of the figured bass is by Alexandre Guilmant (1837-1913), eminent French organist, composer, and editor.

SPOHR, Louis (1784-1859)
Concerto No. 9 in D minor for Violin
Allegro; Adagio; Rondo

Famous and admired in his lifetime and historically important as a violinist, conductor, and composer, Louis (or Ludwig) Spohr has become a rarely remembered musical figure. His name has meaning to the violinist, but even the violinist, let alone other instrumentalists and conductors, is unaware that in practicing and rehearsing he is aided almost daily by an invention of Spohr—the so-called "rehearsal letters" (numbers) that are entered in the score and parts and that enable the players to find quickly a passage to be repeated or studied.

Spohr was born in 1784, at which time Beethoven was fourteen years old, and the greatest works of Haydn, the last symphonies, quartets, Masses, and oratorios were still to come. In the words of Wagner, Spohr's youth was lightened by the sun of Mozart. Only two years older than Weber, he witnessed the advent of Schubert, Mendelssohn, Schumann, and Chopin and outlived them all. He also observed the emergence of Berlioz, Liszt, and Wagner, and when he died in 1859 the scores of *Rheingold, Walküre, Siegfried* (Acts I and II), and *Tristan* were lying in Wagner's desk, and opuses 1-10 of Brahms were already in print. Thus Spohr's artistic career commenced in the period of classicism and continued along the mainstream of German romanticism.

It was at first Spohr the violinist who appeared as a shining star on the musical horizon. As concertmaster at the historic Theater an der Wien he spent about four years in Vienna and established friendly relations with Beethoven. He played under his direction in the large orchestra of Vienna's most prominent musicians assembled for the first reading of Beethoven's seventh symphony and the once-famous "Battle" Symphony. An enthusiastically acclaimed violin virtuoso, he also devoted himself to chamber music, and toured in Italy and Holland. Meanwhile, he engaged increasingly in composition and emerged as an important figure in the German romantic opera after the production of his *Faust* in Prague in 1816 under Weber's direction. In the following year he assumed the conductor's post at the opera in Frankfort, and in 1822 he settled down in Cassel, at the recommendation of Weber, as court conductor, where he remained until his death. Here he produced in 1823 his chief opera, *Jessonda*, which was esteemed highly by Wagner and Richard Strauss and loved dearly by Brahms.

As a conductor Spohr aimed at precision and rhythmical force. Using a roll of strong white paper as a baton, he succeeded, as contemporary reports affirm, in unifying the ensemble and imposing his will upon the orchestra. This kind of direction, also practiced by Weber, caused a sensation in London when Spohr appeared there in 1820. Following the time-honored custom of the eighteenth century, the conductor was supposed to sit at the piano, reading the score and sounding a few chords if the situation seemed to get out of hand. Horrified by Spohr's intention to lead the orchestra with a baton, some of the directors of the London Philharmonic Society protested, but finally consented to a tryout. And then they observed something new—that the tempi were taken firmly, that the conductor indicated the entrances of the wind and brass instruments, and that due to the visible beating of time the orchestra played with a precision never heard before.

Spohr was much in demand as a conductor at German music festivals, and in this capacity he appeared with Liszt in Bonn in 1845 when the Beethoven monument was unveiled. Although he confessed his inability to understand the late works of Beethoven, he hurried to produce another revolutionary work, *The Flying Dutchman* by Wagner, in Cassel in 1843 in the face of strong opposition from the court. He did not know Wagner personally and acted spontaneously, prompted by the desire to further a fellow artist who was inspired by serious intentions and whom he considered the ablest among the contemporary German opera composers.

Spohr's creative activity comprised all branches of music. The character of his music is sharply at odds with his appearance and personality: he was a tall handsome man, the symbol of a German hero, yet his creations often disclose a soft and elegiac quality. When Wagner, in a letter to Spohr written in 1843 calls himself the "pupil full of admiration" of the older master, he is, of course, thinking of certain elements in Spohr's operas that anticipated some technical features of his own, e. g., the treatment of the recitative, of declamation, and of the principle of the leitmotif.

Spohr's music displays a certain nobility, also characteristic of the violin concerto in D minor, the ninth out of fifteen. Keeping the traditional three-movement design, it is not in the manner of the symphonic concerto type of Mozart and Beethoven. Composed in 1820, it was conceived as a vehicle for a virtuoso, and it reflected Spohr's own style of playing—his predilection for trills on notes of small time value, for instance. Yet Spohr's virtuosity was a far cry from the demoniac wizardry of his artistic antipode Paganini. It was a controlled virtuosity, subordinated to expression and to the cantilena, which seems natural for a composer who adored Mozart as his artistic ancestor.

STRAUSS, Richard (1864-1949)
Le Bourgeois gentilhomme (Der Bürger als Edelmann)
Overture; Minuet; The Fencing Master; Entrance and Dance of the Tailors; The Minuet of Lully; Courante; Entrance of Cleonte (after Lully); Intermezzo; The Dinner (Table Music and Dance of the Kitchen Boy)

This orchestral suite writes the final chapter in the troubled history of the opera Ariadne auf Naxos, the third work Richard Strauss created in collaboration with Hugo Hofmannsthal—the others being Elektra (1909) and Der Rosenkavalier (1911). In its original version Ariadne was combined with Molière's Le Bourgeois gentilhomme, for which Strauss also provided the incidental music. Directed by Max Reinhardt, to whom the score is dedicated, and conducted by the composer, the joint production was first given in Stuttgart on October 25, 1912. Salome, Elektra, and Der Rosenkavalier had established Strauss as the most important figure on the German operatic stage since the passing of Richard Wagner, and the musical world looked forward to the première of the new work with great expectation.

The novelty was neither a success nor a failure. The combination of a play with a full-fledged opera did not work very well. It created considerable casting difficulties for the theater management, which had to bring together a fine ensemble of actors and an excellent cast of singers. Hofmannsthal suggested a way out of this dilemma. He proposed scrapping the play by Molière and replacing it with a musico-dramatic prologue to be presented by the operatic ensemble. Thus the new version of Ariadne came into being. First given in Vienna on October 4, 1916, in the midst of the First World War, it is generally called the "Vienna version."

The score of the scrapped incidental music to Molière's play contained too many beautiful pages to be suppressed forever, and Hofmannsthal and Strauss determined to join in a salvage operation. The result was Der Bürger als Edelmann, billed as a "Comedy with Dances by Molière" in three acts.

Strauss incorporated into the play the original incidental music and a few new instrumental numbers and vocal pieces. It was produced under the direction of Max Reinhardt in the Deutsche Theater in Berlin on April 4, 1918. Hofmannsthal modestly remained in the shadow of anonymity, and his name did not appear in the title. Alas, the success for which Strauss in particular had hoped was denied the twentieth-century version of the play that Molière and Lully had collaborated on in 1670. Strauss was bitter about it and considered the failure a "sad chapter."

He fared much better, however, with the success of the suite that he formed from the music. First played under his baton in Vienna on January 1, 1920, it was heard in many concert halls all over the world, and a choreographic presentation was offered by the Ballet Russe in Monte Carlo in New York (1944).

Scored for a chamber orchestra of sixteen strings, twelve wind instruments, harp, piano, kettledrums, and other percussion instruments, the suite consists of nine numbers. The overture portrays Jourdain, le bourgeois, as a clumsy fellow, proud of his riches, and also alludes to a little aria offered by a singer in the play. The following Minuet, cast in pure chamber style, is contrasted with the music of the turbulent scene with the fencing master. This is a very concerted piece with a bravura part for the piano and virtuoso passages for the trumpet, horn, and trombone. In the ensuing Entrance and Dance of the Tailors the spotlight is thrown on a polonaise with a solo violin in the middle section.

A different mood is struck with Strauss' adaptation of a charming minuet by Lully. Then dividing the string body into nine different parts and using harp and piano, Strauss displays in the following Courante an extraordinary splendor of sound within the limited possibilities of a chamber orchestra. He once more turns to Lully as a melodic source in another minuet, whose solemnity is contrasted with a quick trio by winds and triangle. The eighth item is the gracious prelude to the second act. The finale consists of the dinner music and Dance of the Kitchen Boy. Here Strauss wittily alludes to several special dishes with quotations from other works: the wave motif from Rheingold refers to salmon from the Rhein; the bleating of the sheep from Don Quixote to "leg of mutton à l'Italien"; the bird warbling from Rosenkavalier amusingly indicates that le bourgeois also had a little dish of thrushes and larks on his table. Finally, there is served a huge "omlette surprise," out of which jumps a kitchen boy who executes an increasingly wild dance.

Four Last Songs for Soprano and Orchestra

The political developments in Germany during the 1930s and the Second World War brought Richard Strauss the permanent separation from his close artistic collaborators who had gone into exile. Stefan Zweig had taken his life in Brazil, Max Reinhardt, Fritz Busch, and Fritz Reiner went to the United States; so did Lotte Lehmann and Elisabeth Schumann, the great opera singers and interpreters of his songs. The war, naturally, affected him greatly. Strauss's life and activities could not be isolated from the world-shaking events. The première in Salzburg of his last opera, Die Liebe der

Danaë, was canceled, and the authorities permitted only the dress rehearsal on August 16, 1944. "Life has come to its end since the first of September," wrote Strauss, "it would have been best, if the high genii on the Olympus had summoned me on August 17th." The collapse of the Third Reich was accompanied by the breakdown of Strauss's artistic and spiritual world, with the destruction of the opera houses in his birthplace, Munich, and in Berlin, Dresden, and Vienna, where he had wielded the baton for half a century.

Strauss resided in the Bavarian town of Garmisch, which was occupied by American troops in 1945. He left his home for Switzerland in October and spent three and a half years there before he returned to Garmisch in 1949 to celebrate his eighty-fifth birthday on June 11. The most important artistic fruit of his sojourn in Switzerland was the series of four songs with orchestra published posthumously in 1950 under the title *Four Last Songs*.

The idea of writing a song cycle never entered Strauss's mind when he wrote the first sketches to *Im Abendrot* by Eichendorff during the winter 1946/47. Joseph von Eichendorff (1788-1857) was the greatest lyric poet of the later German romantic movement. In his exquisite verses he expressed the mystic meaning of the mood of nature. His name is familiar to vocalists from songs by Mendelssohn, Schumann, Brahms, and Wolf. Strauss only once before had set lines of Eichendorff to music, in a lieder cycle for male chorus and orchestra, *Die Tageszeiten* (The Periods of the Day, 1928), which included a song entitled *Der Abend* (*The Evening*). A spiritual bridge connects the choral song with *Im Abendrot*, which Michael Hamburger's translation renders "The Dusk." Yet the true German meaning is "sunset glow" or "red evening sky" and, if used metaphorically, indicates the declining years of one's life. This was the very interpretation of Strauss, who considered the song as an artistic expression of an autobiographical nature. Witness the last stanza.

Strauss completed *Im Abendrot* in Montreux on May 6, 1948. In the meantime, a friend had directed the composer's attention to the poems of Hermann Hesse. Strauss, who had never before taken notice of Hesse's poetry, caught fire and found a number of poems very suitable for composition. He finally chose three: *Frühling* was completed on July 18, 1948; *Beim Schlafengehen* on August 4, in Pontresina; and the score of *September,* composed in Montreux, was completed on September 20. Strauss may have regretted that he had not previously applied his art to Hesse's poetry. That he felt a spiritual affinity to Hesse can be gathered from an entry in his last notebook. Shortly before Strauss left Switzerland in May 1949, he jotted down a sketch to a choral piece based on a poem by Hesse, which began: "Godly and eternal is the spirit."

The four songs were not published in their chronological order. *Im Abendrot*, the earliest, was placed last because of its biographical meaning. Strauss dedicated *Beim Schlafengehen* to his friends Dr. and Mrs. Adolf Jöhr, of Zurich; *Frühling* to his official biographer, Dr. Willi Schuh, also of Zurich; and *September* to Mr. and Mrs. Seery, of Newark, New Jersey. (Mrs. Seery is the famous dramatic soprano Maria Jeritza, who created the roles of Ariadne and the Empress in *Die Frau ohne Schatten*.) The dedicatee of *Im Abendrot* is the publisher Dr. Ernst Roth, who was instrumental in arranging Strauss's journey to England in 1947 to bring the eighty-three-year-old master once more in contact with international music life.

The first public rendition of the *Four Last Songs* was on May 22, 1950, in London, with Kirsten Flagstad and the Philharmonia Orchestra led by Wilhelm Furtwängler. The event symbolized the reconciliation of German and British musical circles. The songs were heard in Germany for the first time in Frankfurt am Main on September 25, 1950, interpreted by Christl Goltz. They need no particular commentary except for the concluding passage in *Im Abendrot,* where poet and composer raise the question: "Is this perhaps death?" Here Strauss quotes the transfiguration melody from his tone poem *Death and Transfiguration,* which had occurred to him sixty years before, in 1889. Biographically and historically, the *Four Last Songs* are the parallel to the *Vier ernste Gesänge* of Johannes Brahms.

Suite for Orchestra from Harpsichord Pieces by Couperin

Richard Strauss evinced considerable interest in dance and choreography, as some of his creations prove so eloquently. It suffices to recall the "Tanzlied" in *Thus spake Zarathustra,* Salome's "Dance of the Seven Veils," the *Rosenkavalier* waltzes, and the ballets *Josephslegende* and *Schlagobers* ("Whipped Cream"). The dance suite after Couperin, created in Vienna in 1922 and finished on January 6, 1923, is a precious tribute Strauss paid to Terpsichore. It came into being when Strauss, officiating with Franz Schalk as director of the Vienna State Opera, suggested a ballet evening with music of high caliber. The music of this ballet cycle was drawn from Couperin, Ravel, and Johann Strauss.

Speaking of Couperin, we usually mean the most important member of this notable French musician family, the great organist, harpsichordist, and composer François Couperin (1668-1733), who went down into history as *Le Grand.* His harpsichord (claveçin) music appeared in four volumes (1713, 1717, 1722, and 1730).

Strauss's score is not the result of technical and mechanical efforts, but the fruit of study, serious deliberation, and unexcelled craftsmanship. In the selection and grouping of the twenty-three pieces used, paramount consideration was given the demand for contrast and variety. Strauss's orchestra calls for only twenty-nine musicians, smaller than that of the *Ariadne,* which requires thirty-seven. Strauss, the unsurpassed magician of the orchestra, gave Couperin's music an exquisite instrumental garb with colors not dreamed of in the early eighteenth century. The following chart, a table of contents, indicates the titles of the originals and refers in Roman numerals to Couperin's volume numbers to illustrate how Strauss crisscrossed Couperin's output in quest of suitable items.

1. a) Les Graces incomparables, ou La Conti, 4/4   G major, III
   b) La Superbe ou la Forqueray, 4/4   E minor, III
   a) as above

2. a) Courante I, 3/2   G minor, I
   b) Courante II, 3/2   G minor, I
   c) Les Notètes, Les Blondes, 6/8   G minor, I
   d)   Les Brunes, 6/8   G major, I

3. a) Le Carillon de Cithère, 2/4	D major, III
b) L'Evaporée ("The Lighthearted"), 2/4	A major, III
a) as above, with Strauss's additions in the conclusion	D major, III
4. a) Sarabande, La Majesteuse, 3/4	G minor, I
b) Les Sentiments, 3/4	G major, I
a) as above	
5. a) La Fileuse ("The Spinner"), 4/4	E major, II
b) Gavote, 4/4	F sharp minor, IV
c) Les Satires Chevre-pieds ("The Satyrs with the Goats' Legs"), 4/4	A major, IV
d) La Bourbonnoise, Gavote, 4/4	E major, I
e) Princesse Marie, 4/4	E major, IV
f) Coda by Strauss, based on "a" above	E major
6. a) Le Turbulent, 2/4-3/8	F major, III
b) Les Petits Moulins à Vent ("The Little Windmills"), 2/4	D minor, III
c) Les Tricateuses ("The Knitters"), 2/4, with expanded conclusion by Strauss	F major, IV
7. a) Allemande (for two harpsichords), 4/4	A major, II
b) Les Charmes I, 3/4	A minor, II
II, 3/4	A major, II
8. Les Matelotes Provençales ("The Provençal Sailors"), 4/4, with free elaboration by Strauss	C major, I

In three titles Couperin alludes to personages of the French court. *La Conti* is Princess Louise-Elizabeth de Bourbon, *la Forqueray* the wife of the composer Antoine Forqueray (1671-1745), and *Princesse Marie* (Marie Leszczynska) the fiancée of Louis XV.

STRAVINSKY, Igor (1882—1971)
Concerto in D major for Strings
Vivace; Andantino; Rondo: Allegro

Stravinsky composed the Concerto in D major for strings in Hollywood in 1946. He received the commission shortly after he had become an American citizen on December 28, 1945. The occasion for the composition was the twentieth anniversary of the Basler Kammerorchester, which was founded by Paul Sacher for the purpose of promoting contemporary music. Sacher commissioned works from numerous musicians, and he and his group offered the first public hearings of the pieces. The list of composers whose works were played by the Basler Kammerorchester over nearly four decades constitutes an impressive Who's Who of contemporary music.

Stravinsky's D major concerto for strings is cast in the so-called neoclassical vein. Neoclassicism was the battle cry of the opposition to romanticism and impressionism and was directed against expression of emotions and sentiments. It was once described as a "strange mixture of refinement and primitivity, asceticism and exuberance." Stravinsky turned to neoclassicism in the ballet *Pulcinella* (1920); the musical material is derived from Pergolesi and pseudo-Pergolesian themes and motives.

Yet neoclassicism is a misnomer because compositions written in a neoclassical style display more elements of the baroque than of the Viennese classical school. This concerto is a case in point: it is fashioned after the three-movement baroque concerto, and it was Antonio Vivaldi particularly who developed the *concerto per archi* (concerto for strings) in three movements. Naturally Stravinsky followed this pattern in outline only, and he applied to it rhythmical complexities and harmonic turns, which no eighteenth-century composer would have visualized.

One outstanding feature of Stravinsky's concerto is the use of a very short basic motif. Announced at the beginning, it consists of three notes moving in semitone steps—F sharp-E sharp-F sharp—and occurs later in various modifications and disguises. This device is a trait of refinement while the absence of luxurious lyricism reflects the inclination to asceticism. In some passages Stravinsky employs the baroque concerto grosso technique in pitting solo instruments, two violins, violas, or violoncellos against the whole ensemble.

When Paul Sacher requested from the composer an article on the concerto to be published in connection with the first performance on January 21, 1947, Stravinsky declined and excused himself, "being terribly overloaded with work." But he continued: "Besides, what in particular can I tell you about it, (1) that the piece is composed for string orchestra (this, one will perceive immediately), (2) [that] it has three parts (this, in any case, will be in the program), (3) that it is the least atonal piece in the world. But this, do you not think, the audience will have the pleasure of discovering it by itself." This particular point—the tonality—seemed to Stravinsky especially important, for he also said in another context: "I have established in the concerto D major from North, South, East, and West."

Pulcinella, suite pour petit orchestre d'après Pergolesi
Sinfonia; Serenata; Scherzino; Tarantella; Toccata; Gavotta con due Variazioni; Vivo; Minuetto; Finale

In 1919 Sergei Pavlovitch Diaghilev (1872-1929) the creator and director of the famous Russian Ballet, suggested to Stravinsky the composition of a ballet. The dramatic idea and music were to be fundamentally different from the style of *L'Oiseau de feu* (1910), *Petrouchka* (1911), and *Le Sacre du printemps* (1913), works that had established Stravinsky as a leading figure in 20th century modernism and an innovator of the first order. For the scenario of the projected ballet, Diaghilev entered the sphere of the *commedia dell'arte* and chose the story of Pulcinella, a Neapolitan character. To match the color of the place, the musical material was drawn from compositions of Giovanni Battista Pergolesi (1710-1736). Although Pergolesi was not born in Naples, he spent the greater part of his life there, and was artistically a product of Naples.

Diaghilev did not make this proposal for the composition at random. It grew out of practical experiences which had led him to tap forgotten or unfamiliar works of 18th and 19th century Italian composers for choreographic purposes. Cleared of the dust that had accumulated on these scores for almost two centuries, the music provided with modern orchestral garb, proved to be a bonanza for the choreographer and a blessing for the box office. A ballet *Le donne di buon umore* (The Good-humored Ladies) based on the harpsichord sonatas by Domenico Scarlatti, adapted by Vincenzo Tommasini (1878-1950), had achieved great success. So had Respighi's sparkling ballet score *La Boutique Fantasque* fashioned after melodies of Rossini.

Only two works of Pergolesi's musical heritage have successfully withstood the ravages of time: the *Stabat Mater* and the opera *La serva padrona*. A number of small pieces ascribed to Pergolesi have been proven spurious, and the authenticity of others is still a matter of dispute. Stravinsky, in his autobiography, attributed to Diaghilev the "discovery" of "unfinished manuscripts" of Pergolesi found in various Italian conservatories and in London libraries. This claim is highly exaggerated. Actually, the existence of the works which Diaghilev had found, and of which he had copies made, was very well known. So were the collections and libraries where they were preserved.

Diaghilev's idea appealed to Stravinsky who "was always enchanted by Pergolesi's Neapolitan music." Pablo Picasso, to whose art Stravinsky felt a strong attachment, was to do the settings and costumes. Leonid Massine, who had directed *Le donne di buon umore,* was in charge of the choreography. Stravinsky lived then in Morges on Lake Geneva, and frequent trips to Paris were necessary to confer with the producer, designer, and choreographer. These meetings were sometimes very stormy, particularly when Diaghilev quarreled about the costumes or he found fault with Stravinsky's orchestration. Massine worked from a piano arrangement that the composer sent him bit by bit. Sometimes, it happened that the steps and the movements devised by the choreographer failed to correspond to the music and the orchestration. In these instances the choreography had to be altered and adapted to the music, and this procedure naturally annoyed the producer, choreographer, and dancers.

The première took place at the Opéra on May 15, 1920, and brought success to everyone concerned. Stravinsky felt that subject, dancing, and artistic setting formed a coherent and homogeneous whole. He termed the choreography one of Massine's finest creations and his performance in the title role above praise. Picasso "worked miracles" with his enchanting coloring, design, and amazing inventiveness.

Technically speaking, *Pulcinella* stems from the *comédie-ballet* in which the spoken word, the music, both vocal and instrumental, and the dance are blended together. It is a category that bloomed in the time of Louis XIV, thanks to the collaboration of Molière and Lully. *Pulcinella* follows this tradition in the employment of singers who are, however, placed in the orchestra pit. The ballet consists of eight tableaux from which the composer later drew the music for an orchestral suite. Stravinsky's sources were the operas *Il fratello inamorato* (Naples, 1732) and *Il Flaminio* (Naples, 1735), Pergolesi's last stage work, and instrumental compositions (trio sonatas, harpsichord sonatas, and others) several of which are considered spurious. Nevertheless, Stravinsky found them usable for his task.

Pulcinella is Stravinsky's first creation in the neo-classical style that represents a reaction against the late romanticism and attempts to exclude emotional qualities and literary implications from instrumental works. The use of pre-existing material from pre-classical periods ties in with this concept. Although Stravinsky preserves generally the melodic lines and the bass part of Pergolesi, he abandons the harmonic scheme of the early 18th century and provides a more dissonant harmonization of Pergolesi's themes. He also deviates from the metrical symmetry of the original and accentuates the syncopation. For the orchestration Stravinsky turns back to the concept of the concerto grosso by dividing the string body into a soloistically treated small group of five (concertino) and a larger group of eighteen. In the use of pre-classical forms Stravinsky the neo-classicist proceeds with utmost freedom. Witness the quick Toccata that has absolutely nothing in common with the Bach type or pre-Bach models except the name.

TCHAIKOVSKY, Peter Ilyitch (1840-1893)
Serenade for Strings in C major, Opus 48
Pezzo in forma di sonatina; Valse; Elégie; Finale

Tchaikovsky wrote the serenade for strings in 1880. By then his reputation as one of Russia's leading composers was firmly established. Many of his works created by 1880 hold permanent places in the international stage and concert repertory: the opera *Eugen Onegin,* the ballet *Swan Lake,* the fourth symphony, the overture *Romeo and Juliet,* the piano concerto in B flat minor, the violin concerto, and the three string quartets. In a letter of October 22, 1880, to his friend and patroness Nadezhda Filaretovna von Meck, whom he never met, he announced that he had composed an overture and a serenade for strings. "The overture will be very noisy. I wrote it without much warmth of enthusiasm; therefore, it has no great artistic value. The serenade, on the contrary, I wrote from an inward impulse; I felt it and venture to hope that this work is not without artistic qualifications." The overture to which he referred is well-known 1812 *Overture,* and noisy it is. Tchaikovsky even included in the score the ringing of bells and firing of five gunshots.

Naturally, the string serenade in C major is of quite a different disposition. Yet it is unlike the classical serenade type of Mozart—delightful specimens created as light musical fare for social occasions. The common denominator of Mozart's serenades and the Tchaikovsky piece is the lightness of the musical language and the absence of symphonic mentality. The Russian master, nevertheless, did avail himself of the four-movement scheme of the classical symphony. He also applied to the serenade the so-called cyclic principle by quoting in the finale the opening idea of the introductory Andante of the first movement. This Andante passage reappears also as a kind of epilogue to the main portion of the first movement (Allegro moderato) which the composer termed a "Piece in the form of a sonatina." This has to be taken as a disclaimer of any ambition to write a large-scale movement of symphonic character. The serenade quality is obvious in the Valse and Elégie. The finale leads us into the true sphere of Russian music. The national flavor of the theme is conspicuous. Counting on performances abroad, the composer decided to set the words *Tema Russo* in parenthesis as a caption for the finale. The finale, preceded by a delicate Andante section, displays contrapuntal combinations which, nevertheless, do not impair the light quality of the movement. This movement includes the "massive" quotation of the idea heard at the beginning.

The serenade is dedicated to Konstantin Karlovitch Albrecht (1836-1893), inspector of the Moscow Conservatory and an intimate friend of the composer. The first performance was on January 22, 1882, in Moscow, under the direction of the German Max von Erdmannsdörfer (1838-1905), who introduced many works by Russian composers. Tchaikovsky programmed the serenade on his highly successful concert tour, in 1888, of Germany, Austria (Prague), Paris, and London.

TELEMANN, Georg Philipp (1681-1767)
Sonata a quattro for Strings

Success or failure during the creative artist's lifetime does not always signify history's final and irrefutable verdict. Many composers who basked in the sun of fame fell into obscurity after they passed from the musical scene. The fate of Vivaldi is a case in point. Quickly forgotten after his death, almost two centuries elapsed before his greatness was fully recognized. His contemporary Georg Philipp Telemann drew a similar lot. The great fame he enjoyed in Germany and other countries did not secure for him a firm place in the musical life of later generations. When Telemann published some of his works on a subscription basis he found buyers in the upper social strata and among people of high standing in Germany, France, Great Britain, Spain, and even Russia. But since his works have led an archivistic existence for almost one hundred and fifty years, attracting only the historian and musical scholar, they have fallen into dust. As Romain Rolland said in 1920 in a gallant attempt to resurrect Telemann from oblivion, "No dust is as dry as that of Telemann, whom posterity has forced to pay for the insolent victory he won over Bach in his lifetime."

Telemann was born in Magdeburg in 1681. He went to Leipzig in 1701 to study law but soon decided to embrace a musical career. He quickly acquired an excellent reputation and a large following among the students. He aroused the indignation of Johann Kuhnau, the highly respected Thomas Cantor, when he obtained the directorship of the opera while he was serving as organist of the Neukirche. It was considered irreconcilable for a church musician to hold such a position. But Telemann maintained himself successfully, and Kuhnau was the loser inasmuch as the students who helped him out in the church choir preferred to sing in the opera chorus with compensation.

Telemann left Leipzig in 1704, spent several years privately employed in Silesia, stayed from 1708 to 1712 in Eisenach (Bach's birthplace), from 1712 to 1721 in Frankfort in charge of the music at two churches, and finally settled in Hamburg in 1721 as municipal music director.

Telemann was perhaps the most prolific composer in musical history. It is estimated that he wrote more notes than Bach and Handel together. If this estimate is correct, he would have produced enough music to fill one hundred and fifty large folio volumes, requiring fifteen feet of shelf space. He composed operas, oratorios, liturgical music, songs, and instrumental works of all kinds. The requirements of his positions resulted in this mass production. For example, in Hamburg he had to furnish five cantatas for the Sunday service for each of the five churches he supervised musically. It stands to reason that there are many insignificant pieces in this enormous output. On the other hand, a respectable amount of good music came from his never-resting pen. His production is now being sifted, and a number of attractive pieces have been regained for home and concert music. The Sonata a quattro in A major offers an example of Telemann's fine qualities.

Telemann was born when Corelli's trio sonatas, Opus 1, appeared (1681), and died in 1767, the year that Gluck's second reform opera *Alceste* was produced in Vienna. He not only lived and created when the baroque reached its height, but also witnessed the origin and development of the classical style. By 1767 Haydn had already written about thirty symphonies. Telemann, who was subjected to Italian, French, and Polish influences, lived at the turning point of two epochs. This is eloquently mirrored in the piece under review which technically parallels Vivaldi's concertos for string orchestra. Formally it still adheres to the pattern of the church sonata (slow-fast-slow-fast), the second slow movement being reduced to a recitative-like transition to the spirited finale. It is this particular movement in clear-cut rondo form, with three themes and an episode in minor, that definitely veers in the direction of the classical style.

VANHALL, Jan (1739-1813), *Concerto for Viola*
Allegro moderato; Adagio; Allegro moderato

Reference works introduce Johann Baptist Wanhal or Jan Vanhall as a Bohemian, or as an Austrian, composer of Bohemia. Both are correct. The theory is that the family was of Dutch origin (Van Hal) and had immigrated to Bohemia, which was a part of Austria until 1918. Born in the Bohemian village of Nechanicz in 1739, Vanhall was seven years younger than Haydn. Aristocratic patrons sent him first to Vienna, where he was taught by Dittersdorf, and then to Italy. He finally settled in Vienna and quickly established through his industry a fine reputation even beyond the Austrian borders. In fact, he was known in England before Haydn.

When Dr. Charles Burney traveled through Austria in 1772 to gather material for his *General History of Music,* he considered it mandatory to make Vanhall's acquaintance in Vienna. He had difficulty finding the house, which "was in an obscure corner and in a more lofty than splendid situation." Groping his way up "a totally dark, winding stone staircase," the determined British scholar finally found at the summit Vanhall's simple dwelling. Yet the expedition was worth the effort because, as Burney put it, Vanhall's "symphonies had offered me so much uncommon pleasure that I should not hesitate to rank them among the most complete and perfect compositions for many instruments which the art of music can boast."

This statement, which implicitly puts Vanhall's symphonies on a par with those of Haydn familiar to Burney in 1772, must be accepted with a certain reservation. Yet it is a fact that Vanhall's symphonies were once ascribed to Haydn, which proves that the Bohemian was writing proficiently in the classical style. Michael Kelly, the Irish singer and composer who created the role of Basilio in Mozart's *The Marriage of Figaro,* tells in his *Reminiscences* of a quartet session that united Dittersdorf and Haydn (violins), Mozart (viola), and Vanhall (violoncello). Vanhall died in Vienna in 1813. He lived long enough to see his once popular works being pushed into the background by the creations of the giants.

His concerto for viola is a noteworthy contribution to the scanty literature for this instrument. In 1961 the piece was found in the government music shop in Sofia by Reba Mirsky of New York City, in an edition with a piano accompaniment by Stefan Sucharew of the Sofia Conservatory. When Walter Trampler became interested in the concerto, attempts were made to secure the orchestral parts. It was learned that Sucharew had died, and his widow assumed that her husband had lent the score to someone. A search was then instituted; after great difficulty the score was located, the parts copied and dispatched to New York.

VAUGHAN WILLIAMS, Ralph (1872-1958)
Concerto for Violin and String Orchestra in D minor
Allegro pesante; Adagio; Presto

Ralph Vaughan Williams called this violin concerto "Concerto accademico;" in doing so he tagged a puzzle on the score. "Academic" implies scholarly, abstract, unpractical, cold, merely logical—qualities no listener will detect in this concerto. Frank Howes, the leading music critic of the London *Times,* interpreted the subtitle as "an act of defiance of all the big-bow-wow concertos from Beethoven to Sibelius via Mendelssohn, Bruch, Brahms and Tchaikowsky." Whether or not it defies the outstanding nineteenth century violin concertos, Vaughan William's piece harks back not only to the baroque but also to very remote periods of musical history. In this case academism means the observance of time-honored standards and procedures.

True, the concerto follows the three-movement pattern established in the baroque period. It also shows the thematic dualism evolved in the early classical period. The restriction of the orchestra to a string body is in line with the practice of the baroque composers (Torelli, Vivaldi, Bach, Locatelli, Léclair, and Tartini). The opening of the first Allegro refers definitely to Bach's violin concerto in A minor, but on the other hand the striking consecutive fifths recall the ancient organum.

In the second movement (Adagio) we encounter a modern usage of fauxbourdon (a string of sixth chords). Cast in the symmetrical ternary form, the Adagio displays florid arabesques in the violin part and very old techniques. The finale reverts to the once very popular jig, the lively dance that during the sixteenth and seventeenth centuries terminated performances of plays. Vaughan Williams took the capricious main theme from his ballad opera, *Hugh the Drover,* first given in London in 1924. The movement patterned after the old binary type of dance forms is spiced with rhythmic complications (two against three) similar to those we encounter in the gigue of the fifth

Brandenburg concerto. There are two cadenzas in the finale, one midway, and one at the end that dies away in the deftest pianissimo.

Concerto for Oboe and Strings
Rondo pastorale; Minuet and Musette; Finale: Scherzo

Listening to Vaughan Williams's Concerto for oboe and strings, it is very hard to believe that this bucolic composition came into being in 1944 in a country whose population had been subjected to most dreadful tribulations for years and had still to meet the dangers of air raids almost daily. The serene oboe concerto surprised all musicians and music lovers who recalled the violence of Vaughan Williams's F minor symphony (No. 4), of which the composer himself said, "I do not know whether I like it, but this is what I meant." The fourth symphony appeared when many serious people saw storm signals in the invasion of Abyssinia (1935), and Vaughan Williams, aware of the realities of life, held that a composer "must make his art an expression of the whole life of the community." This concept can be applied to the oboe concerto in interpreting the work as the longing for peaceful and serene life after four years of danger, want, devastation, and death.

The piece is in three movements but does not conform to the traditional concerto design. The first movement, entitled *Rondo pastorale*, expresses the pastoral quality in extended solo passages of the oboe, which suggest the improvisations of a shepherd. Of thematic importance is the following idea, which opens and closes the movement and appears in manifold combinations:

In the second movement (Minuet) the composer substituted a *musette* for the trio, and in so doing he injected a folkloristic element. The term "musette" refers either to a member of the bagpipe family, or to pieces whose persistent bass imitates the drone bass of the musette. Here it is the oboe that produces the drone. The quick motion of the finale, subtitled Scherzo, is interrupted by slow contemplative episodes and concludes, after a cadenza of the oboe, with the opening motif of the first movement.

The concerto is dedicated to the famous British oboist Leon Goossens, and was played for the first time on September 30, 1944, in Liverpool. The audience must have enjoyed it thoroughly because the nightmare of the air raids had passed and the armies of the Allies were about to enter Germany.

VERDI, Giuseppe (1813-1901), *Four Sacred Pieces*

As an octogenarian Verdi returned once more to the *musica sacra* to which he had contributed a number of works in the earliest stage of his creative life. As a composer of world renown he had written the grandiose Requiem in 1874. Shortly after the completion of *Otello* (1886) he composed the *Laudi alla Vergine Maria* whose words are taken from the last canto of Dante's *Paradiso*. Two other essays in the realm of religious music were a *Pater noster*

(The Lord's Prayer) for five-part chorus a capella and an *Ave Maria* for soprano and strings based on Dante's paraphrased Italian version of the original Latin text (1879). The favorable reception of these two pieces at a presentation in Milan pleased Verdi who discerned in the success a genuine interest in pure Italian art. Opera goers are familiar with the *Ave Maria* which Verdi set as a preamble to Desdemona's prayer in the last act of *Otello*. The words must have been of no small appeal to him since he set them to music again in 1889. We will have to deal with this setting presently.

After the production of *Falstaff* (1893) Verdi's thoughts moved again in the direction of sacred music. He decided to compose a *Te Deum* as "an act of thanksgiving not for myself but for the public which is free after so many years of necessity of listening to any more of my operas" (1895). The *Te Deum* was finished in February 1896 yet Verdi was determined not to publish it. "I shall join it to the *Ave Maria* and they will repose together, without ever seeing the light of day . . . Amen." As we will see he reconsidered and annulled this solemn promise. Meanwhile his creative mind had turned to the *Stabat Mater*. He had concerned himself with this Latin poem once before when he was only sixteen years of age. Naturally the 83 year old man who was deeply worried about the failing health of his beloved wife entertained different feelings and ideas on Fra Jacopone's poetic glorification of Our Lady of Sorrows than the boy of sixteen years. Consequently the musical approach of the master was unlike that of the apprentice. When he was about to finish the orchestration in 1897 he was not sure what to do with the piece. "I don't want to think about it, because every time I do, I feel more reluctant to exposing myself once more to public opinion. Why should I face that array of argument, gossip, criticism, hate, and love, in which I have no belief whatsoever. Just now I can't say what I should like to do. Any new enterprise seems to me quite useless . . . "

Yet in spite of this attitude Arrigo Boito, Verdi's intimate friend and collaborator, persuaded the composer to agree to a performance of the *pezzi sacri* by the Société des Concerts in Paris during Lent under the direction of Paul Taffanel (1844-1908). Excluding the *Ave Maria* from this presentation, Verdi also permitted the publication and went in January 1898 to Milan, in order to supervise the printing of the choral and orchestral parts. The Paris reading on April 7-8, 1898, was successful. The *Laudi alla Vergine Maria* were presented as a solo quartet. This was also the case in Turin on May 26, 1898, and on April 16, 1899, in the Teatro alla Scala in Milan under the baton of Arturo Toscanini. In Milan the *Laudi* were enthusiastically applauded and encored while the *Stabat Mater* and *Te Deum* failed to cause "an outbreak of enthusiasm" as Boito had expected. Later readings in London, Vienna, Berlin, Munich, and Hamburg included all four pieces with the choral execution of the *Laudi* and *Ave Maria*.

The Four Sacred Pieces hail technically from two different artistic spheres. The *Ave Maria* and the *Laudi alla Vergine Maria* are creations of a musician conscious of the glorious traditions of Italian vocal a capella music while the musical imagery and dramatic qualities of both the *Stabat Mater* and *Te Deum* point to Verdi, the opera composer of the 1880s (Second versions of *Don Carlo* and *Simon Boccanegra*, and *Otello*).

1. Ave Maria

The text of the *Ave Maria*, called the "angelic salutation," consists of the announcement of Christ's incarnation, made by the angel Gabriel to Mary (Luke I, 28), the greetings of her cousin Elizabeth (Luke I, 42) and a prayer. As a devotional formula it was added to the liturgy as early as the seventh century and it assumed greater importance before 1200 when the cult of the Madonna had become widespread. Pope Pius V ordered the inclusion of the *Ave Maria* in the breviary in 1568.

Verdi's third approach to the text was brought about by a curious chance. He came across a *scala enigmatica* which the *Gazetta musicale* in Milan published as a contribution of a sophisticated musician to puzzle the reader.

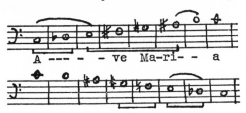

The first step shows the minor second of the Phrygian mode while the ensuing three whole tone steps suggest an important characteristic of the Lydian mode. The descending scale introduces two consecutive augmented seconds (g#- f and e- d♭). Another unusual feature is the sequence of two semitones (#a-b-c and c-b-# a) which occurs neither in the ecclesiastical nor in the major and minor modes. Obviously this scale does not permit a traditional harmonization and the chords derived from the scale cannot be applied to a typical diatonic Verdian melody. Moreover, both the ascending and the descending scales comprising sixteen notes were insufficient to cover the textual total of 31 words of the *Ave Maria*. Verdi solved the problem in a highly imaginative way which recalls the art of the Franco-Flemish Renaissance composers.

He availed himself of a Renaissance *cantus firmus* technique. Assigning the *scala enigmatica* successively to the bass, alto, tenor, and soprano, to the words *Ave Maria*, Verdi treated the text in a strict polyphonic fashion. At the same time he did not emulate the language of Palestrina or Victoria but spoke in the highly chromatic idiom of the late 19th century. His craftsmanship triumphs in the happy union of "modern" and traditional harmony in the concluding *Amen*.

II. Stabat Mater

The thirteenth century, the century of Saint Francis and Saint Thomas Aquinas, produced two religious Latin poems which inspired many glorious paintings and celebrated musical settings—the *Dies irae* which was interpolated into the *Missa pro defunctis* (Requiem) and the *Stabat Mater*. The former deals with the Day of Judgment while the *Stabat Mater* expresses the emotions of Our Lady at the Cross.

The authorship of both poems has been a matter of dispute ever since. Many treatises have been written and many conjectures have been made

The fact that the authorship has even been ascribed to Popes and Saints eloquently proves the high esteem and great veneration the poems enjoyed in the Catholic world. Jacopone de Benedictis, commonly referred to as Jacopone da Todi (c. 1228-1306) is generally regarded as the author of the *Stabat Mater*. The scion of a noble family, he led the usual life of a young nobleman, but the remarkable circumstances which surrounded the violent death of his wife brought about a drastic change in his personality. He withdrew from the world and entered the order of St. Francis as a lay brother, remaining with the order until his death at an advanced age in 1306. Driven by a spirit of fanaticism and fervor, he fearlessly attacked the religious abuses of the day. His uncompromising attitude brought him into serious conflict with Pope Boniface VIII. The result was imprisonment for a long time.

Jacopone's poems were written in Italian and Latin. Hailed as "the most pathetic hymn of the Middle Ages," the *Stabat Mater* is based on the following passages of the Holy Scripture: St. John, XIX, 25, St. Luke II, 35, Zech. XIII. 6, 2 Cor. IV, 10 and Gal. VI, 17. These verses, tender and endowed with rhythmic beauty and melodious double rime which almost defies translation into another language, always made a deep impression when sung at religious ceremonies. Although only officially sanctioned in Pergolesi's time by Pope Benedict VIII in 1727 for use in the office of the Seven Sorrows of the Virgin held on Friday after Passion Sunday, the *Stabat Mater* had long before been in popular use. The flagellants in the fourteenth century had made it known by singing it on their way from village to village and town to town. There is a large literature on the text and its countless translations. The list of composers who set the poem to music includes such very famous names as Josquin des Prés, Palestrina, Lasso, Alessandro Scarlatti, Pergolesi, Vivaldi (only a fourth of the text), Haydn, Rossini, Liszt (in the oratorio *Christus*), Dvořák and Verdi.*

Jacopone's lines (60) must have strongly appealed to Verdi because of their dramatic character and ardent emotionalism. The poem centers on the events of Golgotha and describes the feelings of the actual spectators and at the same time also of those who view the happenings in their imagination. Overwhelmed by the sight of the mother standing at the cross to which her Son is nailed, they launch into an impassioned and fervent prayer to the Madonna.

Employing the 19th century opera orchestra with an array of an 11-piece brass complement, Verdi divides the work in four sections that are clearly defined harmonically (G minor — B major — C major — G major). However, these tonalities are not maintained and the music flows to distant harmonic spheres. The opening with the sharp dissonance g-c♯ sets the stage. A significant feature is the treatment of the lines that tell of the passing of the Crucified: the music fades away pianissimo, *morendo* as Verdi indicates. This episode is markedly contrasted with the gentle beginning of the prayer to the Madonna (B major). It grows in intensity and reaches a powerful climax with the participation of all instrumental forces that, in a typical dramatic fashion, suddenly plunge into the abyss of darkness. There is

* Partly reprinted with the kind permission of Vox Productions, Inc. from the author's introduction to the recordng of Pergolesi's *Stabat Mater* (1956).

another buildup in shining orchestral colors and powerful vocal display to stress the glory of the paradise before the music gradually expires with the restatement of the opening phrase.

III. Laudi Alla Vergine Maria

The *laudi* were songs set to devotional texts and poems in the vernacular and were sung at processions and at gatherings in churches or in oratories. The executants, called *laudisti* or *laudesi*, were plain people—artisans and shopkeepers who organized themselves into confraternities or *compagnie*. In the thirteenth century nine *laudesi* confraternities formed in Florence, often congregating at vesper services of such churches as Santa Maria Novella, Santa Croce, Santa Reparata (the old Duomo), and Santa Maria del Carmine. From Tuscany and Umbria this movement spread to the north of Italy, propelled in particular by the flagellants. Driven by extreme religious fervor, they sang the *laudi* during the rite of flagellation. The poems contain incitations to penance and appeals to divine mercy. Also incorporated into them are narratives of the life of Christ, and of the joys and dolors of the Virgin. Prose or verse in form, the anonymous *laudi* were circulated from town to town and were a source of consolation to many people.

Verdi's *Laudi* deviate from the medieval specimens in one important respect: the historic *laudi* were sung by men but Verdi wrote them for women's voices in order to achieve a gentle and etheric quality that would match the mood of Dante's verses. Although worked out for the greater part syllabically, the piece also displays a few imitative passages and a rich harmonic treatment in accordance with Verdi's *terza maniera,* the musical language spoken in his last operas and the Requiem. The highly transparent opus reflects very tender feelings and in order to enhance the basic gentle mood the composer avails himself of such terms as *calmo, dolce, dolcissimo,* and *morendo.* The tenderness gives way only once to a stormy dynamic accent (the only fortissimo) shortly before the immaterial sublime ending.

IV. Te Deum

St. Paul advocates in Col. 3:16: "Teaching and admonishing one another in psalms and hymns and spiritual songs, singing with grace in your hearts to the Lord." The distinction which separates the hymn from the spiritual songs as well as from psalms is impossible to ascertain. In the fourth century the term hymn was understood to indicate a strophic poem, all the stanzas of which were to be sung to the same melody. There were biblical and non-biblical hymns, and occasionally they were written in prose. The most famous non-biblical hymn in prose is the *Te Deum,* whose authorship has been the topic of numerous scholarly investigations. A legend relates that, in 387, when St. Ambrose (333-397) baptized St. Augustine (354-430), they spontaneously improvised the *Te Deum* in alternate verses.

It is assumed that the *Te Deum* was written in the first half of the fifth century. The text discloses a three-section design: the first part is a paraphrase of Psalm 148; the second is a hymn to Christ and the Holy Ghost, with references to the Incarnation, atoning death, and opening of the kingdom of heaven; the third part is derived from antiphons that are based on Psalms 28, 114, 33, 31, and 71. Many old manuscripts reproduce the text (192 words) without a title, and only sporadically with the heading *Hymnus Ambrosianus* or *Hymnus optimus*. While the former refers to a legendary tradition, the latter clearly reflects the high esteem and veneration these lines enjoyed among the faithful.

The traditional Gregorian melody is by and large coeval with the words. It achieved an extraordinary popularity in Italy. The plain people learned and sang it with fervor almost a thousand years before great masters applied their craftsmanship and artistic personality to a musical setting of the venerated text in extended works for soli, chorus and orchestra (Handel, Haydn, Berlioz, Gounod, Bruckner, and Dvořák). "I know some old settings of the *Te Deum*," writes Verdi in February 1896, "and I have heard quite a lot of modern ones. But to me no performance of this hymn has ever been convincing, quite aside from the quality of the music." Being of a highly personal nature, this statement seems to indicate that Verdi disagreed with the spiritual and technical approach of his predecessors.

What was his guiding concept in musical respect? Verdi strongly advocated the study and performance of the works of Palestrina. He called him "the real king of sacred music, and the eternal father of Italian music" (1891). The score of *Aida* originally included a chorus in the imitative style of Palestrina which Verdi wisely discarded. Late Renaissance polyphony and late 19th century opera do not agree.

The *Te Deum* is not written in strict Palestrina fashion either. However, the eight-voice motets of the Roman master served Verdi as a model in the employment of two four-part choirs that are used antiphonally or in a stirring combination. But here the parallelism ends. The strong dynamic and emotional contrasts as well as the rich orchestral coloring reveal that Verdi, the student of Palestrina, could not exclude Verdi, the opera composer, in his interpretation of the sacred words.

The *Te Deum* opens with the initial phrase of the Gregorian melody

from which several important motifs were derived.

First enunciated gently (a), they appear later in emphatic unison statements (b). A characteristic feature of the piece is the use of very strong dynamic contrasts. To realize his intentions the composer once required the delivery of a certain passage as if it the music would come from afar and die away (*morendo*) in the distance. Witness also the mysterious echo effects in the treatment of the words: "Miserere nostri, Domine." Perhaps the most interesting trait in Verdi's interpretation appears in the treatment of the last lines. He does not close with *Non confundar* but repeats the preceding lines *In Te Domine speravi* which are powerfully exclaimed in the rising E major triad. Yet Verdi leaves the question open whether the hope so confidently expressed will find fulfillment, for the hymn dies away mysteriously and almost imperceptibly.

VILLA-LOBOS, Heitor (1887-1959)
Bachiana Brasileira No. 2
Preludio; Aria; Dansa; Toccata

The art of Heitor Villa-Lobos was deeply rooted in Brazilian life. Born in Rio de Janeiro, he started his musical career when he was only eleven by playing in theater orchestras, motion picture houses, and restaurants. He was attracted by Brazilian folklore and decided to study it at its sources. He went into the jungles along the Amazon River to learn the music of the tribesmen and there collected a wealth of melodic material that he used in his more than two thousand compositions. Villa-Lobos also brought back a knowledge of the instruments of the primitives, mostly percussion, which became essential in many of his scores. Much of this music reflects the impressions he received in the valleys of the Amazon or in the vastness of the states of Mato Grosso and Pará. He portrayed the multiple echoes that can be heard in the Amazon valleys and employed native themes that are imitations of the melodious calls of jungle birds.

A most remarkable feature of Villa-Lobos's artistic profile was his great love of the works of Johann Sebastian Bach, which led to the composition of the series of works he entitled *Bachianas Brasileiras*. Villa-Lobos himself says about the relationship between the music of Bach and the folklore of Brazil:

> This is a special kind of musical composition based on an intimate knowledge of the great works of J. S. Bach and also on the composer's affinity with the harmonic, contrapuntal and melodic atmosphere of the folklore of the northeastern region of Brazil. This composer considers Bach a universal and rich folklore source, deeply rooted in the folk music of every country in the world. Thus Bach is a mediator among all races.

The very mediator between Bach and Brazil is Villa-Lobos himself. The second Bachiana Brasileira is a four-movement suite that includes a prelude and a toccata; here the overt relationship to the baroque and to Bach ends. The rest depends on Brazilian folklore and is a musical depiction of elements of the Brazilian scene that may be compared with Moussorgsky's famous musical gallery. Villa-Lobos was in fact once called the Moussorgsky of Brazil.

Bachiana Brasileira No. 2 is the orchestrated version of three pieces for violoncello and piano and one for piano alone. The composer realized that the descriptive quality of the music as well as its national character demanded a richly colored orchestral garb. Besides the customary strings and wind instruments the score calls for two saxophones, piano, celesta, and a large percussion section with indigenous Brazilian instruments such as the *ganza* (a metal tube filled with gravel), the *chocalhos* (a rattle filled with gourd seeds), and the *reco-reco* (a notched stick).

The first movement, entitled "The Song of the Countryman," has three contrasting segments. The opening Adagio reflects a rather melancholic mood in the saxophone solo

and contains interesting instrumental mixtures; for instance the combination of the violins in the highest position (E flat) and the low violoncellos and trombones. A marchlike rhythmic middle section yields to the melancholy of the Adagio, which dies away in the violoncello.

The ensuing Aria, subtitled "The Song of Our Country," also follows the three-sectional pattern. The full orchestra enters passionately:

This passage is contrasted with a violoncello solo. The strains of a march are heard, first sounded by the saxophone and then taken up by the violins and continued by the saxophone and trombone:

A repetition of the opening section concludes the piece.

The third movement, called "Dansa," is subtitled "Memory of the Desert," and upholds the architectural design of the preceding pieces. It opens with an Andante that displays an extended trombone solo over a vivid string accompaniment:

A rather excited Allegro accentuated by syncopation follows. A repetition of the Andante with the trombone solo ends abruptly with a fortissimo and notes of the lowest register of the piano.

The concluding movement, called Toccata, is subtitled "The Little Train of the Brazilian Countryman." It is difficult to guess why Villa-Lobos ressorted to the title of toccata, since the piece lacks the brilliancy we associate with the baroque toccata. The absence of a strict formal design may account for the title. The subtitle is much more important, for it clearly indicates what the composer wanted to convey—a ride on a train that ran in San Paolo province carrying berrypickers and farmworkers to their villages. Villa-Lobos rode on it once in 1931, and as the train chugged along his creative mind was stimulated by the rotating wheels, the squealing brakes, and the gradual retardation. He jotted down a phrase

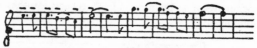

and elaborated on it. It is said that Villa-Lobos tried out the original version for violoncello and piano on the very evening he reached his destination.

Momo Precoce
Fantasy for Piano and Orchestra based on Carnival of Brazilian Children

Momo Precoce, written in Paris in 1929, unfolds a characteristic trait of Brazilian life. Based upon a piano composition, *Carnival of Brazilian Children,* it is a fantasy for piano and orchestra. Here the author attempts to picture this Brazilian carnival, which, in his words, is the most fantastic in the nation. "It is," declared Villa-Lobos in an interview in Paris in 1929, "truly, the most popular fiesta in my country—the most original, typical, the best in Rio. What creates the most vivid impression there, during the three days, is to see in this mad dance the little masked children, rich and poor, aristocratic and bourgeois, all together joined in one idea—to divert themselves freely and with complete freedom." The title of our piece indicates the subject matter: *Momo* represents the God of the jesters and the carnival spirit of Brazil; *Precoce* refers to the children.

Composed for the Brazilian pianist Magda Tagliaferro, who was soloist in the first rendition in Paris, *Momo Precoce* is a freely and rhapsodically constructed piece that constitutes, according to its author, an assemblage of eight episodes: 1. A little Pierrot rides on the handle of a broom; 2. A small red devil with a long tail snorts and jumps; 3. A little Pierrette weeps, afraid of an ugly mask; 4. A young Domino makes shrill sounds with a little bell; 5. The amorous intrigue of a tiny trap-door window; 6. Frolics of a band of masquerading children; 7. The sounds of flutes and horns of the carnival musicians; 8. A wild dance in which the adults also join. Here the piano is the dominating force, but the end comes suddenly.

The first American performance of *Momo Precoce* was given on November 18, 1950 by the Indianapolis Symphony Orchestra. Villa-Lobos's work was played from the manuscript with another Brazilian, Guiomar Novaes, at the piano, and Fabien Sevitzky conducting.

VIOTTI, Giovanni Battista (1755-1824)
Concerto for Violin No. 22 in A minor
Moderato; Adagio; Agitato assai

The eighteenth century was the golden age of Italian instrumental music and violin virtuosi. It was the era of Corelli, Geminiani, Vivaldi, Locatelli, Veracini, Tartini, Viotti, and young Paganini. Greatly admired by their contemporaries, these musicians capture our interest and imagination as both artists and men. Locatelli, Corelli, and Geminiani were collectors of books and paintings, and Tartini wrote scientific treatises. Some were engaged in business enterprises: Geminiani became an art dealer and suffered disastrous financial consequences, Locatelli sold strings, Vivaldi was an opera impresario, and Viotti, who had had appeared before Frederick the Great, Catherine the Great, and aristocratic audiences in Paris and London, became a wine merchant.

Born in Fontanetto da Po, a small Piedmontese village about twenty-five miles northeast of Turin, Viotti was a product of the Turinese school, founded by a student of both Corelli and Vivaldi, Giovanni Battista Somis (1686-1763). Somis's most important pupil was Gaetano Pugnani (1731-1798); steeped in Roman (Corellian) and Venetian (Vivaldian) traditions and also influenced by Tartini (1692-1770), Pugnani became the maestro of the thirteen-year-old Viotti in 1768. A wealthy nobleman provided for Viotti's musical education, which his blacksmith father could not have afforded. His ability developed rapidly. In 1780, accompanied by his teacher, Viotti concertized in Switzerland, Germany, Russia, France, and England. Settling in Paris in 1782, he became accompanist to Queen Marie Antoinette; when her hairdresser was given the privilege of opening an opera house in 1788, Viotti eagerly accepted the appointment of manager. His comfortable life came to an end after the revolution, since, as a friend of the queen, he had to expect serious trouble.

Viotti went to London where his concert appearances were managed by Johann Peter Salomon (1745-1815), the Bonn violinist and successful impresario of Joseph Haydn. Viotti was the soloist in several of the concerts conducted by Haydn during the 1794-95 season. Suspected of political intrigue, he had to leave England, but after several years in Germany, he returned to London in 1801 and made a living as a wine merchant. The restoration of the monarchy enabled him to live again in Paris, where he managed the Italian opera from 1819 to 1822. Overcome by economic failures, he resigned and went back to England, sick and heavily in debt. He died in 1824.

Viotti was a good conversationalist and great reader and was deeply attached to nature. Although he possessed a virtuoso technique, he never used it for the sake of virtuosity or eccentricity, as cultivated by his countryman, Antonio Lolli (1730-1802). As a violinist he was essentially a singer, as his concertos appealingly demonstrate. Eighteen of his twenty-nine concertos were written or published in Paris between 1782 and 1792, two were begun in 1792 and later finished in London, and the remaining nine originated in London between 1793 and 1815. Viotti has been erroneously credited as the first to write violin concertos in "a consciously formulated sonata form." Haydn did this in the 1760s and Mozart in the 1770s. However, Viotti is a true representative of the classical solo concerto as created by Mozart, in which the thematic dualism of the classical sonata form is fused with the instrumental dualism (tutti and solo) of the baroque concerto.

The attractive concerto in A minor was written in London in 1793 and first played in the Salomon concerts on February fourteenth. Dedicated to Viotti's intimate friend, Luigi Cherubini, the concerto, a must for all young violinists, was a favorite of both Brahms and Joachim. Brahms took advantage of this shared enthusiasm in a very delicate personal situation. His friendship with Joachim had foundered, and he wished to restore it. He thought he could achieve this by the musical means of a composition that would serve as an ambassador of his feelings. This composition was the Concerto for violin and violoncello in A minor, Opus 102. In the first movement Brahms alluded to some melodic material of the opening Allegro of the Viotti concerto in A minor. Brahms hoped this reference to a work dear to both since their youth would facilitate their reconciliation. Joachim understood, and the breach was soon healed.

VIVALDI, Antonio (1678-1741)

Concerto for two Violins in D minor, Opus 3, No. 11
Allegro; Largo; Allegro

This very interesting work belongs to a collection that made Vivaldi known in countries north of the Alps; it was published in Amsterdam about 1712 as Opus 3, under the title *L'estro armonico*. Antonio Vivaldi, the romanticist of the baroque, always intent on creating novelties and startling the listener, was fond of giving fancy titles to his compositions. *L'estro armonico*, which is a case in point, means "The Harmonic Whim." The collection comprises eight concerti grossi and four solo violin concertos. In the group of eight concerti grossi, four have a concertino of four violins; two have a concertino of two violins; and two conform to the Corellian (and also Handelian) type and have a concertino of two violins and a violoncello.

The D minor concerto, which is of the Corellian type, has an interesting history. The piece was published in 1844 as an organ concerto by Wilhelm Friedemann Bach (1710-1784) from a manuscript in the handwriting of Johann Sebastian Bach. Wilhelm Friedemann, however, had written on the flyleaf in a shaky hand *"di W. F. Bach"* and added *"manu mei patris descriptum"* (written by my father). Bach's oldest son was very hard up in his last years and engineered several falsifications to get some money. In this particular instance he succeeded very well in enhancing his artistic stature, and posterity accepted the notion that the elder Bach regarded the work of his son so highly that he took the trouble of copying it for himself. The piece enjoyed great prestige as an organ concerto of Wilhelm Friedemann Bach, and a piano transcription by August Stradal became very popular. The truth came out in 1911, when the German musicologist Max Schneider restored the authorship to Vivaldi.

How was it possible that a composition by Vivaldi was known so long as a work by W. F. Bach? The answer is simple. Vivaldi had faded into oblivion after his death in 1741, and knowledge of only a fraction of his works was limited to a few scholars. Because of the lack of reprints of the first editions of the works, of which only a few copies survived, the origin of the D minor concerto was lost. Johann Sebastian Bach was a great student of Vivaldi, and since the works of the Venetian were not available in score, he transcribed ten of them for harpsichord and organ from the parts for his personal use and pleasure. As concertmaster in Weimar (1708-1717) and Kapellmeister in Cöthen (1717-1723), Bach became familiar with the literature of contemporary Italian music and with the compositions of Vivaldi in particular.

Listening to the D minor concerto for two violins and violoncello obbligato, we fully understand why Bach was so attracted to the work, which is, in fact, one of Vivaldi's finest achievements. It displays his contrapuntal craftsmanship, melodic gift, and predilection for the unusual. Vivaldi strikingly demonstrates these qualities at the opening of the first movement, when the two concertino violins obstinately play broken D minor chords and scales, and the violoncello and double bass continue in this fashion, though changing the bass line for a short while. This section is in effect a prolonged cadence, which creates, however, an enormous tension and feeling of expectancy. This device was called, characteristically enough, *perfidia*. The expression alludes to the perfidy of the composer, who delights in subjecting the listener to a protracted suspense before introducing the long-awaited main idea.

In the D minor concerto Vivaldi keeps the *perfidia* through thirty measures. Even after the motion has come to a standstill, he continues the *perfidia* until the entry of the fugal Allegro, which maintains the tension and excitement. The sustained D of the *perfidia* is matched with a long pedal point on A at the end of the movement. The slow middle movement (Largo) is an "aria" for the first concertino violin in siciliano rhythm, framed by a short prelude and postlude. To enhance the transparency and gentleness of the songful piece, Vivaldi silenced the basses. Frequent alternation of the concertino and ripieno occurs in the finale, and the soloists are given ample opportunity to catch the spotlight.

Concerto for Violin in C major

Allegro; Largo; Allegro

This concerto bears the number 88 in Marc Pincherle's *Inventaire Thématique*. Like about four hundred of Vivaldi's instrumental works it was never published in his lifetime. It came to light after Dr. Alberto Gentili (1878-1954), a professor at Turin University, discovered a large collection of Vivaldi manuscripts in a Piedmontese boarding school in 1926.*

Technically speaking, Vivaldi's most important achievement was the creation of what is now generally called the Vivaldian concerto form. Its structural principle is the alternation of tutti (orchestra) and solo and the recurrence of the thematic material of the opening statement manipulated in a related key in the other tutti sections. The first tutti is often repeated at the end of the movement as, for instance, in our concerto. The alternation between tutti and solo, mostly in the ratio 4:3, is still evident in the classical concerto.

Vivaldi was also an opera composer, a fact often reflected in the slow movements of his compositions. The Largo (12/8) of our concerto is a case in point. It is an "aria" for the violin. The quickly moving finale upholds the Vivaldian concerto design with four tutti and three solo sections. The latter display no lyrical quality but stress the virtuoso element in runs, trills, and arpeggios.

* See note on Concerto in G minor for Strings.

Concerto for Lute, Viola d'amore, and Strings in D minor
Allegro; Largo cantabile; Allegro

This concerto, which bears the number 266 in Marc Pincherle's *Inventaire Thématique,* is one of those Vivaldian creations that eloquently testifies to his ingenuity in creating novel instrumental combinations, in this case the lute and viola d'amore. The lute, which attained enormous popularity in the sixteenth and seventeenth centuries, was declining in Vivaldi's day. Nonetheless, circumstances such as a commission from an amateur, the availability of a fine player, or the desire to endear himself to good lutenists prompted him to compose for the lute. The six or seven stringed viola d'amore with "sympathetic strings" that, running under the fingerboard, are not played upon or plucked, but merely vibrate by "sympathetic" resonance, was never a popular instrument, and a comparatively small amount of good music was written for it. The name "love viol" probably stems from the sweet and silvery tone caused by the sympathetic strings.

The viola d'amore became obsolete after 1750; when Meyerbeer employed it in *Les Huguenots* (1836), only one musician in the large orchestra of the Opéra, the concertmaster, was able to play it. Françoise-Auguste Gevaert, the illustrious director of the Brussels Conservatoire, even predicted in his famous *Nouveau Traité Général d'Instrumentation* (1885) that there was no possibility that the viola d'amore would ever regain its former position in Western musical practice. He was wrong, for conditions have changed completely. Today a host of musicians play the instrument as recitalists and in ensembles; Bach's *St. John Passion,* for example, instead of being presented with two muted violas as substitutes for the viola d'amore, can be performed faithful to the original scoring. After the discovery in the late 1920s of seven concertos for viola d'amore by Antonio Vivaldi, this great Venetian composer emerged as the most important contributor to the eighteenth century literature of the instrument. Contemporary composers write for viola d'amore, and it is taught at leading music schools. The renaissance of the instrument is general.

The concerto under review is the only one that had become known in Germany prior to 1930. In June of 1932 it was championed by Paul Hindemith when he played it at the nineteenth Bach Festival in Heidelberg. The original title reads: *Concerto con Viola d'amore e Leuto e con tutti gl'Istromenti sordini.* Stylistically the piece is a concerto grosso, with the viola d'amore and the lute forming the concertino. Because these instruments do not "carry," Vivaldi required the muting of the orchestra (concerto grosso) to counteract the tonal imbalance that could result from the particular quality of the concertino instruments. To ensure the transparency of the solo passages, the violins, with the exception of a few measures, always play in unison, and in the Largo cantabile the accompaniment is limited to a single line, contributed by the violins, the rest of the orchestra silenced. The work displays the familiar three-movement structure, while the Vivaldian concerto form is evident in the first Allegro and the finale (four tutti and three solo sections).

Concerto for Three Violins and Strings in F major
Allegro; Andante; Allegro

This concerto is listed as No. 278 in Marc Pincherle's *Inventaire Thématique*. It is one of the compositions that Vivaldi wrote as part of his duties as *maestro de' concerti* at the girls' conservatory connected with the hospital of La Pietà in Venice. He probably appeared as the leading soloist, and was joined by the most proficient of the young ladies among his students. Like hundreds of other Vivaldi compositions, the piece heard tonight suffered from neglect for two centuries although a copy is in the Dresden Vivaldi collection. This collection was rather easily accessible and investigated by several scholars in the second half of the 19th century. Yet the concerto was reclaimed for present day musical life only after it was issued in the complete edition of Vivaldi's works in the 1950's. The basis of this publication, however, was a copy of the concerto which came to light only as late as the 1920's when Dr. Alberto Gentili of Turin University discovered about 300 Vivaldi manuscripts. They are now housed in the National Library in Turin.

Our concerto is basically a concerto grosso with three violins forming the concertino. The concertino passages, however, demand technical proficiency and, in this respect, go far beyond that required in the concerti grossi of Corelli and Handel. Vivaldi justly calls the three concertino parts *violini concertanti*. In the Andante, Vivaldi silenced the entire tutti and retained only one violoncello and the harpsichord for the accompaniment. The third concertino violin projects the *cantilena* against the arpeggios played by the muted first violin and plucked chords of the second. This passage anticipates a style of instrumental writing that would have aroused the interest of Berlioz and Liszt. This is a daring passage that eloquently reveals Vivaldi's extraordinary imagination, his sense of instrumental coloring, and his romantic spirit. The last movement stresses the motoric element. It is devoid of lyrical passages, and displays a conspicuous rhythmic piquancy in the tutti portions.

Concerto for Strings in G major
Presto—Andante—Allegro

Vivaldi's G major concerto for strings, number 143 in Marc Pincherle's *Inventaire Thématique,* was not published during his lifetime (1678-1741). Like hundreds of his other compositions it fell into oblivion after his death and remained forgotten for almost two centuries until its discovery by Dr. Alberto Gentili in the 1920s and its publication in the *Complete Works*. It quickly became a favorite because of its rhythmic vitality and freshness. The piece is, in terms of orchestration, a *concerto a quattro*; it is cast for an ensemble of two violins, viola, and bass with the support of a harpsichord. Marc Pincherle, the great Vivaldi scholar, considers this category a symphony. He was the first to draw attention to Vivaldi's importance as a precursor of the classical symphony, and he wrote: "It is probably he who most effectively blended the elements furnished by the church sonata, the concerto, and the dramatic overture so as to bring the concert sinfonia into an existence independent of the church and of the theater."

The Vivaldi symphony, or concerto, "in which there is no solo violin," described by Charles De Brosses in *Lettres familières sur l'Italie,* 1739, generally follows the fast-slow-fast design of the Neapolitan opera overture, as does the *Concerto alla rustica.* The title, which explains itself at first hearing, indicates that this work belongs to a group of pieces that reveal the decisive influence of folk music and dance tune.

Although a resident of the city of Venice, Vivaldi was closely attached to the charms of the *terra firma,* the Venetian countryside where the wealthy aristocrats built their beautiful villas. He was acquainted with the life of the peasants who tilled the soil of the Venetian plains and knew their dance tunes. Vivaldi loved nature and even the calls of the birds. This is convincingly reflected in his famous concerto cycle *The Four Seasons.*

The character of the opening movement of our concerto is defined by the constant motion in triplets maintained from the very first beat to the final chord. The short Adagio leads us into a quite different mood over which Vivaldi, the opera composer, exerts his powerful influence. The tension which permeates this episode is resolved with the entry of the Finale that returns to the serenity and cheerfulness characteristic of the countryside.

Concerto in G minor for Strings
Allegro; Andante; Allegro

After having remained forgotten for about two centuries, this composition was discovered with about three hundred other works by Vivaldi in 1926 under most unusual circumstances. The Salesian fathers at a Piedmontese boarding school inquired at the national library in Turin about the value of a manuscript collection that the institution planned to sell to obtain funds for improvements The matter was turned over to Alberto Gentili, professor of music history at Turin University, who requested the material to be sent to him. When he opened the first crate he found before him volume upon volume of Vivaldi manuscripts. He instantly grasped the singularity of the situation and, controlling his overwhelming emotion, realized that these treasures required delicate handling in order to prevent them from falling into the hands of professional dealers with the resultant sale and dispersal abroad. It transpired that the collection had once belonged to Count Giacomo Durazzo, a patron of Gluck (later another substantial portion of Durazzo's holdings was found in Genoa in the home of one of his descendants). A lack of space forbids narrating the various actions undertaken by the Turin authorities and Dr. Gentili in order to secure this precious material for Turin; however Dr. Gentili did succeed in persuading two public-spirited Turinese to acquire these manuscripts in order to donate them to the Turin Library. The two groups of Durazzo manuscripts are known as the Mauro Foà and Renzo Giordano collections. Our piece is an item of the latter.

The discovery of the Vivaldiana of the Durazzo holdings increased considerably our knowledge of Vivaldi's production and broadened our view of his historic position. Until 1926, Vivaldi research had dealt exclusively with his instrumental compositions and in particular with his volin concertos. Technically speaking, his most important achievement was the creation of what is now generally called the Vivaldian concerto form. Its structural principle is that of the alternation of tutti (orchestra) and solo and the recurrence of the thematic material, which, exposed in the opening statement, is then manipulated in a related key in other tutti sections. In other words, the opening idea forms the thematic backbone of the movement.

Having established this technique in numerous solo concertos, the ingenious Vivaldi, always intent on creating novelties, applied this underlying idea, often called the ritornello principle, to his *concerti ripieni* or *concerti a quattro,* which were three-movement pieces for string ensemble (violins I and II, viola, bass) with the essential participation of a keyboard instrument (harpsichord or organ). His contemporaries characterized works of this kind as concertos without a solo violin, and the application of the term *concerto* here conformed with the original meaning of the word—from *conserere,* "to congregate" for the purpose of playing together. The *concerto grosso* obviously differs essentially from the *concerto ripieno*: in the former the chief accent lies in the alternation of tutti and solo (concertino); in the latter it lies in the thematic manipulation. Defining Vivaldi's string concertos as the earliest preclassical symphonies, Marc Pincherle, the eminent French Vivaldi scholar, thus established their technical and historic importance.

Our G minor piece for strings bears the number 394 in Pincherle's *Inventaire Thématique* and was not published until 1959. Conforming to the three-movement pattern of the Italian operatic sinfonia, it discloses a strong rhythmic vitality and diversity that are manifest even in the energetic opening statement. Incisive rhythmic accentuation is characteristic of the Andante, which is not a lyrical or songful piece like many of Vivaldi's middle movements. It reveals a rather marchlike quality, and the dotted rhythm is maintained from the beginning to the end. The finale is a virtuoso movement in *moto perpetuo* fashion. The triplet motion is kept up throughout and spiced with an extended organ point (48 measures), which precedes the conclusion.

Concerto for Strings in A major
Allegro molto; Andante molto; Allegro

The Concerto for strings in A major by Antonio Vivaldi, which bears the number 235 in Marc Pincherle's *Inventaire Thématique,* like hundreds of Vivaldi's other compositions was never published in his lifetime (1678-1741).

This concerto in A major is, in technical and aesthetic respects, one of Vivaldi's finest creations. The most striking feature of the piece is the amazing similarity of the main theme of the finale to a contredanse in C major by Beethoven, published in 1802.

Since Beethoven could not have come across a piece of music that had been buried in an Italian archive for almost a century, the close resemblance of the themes would seem to be purely coincidental. But the ancestry of the Vivaldian tune, undoubtedly derived from a folk dance, can be traced back as far as to a *balletto,* a song suitable for dancing, by Giovanni Gastoldi (c. 1550-1622). The appearance of identical rhythms and phrases in works of composers living in distant countries and separated by scores of years is a phenomenon which strikingly illustrates the importance of popular tunes and rhythms for art music.

WAGNER, Richard (1813-1883)
Adagio for Clarinet and Strings

In the winter of 1833 Wagner began his career as a practical musician as chorus master and coach at the theater in Würzburg, where his brother Albert was a leading singer. The theater was small and so were its musical forces. The chorus consisted of 16 singers. Nevertheless, such demanding operas as Auber's *La Muette de Portici* and Meyerbeer's *Robert the Devil* were given. We wonder how the prisoner chorus of *Fidelio* may have sounded sung by only eight men. In spite of these conditions, Wagner learned a great deal in Würzburg. He must have proven his abilities, since he was offered a position with the theater in Zürich for the summer season. Although his infinitesimal monthly salary of 10 *gulden* ceased in May, he declined the Zürich post and decided to stay in Würzburg over the summer to work on his opera *Die Feen.* To tide him over, his brother Albert, who went to Strasbourg for the summer season, put Richard in charge of his three little children. Moreover, his sister Rosalia provided the 20-year-old Wagner with a little pocket money.

Needless to say, Wagner took his responsibilities very lightly, and instead of minding the house, he preferred to make excursions to the attractive surroundings of Würzburg and enjoy the Bavarian beer and Frankish wine. It was on such an occasion that he met the clarinetist Christian Rummel for whom he wrote the curiosity for clarinet and strings. Wagner was then (1833) no novice as a composer. He could look back to his published piano works, a sonata and a polonaise, and the performances of overtures as well as his C major symphony. The basic quality of the Adagio for clarinet, written in the gentle key of D flat major, conforms to the lyricism of the romantic composers who showed a marked predilection for the clarinet— Weber and Spohr. The piece displays no significant traits that would foreshadow the future creator of *Der Ring des Nibelungen* except for the use of the turn, a melodic formula that we can find in the chain of Wagner's stage works from *Die Feen* to *Parsifal.*

Siegfried Idyll

The musical material of the *Siegfried Idyll* (which in the autograph is entitled *Symphonie*) stems with one exception from two sources: from a movement for string quartet and from the music drama *Siegfried.* The former dates from 1864 when Wagner and Cosima met at Starnberg near Munich.

She was then the wife of Hans von Bülow, the great conductor and pianist and Wagner's most gifted herald. At that time he promised to write a string quartet for her; it never reached the public, but its contents were used in two Wagnerian creations.

The first was the third act of *Siegfried,* Acts I and II having been completed in 1857. In 1866 Wagner moved to Tribschen on Lake Lucerne and was soon joined by Cosima, who had left her husband. Stimulated by the beautiful, secluded surroundings and his happy frame of mind, he completed the Nibelungen tetralogy. Wagner's son "Fidi" (Siegfried) was born in the summer of 1869, and that August he finished the third act of *Siegfried,* using the principle themes of the quartet movement in the concluding scene, namely:

In *Siegfried* this theme appears in 4/4 time. Tapping the quartet was by no means a matter of convenience—Wagner saw the music in a new light, fitting to the moment when Brünnhilde becomes aware of her love for Siegfried.

Occupied with the orchestration of *Siegfried* in 1870, Wagner conceived the idea of a musical birthday present to Cosima, who had become his wife in August 1870. His mind once more turned to the quartet, which he now wanted to convert into a symphonic piece for orchestra. During the events of the past five years the quartet had assumed a deep symbolic meaning to Wagner, signifying the beginning of his relationship with Cosima. To be sure, the circumstances of 1870 were immensely different from those in 1864, for he was then writing the quartet for Cosima von Bülow and now wished to create something for Cosima Wagner. He realized that the scope of the birthday symphony required new musical material that would mirror the present Richard-Cosima relationship and the consummation of their love, personified by Fidi. The former is expressed in the *Idyll* by the horn call of "love's resolution" from the concluding passages of *Siegfried* (Example a) and the latter by the melody of a lullaby (Example b), the only theme that is not derived from either the quartet or *Siegfried.*

Other sections of *Siegfried* incorporated into the *Idyll* are the bird-call and the sleep motif.

As Wagner wanted to surprise Cosima for her birthday on December twenty-fifth, the first performance of the *Idyll* occurred under extraordinary circumstances. Wagner's devoted paladin, Hans Richter, who was to preside over the orchestra at the first Bayreuth Festival in 1876, acted as a "contractor" of a small orchestra recruited from Zürich and held two rehearsals there (December eleventh and twenty-first, 1870). On December twenty-fourth, Wagner himself conducted the final rehearsal in Lucerne at Hôtel du Lac.

Richter, one of two violists, also blew the short trumpet part of twelve measures. A Lucerne musician attending the rehearsal vividly described Wagner's fire, persuasion, and verve of delivery, which was disturbed once by his black Newfoundland dog Russ, whom he reprimanded roughly. Wagner invited a few friends for Christmas Eve, Friedrich Nietzsche among them, and Richter hurried late to Lucerne to bring a double bass and a violoncello to the house.

Assembling on Christmas day before 7:30 in the morning, the musicians placed their stands on the small staircase. Wagner lifted the baton and the music began. The surprise succeeded fully; Cosima listened, deeply touched by emotion and happiness. It was also a big event for her five children (two from her marriage with Bülow and three from Wagner), who christened the piece "Staircase Music" (Treppenmusik). In the evening it was repeated twice, separated by the septet of Beethoven.

At this memorable occasion Wagner led a band of fifteen—eight string and seven wind players—who were crowded into the narrow staircase, but it is a mistake to conclude from this unique performance that Wagner composed the *Siegfried Idyll* for a small body of thirteen or, doubling the violas and violins, sixteen musicians. Anyone who has carefully investigated the villa where Wagner and Cosima lived, now the Wagner Museum, wonders how even fifteen musicians and their stands could find "lebensraum" there, and Wagner, conducting from the landing upstairs, could not be seen by some of the musicians below.

In December 1871, Wagner was to conduct a symphony concert in Mannheim arranged by his friend Emil Heckel. In a letter to Heckel of December 6, 1871, Wagner requested as a "favor and special courtesy" a number of musicians for "playing through a little private composition for a little private entertainment for me and very few friends." For this piece —the *Siegfried Idyll*—Wagner specified a total of twenty-three to twenty-seven players in the string section, which triples those employed in the Tribschen staircase. Thus, performances of the *Siegfried Idyll* in a small or middle-sized hall by an orchestra whose string body approximates that demanded by the composer are logical for the realization of his artistic aims.

Fünf Gedichte
Der Engel; Stehe still; Im Treibhaus; Schmerzen; Träume

In the first years of his stay in Zürich as a political exile, Wagner occasionally conducted concerts in which symphonies by Beethoven figured prominently. Among the patrons of these concerts was, as Wagner relates in his autobiography, a young couple, Otto and Mathilde Wesendonk, who had taken up residence in Zürich in the winter of 1851. Wesendonk carried on a thriving silk business, which was centered in New York. A very friendly relationship developed between the Wagners and the Wesendonks. Mathilde was only twenty-three years old when she met Wagner, who was then forty-three. She was well educated, had some literary gift, and published a number of pieces of prose and poetry. Her husband became a supporter of Wagner, and, as Ernest Newman phrased it, "Wesendonk's purse was always open both for furtherance of his musical plans and for his personal necessities."

Wagner was greatly attracted to Mathilde Wesendonk, who listened eagerly to his artistic, aesthetic, and philosophical plans and ideas, and to his tales of personal afflictions and intellectual distress. The calamities were mitigated considerably when Otto Wesendonk built a villa and put a little house on his property at Wagner's disposal. Beautifully located, it was christened by him the "asylum on the green hill."

Wagner did not enjoy the house for very long. He had to leave it in August 1858, after the situation became untenable. His wife had provoked a clash with Mathilde, and all people involved realized that the Wesendonks could no longer play the hosts; the Wagners had to leave. Although Ernest Newman maintained that "the relation of Wagner and Mathilde [was] wrapped in obscurity," and we do not know what her real feelings were because only a few of her letters were allowed to be published, the importance of this relationship cannot be overestimated. It generated *Tristan und Isolde.* On December 21, 1861, Wagner wrote to Mathilde: "That I wrote *Tristan,* I thank you from the depths of my soul forever and ever."

Yet the influence of Mathilde's personality on Wagner's imagination and creative thinking was not limited to *Tristan.* Mathilde revealed in her recollections, published in 1896, that the sketch to the prelude to *Die Walküre* (1854) bears the inscription G.s.M., meaning *Gesegnet sei Mathilde* (Blessed be Mathilde). Frau Wesendonk owned the sketches to *Rheingold, Walküre,* and *Siegfried,* Acts I and II. Yet what she did not disclose was the existence of sixteen more allusions to Wagner's feelings in the *Die Walküre* sketches, for instance: W.d.n.w.G. for *Wenn du nicht wärest Geliebte* (Were it not for thee, beloved); I.l.d.gr. for *Ich liebe dich grenzenlos* (I love you infinitely); L.d.m.M.? for *Liebst du mich Mathilde* (Do you love me Mathilde?). It is obvious that Wagner saw Mathilde as Sieglinde and himself as Siegmund. The Siegmund-Sieglinde concept was pushed away by the Tristan and Isolde idea, which so completely overwhelmed Wagner that he put aside the *Nibelungen* tetralogy and delved into the work on *Tristan.*

Mathilde expressed her reactions and feelings in five poems, three of which Wagner set to music late in the fall of 1857, and two in the winter of 1858. The spiritual relationship to the *Tristan* mood is obvious, and so are the allusions to the sentiments of the persons involved. Take for instance the very first poem, *Der Engel (The Angel):* Wagner often addressed Mathilde in his letters as "Angel," and she alluded to Wagner in the poem as the angel who took her spirit heavenward. Two songs were designated by Wagner as studies to *Tristan und Isolde: Träume (Dreams),* which contains music for the second act, and *Im Treibhaus (In the Hothouse),* from which the prelude to the third act was developed. *Schmerzen (Griefs)* emphatically reveals Mathilde's frame of mind in that excited time when she saw sorrow as the giver of joy, and, like the rest of the series, was conceived under the impact of *Tristan. Fünf Gedichte (Five Poems),* referred to colloquially as the "Wesendonk Songs," were not published in their chronological order, which is as follows: *Der Engel* (November 30, 1857), *Träume* (December 5, 1857), *Schmerzen* (December 17, 1857), *Stehe still* (February 22, 1858), and *Im Treibhaus* (May 1, 1858).

Replacing the voice part of *Träume* with a solo violin, Wagner orchestrated the song for ten-piece orchestra to offer it as "morning music" on the birthday of Mathilde on December 23, 1857. It was played in the lobby of Wesendonk's villa. Thirteen years later he presented a similar "morning music" to Cosima, his wife, on her birthday, December 25, with the *Siegfried Idyll*. The orchestration of the other four songs is by Felix Mottl (1856-1911), who was coach at the first Bayreuth Festival in 1876 and later became one of its principal conductors.

WEBER, Carl Maria von (1786-1826)
Overture to "Euryanthe"

In 1822 Weber was commissioned to write an opera for the Kärntnertor Theater in Vienna. The impresario of the theater, which was actually the court opera, was the Neapolitan Domenico Barbaja, one of the most interesting figures who ever wielded the directional scepter in an opera house. He started his career as an illiterate bottle-washer, invented the mixture of whipped cream with coffee, which is a favorite item in the Austrian diet, made money as an army contractor in the Napoleonic wars, managed gambling rooms at La Scala in Milan, and finally rose to become its impresario. He also directed the famous Teatro San Carlo in Naples, and in this capacity he engaged a very promising young composer of twenty-three named Gioacchino Rossini.

A very shrewd man, Barbaja had observed the triumph of Weber's *Der Freischütz* and calculated that an opera by Weber held the best prospects at the box office. Weber accepted the commission with alacrity, because it was the ambition of his life to prove that he was more than a composer of a popular singspiel with spoken dialogue. He wanted to create a German musical drama. The libretto that he finally accepted was penned by Helmina von Chezy (1783-1856) and based on a thirteenth-century French tale. The book centers on the tribulations of the beautiful Euryanthe, whose enemies devise a plot to slander her fidelity. Weber was not quite satisfied with the libretto and compelled the author to make many revisions.

The first performance of the "grand heroic romantic opera in three acts" took place on October 25, 1823, with the composer in the conductor's chair. In spite of initial successes, *Euryanthe* failed to hold the stage permanently and became a woebegone child of operatic literature. Weber's enemies christened the opera "Ennuyanthe" (the boring one). Nevertheless, its historic importance is beyond question. Its musical language foreshadows certain features of Wagner's second stylistic period. Weber himself declared that the effect of *Euryanthe* depends on "the united cooperation of all sister arts." In other words, he proclaimed Wagner's principle of the "all-art-work" (*Gesamtkunstwerk*), and in fact, the opera did not succeed because of the weakness of the libretto. *Lohengrin* shows remarkable parallelisms to *Euryanthe,* so much so that *Euryanthe* has been dubbed "Lohengrin's grandmother."

The musical material of the overture is derived from the opera and manipulated along the lines of the sonata form. The brilliant opening foreshadows the introduction to the third act of *Lohengrin*. About midway there is a mysterious slow episode (Largo) for muted strings. Weber toyed with the idea of having the curtain raised at this point and a scene of the plot enacted as a dumb-show, so that the spectator could catch the dramatic meaning. The intricacies of the plot are expressed musically in a fugato that leads to the recapitulation of the main ideas and a sonorous peroration that indicates the triumph of the heroine.

Overture to "Oberon"

By 1824 Weber's prestige as a stage composer, opera conductor, and piano virtuoso was very high; in that year Charles Kemble, the renowned actor and joint proprietor of the Covent Garden Theatre, invited him to compose a new opera and conduct it in London. Although his health was precarious, Weber saw in an acceptance of the commission a highly desirable opportunity to improve his financial situation. The suggested libretto, based on Wieland's epic poem, "Oberon," was written by James Robinson Planché (1796-1880). Though the story suited Weber's artistic individuality very well, he knew the libretto had serious deficiencies; but feeling that he was living on borrowed time, he refrained from making an attempt to have the libretto altered extensively and considered the financial advantage paramount.

Once he had decided to accept the commission he studied English seriously, taking 153 lessons so that he could acquire sufficient knowledge of the language to avoid making serious mistakes in the musical declamation. While he was working on *Oberon* his state of health worsened, and his wife and friends implored him not to undertake the London trip. He answered, "Whatever I do, whether I go or not, I will be a dead man within one year. However, if I go my children will have something to eat when the father is dead and they will be hungry if I stay." He conducted as a farewell *Der Freischütz* on February 5, 1826, left Dresden on the following day, and reached London on March fifth, where he was heartily welcomed by Sir George Smart of the Royal Philharmonic Society, an energetic champion of Beethoven who had introduced the Ninth Symphony in London in 1825.

Weber immediately began working on the finishing touches of the opera. After the composition of the overture he entered into the score the following: "Completed on April 9, 1826, fifteen minutes before noon and thus the entire opera *Oberon. Soli Deo Gloria!!!* C. M. v[on] Weber." Meanwhile he was very busy with the rehearsals. At its premiere on April twelfth *Oberon,* or *The Elf King's Oath,* was greeted enthusiastically; the audience applauded Weber so vigorously after the overture that he had to repeat it. Although his strength declined daily, he conducted eleven performances of the opera. Finally, beset by fever and shortness of breath, he decided to cancel his benefit concert on June fifth and leave for home on the following day. At midnight, while his friends were gathering to discuss preventing his leaving, Weber departed from this world.

Oberon displays elements typical of German romantic opera: a fondness for medieval knighthood and pageantry, the supernatural, and the colorful Orient. Charlemagne and Haroun al Rashid, the Caliph of Bagdad, appear in the story, along with Oberon, Titania, and Puck, whom we know from *A*

Midsummer Night's Dream. The opera is rather a showpiece, and Weber was determined to make a genuine German opera out of it. Alas, the grim reaper interfered, and the work remained a woe-begotten child of managers, stage directors, and conductors. One of the jewels of the score is the overture, whose thematic material is taken from the opera. The introduction opens with the slow call of Oberon's magic horn, then alludes to the elves with the quickly moving figures of the woodwinds, and indicates by the trumpets the march tune heard in the palace of Charlemagne. The stirring Allegro in sonata form also employs the fiery phrase from the conclusion of the famous "Ocean Aria." The melody reappears with irresistible élan in the dashing coda. It seems incomprehensible that a gravely sick man, being aware of his impending doom, could create a piece of such vitality. This vitality and the beauty and poetry of the lyrical passages have secured the overture to *Oberon* a firm place in the concert hall.

WEIGL, Karl (1881-1949)
Concerto for Violin in D major
Allegro; Largo; Allegro molto

Karl Weigl received his superb musical training in Vienna as a piano and theory student at the conservatory and a student of musicology at the university. He also studied composition with Alexander von Zemlinsky, who had tutored Arnold Schönberg. After Weigl had received the doctorate of philosophy in 1903, he was engaged by Gustav Mahler in 1904 as a coach for the court opera. Weigl resigned this position in 1906 and devoted himself to composition and teaching. He taught at the New Conservatory of Music in Vienna and gave special courses for English and American students during the Salzburg Festival. Weigl came to the United States in 1938 and taught theory and composition in various schools and colleges in New York, Hartford, Boston, Philadelphia, and Chicago. Kurt Adler, the chorus master of the Metropolitan Opera, and Frederic Waldman were two of his numerous students, a group that included composers, pianists, violinists, scholars, and conductors. Weigl was the recipient of important prizes that testify to his artistic stature. He received the Beethoven Prize of the Society of Friends of Music in Vienna in 1910 and the Prize of the City of Vienna for the large symphonic cantata *Weltfeier* ('World Festival') in 1924. Outstanding conductors and performers such as Wilhelm Furtwängler, George Széll, Elizabeth Schumann, and Ignaz Friedman programmed Weigl's compositions.

As a creative artist Weigl belonged to the circle of young Viennese musicians who gathered around Gustav Mahler and Arnold Schönberg. His impressive life work includes six symphonies, concertos for piano, violin, and violoncello, smaller orchestral pieces, eight string quartets and other chamber works, large-scale choral compositions, and about 120 songs. Richard Strauss, Bruno Walter, and Schönberg held Weigl in high esteem. Schönberg, speaking of the Viennese musicians active in the early twentieth century, wrote in 1939: "I always considered Dr. Weigl as one of the best composers of this older generation: one of those who continued the dignified Viennese tradition."

The violin concerto, first performed in Vienna by Joseph Wolfsthal in

1930, was praised by Furtwängler "as an excellent work and a very effective piece." In its three-movement design, key, and some details it upholds the classical tradition. Note the thematic tie of the solo part to the preceding orchestral introduction. The songful quality of the slow middle movement also complies with the time-honored tradition of the concerto literature, while the frequent changes of tempo and key lend a more rhapsodic quality to the speedy finale.

WOLF, Hugo (1860-1903)
Italian Serenade

Hugo Wolf, the great master, of the German *lied* left only three instrumental works of consequence: the symphonic poem *Penthesilea*, a string quartet, and the *Italian Serenade*. *Penthesilea* (1883-1885) never acquired a firm place in the orchestral repertory. Following the road laid out by Liszt it was eclipsed by the masterpieces of Richard Strauss. Wolf's string quartet (1878-1884) is rarely heard, but the *Italian Serenade* has fared better. Wolf was very much attracted to the spirit and milieu of two countries within the Latin orbit— Spain and Italy. A substantial number of his creations eloquently reflect this significant trait of Wolf's personality: the *Spanish Song Book* (44 songs), the opera *Der Corregidor,* based on a tale of Pedro Antonio de Alcarón (1833-1891), the unfinished opera *Manuel Venegas* (after Alcarón), the *Italian Song Book* (46 songs), and the *Italian Serenade.*

The original version of the *Italian Serenade* was composed in 1887 for string quartet. It was held back by the author who, in 1892, decided to use the piece as the first movement of a larger work "for which two further movements must be composed" (from a letter of April 2, 1892). This plan never materialized. Among Wolf's sketches are a fragment of a slow movement in G minor (1893), another of 1894, and 40 measures of a Tarantella projected for the finale and jotted down in 1897. This was the year of his mental collapse, after which he had to be confined to an institution. The plan of an orchestral serenade occupied Wolf's mind from 1892, when he recast the string quartet movement for a small orchestra, until 1897, the year of his collapse. In his last attempt—a fragment of about 170 measures—Wolf used Luigi Denza's enormously popular song *Funiculi, Funicula* which Richard Strauss had introduced in his symphonic fantasy *Aus Italien* in the belief that it was a folk song.

All that is left of Wolf's endeavours to write a large-scale *Italian Serenade* is the well-known, light-footed, and delicate one-movement piece in G major. Published post-humously, it is performed in both the original version by string quartet and in the orchestral attire. The orchestral version which is eight measures longer, originally included a soloistically treated part for the English horn, but Wolf entered a remark in the score to the effect that "a solo viola is to play instead of the English horn throughout." It does not require much imagination to realize what Wolf intended to depict: the preliminary strummings (of the guitar) by serenading musicians, the declaration of love accentuated by impassioned recitative-like phrases, amorous sighs, and fiery utterances. Finally, the serenaders disappear noiselessly into the darkness from whence they came.

INDEX

PERGOLESI, G. B.

POULENC, F.

RAVEL, M.